Jayne Whitcraft
433 Decker

THE Nursery School

Human Relationships and Learning

KATHERINE H. READ

Formerly of the School of Home Economics
Oregon State University

Sixth Edition

1976

W. B. SAUNDERS COMPANY   Philadelphia London Toronto

W. B. Saunders Company: West Washington Square
Philadelphia, PA   19105

1 St. Anne's Road
Eastbourne, East Sussex BN21 3UN, England

833 Oxford Street
Toronto, M8Z 5T9, Canada

Listed here is the latest translated edition of this
book together with the language of the translation
and the publisher.

Danish *(2nd Edition)* — Gyldendal, Ltd., Copenhagen, Denmark.

Hebrew *(3rd Edition)* — Israel Teachers' Union of Tel-Aviv, Tel-Aviv, Israel.

Italian *(3rd Edition)* — Armando Editore, Rome, Italy.

Japanese *(3rd Edition)* — Frebel Kan, Ltd., Tokyo, Japan.

Swedish *(3rd Edition)* — C. W. K. Gleerup Torlag, Lund, Sweden.

German *(5th Edition)* — Otto Maier Verlag, Ravensburg, W. Germany.

Norwegian *(5th Edition)* — Technologisk Sorlag, Oslo, Norway.

Library of Congress Cataloging in Publication Data

Baker, Katherine Read.

The nursery school.

Bibliography: p.

1. Nursery schools.

LB1140.B27 1976   372.21'6   75–28801

ISBN 0–7216–7488–7

The Nursery School: Human Relationships and Learning   ISBN   0-7216-7488-7

Last digit is the print number: 9   8   7   6   5   4   3   2   1

To my daughter

ANN

PREFACE

The first edition of *The Nursery School* was written to help students gain more understanding of human behavior. The sixth edition has the same objective. The need for better understanding of human relationships remains as great, if not greater, today.

The sixth edition also reflects the growing need to help students become more aware of the opportunities that exist to promote learning as they guide young children at home or in the centers for children under five years of age. Care-givers in homes and in centers everywhere need to be able to use wisely what is now known about learning, cognitive as well as social and emotional.

The field of early childhood education has expanded greatly in the last 25 years. The number of centers serving the needs of young children has increased, as has the research being done in the field of early development. Many students today are pursuing careers that involve working with young children. Head Start programs, day care centers, nursery schools, parent cooperative groups, and play groups all need teachers who understand children as developing persons and who are adequately trained to guide them in learning. Observing young children as they play, providing what they need for healthy growth, and guiding them in learning and growing are avenues for expanding one's understanding of others and of oneself. Men and women gain personally and professionally from a better understanding of the needs of young children. As care-givers they can also promote healthy growth.

In writing this book I have used the pronoun "she" in referring to the adult and "he" in referring to the child as a matter of convenience in a general context. I continue to do this in this edition, although, I am glad to say, there are now more men in the student and teacher roles. I apologize to those who question this practice and who are rightfully concerned with a more equal treatment of the sexes; but until we have a pronoun that refers to both sexes, I prefer to avoid the cumbersome repetition of two pronouns each time.

Many people have given me help in the preparation of this edition, and I am grateful to each one even though I cannot name them all. Special thanks, however, go to Betty Lark-Horovitz, who has generously shared from her large collection of children's drawings and paintings the pictures which appear as chapter openings and on the covers. Mrs. Lark-Horovitz is an artist herself and a teacher who writes in the field of art education. Her publication, *The Art of the "Very" Young. An Indicator of Personality and Individualism* (Columbus, Ohio, Charles E. Merrill Publishing Company, in press), is a longitudinal study of very young children's art with many illustrations.

My appreciation goes to Jean Berlfein, who provided a large number of photographs for this edition. Mrs. Berlfein spent some time in 12 different centers, taking pictures of children performing a variety of activities. She selected significant incidents which supplement the text well. She herself has worked in nursery schools and has a film strip on block play.* I am also indebted to the 12 schools in which the pictures were taken. The cooperating schools, all located in the Greater Los Angeles area, were John Adams Child Development Center, Kids Unlimited, Pacific Oaks Children's School, Henrietta Endore's Nursery School, Ocean Park Children's Center, Children's Center for Educational Therapy, Center for Early Education, Modern Playschool, Culver City Children's Center, Echo Park Head Start, Echo Park–Silverlake People's Child Care Center, and University Elementary School at UCLA.

Excellent photographs came from other sources too, such as the sensitive photographs taken by Susanne Szasz and Myron Papiz. Carol Sharpe sent pictures from her nursery school class at Bakersfield College, taken by Jim Fisher and Pat Schroeder. Dr. Dorothy Hewes contributed pictures taken by a student, Jim Hollander, in the Child Development Laboratory at San Diego State University. Carol Harris kindly supplied pictures from the Santa Monica Child Development Center and Laboratory Preschool. I am grateful for all these pictures.

I also wish to express my gratitude to Jane Martin, who supplied the observations used in the "Situations for Discussion" at the end of some chapters. Mrs. Martin, a home economics teacher in a high school, recorded these in a play group she conducts with her students. The observations illustrate some of the relationships between young students and children.

During the preparation of this manuscript I have profited from the constructive suggestions and the encouragement given to me by Baxter Venable, psychology editor at W. B. Saunders Company. His interest and his generous help have been of great value. My thanks also go to the members of the staff who have taken part in the production of this edition, and to the authors and publishers who have given their permission for the quotations used in the book.

---

*"Where are your blocks?" Learning while playing with blocks. 15-minute film strip and cassette. Available from Berlfein Films, 551 S. Beverly Glen Boulevard, Los Angeles, California 90024.

Katherine Read Baker

CONTENTS

Part One
EARLY CHILDHOOD EDUCATION: THE NURSERY SCHOOL...................... 1

Chapter 1
INTRODUCING THE PEOPLE IN THE NURSERY SCHOOL OR CENTER..... 3

Chapter 2
THE NURSERY SCHOOL AS IT FUNCTIONS: PROGRAM AND TYPES
OF CENTERS... 24

Chapter 3
BACKGROUND AND PHILOSOPHY OF EARLY CHILDHOOD
EDUCATION 45

Chapter 4
THE CHILDREN AND THE TEACHING STAFF............................ 64

Chapter 5
THE BUILDING: THE EQUIPMENT: THE USE OF SPACE AND TIME 79

Part Two
BASIC TEACHING SKILLS... 95

Chapter 6
INITIAL SUPPORT THROUGH GUIDES TO SPEECH AND ACTION........... 97

Chapter 7
USING DISCIPLINE... 114

Chapter 8
MAKING OBSERVATIONS.. 124

Part Three
GUIDANCE IN EXPERIENCES COMMON TO EVERYONE 133

Chapter 9
HELPING CHILDREN ADJUST TO NEW EXPERIENCES............................. 135

Chapter 10
HELPING CHILDREN IN ROUTINE SITUATIONS..158

Part Four
THE PROGRAM 181

Chapter 11
THE ROLE OF THE TEACHER...183

Chapter 12
THE ROLE OF PLAY 196

Chapter 13
THE PROCESS OF LEARNING IN EARLY CHILDHOOD..............................208

Chapter 14
AREAS OF LEARNING IN THE PROGRAM..224

Part Five
UNDERSTANDING BEHAVIOR 277

Chapter 15
FEELINGS OF SECURITY AND CONFIDENCE 279

Chapter 16
FEELINGS OF HOSTILITY AND AGGRESSIVENESS.....................................303

Chapter 17
AUTHORITY AND THE SETTING OF LIMITS...323

Chapter 18
RELATIONSHIPS IN GROUPS...337

Chapter 19
DRAMATIC PLAY — AVENUE FOR INSIGHT 357

Part Six
HOME — SCHOOL — COMMUNITY RELATIONS 369

Chapter 20
TEACHERS AND PARENTS WORK TOGETHER...371

Chapter 21
ACCEPTING OUR COMMON RESPONSIBILITIES 387

Index 391

PART ONE

EARLY CHILDHOOD EDUCATION: THE NURSERY SCHOOL

CHAPTER 1

Baseball Players (boy, 3 years)

INTRODUCING THE PEOPLE
IN THE NURSERY SCHOOL
OR CENTER

Education shall be directed to the full development of the human
personality and to strengthening of respect for human rights
and fundamental freedoms.*

DECLARATION OF HUMAN RIGHTS, UNITED NATIONS

INTRODUCTION

"The single most important thing in human cultural behavior is literally and
specifically the way we bring up our children."* This statement, made up by an
anthropologist, points to the significance of the task of those responsible for

---

*LaBarre, Weston: Wanted: A pattern for modern man. Reprinted from Mental Hygiene, April,
1949, by The National Committee for Mental Hygiene.

bringing up children, whether they are parents or teachers or members of any other group dealing with young children.

There has always been concern among people about meeting the needs of children. Today this concern is based on more knowledge. However, with more knowledge comes increased responsibility for providing each child with what he needs for sound growth. Research findings have emphasized the importance of the first years of life and the necessity of meeting adequately the physical, social, emotional and intellectual needs of young children.

The education program we shall be considering is the nursery school or child development center. It is a place where young children learn as they play and share experiences with other children under the guidance of adults who have an understanding of child growth and development and of the learning process. It is a place where adults learn more about behavior and human relationships as they observe and participate in the program of the school.

The Educational Policies Commission of the National Education Association believes that early education is advisable for all children, and also that "Early childhood education, properly conducted, promises significant benefits to American life; poorly conducted, it can do more harm than good.*

What is a well-conducted program of education for young children? What do teachers need to know about child growth and development and about learning? What skills do they need in guiding young children? We shall be looking for answers to these questions and to others—even though the answers may often be incomplete.

The material presented here is addressed specifically to those who are beginning a teaching experience in a nursery school, a child development center, or a day care center; but it can also serve those who care for young children anywhere. Young children have the same developmental needs whether they are at home or in day care centers or in nursery schools. Anyone working in an educational program for young children, even the most experienced person, needs to be learning as well as teaching. The two processes are inseparable.

The order of the material in this book is not an indication of degree of importance. The order is only a reflection of the fact that one must begin somewhere. Some matters of more immediate importance appear first and later are developed in more depth. Although we may wish that we could start out with a complete background, we must be content to be learning each step of the way. The more knowledge we have, the more we perceive there is to know. We must spiral our way up, going over subjects at new levels. The going demands our best efforts. It is never dull. It remains challenging. It is always rewarding.

THE CHILDREN

A center for young children is a place where people are important. We will start by introducing the people one finds there, beginning with the children.

---

*Universal Opportunity for Early Childhood Education. Washington, D.C., Educational Policies Commission, National Education Association and American Association of School Administrators, 1966, p. 7.

We Learn from Children

The children are the most important people whom we will meet in the school. They are the people from whom we will learn the most, not just because they are the most active and the noisiest, but also because they show us most clearly how they feel. Their responses are relatively simple and direct. They act as they feel. When a child is angry, he may cry or kick or throw something, or he may yell at his mother or his teacher, "Go away, I don't like you." He has neither the capacity nor the inclination of the adult to modify his responses. His patterns of behaving are less likely to be influenced by a fear of consequences.

We learn from children for another reason. Their behavior changes rapidly. In different environments or under different circumstances they blossom forth with quite different behavior. We can see more clearly what our handling is accomplishing when we watch a child's response.

Watching children, we see, too, that they are surprisingly different. Each one has his own way of meeting situations. Let us introduce some children, so that we may feel acquainted and thus be better able to understand what may lie behind the behavior of other children with other names whom we will meet in the nursery schools where we may be working.

Charles, Who Is Fighting to Find His Place

Charles is a rosy-cheeked, brown-eyed boy of three and a half. He comes running into the nursery school in the morning, greeting the teachers and the

Children enjoy creating shapes in damp sand.

Courtesy of Jean Berlfein.

children with enthusiasm and plunging into activity. Everything catches his attention, a new book on the table, a bird's nest brought by one of the children, the pin on the teacher's dress, the garage of blocks that the children are building. Observed over one fifty-minute period, he engaged in more than thirty activities with a show of wholehearted interest.

He is eager to join other children in whatever they are doing and makes many attempts to get others to join him. He directs any play that he is in with a flow of excellent language and a vigor and enthusiasm that overwhelm opposition. But the other children drift away from him or reject his advances, perhaps because he cannot brook opposition. He hits or bites when blocked or even when there is no apparent provocation. He is impulsive and quick, so that it is difficult for the teachers to keep him from attacking others. He is constantly taking things from other children. If he sees someone using a tricycle, he immediately wants it. If he sees someone swinging, he wants to use the swing himself.

He has picked up many adult verbalizations which he understands only partially, but he knows that words are often used to justify acts. "I want to swing," he cries, as he sees Jill in the swing. "Why?" asks Jill reflectively. "Because I have to learn how," he answers her. He quickly gets on the tricycle that Bruce has left for a minute. When Bruce cries, "I want it," his answer is, "When people get off trikes, I have to get on and ride around." Usually he does not wait until people get off. When he is absent with one of his rare colds, Mary's comment is, "I'm glad. Now he won't bite me today."

His behavior often surprises the teachers as well as the children. One morning as he started to pour a drink, he said to the teacher cheerfully, "Do you know what I'm going to do?" To her negative reply, he answered, "I'm going to pour this water on the floor." He did just that before her startled eyes and immediately mopped it up willingly, becoming absorbed in watching the way it ran down the corridor, exclaiming, "The water doesn't wait for me."

His observations and his attack on problems reveal a superior intelligence. He loves books and listens to reading with sustained attention. He accepts adult suggestions readily and is quick to see their point. One gets the impression that he can see the value of constructive ways of managing people, but that his own feelings get in his way and are often more than he can manage. Eager for social contacts but carried away by his impulses, he appears genuinely sorry when he hurts another child.

Typical of Charles' behavior is the following incident. As he came on to the playground one morning he saw Bill on a tricycle. He ran to him, grasping the handlebars firmly and saying in a persuasive voice, "Give me your trike, Bill. I want to pull you." Bill made no move to give up the tricycle and Charles repeated the request several times in the same persuasive tone. Then still talking, he pushed Bill off and rode away, calling back, "I'll be right back, Billy. I'm only going to take a little ride." But Bill ran after him and grabbed for the tricycle. Charles hit him, and the teacher had to intervene and help Bill recover his tricycle. Deprived of the tricycle, Charles threw himself on the ground, crying loudly. Suddenly he jumped up and ran to the shed where the toys were kept, calling to Bill to wait for him. He came out with another tricycle and rode off after Bill, trying vainly to get Bill to play with him.

The demands for adjustment have been heavy for Charles in his home. The family has moved many times. They have expected adultlike behavior from this

Courtesy of Jim Fisher, Bakersfield Community College.

Three space men, well-equipped, use their imaginations.

little boy. He has been spanked, threatened, made to sit on a chair, and reasoned with. His parents think he is a difficult child to manage. They appear to have little understanding about what a load their expectations have been for him or how often he has been confused about what is expected. A new baby at home has complicated the situation further. Again, his parents have not recognized what the coming of the baby has meant to Charles. They have succeeded in making him hide his feelings to such an extent that they report that "he adores his baby sister and is very sweet to her." His biting at nursery school is probably related to this situation at home.

Anxious to conform to adult standards and be accepted, eager for friendships with children but often meeting rejection here as with adults, with strong drives and confused feelings which are more than he can cope with constructively, Charles is very much in need of guidance and quite able to profit from it. He needs to be with people who will reduce the difficulties he has to face, who will give him suggestions for solving his problems acceptably, and who will interpret the needs of others to him. Bound to be a force in any group because of his intellectual capacity, his strong drives, and physical vigor, he will be a damaging influence or an inspiring one, depending on the guidance he is given. With the qualities of a leader, he may go in either direction.

Jean, Who Has Lived Under Favorable Conditions

Jean is a small, sturdy looking child. She is one of the younger children in the group, but she is independent and resourceful and plays with all the children. She entered the group several months after school had begun, but she was soon acquainted with everyone and everything. Being the youngest in a family of four children may have helped her.

Jean appears to like people and to trust them. She approaches other children easily and is not defensive in her responses to their approaches. If they reject her, she turns to something else. She is seldom rejected, however, for when she joins a group it is with a purpose in mind. She brings an idea or some new material. She is primarily interested in activity and joins groups of active children who are carrying on projects.

Jean has many interests. She loves music and, although a vigorous, active child, will occasionally spend as much as half an hour listening to music. She paints, uses clay, builds with big blocks, and is often busy in the housekeeping corner. She stands up for herself and will hit another child who tries to take something from her. Her social skills are excellent and seem to reflect a very realistic appraisal of what other children are like. She solves her problems well, both with materials and people. She is matter-of-fact and impartial in playing with other children. Her sympathy is apparent and intelligently given. One day, for example, she took a child with a scratch to the first-aid cabinet to get a Band-Aid.

An example of how she copes with experience occurred on the second day she stayed at school for lunch. She followed the teacher's directions carefully and seemed to enjoy the experience very much, taking additional servings of everything, including dessert. The dessert consisted of fruit and cookies that the children had helped make earlier in the morning. When Jean asked for another cookie, the teacher told her to go to the kitchen and ask the cook for one, since there were no more on the table. This teacher was not aware that plans had been made to let each child take a cookie home after lunch. Jean trotted off in the di-

Courtesy of Earl Dible.

This group is re-creating family roles in play.

rection of the kitchen. When the teacher glanced up two or three minutes later, she saw Jean again going in the direction of the kitchen, but this time she had her coat on. For a moment the teacher was puzzled, and then she realized what must have happened. The cook, when asked for a cookie, had told Jean, "You may have one when you have your coat on ready to go home." So Jean trotted to the coat room, put on her coat, and was returning. She must have felt that adults make queer requests! She was given her cookie. With it in her hand she went back to the coat room, removed her coat, returned to her place at the table, and happily ate her cookie.

Jean had kept her purpose in mind and carried out the confusing directions. She accepts things as they are!

Jean's confidence spills over to others. She takes care of herself, faces problems, and feels comfortable. Others are more comfortable and confident and purposeful because of her presence. Without actively leading, Jean is a strong force in the group.

Juan, Who Watches Others

Juan is a beautiful, dark-eyed boy who gravely watches what goes on around him in nursery school. His mother was very glad when Juan was able to enter school. From the time he was an infant, she had been taking him with her when she went out to do housework in various homes. He had been a good baby and cried very little, but it had not been easy for her to manage. She was alone and was supporting herself and the child. As Juan grew older, he played quietly or watched her as she worked. He understood that he was not to touch the things around him or to disturb other people. By the time he had reached the age of four, his mother felt that he needed to be with other children and to start learning more than she could teach him. She had already tried to teach him his letters, without much success. She was relieved when she found that the school would accept Juan.

When Juan entered nursery school, he was able to let his mother leave after the first day. He made no protest. But now, after several weeks in school, he is still a "watcher." He seems interested in what the other children do, but when they approach him or make an effort to draw him into play, he smiles shyly and withdraws. He seems bewildered and prefers to play alone.

Juan is skillful in manipulative play with puzzles or in stringing beads. He does not often use the large blocks or engage in any vigorous play. He follows the teacher's directions and fits into the routines of the school. He sits quietly at the table at lunch time and rests when it is time. He remains rather passive, doing what is suggested but initiating very little on his own.

What is Juan really like? The teachers feel that they do not know. He presents them with challenges. How can he be helped to do more exploring and discovering and creating on his own? How can he be helped to develop the language skills for communicating that he will need so much in learning, later as well as now? How can he be helped to discover how to play with other children?

The teachers are slowly finding ways to win his trust. They hope to help him change his passivity into a confident zest for experience. They hope to help him find friends. They hope to help him discover his own individual patterns of learning as he grows in the nursery school world.

A child expresses his thoughts and feelings in painting.

Nettie, Who Wishes She Could Be Important to Someone

Nettie is the fourth child in a family of five. Her home is a busy, crowded place where relatives come and go. Nettie is often brought to school by these relatives and never seems to know who may be coming for her. Her mother seldom comes. If her mother does come, she usually waits outside, sending an older sister in to get Nettie.

Nettie has no close friends among the children. She seems to feel that no one likes her. It is easy to see why. When she plays with children, she wants the biggest share of everything, or she teases and runs off with some favorite item. The children soon refuse to let her play with them.

She is restless and distractible in her play, going from one piece of equipment to the other. Here is a sample of a few minutes of activity. She sees a spoon in the sandbox, jumps in and digs with it, then drops it as her eye falls on a red truck another child has just left. She pulls the truck across the yard but leaves it to climb on the bars for a minute. Then she turns to the workbench where a group is pounding and sawing, but she does not wait for a turn with the tools. She wanders over to the housekeeping corner where she kicks at a doll buggy, bringing an angry response from the child whose "baby" is in the buggy.

Nettie seems to invite rejection from the children, but she continually seeks attention from the adults. When there is a visitor in the school, Nettie will follow him or her around, talking and clinging to the visitor. She demands attention. She is not satisfied. With three older sisters and a younger brother at home, one suspects that she has not had much attention. Her contacts with people are on a superficial level. She seems always to be seeking something and never finding it. Learning and achieving do not interest her.

What can the school do for Nettie? Nettie's attendance at nursery school has been rather irregular during the three months she has been enrolled. The staff is not satisfied with the progress she has made. They feel they must take another look at what is happening to her. They realize that it is not easy to give attention to a child who is always demanding it. Perhaps the best answer may be to let someone volunteer to be Nettie's "special" teacher, one who will devote herself to building a firm relationship with this little girl who has never felt sure that anyone thinks of her as an important person.

If Nettie can feel valued in a relationship with someone, she may be free to give her attention to other experiences, to develop skills in activities and in communicating with others. Nettie needs help from the teachers in seeing herself as a valued person. She needs help in becoming independent and resourceful in making use of the opportunities to learn and grow at school. She needs to feel the satisfactions of achievement and competence.

Ellen, Who Finds It Hard to Trust the World and the People in It

Ellen is a child who was born with a physical deformity requiring corrective surgery. She was in the hospital several times as an infant and very young child. When Ellen was in the hospital, her mother was not allowed to stay with her but could only visit during visiting hours.

This girl plans with care and constructs.

Courtesy of Jim Fisher, Bakersfield Community College.

Ellen is physically normal now, but she bears both the scars of her operations and the psychological scars left by the experiences she had. These experiences came at a critical time in her development when she should have been learning to trust herself in the world. Instead, she learned to be suspicious and unsure of herself. She is very jealous of a younger brother who had been born shortly after her last hospital experience.

Ellen's parents were eager for her to enter nursery school. The bonds of affection between Ellen and her parents were close, but they felt that she would gain a great deal from being in school. They were delighted when she was enrolled.

When Ellen entered school, she moved rather clumsily and often had a pouting expression on her face. She was a heavyset, stolid-looking girl with thick dark hair. Her motor coordination was poor for a child of her age, and she avoided active play. She did not join the children in playing on the jungle gym or the ladders. She seemed aware of her lack of skill and was defensive about it.

Ellen needed her mother when she entered nursery school. She did not remain near her mother, but she would protest vigorously if her mother indicated that she was going to leave. She seemed to want to be sure that she could control the matter of her mother's leaving. Both the staff and the mother felt that it was a good thing for Ellen to feel she could keep her mother there. They knew that she would feel sure of herself in time. Meanwhile, the teachers tried to build good relationships with Ellen. She had accepted help from them from the beginning, but seemed to keep this on an impersonal level. She was suspicious of people.

Courtesy of Robert Overstreet.

All children enjoy playing with sand. Notice the storage shelves for sand toys.

Over a period of many weeks, the teachers continued trying to maintain warm, friendly relationships with the child, giving her extra encouragement when she tried something new or was successful in any motor skill. They also let her decide as many things as possible. When they had to refuse to comply with what she asked, they did so firmly and matter-of-factly, explaining the reason and adding, "I would like to let you do it, but I can't because . . . ."

In addition, they made a point of including many items for dramatic play of the doctor-nurse-hospital variety. They found stories about children and hospital experiences. It was a long time before Ellen was interested in these books, not until she had enjoyed a lot of messy play — getting her hands into sticky clay, and playing with water. By this time she had also picked out one teacher as her special friend. She seemed more secure then, and began using the dramatic play materials.

The change in Ellen by the end of the year was rewarding to everyone. She was enjoying active play, using her body freely and keeping up with the other children in climbing, riding a tricycle, and other large muscle activities. She sometimes talked with the teacher about her experiences in the hospital as though these were really a thing of the past for her. She was steadily making progress in learning about the world and the people in it and in finding it good to achieve and master experience. The nursery school had been successful in providing Ellen with what she needed.

PARENTS

Parents Are Important People

Next we will look at some of the parents we may meet. Parents are important people. They are the child's first teachers. The give the child his first experiences with loving relationships. They serve as his first models. They direct his first learning experiences.

They are also important because they are people with feelings and needs. They must cope with difficulties and seek personal satisfactions. Their relationships with the child are loaded with some of the deepest human feelings there are. We need to know something about parents and to respect the part they play in bringing up the children we meet at nursery school.

Parents are all different. What are they like? What does nursery school offer them?

Charles' parents are glad to have him attend nursery school. They are both very busy people. While they are proud of the handsome little boy and love him very much, they often find him difficult and trying. He does not fit easily into the dream they have of a well-behaved child who does them credit. They look forward to the time when it will be easier for him to understand what they want. They are glad to shift the burden of caring for Charles to the school for a time. Charles' father has never come to the school, and the mother seldom has time to visit. She has to get back to the baby or on to some engagement.

Jean's parents lead a full life. At the moment it is full because of four active children, and they enjoy them all. Jean has a special place because she is the baby, even though she is well able to hold her own with the others. The mother really wanted to keep her at home, but she knows that Jean wants to play with children and is eager to go to school. The mother often drops in for a visit and has stepped in quietly to help on occasions. She thinks that teaching in a nursery school would be a delightful experience and wonders if it might be possible for her to do this later when her children are older.

Juan's mother misses him, but she is relieved that he can be in school. Having him at school makes it much easier for her to manage her work, and she feels that he needs school. She hopes he will be a good boy. She wants Juan to do well and to have some of the opportunities that were denied her. She sometimes worries about him, but she hesitates to talk with the teachers. She doesn't find it easy to talk with people. She and Juan have been close to one another without using many words. She is not very clear about what nursery schools are like, but she knows that Juan enjoys going there.

Nettie's mother is very relieved to have Nettie in school. Nettie was always a fussy child and often cried. Even a hard slap was not enough to stop her. Nettie's mother does not believe in "babying" children and she did not "baby" Nettie. She herself had never had much mothering. Her own mother died when she was a child, and she was sent to live with an aunt who never really wanted her but who tried to do her duty by the child. Nettie's mother had married young, probably to escape from what must have been a loveless home. She was proud and pleased with her first baby, but then things became difficult. Her husband left her. Nettie's father is her second husband. Even though there are many members of his family in and out of the house, she often feels lonely and unwanted, as she did when a child. She gets depressed. She is sure that the women who teach at the school must look down on her. But she is glad to have Nettie there just the same.

Ellen's parents are very grateful to have Ellen in the nursery school. They feel that she is thriving in this experience, so different from her earlier separation experiences.

Ellen's mother was glad to stay with the child as long as the teacher felt it helped Ellen. Her husband willingly carried the extra work at home. The mother observed with interest what the teachers did at school and how they guided the children. She feels that she learned many things that have helped her understand better what Ellen needs and how she and her husband can encourage Ellen's development at home. Both parents feel that the teachers care about Ellen and are watching her development with pleasure. The burden of concern they had known earlier is lifted. They welcome conferences with the teachers and are glad of the help they have received.

As we can see, all of these parents have different needs. They look at the school and the teachers in different ways. But for all of them the school and the teachers play an important role in their lives.

Charles, Jean, Juan, Nettie, and Ellen are like some of the children whom we will meet in the nursery school. Their parents are like some of the parents there. Who are the other adults in the nursery school, and what are they like?

ADULTS IN THE CENTER

ADULTS ARE PEOPLE WITH FEELINGS THAT NEED TO BE UNDERSTOOD

Adults are people with the same kinds of feelings as children, but they are likely to express their feelings less directly and less openly. Their responses have been modified by many experiences that have taught them to control and often to conceal their feelings even from themselves. An adult who is angry seldom hits or throws, but the he may do the next job poorly or may be critical of someone else for no apparent reason. Many times the adult's responses are as inappropriate and as unacceptable as the child's, but they are harder to relate to the cause. The adult's responses do not change as quickly as the child's, perhaps because in part they are patterns that have been in use for a long time.

But there is one difference between the child and the adult that gives the adult a real advantage. The adult has a greater capacity to be objective, that is, to look at his own feelings and his behavior. Because of this capacity he can modify his responses and make them more appropriate as he comes to understand them. Understanding ourselves, what we feel and why we respond as we do, is very important to all of us. We need to understand ourselves, for our feelings will influence the relationships we maintain with other people.

Self-understanding is especially important for teachers because children are influenced by the feelings of teachers. It is important for us as teachers to learn to understand our feelings, so that we can be honset and realistic and respond in appropriate and constructive ways to situations. We are in a better position to help children understand themselves when we understand ourselves.

We Are Likely to Feel Inadequate in a New Situation

We will start by looking at how students or beginning teachers will probably feel as they start working in a school. We will try to understand these feelings because it may help us understand the feelings of the children as they, too, begin a nursery school experience.

In beginning work in the nursery school or center most students are going into a situation that is new to them. They may not be sure what to do. They do not know the children or the teachers. They do not know what the procedures are in the school. They may not know simple things like where the paints or the mops are kept. Even though they have been given directions and have been shown through the school, they are sure to find that they have forgotten or were not told many of the things they need to know. Unexpected things keep happening, things for which they are not prepared.

In these situations a student may try something that does not work out the way she expects. She* may greet a child cheerfully only to have the child reply, "I don't like you." She may follow the example of the teacher in approaching a group with the words, "It's time to put things away now," but she may get a different response: "We're not going to," the children reply to her.

She has many questions. Should she interfere when one child hits another? Should she just watch? Should she ask an experienced teacher for help? What should she do?

It is not comfortable to feel unsure and inadequate. It is easy to blame some-

---

*In our general discussions, for purpose of convenience, and to avoid tedious sentence structure, we will use the pronoun "she" for the adult and the pronoun "he" for the child. We realize that half of the children are likely to be girls and some of the adults will be men. No discrimination is intended in either case.

one or something as a defense against this feeling. A student may become critical, disapproving of the teachers and the program and what the children are allowed to do. Or she may turn away from the unfamiliar or difficult situations. She may busy herself with familiar things or spend time with the passive, easy children. She may do a great deal of needless talking or giving directions as a way of reassuring herself. She may even blame herself for not knowing what to do. This may make it harder to become more adequate.

We Need to Feel Comfortable About Being Inadequate in the Beginning

All these responses are natural. In a new situation everyone has feelings of inadequacy. These feelings are not easy to face. The important thing is to realize how we feel and something about why we feel as we do.

First of all, students can expect to feel inadequate when they begin their experience in the nursery school and probably for some time after that. They cannot possibly be prepared for all that may happen. No one can give instructions that will cover everything, certainly not in the time they may have had for preparation. Of course they will not feel sure of what is expected of them or of what they are supposed to do. The teacher who is guiding them may not be sure of that herself. She does not know them yet or know what is possible for them.

What we can do about the feeling of inadequacy at this point is to feel comfortable about having it. We will be inadequate when we start if there is something to learn, and we might as well accept this as a reality. It is all right to be inadequate when one begins a learning experience. No one should expect to know in the beginning what will be learned in time. We do not need to expect it of ourselves.

There is a lot to learn at first. There is no need to fight against feeling inadequate or to deny the feeling. It is part of the experience. We might as well try to live as comfortably as we can with the feeling and enjoy our successes as we begin to have them.

We Have Other Feelings, Too

The feelings we must face and deal with first are usually the feelings of inadequacy. But there are other feelings that encourage us. We have some successful experiences, too. A child's face lights up as he sees us come into the room. We know that our relationship with him is a source of strength. He is seeing us as someone who cares, who can be depended on, and who has something significant to give to him. It makes us feel good inside to be this kind of person for a child. It gives us confidence.

Or, a child may bring us a drawing he has made, saying softly, "It's for you." It is the kind of gift that warms the heart. We are rewarded, too, when we watch a child struggle and then succeed in actually cutting through the piece of wood with the saw or in making the bridge stand, all on his own. The glow of satisfaction on his face or expressed through his body makes our teaching effort seem worthwhile. We share in his accomplishment. We can truly feel that we are engaged in "the most important thing in human cultural behavior" as we succeed in helping the children.

WHAT DO WE NEED TO UNDERSTAND ABOUT OURSELVES?

Probably the most important adult each of will meet in the nursery school is ourself. It is important for us to understand this self if we are to understand others. We are all alike in many respects. We all have some common experiences that may influence our responses.

We Were All Children Once

In the first place, all of us were children once. We can never escape that fact. What happened to us then still influences what we are like now. Some of us may wish that things that happened to us in childhood had been different. Others may feel grateful on the whole for the experiences that were theirs. But whatever happened still matters tremendously. That is why we can understand ourselves and other adults better by trying to understand what children are like and by watching the effect on them of the things that happen.

We are probably still being influenced by the fact that we started out tiny and helpless, dependent on the adults around us. The way our needs were met during this period of dependency is still affecting what we do. If we lived with people on whom it was good to be dependent because of the warmth and abundance of their giving, if we were fed when we felt hungry and played with and loved when we wanted attention, we were *satisfied* during this period. If the adults around us

Courtesy of Santa Monica College.

A student helps a group of children make pancakes.

were themselves satisfied people who did not try to prolong needlessly our dependence, we were free to become independent when we were ready. Growing up under conditions like these, we are now neither fighting against being dependent nor seeking reassurance by demanding more protection than we need.

Others of us may have lived with people on whom being dependent was not such a pleasant experience. We were not fed when we felt hungry. We were left to "cry it out" when we felt helpless and alone. There may have been many reasons for such handling by our parents, such as ignorance of the real needs of infants, poor health, too many responsibilities, or the influence of our parents' own childhood experiences. Under this handling, however, we may have fought against being dependent, finding it hard later to accept the necessity of being dependent under any circumstances. Or, we may have continued seeking to have our "dependency needs" met by trying to be more dependent than we needed to be, as though to make up for what we did not have earlier.

We Were All Members of Families

Another factor influencing our behavior is the position each one of us held in our families. Some of us were only children; others were oldest or youngest or any number of middle positions. The position meant different things in different families. Families are likely to be competitive places. Children want attention and compete for it from their parents or from each other. Some are more successful than others in getting it.

In the nursery school, for example, a student who happens to be the youngest in her family may identify herself with the baby in the school and resent seeing her teased. She may want to see the aggressor punished just as she wanted to see punishment given to those who teased her in her childhood. Under the guise of wanting to be "fair," she may try to impose a "justice" that really belongs to a situation from her own past from which she has not yet succeeded in untangling herself. Recognizing that patterns of past feelings still exist gives a person a better chance to handle situations in the present with understanding.

We All Met Frustrations in the Growing-up Process

Let us take one more example of the way our childhood patterns enter into how we feel and behave in the nursery school, or anywhere else. As a result of the frustrations that are an inevitable part of the growing-up process, we all have feelings of resentment and hostility, and we handle them better if we can recognize them. It is needless, and may be damaging, to try to deny these feelings. We all have them because we were babies once. The baby is subject to many limitations. He can't reach the toy he dropped. He trips and falls when he tries to walk. He isn't allowed to touch interesting objects. Frustration rouses resentful, often hostile, feelings.

How much hostility a child feels depends somewhat on whether the adults in his world help to minimize the inevitable frustrations, or whether they aggravate and increase frustation by a mistaken idea of "teaching" the child. If the necessary limitations are imposed with gentleness by a comfortable, confident, loving person, they will not rouse much resentment; but if limitations are imposed by one who is cross, confused, and struggling with his own feelings of hostility, they will rouse a great deal of negative feeling in the child. The child will want to fight and hurt in return, and these feelings will spill out in many situations against anyone who interferes with him.

Few of us are fortunate enough to have been handled all the time by people who tried to decrease the feelings of hostility and resentment that are part of the growing-up process. Most of us feel more resentment than we can manage comfortably on all occasions. Our feelings spill out in inappropriate ways in many situations. When these negative feelings spill out inappropriately, they may make us feel guilty and afraid without knowing what is wrong. They may keep us from learning things that we may really want to learn.

All of Us Have Negative Feelings That Need Draining Off

We all have a store of negative feelings. These feelings need to be drained off through vigorous activity, or through some satisfying expression in art or music, or in "spilling things out" by talking to a friend, or in doing something that makes us feel more adequate. When we have such outlets, we keep our negative feelings down to manageable proportions.

All of Us Need to Identify the Negative Feelings We have

If negative feelings are not drained off, they may come out later in ways that are difficult to identify. Feeling very strongly about a thing, for example, is an in-

Courtesy of Suzanne Szasz.

A student sings with the group in a center.

dication that it is serving as an outlet for extra emotion, especially if most people do not seem to feel as strongly as we do about the same thing. It may be a good thing to stop and ask oneself, "Why do I feel so strongly about this thing?" We can direct strong feeling more safely when we understand why we feel as we do. The likelihood of our meeting the needs of the child is increased if we understand our own needs and feelings.

For example, a student finds herself feeling very indignant that a child is allowed to play with his food at the table and even leave some of it uneaten. She may feel this way because she was not allowed to play with her food when she was a child. Now that she has accepted adult patterns and identified herself with the adults in this situation, all the resentment that she felt at being denied the delightful experience of playing with food, as well as tasting it, is turned into her feeling about seeing a child permitted to do what she was not allowed to do and what she was forced to consider "bad." It is not easy to take on values, and we often pay a heavy emotional price when they are forced on us too early. We cannot bear to see others getting by cheaply.

We shall not discuss here whether or not a child should be allowed to play with food. We are only pointing out that it is important to be able to decide this on the basis of its meaning for the child and whether or not it is a good thing for him, instead of on the basis of our own personal conflict. In other words, it is important to be able to identify the emotional forces that lie behind our reasoning.

All of Us Tend to Resist Change

A characteristic that we all have in common is that of resistance to change. In spite of ourselves we find all kinds of reasons for avoiding real change in our thinking and in our behavior. New ways of behaving, no matter what their merit, are rejected until we manage to handle our resistances. Most resistances are the result of childhood experiences. Recognizing this, a student can handle her resistance more appropriately, saying to herself, "I don't have to feel and behave as I did when my mother—or my big sister or my father—was bossing me. I'm no longer a child. I'm grown-up, and I'm free to use a suggestion if I think it is a good one or to reject it if I think it is a poor one." She can free herself from the control that childhood patterns may still be exerting over her in adult life.

The more insecure we are, the less likely we are to feel that we can afford to change, for change involves uncertainties. Even a too-ready acceptance of a new point of view may mean only a superficial acceptance, in itself a defense against any real change. It is important for us to be aware of this universal tendency to resist the new, the different, so that it will not block us when we try to profit from the thinking of others. We must assert our right to use experience, whether it is a morning in the nursery school, a discussion period, or the reading of a book, to reach our own conclusions.

We Need to Accept All the Feelings We Have

It is essential for all of us in the nursery school not to feel ashamed or guilty about the feelings we have. We have been taught so often that we must be "good" that we may be afraid to face the negative feelings that exist in us. They go unrecognized and interfere with our thinking more than they would if we had accepted them.

As adults we can afford to look at our feelings because we have more capacity for managing them than we had as children. As children we felt strongly, and our feelings overwhelmed us. Anger turned into a violent temper tantrum, perhaps. We may have felt guilty and afraid, and we may not have had much help from the adults around us at this point. Now that we are grown, we have less need to feel so afraid. We are not as helpless as when we were children. We have more ability to handle feelings when we know that they exist.

We Need to Recognize the Ambivalence of Feelings

It is also essential to be aware of the ambivalence of our feelings. Feelings are usually mixed. Feeling comfortable or uncomfortable, enjoying and not enjoying, loving and hating are all mixed together, although we may be aware of only the feeling that is strongest at the moment. We may be surprised at sudden changes in feeling because we have not been aware that other feelings were present all the time. We may want to learn more about people and yet resist learning. We may like and dislike the same person; and he, in turn, may have some of both kinds of feelings about us. We seldom feel all one way or all the other way about a person or an experience.

We Need to Try to Understand, Rather Than Judge, Ourselves and Others

It is not for us to say whether or not people ought to feel and act as they do. We make very little progress when we blame or praise them or ourselves for the way they or we feel and act. We make progress when we try to understand why we behave as we do. Getting angry or discouraged with ourselves or anyone else is usually unprofitable. It is tremendously profitable to recognize that we can do something to change our ways of feeling and acting if we are willing to try.

Some of the things that we learn about ourselves and others will be confusing and disturbing. Human behavior is complex and difficult to understand. It may be important to talk things over with someone. Certain questions may be brought up for discussion in the group. Some less clear or more personal matters may be talked over with a teacher whose longer experience has added to her understanding of behavior.

EACH GROUP SHARES COMMON PROBLEMS

The whole school is thus full of human beings who must understand and accept their feelings and those of others in the school. Each group shares some common problems.

Students, as they start teaching in the nursery school, have the problem of facing and accepting the almost inevitable feelings of inadequacy that a new situation brings.

Parents whose children are in nursery school face the problem of being able to leave the child free to take the step toward greater independence that going to school represents. Their confidence in what they themselves are as parents and the degree of security that their past experiences have brought them will play a part in the ease with which they face their new role of parents with children attending nursery school.

Teachers must continue their professional growth, deepening their understanding of the ways to meet the needs of children and parents in the nursery school.

The *cook* must share in the goals of the school, too. She must find satisfaction in what she is doing for and with the children as she prepares and serves the food.

The *janitor* must be able to understand and accept the needs of the children if he is to see his job as one of making the school a good place for children instead of merely a good place for a janitor.

For everyone, the nursery school can be a human relationships laboratory. It can be a place where we learn more about ourselves and about others as we gain skill in guiding children's development.

PROJECTS

1. As you observe in a nursery school, see if you can identify characteristic patterns of behavior in any of the children there. For example, is there:
   (a) A child who seems to feel confident and to like himself?
   (b) A child who seems timid and lacking in confidence and who may frequently ask for unnecessary help?
   (c) A child who tends to be an "onlooker" and who approaches people or activities with reluctance or caution?
   (d) A child who plunges almost immediately into activities, getting involved in a wholehearted way, and approaches people directly?
   (e) A child who seems distractible, who goes from one activity to another without becoming deeply involved in anything?

Give incidents to illustrate your conclusions. In later observations see if you come to the same conclusions about what is characteristic behavior in these same children. If your conclusions are different, what might the reasons be?

2. Recall and report an incident in your own childhood when you were about the same age as the children you are observing. What significance do you think this incident had for you?

3. What were your favorite toys or play activities? What did you dislike or what frightened you as a child?

4. List some of the things that children do that you find annoying. List some of the things that you enjoy watching children do. Keep this list and check it later to see whether or not your feelings have changed. If they have, how would you explain the changes.

REFERENCES

General

Menninger, William: Self-Understanding—A First Step in Understanding Children. Chicago, Science Research Associates, Inc., 1951.

Ornstein, Allan: Who are the disadvantaged children? Young Children, May, 1971.
Senn, Milton: Early childhood education—For what goals? Children, January-February, 1969.
Zigler, Edward: Contemporary concerns in early childhood education. Young Children, Vol. 26, No. 3, January, 1971.

Case Studies

Axline, Virginia: Dibs: In Search of Self. Boston, Houghton Mifflin Company, 1964.
Coles, Robert: Children of Crisis: A Study of Courage and Fear. Boston, Atlantic-Little Brown, 1967.
Coles, Robert: Uprooted Children. Pittsburgh, University of Pennsylvania Press, 1970.
Greenfield, J., and Greenfield, F.: A Child Called Noah: A Family Journey. New York, Holt, Rinehart and Winston, Inc., 1972.
Grey, Catherine: Four children. Children Today, Vol. 1, July-August, 1972.
Phillips, Doris Campbell: The one and only Jimmy. Young Children, Vol. 20, No. 3, January, 1965.
Rubin, I.: Jordi and Lisa and David. New York, Ballantine Books, Inc., 1968.

CHAPTER 2

Going to School (girl, 4 years)

THE NURSERY SCHOOL AS
IT FUNCTIONS: PROGRAM
AND TYPES OF CENTERS

CHILDREN'S EXPERIENCES IN SCHOOL

Characteristics of a Nursery School

The nursery school as we will define it is a school serving the needs of two-, three-, and four-year-old children in today's world by offering them experiences adapted to what is now known about growth needs at these age levels. It shares with parents the responsibility for promoting sound growth and learning in a period when growth is rapid and significant. Respect for the individual child and his needs is the basis for a good nursery school program.

In a good nursery school the groups are small. Children are seldom all together, doing the same things at the same time. They work or play in groups of two or three or four. There is a great deal of talking, for language skills are valued.

The nursery school is a place for activity. One group may be playing in the housekeeping corner, carrying on a variety of homemaking activities. Another group may be building with blocks. A child may be working on a puzzle by himself. Another group may be playing a "matching game" under the guidance of a teacher, while another group may be outdoors with a teacher.

Play is the great avenue for learning in the nursery school. "The curiosity, inventiveness and spontaneous energy of young children are sources from which a lifetime of learning can develop," comments the Educational Policies Commission in a statement referred to earlier.* Young children must see, touch, taste, and hear if they are to learn. Young children play to discover and master experiences. Discovery is an active process for them, even discovering about liking and not liking things and people, or about managing feelings.

Most of the teaching in a nursery school is done indirectly. The stage is set for learning through the varieties of materials the teacher provides and the range of experiences she makes possible for the children. She extends and enriches these by her guidance. She makes comments or asks questions and, above all, she listens. She is ready to prohibit and restrain when necessary.

Throughout her teaching the teacher respects the individual interests, styles, and rates of learning of the children. She encourages children's independence and initiative and helps increase their awareness of the world around them.

---

*Universal Opportunity for Early Childhood Education. Washington, D.C., Educational Policies Commission, National Education Association and American Association of School Administrators, 1966, p. 9.

Courtesy of Jean Berlfein.

Discovering and observing a snail with the teacher's help.

A child works steadily shoveling the sand.

Courtesy of Sam Hollander, San Diego State University.

Every group in the nursery school will have more than one teacher. Young children need individual attention. The teachers will work as a team, planning together and carrying out the program in the light of the children's needs. There is an order or structure to the day. A schedule exists, and because it exists, it can be modified. The structure will depend on the needs of the individual children in the group, on the limits and possibilities in the school itself and in the community around it, and on the interests and skills of the teacher.

The Program as It Functions for a Child

We will describe what school is like for a child by following a hypothetical child through a morning. His program might be something like this.

Our hypothetical child, a three-and-a-half-year-old, arrives with his mother. After greeting the teacher who is checking the children on arrival, he runs outdoors and plays for half an hour, riding a tricycle vigorously for a while and then joining a group in hauling the building blocks to a corner of the playground to make a building. All the children on the playground share in working on this project for a time. A swing and a climb on the jungle gym complete the cycle of outdoor activity for our child.

He comes inside and takes off his outside wraps with very little help. Then he uses the toilet and runs into the playroom where he is accepted by two girls who are playing in the doll corner. He joins them and takes on the role of "father." He

sweeps busily; he wheels the doll buggy around; he converses over the toy telephone about an evening engagement. Then the group has trouble over who is to
use the iron, and he loses interest. He turns to painting at the easel and grows absorbed in his painting. He is a child who seems very sensitive to color. He paints
large areas with vivid color, covering the paper. His painting on a second sheet
of paper is quite similar to that on his first. In a businesslike way he removes his
finished paintings and puts them away to dry. Relaxed and content, he leaves the
easel and goes to the table for a cup of fruit juice which is served at the end of the
first hour in school. He finishes his juice quickly and returns his cup to the tray.
Then he joins a group who are marching to music which the teacher is playing
on the piano. Our child tries the drum and then the bells as he marches. When
the marching stops, he stays with a group around the piano who have begun to
sing with the teacher.

   Soon he notices that some children are outside and runs and gets his wraps,
needing some help with his boots. The children outdoors are busily engaged in
digging, each in his separate hole, some filling pans and some transferring the
dirt to a big pile. They comment to each other as thoughts occur to them. They
have occasional conflicts, most of which are settled without help from the nearby
teacher, because they are all satisfied in their activity and are enjoying being
together. Someone finds a worm and the teacher explains how the worm eats and
digs. By the time the group begins to grow weary, it's almost noon. The teacher
steers them inside to get cleaned up in time to hear a story before lunch.

Courtesy of Myron Papiz.

Finger-painting is a satisfying activity.

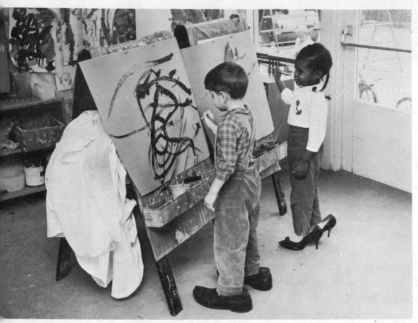

Artists work together after putting on "grown-up" footwear.

When his wraps are off, our child uses the toilet again, spends some time enjoying washing his hands—and they really need washing! Then he joins the group listening to stories. The teacher has a book with pictures of animals, including insects and worms. She reads the paragraph on earthworms. Our child eagerly adds his account of a worm, as do others. They speculate about what it might be like to be a worm. Our child demonstrates wiggling on the floor. The teacher recalls an experience with worms in fishing. They decide to try a fishing game, and the teacher assures them that she will see that there are fishing poles ready in the morning. Now she has another story to read on the subject. They listen and comment, sometimes relevantly and sometimes not, as the teacher listens, too, and then turns their attention back to the reading.

By the time everyone has "toileted" and washed, it's time for fifteen minutes of rest on cots while the tables are being set for lunch. While the children are resting, they listen to recorded music. It's been a good morning and they are relaxed and comfortable.

Being active and vigorous, our small boy enjoys most of his lunch. He dislikes squash but manages a bite on the teacher's suggestion and takes a second helping of everything else. He drinks some more milk, too. As his interest in food wanes, he gets a little too sociable and tries to get the attention of his quieter neighbor by poking him with a spoon. The teacher gives him her attention by asking if he has finished digging his hole outdoors. He decides to do some more digging and finishes his dessert quickly, runs to the coat room, and gets his wraps. He is outside digging when his father comes; and he has to leave, a little reluctantly, to go home for his nap. The day at nursery school is over.

The Pattern in a Day Care Center Will Be Different

In a day care center, the day will be a longer one. It must fit the working hours of parents. The program will include more of what a home offers, meeting more the child's needs for learning, for personal relationships, and for rest.

The morning will probably start more slowly. The children who arrive first may play quietly inside, and the teacher will help them make the transition from home to school as a place to live. She may put an arm around one, give another a pat, and listen to another talk about what happened at home. She may have a snack ready for the children to supplement their hurried breakfast. As more children arrive, they will separate and go to their different groups.

If the center is large and has several groups, the schedules of the teachers will differ. The "morning" teacher may leave early, and in the late afternoon there will be another teacher with the children who stay later than others. The activities at the end of the day will take into account the children's long day together. The teacher may plan special activities such as telling a story, singing folk songs, perhaps with an autoharp accompaniment, or using finger plays. She will recognize the children's need for a relaxed, quiet period, calling for less initiative and activity on their part. Talking over the day, listening to music, playing table games like lotto or puzzles, or engaging in some special activity like blowing soap bubbles through straws, which involves little equipment or group effort, helps relaxation

Courtesy of Myron Papiz.

A group enjoys a story in a homelike atmosphere.

and gives a sense of bringing the nursery school day to a close. Putting things in order and washing hands will be part of the routine. Parents will appreciate being welcomed by a child who is not too tired and a teacher who is still enjoying him and a room which looks lived in but not discouragingly disordered at this point.

The long day will include both a morning and afternoon snack as well as a main meal at noon. There will be a nap period with a rest of perhaps an hour for those few not sleeping and often a much longer rest for those who fall asleep. Here again the teacher will recognize the need to give more "mothering" to children who may need it as they settle down to sleep. The children will spend most of their time in their own group with their own teachers, but there may be times when groups are together on the playground or on trips outside the school as well as at the beginning and the end of the day.

Planning for a full day means that the school is providing a larger share of the children's experiences. There will be excursions to visit the park, a farm, the city zoo, the grocery store or to see construction of a building or of a new sidewalk. There may be visitors to the school—a friendly police officer, or a firefighter who comes by arrangement with a fire truck, or people who play different kinds of instruments, people with pets to show or with other interests to share with children.

Through the days and weeks, children need new experiences to talk about, to broaden their concepts of the world, and to stimulate their thinking. The teachers will encourage conversation. Children need experience with verbal communication and the clarification of ideas which comes through expressing them. In

Playing the role of a mother in a lively telephone conversation.

Courtesy of Jim Fisher, Bakersfield Community College.

a day care center especially, they must depend on finding this in their nursery school experience.

Scheduling includes attention to the needs of teachers, too, if they are to meet the children's needs. Opportunity for rest, provision of efficient, convenient work areas, sufficient help with materials, equipment, and with cleaning are important so that there may be time and energy to meet the children's demands. Professional recognition as well as stimulation is needed, too, so that there is a feeling of worth and a sense of learning and growing as one works. Regular staff meetings are part of the week's schedule, as is time for conferences with parents.

The all-day program requires more administrative planning than the half-day program. But the teacher herself will carry through her full day by working with her fellow teachers and the children in the same way as in the morning program. She will try to be aware of what each child is doing, keeping the needs of individuals in mind but being aware of the needs of the whole group. She will not interfere in the play, but she will contribute to it and to the learning opportunities there. She will provide a structure to the day, with special attention to transition points and to the children's need at times for feeling close to an adult. She will strive to give the children the same sense of sureness about what happens in a nursery school day.

Patterns in All Good Centers

From this description of the morning or full-day program we can see that the atmosphere of the school is a homelike one. There is a free flow of activity, indoors and out, with very little regimentation. There is companionship with others, both children and adults. The adults give security and order to the day and extend experiences for children. A child fits easily into this world. It is equipped to suit his needs. It offers wider experiences and more freedom than most homes can. The teachers are burdened with fewer other responsibilities than most parents are.

The teacher makes notes and keeps records to help her in her evaluation of each child's needs and the progress he makes, as well as in her evaluation of the program and her contribution to it. Learning takes place in the regular staff discussions in which members share their experiences, plan for future activities, and evaluate what has already been done. It also takes place as teachers work with parents, learning from them about individual children, and interpreting to them the philosophy and methods of the school or center. In a good nursery school or day care center the teachers and the parents are in close touch.

TYPES OF PROGRAMS

There are many different types of programs today giving care to young children. No one type of program meets the needs of all children or their parents, but all programs should meet the universal need of children for good physical care with ample opportunity to develop their potentialities, socially, intellectually, and emotionally, and to overcome as far as possible any handicaps that may exist. Different programs offer somewhat different methods of trying to reach these goals, emphasizing different aspects of development.

Courtesy of Jean Berlfein.

The teacher reads a story to the children while they rest.

Day Care Centers

The type of program receiving the most attention today is that of day care. A recent book, *Day Care in Context*, defines day care as "What happens when the child, his family, and a community resource come together."*

Day care centers, or day nurseries as they used to be called, have been in existence in America for more than 150 years. They were established first to meet the needs of children for education and training but soon shifted to meeting the need for care for those children whose parents were unable, because of outside employment, or illness, or inadequate living conditions, to give them adequate care at home. Day care in this country has been a "sensitive barometer of national crises,"† with the number of centers multiplying during wars and periods of depression. Today the numbers are increasing as more women seek employment outside the home.

The philosphies of the day care center and the nursery school grew more similar in the 1930's as more people trained in early childhood education joined the staff of day care centers. The goals for good day care have been given as, "Good day care provides educational experience and guidance, health services, and makes available social services needed by the child and his family. It safeguards children and helps parents to maintain the values of enriched family life."† But

---

*Fein, Greta, and Clarke-Stewart, Alison: New York, John Wiley & Sons, Inc., 1973.
†Newsletter, National Committee for Day Care of Children, Vol. 5, No. 4, Spring, 1955.

serious problems exist because of the large numbers of children needing full-day care, the high cost of good care, and the lack of adequately trained staff.

Day Care Centers Serve Working Parents

The majority of children in day care centers are children whose parents are working outside the home. Many of these are from one-parent families, homes broken by death, divorce, or desertion. Many are from low-income families facing crises such as illness, unemployment, inadequate housing. Some are from minority groups; some speak a language other than English at home. They are children who need the best program that can be made available to them; but, unfortunately, few centers have the resources to give this. Until recently little attention has been given to adapting programs in centers to meet the needs of particular groups of children.

The cost of good day care is high, especially for any center which cares for children under two years of age. Budgets in most centers are inadequate. Support comes mainly from philanthropic or governmental agencies, although there are also centers run privately for profit. Some churches are operating day care centers. Most groups charge a fee on a sliding scale, according to family ability to pay, with the agency making up the balance.

Lincensed centers are required to meet state and local health and safety regulations, but enforcement is often inadequate. Few states have regulations relating to educational standards. Many centers still remain unlicensed.

Recent surveys* indicate that standards are far from acceptable in the majority of centers. Too many of them remain largely custodial. They are often regimented, partly owing to inadequate staffing and untrained staff. Housing is often poorly adapted to the needs of the center, and adequate space, especially outdoor space, is lacking.

A New Staff Category

A training program for a new staff category, Child Development Associate, now under way in some pilot centers, may be of help in staffing centers. In this experimental program credentials are awarded on the basis of demonstrated competence in work with children rather than solely on the basis of college credits. If successful, the program may lead to improved standards in the centers. Such competency may be difficult to evaluate, but the training program opens up possibilities for enlisting men and women with practical experience gained in their own families for work as "care-givers" in day care centers.

Having the Choice of Using Day Care Services

The question may be raised here as to whether it is not more desirable to give support to the mother who needs financial aid but prefers to stay home while her children are young rather than to require her to take a job outside the home. The evidence is clear that having a mother home with her child, if this is what the

---

*For example, Ruderman, F. A.: Child care and working mothers; A study of arrangements made for daytime care of children. New York, Child Welfare League of America, 1968.

mother wishes, contributes in significant ways to the child's sound development. It is very costly to provide a center that can compare with parental care-giving in the first years of a child's life. While the woman who wishes to work outside the home should be assured of having good care available for her child while she is at work, the woman who prefers to stay home should be encouraged to do so.

Helping a mother care for the child at home should not deprive the child of the advantages of a group experience for a few hours a day by the time he is three or four years old. Limited attendance may meet the needs of both mother and child.

The growing number of women at all levels of society who are now employed outside the home increases the need for day care programs, available for all parents, not just those with low incomes. The Department of Labor estimated in 1973 that 4.5 million women with children under six were working in the United States.* The differences which have existed in the socioeconomic levels of children in day care and those in nursery school may tend to disappear as more professional women continue to work outside the home and the use of day care centers for their children increases.

Communities must accept the fact that parents need more support from the community than is usually available to them. The much discussed question of "battered" children is an example of the breakdown in parenting which can occur when social supports are lacking and the problems facing families become too great for them to meet alone. Maintaining an adequate number of good day care centers should be a matter of great community concern. Day care presents a challenge to communities and to the nation because of its great potential for helping families with children.

A national commitment to longterm planning, development, and research is needed if day care is to contribute to the education and development of young children. Without such a commitment "the ever present danger is that day care will itself become an educationally depriving environment."†

Federally Supported Programs

Early Federal Programs

The federal government first gave support to nursery schools in the 1930's under the Works Progress Administration. The purpose then was to mitigate the effects of the depression on low-income families and to provide employment for teachers and other unemployed people. Well-balanced hot meals, health care, a clean place to play and to rest, and play materials were provided. Some training was given to staff to help them plan appropriate experiences for the children. These W.P.A. schools were disbanded as the economy began to improve. With our entry into the Second World War the federal government supported nursery schools again under the Lanham Act. The purpose this time was to encourage

---

*Day Care Facts. Women's Bureau Pamphlet No. 16. Washington, D.C., Department of Labor, 1973.

†Fein, Greta, and Clarke-Stewart, Alison: Day Care in Context. New York, John Wiley & Sons, Inc., 1973, pp. 289–290.

mothers to take jobs in war-related industries. The Lanham schools were closed abruptly with the ending of the war.

Head Start Programs

Head Start programs for preschool children opened as summer programs in 1965 and then were extended to full-year programs in 1966. They were funded under the federal Office of Economic Opportunity with local sponsors and matching funds contributed by local sources. These contributions sometimes took the form of services and use of community buildings. Federal support was steadily reduced during the early 1970's; some programs lacking community support closed.

The federal government took another step in 1969 when an Office of Child Development was added in the Department of Health, Education, and Welfare, with the directive "to take a comprehensive approach to the development of young children, combining programs which deal with the physical, social, and intellectual."

The purpose of Head Start has been to give preschool children the kinds of experiences they need in preparation for school. Educators and parent groups everywhere had become concerned about the large numbers of children who were falling behind in school, especially those from low-income families and minority groups. Head Start programs were designed to help children who have had limited firsthand experiences, limited play opportunities, little experience with books, or who lack competency in using English. The plan included checking for and correcting physical defects in such things as hearing and vision, improving the child's general physical condition, giving the child a feeling of confidence and self-respect, helping him acquire social skills and a good background for concept development and for reading readiness. Parents and members of the community have been expected to become involved in the Head Start program as volunteers or paid assistants.

Home-based programs are being tried in which a teacher visits the child at home and instructs the parent in good guidance practices including ways of stimulating cognitive growth. There is also more emphasis on including physically and mentally handicapped children in Head Start programs. The federal government also supports some "pilot projects" in the field of early childhood education. An example is centers where the staff investigates the competencies needed for the credential of Child Development Associate and methods of evaluating these competencies.

Evaluation of Federally Sponsored Programs

The success of these ambitious programs and of the later Follow Through program has varied greatly, depending on the resources in individual communities. The programs were admittedly hastily conceived with only meager training given to teacher and helpers at first, but many children obviously benefited greatly from the improved conditions for play, from contacts with other children, and from the guidance and the wider experiences available. Where the medical profession was cooperative, defects were often corrected. But the results were disappointing when later school performance was evaluated.

It seems likely that in those programs where the goals were understood, where there was leadership from people trained in early childhood education, where resources were adequate and the experiences offered to the children were appropriate to their developmental levels, the gains were significant. In other programs where these factors were not present and the children were merely introduced to a regular school program earlier, the gains have been limited. Objective measurement of social and emotional gains made by children and their parents is very difficult.

There have been important broad benefits from Head Start, however, in encouraging wider recognition and acceptance of children's need for group experience before six years of age, greater awareness of the need for change in the primary school program itself and the need for better understanding of what good education for young children really is, as well as more recognition of the need for adequate training for teachers or care-givers in all programs.

As federal funding is being reduced, many states and localities are still continuing to offer educational opportunities to young children.

Head Start and Follow Through programs are basically compensatory programs. The need remains for programs which contribute to the child's optimum individual development at each stage of growth, while society strives to overcome the conditions contributing to deficits in development.

Legislation for a "Comprehensive Child Development Program," supported by the professional organizations concerned with the education and welfare of children, was passed by Congress in 1971 but received a presidential veto. It is hoped that some such bill will be passed and approved in the near future. No nation can afford to ignore the needs of its children.

Laboratory Schools

The college or university laboratory schools were among the earliest nursery schools established in the United States, opening shortly after the First World War. They remain focused on preparental education, teacher training, and research; and they may serve as centers for mobilizing the resources of an area to meet the needs of young children. Some of the better nursery school programs for young children today are those maintained by colleges and universities. They set standards and add to the knowledge we have about young children. They usually are financed mainly by the institution itself and are an important part of nursery school development in the United States.

Other Programs Receiving Some Federal Support

Many community colleges and junior colleges have opened laboratory nursery schools where students can receive some training for work with children as "aides" in day care centers, Head Start programs, or other types of centers. These laboratory schools also serve as centers for preparental education for students. The federal government is encouraging preparental training through its "Training for Parenthood" programs, described in the March-April, 1973, issue of *Children Today*. These laboratories contribute to education for parenthood programs.

High schools, too, are involved in education for parenthood as well as in training for work with young children. Some high schools provide experiences with children for their students. A few have a well-run day care center on or near the campus where students may work under supervision, with class discussion of their experiences. Other high schools organize temporary "play groups" to give some experience to their students.

Programs for Handicapped Children

Some nursery schools are offering programs for children with physical, mental, or emotional handicaps. In most cases it is considered desirable to have the child with a handicap in a regular nursery school group, if this group is staffed well enough so that his needs and those of the other children in the group can be met. A blind child may be enrolled in a group of sighted children, for example; or a child with a handicap, such as cerebral palsy or mental retardation which is not severe, may be enrolled in a group of normal children. With a trained person who understands the handicap and can help the parents and the other children in the group to deal constructively with the questions and anxieties a normal person inevitably feels, the experience may be a rewarding one for the group as well as for the handicapped child. Head Start programs may include children with mental or physical handicaps.

Children with behavior disorders ranging from eating problems to more serious problems usually profit from nursery school experience. Emotionally disturbed children often gain from a nursery school experience, as is evident to anyone who has read the story of *Dibs: In Search of Self* by Virginia Axline. If staff members have a chance to discuss the problems they face with a psychiatrically trained consultant, they not only provide more effective help for the child, but they also grow in their own understanding. A few nursery schools are designed to give therapy to seriously disturbed children. Specially trained teachers work with the psychiatrist as part of treatment. The evidence suggests that much more can be done in this respect than has yet been done with the therapeutic type of nursery school.

The number of nursery school groups that accept mentally retarded children is increasing. These children and their parents gain a great deal from the experiences a nursery school offers.

Cooperative Nursery Schools

Another type of school is the cooperative type of school, organized by parents who employ a trained teacher and assist her in carrying out a school program. With good professional leadership and a seriously interested group of parents, these schools have often developed sound programs at somewhat less cost than the private school. Many of these groups have found adequate quarters in churches. Some well-established groups have built their own buildings.

The cooperative nursery school parents face special problems in the relationship with their own child because of the dual role they play as assistant teacher and parent. Careful attention needs to be given to working through the conflict which this dual role may present to both child and parent. When this is done, parents and children both gain from the school experience. The close contacts with other parents who have children at the same stage of development, the sharing of responsibilities, and the need to face and talk through problems as they arise in the school mean a great deal to parents, especially parents of only children or parents with their first child. Because of the complexity of relationships in the setup, cooperative nursery schools often benefit from using the help of a psychiatrically trained consultant.

Many churches have a nursery school run by a trained staff as a service to young children and their parents, or they may provide quarters for a parent-operative school, as we have mentioned.

Parents have also arranged informal neighborhood play groups which run for a short time and meet the needs of the neighborhood group at the time.

Parent Education Programs

Parent education plays an important part in all types of nursery schools. In some communities, school boards run nursery schools as part of a parent education program. Parents participate in the nursery school program and also enroll in study-discussion groups under the direction of a professionally trained parent educator. The interest in such programs indicates the extent to which parents feel the need to find answers to some of their questions and to be better informed about findings in the field of child development.

Private Schools

The number of private nursery schools has grown rapidly in the last few years. Because of their cost, these schools offer nursery school experience to children from wealthier families. When private schools are staffed by competent, trained people, they provide good care for a limited group of children. Very few states, however, set adequate standards or give educational supervision to private nursery schools. The result is that there is little assurance for parents and children that such schools are always good schools. Parents themselves must depend on becoming qualified to judge whether or not a school offers a constructive experience, if they wish to protect their children.

Schools that emphasize one aspect of experience, such as music, or one method of teaching, such as "Montessori method," often make less use of the knowledge and insights available today and tend to be less valuable in promoting all aspects of development. But in any particular school it is likely to be the teacher as a person who is most important to the child attending the school.

There is little need to include here the parking places for children that have been developed solely as commercial ventures and that do not meet educational standards. Children left in such parking places often suffer damage.

SELECTING A SCHOOL OR CENTER

Because there are many types of schools, just as there are many different needs of parents and children, it is important to be informed about what good early childhood education is in order to select a school. There are sources of help, such as the Public Affairs pamphlet by Burgess: *How to Select a Good Nursery School*. But every parent planning to enter a child in a group must visit the school first and decide whether the school provides the climate in which his child can grow best. One of things we shall try to learn is how to identify a good early childhood education program.

HOME-SCHOOL CONTACTS

Whatever the type of school selected, there should be close contacts between the home and the school after the child enters. Teachers and parents need to depend on each other. Parents are under pressures; teachers are under pressures. They need each other's support in the jobs they have to do. The nursery school or child development center can be an important resource for helping both groups face these pressures.

Parents as well as children need to feel at home in the school or center. They should be welcomed and encouraged to stay to observe whenever they wish. The teachers will consult often with the parents, sometimes by telephone and often in the daily contacts they have as parents bring and call for children. They will share accounts of incidents that seem important, so that each may understand the child better. The parents should feel free to consult the teacher. Parents and teachers may plan and make decisions together about what the child may need. The home and the school are working for the same goals.

Consistency and compatibility are important as home and school work for the sake of the children. Teachers and parents each need to be sympathetic to the problems of the other. They need to respect the values and the methods of the other. Exchange of information and frequent discussions are necessary, especially if there are any differences in their expectations for the child.

The value of a parent's visit in the school is increased when the teacher has time to interpret to the mother or father something about what is taking place, explaining the purpose of an activity or of the method used in meeting a situation. Misunderstanding is prevented by such discussion. The parent may be better able to support and extend the work of the school for the child when he is at home.

Parents Often Feel Inadequate

Parents often feel inadequate and defensive as they try to meet the new demands made of them. The gap between what they have experienced and what their children may experience is a large one and not easily bridged. Yet it is more important than ever that parents be able to maintain their values and behave responsibly with their children. If teachers are understanding and sympathetic the school can be a support to parents as they carry out their task. Both parent and child should find satisfaction in the "growing-up" process; and for this parents need encouragement, positive guidance, and an environment that makes possible constructive solutions to problems. Teachers can meet some of these needs for parents just as they do for children.

Teachers Often Feel Inadequate

Teachers, too, often feel inadequate and defensive as they try to meet the new demands being made of them. They need the support of the parents if they are to plan and carry out sound programs. A teacher needs to learn from the mother more about what the child is like, the kinds of experiences he has had, what his interests are, and how he responds at home if she is to understand him well at school. With the help of the mother, she can plan more wisely for this child. The mother needs the teacher's help in keeping in touch with her child. She needs to know what he is like at school and what the nursery school is offering him if she is to understand his growth and to give him the help he needs at home.

Contacts Between Parents and Teachers

The nursery school offers parents the chance to learn, through observation in the school, more about child growth and development and about ways of guiding children's growth. There are many opportunities for contact even when parents do not participate in the program directly. There will be *informal conversations* daily, as parents come and go. These may be short, but they are often significant to both parent and teacher because of the information exchanged and the friendly climate created. Car pools or group arrangements for transportation are a handicap because they cut down on the number of such contacts. There are also *conferences* that the teacher and parent can arrange together, usually outside of school hours when there is a chance for uninterrupted conversation. *Group meetings* of fathers and mothers and staff members are ordinarily held regularly. They offer opportunities for bringing up questions and for talking over subjects of general interest. Usually these meetings are discussion meetings. Occasionally there may be a speaker who answers questions after giving a talk on child nutrition or on some phase of development.

Participating in the school program offers parents a chance to learn more about children and about guidance. Parents may take part as volunteers or as paid workers, paraprofessionals, or aides. By participating they may help broaden the program or meet the needs of individual children.

Regular group meetings are essential when parents are participating in the school program. Staff and parents need to talk over experiences, make plans, and discuss procedures. They need to learn together as they develop the program of the school. Fathers, too, can participate in these discussions and take part in the work of the school, perhaps in a Saturday "work day" held to help with maintenance or the making or repairing of equipment.

Besides its educational value for parents, the nursery school can be of value because it offers parents and children a chance for some experiences apart from each other. There is a real need for time apart when families live in small homes or apartments under crowded conditions. When there is little outdoor play space available and no help from relatives, parents and children need some separation. With a child literally underfoot almost constantly, a mother is likely to find it hard to be loving and patient or to keep from overwhelming the child with too close or too anxious attention. The child in a small family may carry a heavy burden in the

Courtesy of Jean Berlfein.

Lunch is served in the full-day program. This group is served "ethnic" foods.

anxiety, irritation, or attention centered on him, undiluted and undivided. Nursery schools give both parents and child the opportunity to have some freedom from contacts that may be limiting because they are constant and close.

Community understanding and support are important for every school or center. The school is of value to the community and needs support from the community. Teachers need to help citizens become acquainted with their school and with its purposes.

In a later chapter we will discuss further the methods by which parents and teachers may work together in a community.

SITUATION FOR DISCUSSION

*Incident in the Homemaking Area**

One of the most important areas in any center is the homemaking area. Here is a record of play there. The children had time to play out their purposes in this situation.

10:20 In the homemaking corner the small kitchen table is covered with play dishes, pots, and small cars. At the sink Lena (2–11) is busy turning the

_____

*Recorded by Jane Martin.

faucet and swishing her hands as though there were water there. Her head is slightly bent and she hums softly.

Shaylan (3–1) and Davie (4) come into the area and stop by the table. Davie looks over the toys carefully and picks up the new cooking pot. He holds it out, looks at it from all angles, then tucks it under his arm and turns toward Shaylan who is now watching Lena. Softly he calls to Shaylan, "See what I have." Shaylan turns, looks at Davie, and smiles. Then suddenly she scoops up an armful of dishes. The clatter startles Lena who turns wide-eyed to watch Shaylan. Holding the dishes close to her chest, Shaylan goes to the stove, dropping several dishes as she leans over and opens the oven door. She arranges the dishes carefully on the rack.

Lena leaves the sink and excitedly grabs the rest of the toys from the table and puts them in the refrigerator. She returns to the sink, leans down, and opening the cupboard door under the sink, gets out several cups and saucers and drops them with a clatter into the sink. She noisily swishes them around.

Shaylan walks over to watch her. A frown crosses her face as she climbs into the cradle which is next to the sink. She sits, covers her legs with the blanket, and turns to watch Lena who is still swishing the cups and saucers around in the sink. Then Shaylan quickly hops out of the cradle and grabs for the saucers in the sink. Lena tries to push Shaylan away, using her whole body, while she says, "No, no." Shaylan looks at her with a scowl. Lena drops her head and then hands Shaylan a saucer, "Here." Shaylan takes it and carries it to the oven.

Davie, still holding the cooking pot, has been watching the girls. He calls, "Shaylan, Shaylan." Shaylan appears to pay no attention to him but starts rearranging the dishes she had put in the oven. Davie puts the pot down, walks around the table, and sits down. He puts his elbows on the table with his chin in his hands. As he looks towards the block corner, he puckers his lips, making sounds, "choo, choo, choo." Lena leaves the sink, picking up the telephone as she passes the ironing board. Holding the receiver to her ear and carrying the phone, she leaves the homemaking corner. Davie, still making a "choo, choo" noise, gets up and follows her. *10:26*

Comment

Here is an account of a play episode lasting six minutes in the homemaking area in a play group. We see the shifting interests characteristic of this age level, the varied uses of the equipment, the types of social relations the children have, and the roles they try to enact.

Davie who is older than the others selects a particular toy, the new one. He discriminates, in contrast to Shaylan who just scoops up an armful of cups. He uses sentences, "See what I have." He depends on language to call attention to a thing rather than pushing or pulling as the younger children do. When Davie finds he cannot promote sustained play with the group, he leaves the situation.

We note the quality of relationships among these children. Shaylan responds to Davie's attempt to interest her by doing something herself, scooping up a lot of dishes. Then she seems to develop a purpose. She puts the dishes in the oven. Her action suggests something to Lena in turn. Lena puts the rest of the dishes in the refrigerator. Social responses and interest in manipulating materials are both operating. Shaylan and Lena are at about the same stage of development. Lena makes an interesting adjustment when she tries to prevent Shaylan from taking her dishes and then offers her one; but Shaylan is not won over, and Lena then turns her attention to the telephone. Relations are short-lived at this age.

Shaylan is interested in arranging dishes, but at the same time she drops them, paying no attention to those she has dropped. Only Davie takes time to select what appeals most to him. The playing out of activities observed at home is clear, as is the interest in the "baby" role. To *play* being a baby may make more manageable the reality of being a baby, in other people's eyes, at least. The mother role seems important too.

Discussion

What have you learned about these children? How do you feel about the "climate" of this group?

PROJECTS

1. In the nursery school where you are observing or participating, use the check list, "Some Ways of Distinguishing a Good School or Center for Young Children,"* to evaluate the school. In what respects is the school adequate? Are there any respects in which the school is lacking?

If possible, discuss the evaluation with the head teacher and ask her to confirm or explain points to you.

2. What needs does this school serve in the community?

3. Make a survey of the community, and report on the number and types of schools or centers that serve the needs of young children. What are the provisions for the care of young children whose mothers are working?

4. Visit a day care center and a Head Start program, and evaluate these using the same check list. How well do you think the goals of these groups are being met?

REFERENCES

Day Care

Caldwell, Bettye M.: Can young children have quality life in day care? Young Children, April, 1973.
Day Care for Your Children. Washington, D.C., Department of Health, Education, and Welfare, Office of Child Development, Children's Bureau, Pub. No. (OHD) 74–47, 1974. 13 pp. (Single copy free from OCD, P.O. Box 1182, Washington, D.C. 20013.)
Fein, Greta, and Clarke-Stewart, Alison: Day Care in Context. New York, John Wiley & Sons, Inc., 1973.
Keyserling, Mary: Windows on Day Care. New York, National Council of Jewish Women, 1972.
Prescott, Elizabeth, and Jones, Elizabeth: Day care for children—Assets and liabilities. Children, Vol. 18, March-April, 1971.
Prescott, Elizabeth, and Jones, Elizabeth: Day Care as a Child Rearing Environment, Vol. 1. Washington, D.C., National Association for the Education of Young Children, 1972.
Sole, June Solnit: Family day-care—A valuable alternative. Young Children, Vol. 28, April, 1973.
Sulby, Arnold, and Diodati, Anthony: Family day care: No longer day care's neglected child. Young Children, Vol. 20, May, 1975.
Van Loon, Eric: Perspectives on Child Care. Washington, D.C., National Association for the Education of Young Children, 1974.

---

*NAEYC Publications Department, 1834 Connecticut Avenue N.W., Washington, D.C.

Meeting Special Needs

Keister, Mary Elizabeth: "The Good Life" for Infants and Toddlers. Washington, D.C., National Association for the Education of Young Children, 1970.

Klein, Jenny, and Randolph, Linda: Placing handicapped children in Head Start programs. Children Today, Vol. 3, November-December, 1974.

Lewis, Eleanore: The case for "special" children. Young Children, August, 1973.

Provence, Sally: Guide for the Care of Infants in Groups. New York, Child Welfare League of America, 1967.

Rafael, Berta: Responding to Individual Needs in Head Start: Part 1: Working with the Individual Child (Focuses on Handicapped). Washington, D.C., Project Head Start, Office of Child Development, P.O. Box 1182.

Selecting a School or Center

Burgess, Helen S.: How to Choose a Nursery School. Public Affairs Pamphlet No. 310.

Some Ways of Distinguishing a Good Early Childhood Program. (New and revised edition.) Washington, D.C., National Association for the Education of Young Children.

What Are Nursery Schools For? Washington, D.C., National Association for the Education of Young Children, and Association for Childhood Education, International.

Program

Elvardo, Phyllis, and Caldwell, Bettye: "The Kramer Adventure"; A school for the future? Childhood Education, Vol. 50, No. 3, January, 1974.

Harms, Thelma: Change-agents in curriculum: An overview of innovative programs in American schools for young children. Young Children, Vol. 19, July, 1974.

Kellog, E., and Hill, D.: Following Through with Young Children. Washington, D.C., National Association for the Education of Young Children, 1969.

Landreth, Catherine: Preschool Learning and Teaching. New York, Harper & Row, Publishers, 1972.

McFadden, Dennis (ed.): Early Childhood Development: Programs and Services: Planning for Action. Washington, D.C., National Association for the Education of Young Children, 1972.

O'Keefe, Ruth Ann: Home start: Partnership with parents. Children Today, January-February, 1973.

Prescott, Elizabeth: Approaches to quality in early childhood programs. Childhood Education, Vol. 50, No. 3, 1974.

Winnicott, D. W.: The Child and the Outside World. New York, Basic Books, Inc., Publishers, 1957. pp. 3–28.

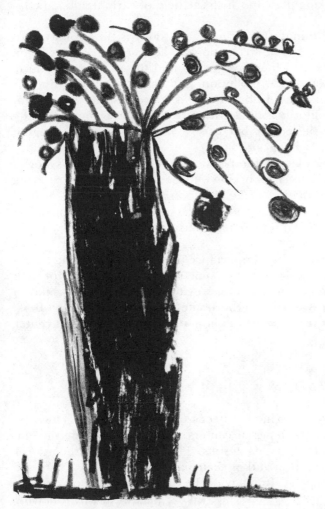

CHAPTER 3

Tree (boy, 4 years)

BACKGROUND AND PHILOSOPHY OF EARLY CHILDHOOD EDUCATION

BACKGROUND

To understand the nursery school program and the philosophy on which it is based, we must see it in relation to the twentieth century world and the people whom it serves. We need, too, to consider some of the theories of educators and clinicians who have influenced thinking in early childhood education. An "information explosion" has been taking place in which the field of early childhood education is sharing.

One of the most striking things about the world today is the rapidity with which it is changing. The tremendous technological advances that have been made in this century have changed the way we live and the problems we face. There are problems of overpopulation, pollution, and the possibility of nuclear destruction. Balances of power are shifting. There is more respect for cultural differences and the rights of minority groups. New life styles are being tried. The family remains the basic unit of society, but it is adapting itself to a changing world.

One of the changes taking place is the position of women in today's world. More and more women of all classes are working outside the house as labor-saving devices and birth control information make this possible. Families are smaller. Men are sharing with women more of the home responsibilities. Women are gaining a more nearly equal status with men in the business and professional world as well as in the general labor market.

Good child care centers assume new importance under these changing conditions. Women who decide to work outside the home need adequate care for their young children while they are at work. There is evidence, too, that all children may need some group experience outside the home by the time they are four, and almost all parents can use the support that a good child development center can offer.

DIVERSITY IN TYPES OF CENTERS

While the number of centers serving the needs of young children is increasing, there is also an increase in the types of centers. We are in an experimental period, exploring methods and evaluating results. The interests and theories of educators vary. The needs of children and of their parents differ also. There are different "models" in existing centers. In many of the programs today parents are more involved than in earlier periods. They are taking part in decision making. They have more options as to the kind of center their child may attend, at least in the urban areas.

Early Nursery Schools

The first nursery schools were activity centered, in contrast to the traditional educational model of the period. One of these early schools grew out of the work of Maria Montessori. Montessori first worked with retarded children in Italy at the beginning of the century. She was convinced that children learned best through activities, by doing, not by sitting and being talked to. In this her ideas were similar to those of John Dewey in America. But, unlike Dewey, she developed sets of materials, which were self-correcting and could be used in sequence from the simple to the complex, or "programmed," needing little supervision. Montessori was interested in children's intellectual development and in developing good work habits. She was less interested in social and emotional development of children or in the creative aspects of experience. She worked mainly with disadvantaged children. Most Montessori schools today have modified her approach, but almost all types of schools make some use of the step-by-step principle in learning.*

One of the first nursery schools to open in the United States was the City and Country School founded by Caroline Pratt and directed by Harriet Johnson with the assistance of Lucy Sprague Mitchell. This school later became the demonstration school for the Bank Street College of Education, New York City. Its founders felt that "the power to deal effectively with his environment accrues to a child through the free use of constructive materials."† They made extensive use of unit blocks and followed the ideas of John Dewey in their activity-centered approach.

Another laboratory school was opened in the early 1920's at Columbia University Teachers College by Patty Smith Hill, who also considered blocks to be important. Her specially designed blocks were used in many schools.

About the same time, the Merrill Palmer Institute, Detroit, under Edna Noble White, a home economist, opened a nursery school to be used as a laboratory for training young women from different institutions throughout the country in the subject of child care. In Boston a day nursery at Ruggles Street became The Ruggles Street Nursery School, headed by Abigail Eliot, in 1922. The program of both these schools was modeled after the school run by the McMillan sisters in England. The McMillan's school in London was one of the first nursery schools to be established, opening before the First World War.

Another early school which also followed an activity-centered approach but had a research interest was a small school operated by Susan Isaacs in the 1920's for advantaged children in England. Isaacs kept full notes of her observations of children's responses. She was interested in the social and emotional aspects of development, in addition to the intellectual aspects, and interpreted her observations with insights from Freudian theory as well as from Piaget's work. Her goal was the development of the whole child. Isaacs provided the children with a rich variety of practical experiences and encouraged children to explore these in their play. She guided the children's spontaneous activities with skill. Her careful observations and reports on the children's learning and on their social development are useful today.‡

Present Day Nursery Schools

Most of the present day nursery schools are child centered and activity centered. The differences in schools lie largely in the amount and kind of guidance given by the staff. Some schools give more directed guidance than others, based on somewhat different assumptions.

The methods in some centers, for example, are influenced largely by the

---

*Montessori, Maria: The Montessori Method. (Reissued.) New York, Schocken Books Inc., 1964.

†Johnson, Harriet M.: Children in the Nursery School. (First published 1928.) New York, Agathon Press, 1972. p. 183. Copyright 1972 by Agathon Press and used with permission.

‡Isaacs, Susan: Intellectual Growth in Young Children (1930). (Reissued.) New York, Schocken Brooks, Inc., 1966; and Isaacs, Susan: Social Development. (Reissued.) New York, Schocken Books, Inc., 1972.

work of the behaviorists, depending on stimulus-response (S-R) conditioning. These schools are less concerned with the "whole child." They are usually more concerned with cognitive aspects of development and with behavior modification. Their methods have been successful in producing short-term gains in some competencies. Long-term gains and the effect on all areas of development are open to question.

One principle, however, which this group has stressed and which is used in all types of centers is reinforcement. The teacher reinforces desired behavior, by giving attention, approval, a privilege, or an object wanted by the child, when the child acts in the desired way or accomplishes the task. The teacher withholds approval or punishes when the child acts undesirably or fails to act. In helping a child develop a skill, for example, such as buttoning his coat or pounding a nail, the teacher may reinforce by her verbal approval each correct step the child takes, thus reinforcing his learning and leading to successful performance of the task. All teachers and parents make use of reinforcement in some way, at some time.

Some schools today depend on published "lesson plans" and on mechanical learning aids. While these may be beneficial for the school-age child, their use at the preschool level is questionable. They are often used because of a lack of adequate training for staff or because of pressure from anxious but uninformed parents. One consequence has been a flood of published material, profitable for publishers. Using lessons planned for children in general does not represent the kind of individualized teaching we are describing. It may even distort the learning process for individual children. Neither "canned" planning nor unplanned programs result in quality education for young children.

The nursery school we are describing is an informal, comfortable place where children and parents can feel at home. Learning for the children takes place through their experiences in daily living with a group in an environment where there is much to explore and wonder about. There is guidance, too, in solving the problems and answering the questions which arise. Independence, initiative, and individual differences in growth rates and "styles" of learning are respected. The goal is to promote the optimum development of the individual child.

EVALUATION

The diversity in types of programs and in teaching methods today makes evaluation a necessary part of any early childhood education program. It becomes important to consider *what* we try to evaluate as well as *how* we evaluate. Evaluation of goals such as building a healthy personality, increasing awareness, improving strategies for problem solving, or exercising imagination is not easy. It is far easier to evaluate more limited or specific goals. But both kinds of evaluation should be attempted. Evaluation is necessary and must be constantly carried on. We are interested in the "accountability" that gives consideration to personality growth, attitudes, and approaches to learning, as well as to cognitive achievements.

Teaching, as we are describing it, is a demanding job, calling for resourcefulness and understanding along with concern for the child as a person and for all aspects of his development. This is a broad, inclusive goal, and the teacher is the key to its accomplishment.

The teacher herself learns through evaluating. It is rewarding to a teacher to look back over a period of time and note the changes that have taken place in a child or in the group of children. It gives her "leads" for planning. It shows her what is of value or what simply didn't work as she had expected. She improves her teaching. Evaluation also takes place in staff discussions and in consultations with parents, to be described later. It is always an important part of any good program.

In order to evaluate we need to have our goals clearly in mind. We will outline assumptions in a philosophy for early childhood education after we have considered the theories of some people who have influenced the field of early childhood education.

THEORIES INFLUENCING PROGRAMS

THREE PEOPLE WHOSE THEORIES HAVE INFLUENCED EARLY CHILDHOOD EDUCATION

Among the many investigators in the area of child growth and development we have selected three whose thinking has contributed to our understanding of human behavior, Sigmund Freud, Erik Erikson, and Jean Piaget. Many other investigators have, of course, made important contributions, but they have not developed such comprehensive theories. The theories of these three men were based on careful observation of human behavior, much of it done under natural rather than laboratory conditions.

Contribution of Sigmund Freud

The theories of Sigmund Freud have greatly influenced our understanding of personality development. His work in the late nineteenth and early twentieth centuries has been carried forward by many others and has become part of our thinking about personality. It includes the concept of the Unconscious, that great reservoir of universal feeling within us which we can never be directly aware of, but which influences what we do. It also includes an emphasis on the significance of the individual's earliest experience in determining attitudes and patterns of behavior, and the existence of infant sexuality.

Freud described the early stages in sexual development as the anal, the oral, and the phallic, with their respective sources of excitement and satisfaction, followed by a latency period lasting until adolescence. He pointed to the male and female components in the personality of every individual, and the process a child goes through in establishing his or her sex identification.

Freud developed the method known as "psychoanalysis" for gaining insights into the defenses built up by an individual which block the creative use of energies. Psychoanalysts working with disturbed young children have used "play therapy" as a method of treating children's emotional disturbances. Play therapy is based on the principle that in play children often reveal indirectly or symbolically the conflicts they are feeling. Among these therapists is Anna Freud, the daughter of Sigmund Freud, who has made important contributions to our understanding of children.

The process of discovering and accepting one's sex, according to Freudian theory, takes place in the first years of life and becomes the basis for normal sexual adjustment later in life. In the beginning, all infants relate closely to the mother, the care-giver. Later, each moves toward identification with the parent of his or her own sex, male or female. The struggle of the male child to shift identification from the mother to the father is known as the "oedipal conflict" and is most acute in the third, fourth, and fifth years. We see boys of this age asserting themselves in vigorous, aggressive ways, imitating males and needing to have their father's attention and approval.

We can understand, too, the serious problem of young boys in families in which the father is absent. They have a real need for contact with a man from whom they can learn male attitudes and ways of behaving. Day care centers and nursery schools should have men as care-givers to meet this need, as regular staff members or as volunteers. The staff in a preschool center will always be predominantly female, but it should not be exclusively so. Girls, too, need contacts with a man if they are to develop their femininity. Girls shift to a new relationship with their mother, identifying with her as a female, but the shift is more gradual for them.

In the nursery school we observe the interest that children have in each other as they use the toilets together and discover differences in the sexes. Girls may be interested in the boy's penis and wonder why they lack one. All children are interested in the subject of babies and where they come from. They have many misconceptions which can slowly be cleared up by offering the correct information as it is wanted. Both boys and girls try out male and female roles in their sociodramatic play as they seek to discover more about what these roles are like in the grownup world.

Contribution of Erik Erikson

Erikson's interest in personality development led him to observe people in different cultures. From his studies he formulated a theory of stages in personality growth, with each stage having a major "task." He presented an outline of these stages at the 1950 White House Conference in Washington. According to Erikson, a "task" consists in resolving in a favorable direction the conflicting impulses that characterize the stage. For example, in the first stage, during the first months of life, the major task in personality development is to ensure a sufficient balance of trust over mistrust. The task of establishing a large measure of trust rather than mistrust in feeling is not completed in the first months of life, but its most significant growth takes place during this period, the "critical" period for this task. We will consider the crises and tasks of the preschool years as Erikson has outlined them.

Personality Tasks in Childhood as Formulated by Erikson

The first and most basic task in healthy personality development is achieving a *sense of trust outweighing the sense of mistrust*. In the first year or more of life the infant needs to feel that the world is a trustworthy place and that he himself is trust-worthy. This sense of trust will grow out of the experiences the infant has with his mother and later with other significant people in his world. Out of many experiences of having his needs met, being fed when hungry, being kept warm and safe, and being handled with loving care, he begins to trust the world. This feeling enables him to meet the new, the unexpected, the frustrating experiences that come later. Because of these good experiences, the individual learns to trust his own capacity to meet what comes.

Understanding of the importance of early good mothering, and its influence on personality development, has been carried further by D. W. Winnicott, an English pediatrician who later became a psychoanalyst. Winnicott pointed to the importance of a mother's adaptation to her infant in the first weeks and months when, by her sensitive management, she adapts completely to the infant at first and then gradually withdraws this complete adaptation as she senses that the infant is ready to tolerate delays and frustrations—in other words, when he has developed sufficient trust. By presenting the world to him "in small enough doses," she enables the infant to build a sense of trust over mistrust which is the cornerstone of a healthy personality.

All through life we continue to need experiences which contribute to our feeling that the world is a place where we can feel comfortable and trust ourselves. But the most critical point, the crisis point for the development of this trait, is in the earliest months of life. The infant needs protection then from experiences that produce mistrust which may overpower him. Separation from the care-taking person, for example, may be overwhelming to an infant even when it is brief. It may seem an eternity to him because of his undeveloped sense of time.

Mutual adaptation is an important element here. As the weeks and months go by, the infant under favorable circumstances builds up a large "bank account" of trust on which he can draw. His mother can then expect him to make adaptations to her needs and the needs of others. In doing this she shows her trust in him and in his growing capacity to delay satisfaction.

Infants differ in their responses. Some seem to grow to trust easily and others find it more difficult, but it is the mother's sensitive management that enables them to succeed in developing a healthy balance of trust over mistrust. We can see the results in children's behavior when they reach nursery school. The task of continuing to build trust remains important throughout the preschool period. In fact, all our lives, as we suffer disillusionment, we need at times to restore our faith in ourselves and in the trustworthiness of others.

The second task in healthy personality growth is that of developing a *sense of autonomy outweighing the sense of shame or doubt.* Already toward the end of the first year we can see evidence of the child working on this task. It becomes the major task of the second and third years. The mother or other care-givers must be sensitive to the great need of the child to assert his independence at this time. It is the "Me do it" stage, and if he is permitted to "do it," the child has the chance to begin to take steps in organizing himself as a learner. It is the stage in which Spock says the child asks himself, "Am I a man or a mouse?" It is the age of "No" and frequent "contrariness," but out of this is born an independent individual capable of feeling "I *am* someone."

Mutual adaptation is again important here, if this task is to be accomplished with sufficient autonomy to balance the necessary dependence and doubt. It is a

Courtesy of Jean Berlfein.

Pouring one's own juice is a step in independence.

period when the discipline should be mild and reserved for the most necessary points. If we can accept the self-assertion, we find the child usually does what we want because he can feel that *he* is deciding to do what we have asked. Giving him choices, avoiding issues, and introducing a play element all work better than issues at this stage. In this way we are protecting him in his task of beginning to feel himself an autonomous person, "I *am* and I am important and powerful," in his own small world. Feeling autonomous is better than feeling helpless as one faces life.

The third task in personality growth as outlined by Erikson is that of developing a *sense of initiative outweighing the sense of guilt.* It is the important personality task of the child of three, four, and five years, although we see many signs of initiative earlier. In this stage the child is more actively exploring and investigating, he is beginning to ask questions, to think new thoughts, to try himself out in all kinds of ways, to take the initiative, in other words. He is also developing a conscience, a sense of being responsible for actions as an autonomous person. A conscience is necessary and valuable, but it should not carry too heavy a load at this point in healthy personality growth. A four-year-old can easily feel *too* guilty for some transgression or guilty for the wrong things. It is important that his sense of initiative, of being able to forge ahead and try, should outweigh his fear of wrong-doing. Understanding guidance is needed in this period if the child is to emerge with a large measure of initiative outweighing but still maintaining his capacity for guilt.

In this stage the child has an urge to make and to do things. It is a creative period in personality growth. A four-year-old who may be helping to carry the blocks back to the shelves where they belong may suddenly discover the interesting patterns they make as they tumble from his wagon or the way in which they can be stuffed into the holes in the fence. He begins a new and imaginative form of play. He will need a reminder about the job in hand and perhaps some help in getting on with the task, but we can do this with an appreciation for what he has discovered and for the excitement he feels for his discovery. Life should be made up of such experiences when one is four.

This period is an important one for intellectual development. The groundwork is being laid for the child's learning in school. With a firm foundation of trust and a sense of being an autonomous person, he exercises his initiative, taking hold of experiences as they are offered and making something out of them. This is the period in which most nursery school children are when we meet them. We consider this task as we guide them. There will, of course, be unfinished business left over from the earlier stages for almost all children. We need to give help with all these tasks if sound personality growth is to continue, but the major task of the period is to encourage and support the child's sense of initiative.

The next stage, the development of a *sense of industry outweighing the sense of inadequacy or inferiority* is the important task of the school-age child, carrying through to adolescence. At this stage the healthy child sees himself as a "worker" and a

Courtesy of Jean Berlfein.

A sensorimotor experience: a child explores a new material, clay.

"learner." Games with rules, skill in sports, group activities become important. He is a school child ready to accomplish in learning under favorable circumstances. He is in the intellectual stage of "concrete operation," in Piaget's words.

As we work with nursery-school-age children, we will keep in mind these personality tasks and the help we may be able to give children in order that the crises may be resolved in ways favorable to healthy development. We will adapt our methods so we can support the balance of trust over mistrust, the balance of autonomous feeling over doubt, the balance of initiative over guilt; and we will value the child's developing sense of industry over inferiority as he becomes more of a learner and worker.

Contribution of Jean Piaget

Piaget, a psychologist, became interested in observing the development of his own children and devoted himself to studying their behavior, especially the evidences of reasoning and judgment. He continued by observing and interviewing many children. He ended with a theory of how children think and learn. His work has greatly influenced the program of the British Infant Schools. He was well known in Europe before he was "discovered" by American educators in the late 1950's.

Piaget has contributed to our understanding of the stages through which a child goes in the development of his intellectual capacities. On the basis of his detailed observations of children, Piaget has described the following stages.

1. Stage one, from birth to around two years, Piaget calls the *sensorimotor stage.* In this stage, the infant or toddler is looking, listening, touching, smelling, tasting, and moving in response to stimulation of his senses. He learns in sensorimotor ways. Thought consists of patterns of action or sensorimotor schemata. These schemata are ways of behaving that he can apply to a variety of ob-

Courtesy of Robert Overstreet.

These projects call for planning, motor skills, concentration—and facing consequences.

jects or situations, behavior like grasping, shaking, banging. He develops these schemata through "assimilation" or taking in of sensory impressions, and through "accommodation" or modifying his action patterns to fit changes in the situation such as a rattle presented in a different position. He comes to "know" an object like a rattle by having many different experiences with it, fingering it, mouthing it, banging it. Through all these experiences he stores up impressions and nourishes his zest for exploring.

During this stage he becomes aware of the permanence of objects. He begins to look for the rattle he has dropped. He realizes it still exists even when he no longer sees it. His mother is somewhere even when she is not within his sight. His mother is important to him because good relationships with her, her attention and care, enable him to feel enough trust to reach out for new experiences. Her interest and encouragement support his learning and may be as necessary for learning as the experiences themselves.

2. Piaget calls the second stage, from about the age of two to about the age of six or seven, the *preoperational stage.*

In the preoperational stage the child continues to take in impressions but his range of impressions is greatly extended because he can talk, explore wider territories, and participate in more activities. He is having a greater variety of experiences. Assimilating these requires more complex thought processes. He begins organizing his impressions into classes or categories. He perceives similarities and differences. He makes things happen in purposeful ways. He has mental images and uses symbols. He does something and watches to see what will happen. He is no longer so surprised by what happens. He is extending his thought processes. He no longer perceives only in terms of sensorimotor schemata such as implied in, "A hole is to dig." He can think of a hole in many ways, a deep hole or a hole in the street or in the garden where it is muddy.

In this stage the child is assimilating perceptions and accommodating or restructuring his thinking to fit his new level of understanding. For example, he may know that a dog and a cat are "animals." His concept of animal at this point may be of something that has a furry feel, that runs around, that makes a variety of sounds. Then he meets the large, hard-shelled turtle at nursery school. It has a very different feel. It moves very slowly or hardly moves at all and does not make any kind of noise. He is told that it is an animal too. He must "accommodate" these perceptions, changing his concept of "animal" to include this new dimension.

The child at this stage may pretend he is a father and play out the role as he has observed it. A father is a man who goes to work. Then he discovers that Jane's father goes to school. Not only children but also grownups go to school. He has added new dimensions to his concepts of "fathers" and "school."

He accommodates his actions to his perceptions. The child of this age who throws a ball down a slope runs after it to retrieve it, but he may notice that it rolls back to him if he throws it up a slope. He changes his patterns of action to accommodate this new perception. As he plays with different objects in water, we see his play change as he perceives the different properties of objects. Later, as the child begins to move toward the stage of concrete operations, he begins to develop ideas about the general properties of matter and about forces. He enters a transitional period in his thinking.

The Development of Speech.   The development of speech gives the child a new tool for remembering and storing impressions. He can begin to learn from the experience of others, rather than just from his own experience. He can understand simple explanations if they are put in terms of his mode of thought. He is asking questions and seeking answers to "why," but he continues to assimilate and accommodate, to adapt what is perceived or experienced to new patterns of action.

There are steps in the growth of his perceptions. He perceives differences in the way things behave, but it is some time before he can "conserve," or perceive that an amount is the same whether it is in one piece or divided into parts. He knows which is big and which is small, but he is not yet able to seriate or place objects in order from largest to smallest.

Reaching a high level of competence in a field of thought seems to depend on having completed necessary experiences at earlier levels. Brearley and Hitchfield, in discussing the field of measurement, put it this way: "It may well be that a true understanding of measurement at *every stage* needs to be prepared for by experience which provides *implicit* knowledge as a basis for explicit training."* The child may know how to count to ten or to twenty, for example, but he may have implicit knowledge only as far as four on which to base a true understanding of the numbers.

---

*Brearley, Molly, and Hitchfield, Elizabeth: A Guide to Reading Piaget. New York, Schocken Books, Inc., 1969 (paperback). p. 38.

Implicit knowledge: this girl understands the meaning of the word "heavy."

Courtesy of Jean Berlfein.

Problem solving: an achievement based on implicit understanding of balance and space.

Courtesy of Marcy Hull.

3. The third stage Piaget calls the stage of *concrete operations,* with the word "operations" defined as "a means of organizing facts already internalized about the real world so that they can be used selectively in the solution of new problems."* In this stage the child can deal with properties of matter or its stability or invariance in spite of changes in appearance. He gradually extends this understanding to length, weight, and volume.

4. The stage of *formal operations* may begin around the age of eleven or twelve, or later. In this stage, formal or abstract, as well as concrete, operations can be carried out.

As Brearley and Hitchfield point out in their very useful book, Piaget's work has value for teachers because he has shown "the fundamental *connection* between action and learning and the extent to which true learning is dependent on the activity of the learner. 'Activity' is no fanciful addition to the curriculum to give children more enjoyment (although it does) but the necessary element in all learning skill. Piaget has helped us to understand what we mean by activity, by revealing its role in the genesis of mental structure and therefore of 'mind' itself."†

BUILDING TEACHING STRATEGIES ON A FRAMEWORK OF THEORY

Our observations of children hold more meaning when we see, not just an incident standing by itself, but one which is related to a scheme of development, a

*Ibid., p. 168.
†Ibid., p. 166.

part of a whole growing person, appropriate to the stage and giving evidence of an achievement in the total growth pattern.

We recognize that a two-year-old who refuses our proffered hand on a steep slope is exercising his urge to be autonomous. When he pokes his finger into every hole or must touch every object he meets, we recognize that he is in the sensorimotor stage in his learning. We make use of the principle of reinforcement as we direct his efforts to open a latch or lace up his shoe, and we recognize it as such.

When a four-year-old digs up some of the seeds recently planted in the garden to discover what is happening to them, we can accept his behavior as in line with the "initiative" stage of development. We may explain and define some limits for the future, but we do not condemn his behavior and add to his sense of guilt. We observe him building with blocks and we see evidences of "accommodation" and planning as he adjusts to what will work in his scheme and selects just the right block for his bridge. He has a concept of "bridging" spaces. His questions are not just words to us, but evidences of intellectual growth taking place.

The group of four-year-olds arguing in the housekeeping corner are using language to communicate and reach a compromise, each adjusting to the ideas of others, an evidence of a new stage of growth. A year or more earlier the same children would have been pursuing their own purposes in parallel play and might have resorted to blows in case of conflict.

The help that they need from us is different in each stage of social development. We have a framework of theory into which we can fit our observations and on which we can build our teaching strategies.

TENETS IN A PHILOSOPHY OF EARLY CHILDHOOD EDUCATION

The way we undertake to educate children will depend on what we believe to be most essential or important for an effectively functioning human being in a democratic society. It will also depend on what is known about growth and development of young children. A philosophy is based on beliefs and on knowledge.

The following assumptions are common to most early childhood education programs. They embody principles we will be using as we work with children individually or in groups. They are tenets in a philosophy of early childhood education.

The *overall* goal of early childhood education is to provide a child with an environment which will promote his optimum development at a period when growth is rapid and the child is vulnerable to deprivation of appropriate experiences.

All aspects of growth are considered in the program, *physical* development, the development of *social* relationships or the capacity to enjoy and get along with other people, *emotional* development including confidence in and understanding of oneself as a person, and growth in ability to express thoughts and feelings and manage impulses, and *intellectual* or cognitive development, including language competency, nourished through guidance in a stimulating environment.

Some of the basic assumptions and tenets underlying a program are these:

1. *Every child is an individual* with his own rate and style of learning and grow-

ing, his own unique patterns of approach to situations, and his own innate capacities. His genes and his experiences have made him unique. His family experience is different from that of any other individual, with its strengths and its vulnerabilities. Some of these differences may seem "deficiencies" if aspects fail to fit the expectations of a particular situation. A child from a Spanish-speaking home, for example, may seem "backward" when compared with children in an English-speaking group. We need to accept each child as an individual within his own "frame of reference" and values, without employing any limited or preconceived standards. A child skillful in cooperation with others may not be successful in competitively motivated situations, for example; a child with manual skills may be considered "deficient" in an academic setting. To do justice to individuals we need to broaden our horizons to include respect for the strengths of individuals.

Every child needs experiences adapted to his individual needs, with respect for his individuality. For example, Juan, described earlier, waits and watches before entering an activity; while Jean, on the other hand, plunges into new experiences without waiting to watch what others are doing. Guidance for children takes into account their differences and their varying backgrounds of experience.

2. *The genetic constitution and the environment together determine the course of development of an individual.* We may say that the genes determine the limits of develop-

Courtesy of Sam Hollander, San Diego State University.

The child is giving whole-hearted attention to investigating a sponge.

ment and the environment determines how much of what is possible will be achieved. A normal person is born with the capacity for developing speech, for example, but he does not learn to talk unless he is with people who use speech. The kind of language he learns, and how well he uses the language, will depend on his environment.

A normal person is also born capable of a range of feelings. What he will feel, his biases and prejudices, his loves and hates, will grow out of his experiences. In the nursery school we influence the direction and the extent of development in the children we teach.

3. *Intelligence develops as it is nurtured.* Cognitive development depends on adequate and appropriate physical, mental, and social nourishment supplied by the home, the school, and the community. The "critical period" for nurturing intelligence seems to occur early in the life of individuals. The individual needs a range of suitable experiences and opportunities to act on these. He needs to feel secure and valued by people who also value learning.

Intelligence is not just a single entity, although it is part of the whole child. There are varieties of intelligence. Among the children we meet in the nursery school, there will be some who have been well-nurtured intellectually and others whose nurture has not been adequate. Making up for deficiencies may be an important part of the program for many children. Play, both the informal and the more organized types, is significant in nurturing intellectual growth.

4. *All aspects of development are interrelated,* physical, social, emotional, intellectual. The child develops as a whole, with each area influencing and being influenced by what takes place in other areas. In planning a program, we consider the child as a whole, not just one aspect of his development. For example, in planning equipment for developing body skills we are also interested in how these build self-confidence and increase opportunities for contacts with other children and add to the child's knowledge of physical forces.

5. *Growth means change.* Changes take place not only in a child's height and weight but also in his capacities and characteristics. Changes are often accompanied by conflicts or disturbances until a new equilibrium is reached. During these periods of change the child is likely to respond well to appropriate guidance or help. Our role is to influence growth changes in positive, healthy directions, physically and psychologically.

Children's behavior changes as circumstances change. When a child is tired or ill, for example, he behaves differently than when he is rested or well. When we say that a child is "dull" or "lazy" or "selfish," we are reporting *only* what we see at the moment. In time, or under different circumstances, or in someone else's view, the child might be described very differently. We change too. With more experience and more understanding, we perceive different meanings in children's behavior.

6. *Growth takes place in orderly sequences or stages,* with each successive stage depending on the outcome of previous stages. No stage can be skipped without handicapping the child. Rates of growth differ for individual children, but the sequence of stages is uniform. A child sits up before he walks; he laces his shoes before he can tie his laces. Age gives only a general indication of what to expect because children differ in the time they take to complete a stage, but not in the order in which the change takes place. For example, most six-year-olds and some five-year-olds can tie shoe laces but very few four-year-olds can.

Having time to complete each stage, with a variety of experiences appropriate to the stage, enables the child to leave one stage behind and move on, fully prepared for the next. Pressure or "nudging" to move on before a stage is completed inhibits sound growth just as blocking the forward movement does.

In every stage there are certain aspects of development that are "critical," most vulnerable to deprivation at this point, and most likely to benefit from optimum conditions. Severe protein deficiency in the diet of the twelve to twenty-four-month-old child, for example, will impair physical and intellectual development but the same deficiency may have only a temporary effect on an adult. Between six months and twelve months, for example, the infant is at a critical stage in his development of a feeling of trust. He is more disturbed by an extended separation from his mother at this point than he will be later.

7. *Play is an important avenue for learning and for enjoyment.* Children learn through active experiencing in play, using all their senses; through doing things to and with materials; through representing concepts in play, rehearsing roles, and thus clarifying them. Children test out, explore, discover, store up impressions, classify, organize, assimilate, and accommodate to experience.

Discovery and mastery are part of play, as are sustained attention and effort, the characteristics needed in learning. Play calls for initiative, imagination, purposefulness. It calls for motor skills and for social skills. Beginnings of symbolic thinking occur in play. Play with other children is considered essential for healthy personality development. The values of play are increased by informed guidance and a wide variety of appropriate materials and equipment, as well as space and uninterrupted time.

8. *Attitudes and feelings are important in learning and in healthy personality growth.* The attitude of the child toward himself, the way he feels about himself, is an important factor in his learning and in his mental health. If he is to develop well, a child needs to feel that the significant people around him like him and feel that he is an able person. A positive self-concept or self-image enables the child to use his capacities well.

Becoming aware of one's own feelings and those of others and finding avenues for expressing feelings in constructive and creative ways are other important aspects of learning. They can be fostered by understanding guidance. Self-control results from being aware of one's impulses and having avenues into which negative impulses can be channeled. Imagination and its expression in art and language and its use in problem solving can also be stimulated through a favorable environment.

9. *Behavior is motivated by extrinsic and intrinsic factors.* Extrinsic forms of motivation consist in giving attention, approval, or reward for a specific behavior or in withholding attention, in disapproval, or in punishment to reinforce behavior or to make it more likely that the child will repeat or desist behaving in some way. The effectiveness of the reinforcement will depend in part on the relationship existing between the child and the one who reinforces. Personal relationships play a large part in motivation.

Intrinsic motivation comes from inside the child, arising out of his curiosity, his drive towards competence, his past experiences in finding satisfactions or in not finding them. In using a hammer or a saw, for example, the child may persist because he has an end in mind or because he finds satisfaction out of the increasing competency he feels in doing the job.

Timing of reinforcement and type of reinforcement used at any point are important. The child who is doing something because he wants to do it does not need reinforcement, as does a child who is doubtful about himself and his ability. The first child may want to be sure of the teacher's interest, but he is not dependent on her external reinforcement.

10. *Understanding, responsible guidance is necessary* if the child is to develop his potential. In his early years the child needs care-givers who like him, who are generous and warm in feeling, who can assume responsibility for setting limits, who are informed and resourceful in providing him with a favorable environment, who enjoy learning themselves, who can feel respect for the child as well as for themselves, and who can communicate with children. Learning is personal for the child and is influenced by his relationships with those who provide for him and guide him. Personality development depends, too, on personal relationships with care-givers who serve as adequate "models" for the child.

Parents are the child's most important teachers. Teachers need to work with parents. Teachers and parents learn from each other. Early childhood education programs respect the parent-child relationship. Teachers have responsibility for interpreting programs to parents as well as understanding the expectations of the parents about the education of their own child.

11. *The development of a young child suffers if there are deficiencies* in nutrition and health care, in attention and loving care, in opportunities for play which nourishes social, emotional, and intellectual growth, in richness and variety of appropriate firsthand experiences. Some apparent "deficiencies" are only differences in experience, such as those in language competency where English is not the first language. When real deficiencies do occur, they can best be compensated for by going back and supplying what was lacking in earlier stages, giving the chance for sound growth to take place, rather than pushing a child on to the next stage.

12. *A healthy environment is the right of every child and the first responsibility of the community, the state, and the nation.* A healthy environment provides adequate health care, food and shelter, and community services including schools and services that offer support to families. It includes a family life free from excessive burdens of economic insecurity, deprivation, and discrimination, and with adequate provision for satisfaction and stimulation for all members of the family. A child development center is one of these community services. It contributes to the child and the family at a critical point in life.

Throughout the rest of our discussion, we will try to apply these assumptions or tenets to programs that meet the developmental needs of young children.

PROJECT

Select an individual or an organization or agency and report on the contribution this individual or group has made to the field of early childhood education.

REFERENCES

Goals and Methods

Baratz, S., and Baratz, J.: Early childhood intervention: The social science base of institutional racism. Harvard Educational Review, Vol. 40, Winter, 1970.

Biber, Barbara: Challenges Ahead for Early Childhood Education. Washington, D.C., National Association for the Education of Young Children, 1969.

Biber, Barbara: Goals and methods in a preschool program for disadvantaged children. Children, January-February, 1970.

Katz, Lilian: Teaching in preschools: Roles and goals. Children, March-April, 1970.
Moskovitz, Sara: Behavioral objectives: New ways to fail children. Young Children, April, 1973.
Murphy, Lois B.: The stranglehold of norms on the individual child.Childhood Education, Vol. 49, No. 7, 1973.
Piaget, Jean: To Understand is to Invent: The Future of Education. New York, Grossman Publishers, 1973.
Zigler, Edward: Contemporary concerns in early childhood education. Young Children, Vol. 26, No. 3, January, 1971.

History

Almy, Millie: The Work of the Early Childhood Educator. New York, McGraw-Hill Book Company, 1975.
Braun, Samuel J., and Edwards, Esther P.: History and Theory of Early Childhood Education. Worthington, Ohio, Charles A. Jones Publishing Company, 1972.
Engstrom, Georgianna (ed.): Open Education: The Legacy of the Progressive Movement. (Conference led by Bernard Spodek.) Washington, D.C., National Association for the Education of Young Children, 1970.
Fein, Greta G., and Clarke-Stewart, Alison: Day Care in Context. New York, John Wiley & Sons, Inc., 1973.
Johnson, Harriet: Children in the Nursery School (1928). (Revised with an introductory essay by B. Biber.) New York, Agathon Press, Inc., 1972.
Klein, Jennie, and Williams, C. Ray: The development of the Child Development Associate (CDA). Young Children, Vol. 28, No. 3, February, 1973.
Montessori in Perspective. Washington, D.C., National Association for the Education of Young Children, 1966.
Murphy, Lois Barclay: Child development then and now. Child Development, January, 1966.
Standing, E. M.: Maria Montessori: Her Life and Work. New York, The New American Library Inc., 1972.
Synder, Agnes: Dauntless Women in Childhood Education. Washington, D.C., Association for Childhood Education, International, 1972.

The Profession

Almy, Millie: The Work of the Early Childhood Educator. New York, McGraw-Hill Book Company, 1975.
Hymnes, James L.: Early Childhood Education—An Introduction to the Profession, 2nd ed. Washington, D.C., National Association for the Education of Young Children, 1975.

Some People Whose Theories Have Influenced the Profession

Erikson, Erik: Childhood and Society. New York, W. W. Norton & Company, Inc., 1950.
Erikson, Erik: Identity and the life cycle. New York, International Universities Press, 1959. Vol. 1, No. 1.
Freud, Anna: Psychoanalysis for Teachers and Parents. (B. Low, tr.) New York, Emerson Books, Inc., 1935.
Freud, Anna: The ego and the mechanisms of defense. In The Psychoanalytic Study of the Child, Vol. 1. New York, International Universities Press, 1945.
Freud, Anna: Normality and Pathology in Childhood. London, Hogarth Press Ltd., 1965.
Freud, Sigmund: The Ego and the Id. (Revised and edited by James Strachey.) New York, W. W. Norton & Co., Inc., 1960.
Freud, Sigmund: The Unconscious. (Standard edition.) London, Hogarth Press Ltd., 1957.
Inhelder, Barbel, and Piaget, Jean: The Early Growth of Logic in the Child. New York, W. W. Norton & Company, Inc., 1962.
Inhelder, Barbel, and Piaget, Jean: The Psychology of the Child. New York, Basic Books, Inc., Publishers, 1969.
Isaacs, Susan: Intellectual Growth in Young Children. New York, Schocken Books Inc., 1966.
Isaacs, Susan: Social Development in Young Children. New York, Schocken Books Inc., 1972.
Piaget, Jean: The Child's Conception of Number. New York, Macmillan Publishing Co., Inc., 1965.
Piaget, Jean: The Language and Thought of the Child. New York, Basic Books, Inc., Publishers, 1954.
Piaget, Jean: Play, Dreams and Imitation in Childhood, New York, W. W. Norton & Company, Inc., 1962.
Piaget, Jean: The Psychology of Intelligence. New Jersey, Littlefield, Adams & Co., 1966.
Winnicott, D. W.: The Child and the Outside World. New York, Basic Books, Inc., Publishers, 1957.
Winnicott, D. W.: Playing and Reality. New York, Basic Books, Inc., Publishers, 1972.

CHAPTER 4

Lady and Dog (girl, 3 years)

THE CHILDREN AND THE TEACHING STAFF

We have described the characteristics of a good nursery school program; we have followed a hypothetical child through a program; we have listed types of centers serving young children; we have outlined the basic beliefs and tenets in a philosophy of education for young children. We will look now at factors to be considered in the more detailed planning for a program.

Group experience should supplement the child's home experience, supplying a variety in experiences not possible to the same extent at home, companionship with other children, and guidance by trained adults who care about children. For children in a full-day program, the school not only supplements the home, it also contributes some of what the home is unable to provide because of limitations in time, space, or opportunity.

THE CHILDREN

Selecting the Children

Part of the answer to questions about selection of children attending the school or center will lie in the type of school and the needs it serves in the community. A Head Start school, or a school for physically or mentally handicapped children, or a laboratory school is planned to meet special purposes. The children are selected with these particular purposes in mind. Many schools, on the other hand, will decide to meet a variety of needs, enrolling some handicapped children, for example, or children from a diversity of cultural backgrounds.

Schools are fortunate if they can include children of different races and socioeconomic backgrounds. Under the guidance of understanding teachers, such diversity brings significant enrichment in the experiences of all children. Children are sensitive to the feelings and attitudes of others. Under favorable conditions they develop constructive and realistic attitudes that can lead to better human relationships and perhaps to less complacency about discrimination on the part of society in the future. Attitudes begin in the nursery, and the first steps in their disappearance can be taken in the nursery.

In any particular school there will be decisions to be made as to the number of children to enroll, the ages and the ranges in age, and the length of the school day.

The Number of Children in a Group

In a good school the number of children in any one group will not be large. Space arrangements, the ages of the children, the length of the school day, the purposes of the program, and the experience of the staff will be among the factors determining the exact numbers of children. There will be less than twenty children in any one group, for large groups create strains and reduce the contribution that the school can make to individuals. The group will be smaller if

Courtesy of Marianne Hurlbut.

Using blocks together. Notice the shelves for organizing and storing the blocks.

there are many two-year-olds or young three-year-olds in it. It will be smaller if the program is set up to meet special needs, such as needs of handicapped or deprived children.

Ages of Children

The nursery school serves the needs of two-, three-, four-, and sometimes, five-year-olds. Most fives, however, are ready for a good kindergarten experience, one that builds on the child's nursery school experiences.

The best evidence that we have at present indicates that most children are ready for group experience when they are around the age of three years. Unless they can enter programs especially adapted for infants and toddlers,* children seem to need three years in which to "live out" the period of dependency on parents, to achieve sufficient security in the home and with their parents to be ready to belong to a school group and to identify with adults outside the home. Taking this step too soon may distort growth as much as failing to take it when the time is ripe.

Every mother will, of course, recognize in her child an eagerness to be with

---

*See Keister, Mary Elizabeth: "The Good Life" for Infants and Toddlers. Washington, D.C., National Association for the Education of Young Children, 1970.

Homemaking play is important for both boys and girls.

Courtesy of Jim Fisher, Bakersfield Community College.

other children long before he is three. This readiness can be met by informal experiences with children, visiting or having another child visit. These informal experiences help prepare the child for regular, sustained group experiences later.

Many two-year-olds gain from a program planned especially for their needs. The program will probably be one or two hours, or less, a day, perhaps only two or three days a week, with mothers present most of the time at the beginning of the experience. Some schools are exploring the possibilities of this type of program. The real satisfaction that children of this age have in playing beside other children, the benefits they gain from play in an environment rich in opportunities for sensorimotor explorations, and added language experiences make such programs well worthwhile.

Age Range in a Group

Most schools are flexible in the range of ages, the age span depending on the goals of the school, the needs of the community, and the children served. There is some evidence that a narrow age range in a group may increase competitiveness among children and offer less chance for the learnings that come from being with children who are both younger and older. On the other hand, it may be easier for teachers to provide experiences adapted to the children's needs when the age range is narrow. Chronological age is not, however, the only measure of maturity, and the range in levels of development is large in any group, whatever the range in age.

In a "family type" group in which the ages are mixed, the younger children have the chance to learn through watching and playing with older children. The

Singing: "This is the way we wash our face."

older children, in turn, may gain from helping the younger ones and playing with them. Cooperative play seems to occur more easily. The mixed age group at times takes skillful teacher help to prevent the younger child from continually taking a passive role or to prevent the older children from interfering in the play of younger children. Patterns of adjusting to siblings at home may be repeated in the school.

We can only conclude on the evidence we have at present that the optimum range in age may depend on the preferences of the teachers or on the needs in particular situations.

Length of the School Day

The length of the school day varies in different schools. The nursery school age child gains most from school experience that supplements his home experience. Three or four hours a day spent away from home with other children in school serves this purpose for most children. In cases where the needs of the family make a longer school day necessary, as in day care, the program will adapt its pace to meet the demands the longer day makes on the child. It will give him more of what the home cannot provide. He will have a nap at school or at least a longer period for rest. More of his nutritional needs and more of his dependency needs will be met at school.

Where the program serves children whose parents are working outside the home, it must be in session during the hours when the parents may be at work.

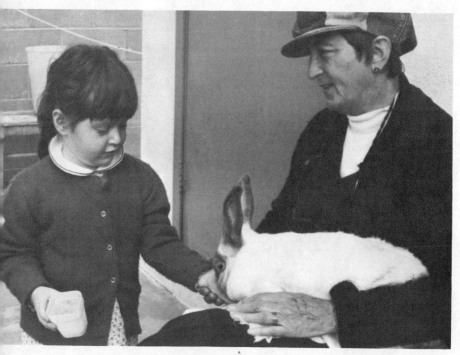

Courtesy of Jean Berlfein.

The teacher and child share a satisfying experience.

THE STAFF

Number and Type of Staff

The number and type of staff members in a school will depend on the size of the school and on its purposes. In a large school there will be a variety of staff members—a head teacher, assistant teachers, aides, students in training, and volunteers who may or may not be parents. There will also be a cook and housekeeper, a person responsible for the cleaning and maintenance of the building, and possibly a "handy man" on a part-time basis. There may be people from other professions such as a social worker, a nurse or doctor who visits regularly, and perhaps a psychologist or psychiatrist who acts as a consultant.

Most of the staff members will be women, but it is very desirable to have men as members of the staff whenever possible, as we pointed out earlier. A man may be a volunteer, on a part-time basis, but he gives the children an added and valuable experience. Some schools are fortunate enough to have men as full-time staff members.

Number of Staff

In a good nursery school there will be more than one adult with each group of children, regardless of the size of the group. There will be one teacher to every eight or ten children. The ratio will be lower if there are children with special needs or if there are very young children.

Courtesy of Jean Berlfein.

Children at the work bench with a teacher ready to help.

Additional staff is needed when two-year-olds are enrolled in the group. The two-year-old needs attention and individual care from a teacher, help in dressing, in using the toilet, and even in eating, at times. He needs to have someone to turn to for encouragement or for comfort. His teacher must be reliably there when he needs her. She must be a person who enjoys the dependency of a young child, without fostering this dependency.

When children with physical or emotional handicaps are enrolled, the school needs additional staff. A blind or partially sighted child, a deaf child, a spastic child, or a mentally retarded child requires more help from a teacher than does a child without a handicap. Emotionally disturbed children need more help. All these children may gain from being in a group of normal children and may contribute to the experiences of the other children when the situation is well-planned and well-staffed. But a balance must be maintained between meeting the needs of special children and the needs of the rest of the group. For the good of all, the group should not be overweighted with handicapped children, or the gains will be less for everyone.

We will discuss in a later chapter the special needs of children whose experiences have been deficient in opportunities for cognitive learning. Additional well-trained staff may be needed if these children are to be helped. A teacher cannot try to meet the needs of too many young children if she is to help them grow and learn as they should.

The number of staff needed is also influenced by the physical setup of the school, the convenience of its plan, and the ease of supervision. If supplies are stored near where they are used, if there are no "blind spots" to hide viewing, teachers have more time to give to meeting the needs of children.*

Personal Characteristics of Teachers

There is ample evidence that the teacher as a person is the most important single factor in determining what nursery school experience will be like for children. Not only a teacher's skill but also her attitudes and feelings will influence what she does for and with the children.

What are the characteristics of a good teacher?

First of all, a teacher needs to be in good physical health and to get adequate rest if she is to meet the daily demands of a group of active young children.

A teacher also needs to be emotionally stable and able to manage her moods and depressions so that they do not interfere with her responses in the teaching situation. She needs to have confidence in herself and in others, a capacity for warm personal relationships, and a zest for living and learning. A sense of humor and a "light touch" will help her keep a perspective as she meets the daily crises in work.

A good teacher is flexible, resourceful, independent in her thinking, realistic, and capable of sustained effort. She is sensitive and responsive but able to use authority in constructive ways. She trusts herself enough to experiment and to act

---

*Cf. Kritchevsky, Sybil, and Prescott, Elizabeth, with Walling, Lee S.: Planning Environments for Young Children: Physical Space. Copyright © 1969, National Association for the Education of Young Children, 1834 Connecticut Avenue N.W., Washington, D.C., 20009.

with spontaneity. In addition, she has a sense of order, an appreciation for beauty and the wonder of life, and a strong faith.

It takes time for a teacher to grow in understanding and skill, just as it takes time for a child to grow. We will find that becoming a good teacher is a process that continues throughout one's teaching experience. There will be teachers in different stages of "becoming" in any group. Learning is partly a matter of becoming more aware of the significance of more and more aspects of experience, as well as of gaining skills in the techniques of teaching. One cannot skip any stages in growth. The attempt to take short cuts may preclude the possibilities of growth in later stages.

We come as human beings to the task of teaching, with our strengths and our weaknesses and our past experiences. The more we understand ourselves as people, the better we help the children understand themselves and others. We serve as models for them in many different ways. As we work with young children and guide their learning, we grow in our own understanding of human relationships. We need to be aware of our feelings and to be patient with ourselves. We need to enjoy making discoveries and learning.

Qualifications of Teachers

The *head teacher* in charge of the group should be well-trained, with previous experience in nursery school teaching. Her training will include a college or university degree with a major in early childhood education or its equivalent. This will include courses in science, social science, and the humanities, with special emphasis in the fields of psychology and education, art and music, and nursery school subjects, including laboratory experiences in working with groups of preschool children. The more extensive her training and experience, the better she should be able to do her job and make good use of her staff.

The *assistant teacher* should also have a background of training in child growth and development and in nursery school methods. She should have an understanding of personality development and the learning process in young children. As part of her training, she should have had laboratory experiences with groups of young children, working with a trained and experienced teacher.

A new professional category is *Child Development Associate.* Training for the CDA in the twelve pilot programs now funded by the federal government is geared to the needs of the individual trainee. One requirement is that a minimum of fifty per cent of the training time be spent in supervised field work, actual experience with children under a competent teacher "model," with regular discussion of these experiences. A certain amount of academic work is coordinated with the field experience.

The credential is based as much on performance with children as on the completion of a prescribed number of credit hours.* *A Guide for Training* for this new professional category of Child Development Associate lists six broad areas of competency needed by CDAs. These competencies are listed as follows:
  1. Setting up a safe and healthy learning environment;
  2. Advancing physical and intellectual competence;

---

*The CDA Program. Washington, D.C., Department of Health, Education, and Welfare, Pub. No. (OCD) 73–1065.

The teacher encourages.

Courtesy of Marianne Hurlbut.

The child succeeds.

Courtesy of Marianne Hurlbut.

3. Building positive self-concept and individual strength;

4. Organizing and sustaining the positive function of children and adults in a group in a learning situation;

5. Bringing about optimal coordination of home and center, child-rearing practices and expectations; and

6. Carrying out supplementary responsibilities related to the children's programs.

These are competencies needed by everyone who works in a center for young children.

Aides

Some schools use aides as assistants to supplement the professionally trained staff members. These aides may work on a full- or part-time basis. They may be young men or women interested in children, or older men or women whose children are grown.

Aides contribute to the program in many ways. They may help with housekeeping duties, keeping things in order, cleaning up after messy play, preparing the paints or clay supplies, or using their skills in repair of equipment. They may supervise to make sure children are safe and may assist teachers by reading or telling stories, by singing or playing an instrument in a music period, and, above all, by spending time with individual children who need extra attention.

The contribution an aide makes can have special value in a school where there are underprivileged children. Every child needs to feel that there is a special place for him. He needs to feel that he is valued by someone. Some children have had little attention because their parents were ill or are burdened with work or the demands of a busy social life. A teenager or an older woman may be able to help this child by giving him a big dose of attention. She can help him in play, talk with him, enjoy books with him, and broaden his experience in many ways.

When there are assistants or aides working in a school, it is important that they understand clearly what is expected of them. They need to know such things as where materials are kept, how they are to be prepared, and what rules about their use are to be enforced. Aides need to be given enough help to be successful for the sake of both the children and themselves.

The successful use of aides will depend on the care taken in their selection, in considering the fitness of their personalities and their motivations. It will also depend on the opportunities they have for "in-service" training. After they begin work, as with all staff members, aides or assistants must have opportunities to talk over situations that concern them, voice their uncertainties, ask questions. They need to see the relation of what they are doing to the whole and to feel that their contribution has significance. They need to discover the intrinsic satisfactions in developing competence.

Volunteers

Volunteers may be very useful in enriching the program of the school. They may come regularly, carrying out duties similar to those of an aide, or they may come for special purposes. One may come in occasionally to play an instrument, a violin or a flute or a horn, for example. There may be one who loves animals and can bring a pet to school or invite the children to visit and get acquainted with the animal at home. Someone who has a collection of interest, such as a shell collection, may bring some bits to share with the children.

Volunteers can contribute needed services, too, helping with transportation on excursions, or coming into the school to prepare snacks or to work with special children. Parents may welcome the opportunity to participate in such ways. They gain from taking part in the program. We will discuss this at greater length in the section on parents.

Assistants, either aides or volunteers, whatever their age, bring their individual capacities for human relationships. When they are able to offer a warm, loving, "caring" type of relationship to a child, they bring him something of great importance. If they are to be successful, there must be someone responsible for giving them adequate directions and a background for understanding individual children, as well as some knowledge about how a child learns and what a child needs to learn. This must be done without diminishing their spontaneity or interfering with their own "style" of relating to children. Success with even one child opens up the possibilities for success with other, different children. For teenagers it may open up new possibilities for success with their own children some day.

Professional Growth Experiences for Staff Members

All teachers need continuing opportunities for professional growth experiences. Some of these will be within the school setting itself. There will be regular staff meetings for planning and for discussing questions that arise about the program, about individual children, and about the philosophy of the school. These meetings make possible a pooling of experiences and an exchange of viewpoints. They help build understanding and improve relationships within the staff. Some staff meetings will include all those who work in the school. Others will include only the regular staff members who are working with the children. Parents will participate in some meetings.

In a large school there will be individual conferences between the director and the head teachers. The school may bring in consultants, preferably on a regular basis, to discuss aspects of growth and development or the problems of individual children.

Other professional growth experiences will be with professional people outside the school, for instance through membership in the professional organization—the National Association for the Education of Young Children—and through attendance at lectures, discussion groups, seminars, and other meetings. There should also be time for things like attending a concert, taking an art class, dancing, skiing, or traveling. These experiences help a teacher return to the job relaxed and renewed.

Staff Discussions: A Method of Evaluation

The staff discussions that are held regularly as part of the program in every good nursery school will center around planning, evaluating, and increasing insights. Group discussions contribute to the professional growth of staff members.

Planning.   In discussions staff members may spend time planning for future activities, such as cooking with the children, deciding what supplies may be needed, how they will share the responsibilities, and what the purposes and outcomes may be. They may discuss how the budget may be allocated to meet needs best. If a trip is planned, there will be arrangements to be made. What and how will these be done? They may evaluate a recent activity, or decide on a change in the arrangement of the housekeeping corner or the placement of the easels.

Improving Insights.   Staff members will also raise questions. One may ask, "I wonder what happened today when the boys were fighting over the wagon outside?" In describing the incident, another member may suddenly realize more clearly just what did happen and the part she may have played in it. Insights into situations and into the needs of individual children grow as a result of thoughtful consideration like this.

As they recall a number of incidents about a particular child, the staff members may begin to understand more clearly the meaning of his behavior. They may develop a more consistent and constructive plan for dealing with his behavior. On the other hand, they may realize that there is much more to understand. They may decide to observe and make notes on this child and to discuss his problems again at the next staff meeting.

Another staff member may comment, "I realized today that I have never given much attention to Jane. She doesn't seem to need it. Now I'm beginning to wonder if she is missing out somehow. She hasn't changed much since she entered school." The staff pools their impressions and observations on Jane, trying to assess her behavior to see whether her patterns are those of independent competence or of passive avoidance of difficulty.

Then someone may comment, "I really felt angry when Jim kicked me today and told me to go away when I was trying to help him." Others assure her that Jim has made them angry, too, and they have felt frustrated and uneasy about their responses to him. In talking about the situation, they feel some relief and can begin to smile at themselves. He is such a little boy, rejecting these big grown-ups. But they begin to wonder what the world must be like for Jim if he sees everybody in it as an enemy. Why does he feel and act this way? What can they do to help him change his perceptions of people and of himself? How is one friendly and firm with such a child?

Staff discussions are one of the ways in which teachers evaluate what is taking place in the school and plan the next steps as they assess what has happened.

Maintaining Relationships.   Staff members become better teachers through such discussions, but discussions like this depend on good staff relationships. The development of good relations may be helped by drawing up some "ground rules" for conducting a discussion, something like these:

It is understood that all members:

1. Agree to respect individual differences in feeling and in "styles" of working and to accept the fact that there are many possible ways of reaching a goal.

2. Agree to refrain from passing judgment on what another person does. Instead they agree to join in looking at questions and in thinking about them, rather than condemning or criticizing. One may ask, "I wonder why you did that?", attempting to understand; or, "I wonder what else could have been done?", attempting to seek other possible solutions.

3. Agree, as a matter of "professional ethics," to respect as confidential the personal things that are discussed in the staff meeting and not to repeat these outside of the professional setting.

In the climate of acceptance set up by such agreement, staff members are better able to be honest and objective in looking at behavior, both their own and the children's. They are better able to function with competence, channeling their energies into common goals, less entangled by the universal problems of jealousy and rivalry. They are better able to work out ways of facing the problems of authority that everyone must face. They are freer to grow in their insights into human relationships, just as they hope to help the children grow in understanding the problems of relationships at their level.

SITUATION FOR DISCUSSION

Davie and a Book*

Davie, wearing a blue knit cap, entered the room slowly and looked around. He did not answer the teacher's, "Hello, Davie," but walked slowly across the room to a low table where several books were scattered haphazardly. Opening the one nearest to him, he slowly turned the pages. A frown appeared on his face and he pursed his lips as he looked intently at each picture.

"Look what I found here, teacher," he finally said to the teacher who was standing near watching a group building with blocks.

Teacher: "What is it, Davie?"

Davie: "It's a choo-choo train."

Teacher: "Where do you think the train is going?"

Davie: "Don't know."

Teacher: "Is there another picture of the train in the book?"

Davie (hurriedly turning the pages): "No train."

Pulling out a chair, Davie then sat down at the table. He turned several more pages and then put both elbows on the book and looked toward the homemaking area. A slight frown remained on his face.

Shaylan, a two-and-a-half-year-old, pulled up a chair next to Davie and sat down, saying, "Train." Davie turned toward her, "No, car. There's a horse," and he pointed to the picture in the open book. Shaylan looked questioningly at Davie and asked, "Horse?" Davie answered, "No, it's a cowboy."

At this point the teacher left the area to answer a knock at the door and Shaylan began to cry, "Jeannie, Jeannie," she sobbed. Davie shoved the book in front of her, "See, Shaylan." She pushed the book away and continued to cry for her sister. Davie watched her.

A student came to the table, stooped down and put her arms around Shaylan, saying, "Mrs. M. will be right back. She is anwering the door. You know, Shaylan, that Jeannie has gone to her class and this is your class." Shaylan's sobbing subsided. Davie closed the book and pushed it to the center of the table. He got up and went over to the homemaking corner.

Comment

This observation is of a three-year-old boy who seems to enjoy looking at books. It consists of two parts, the child looking at the book himself and the child sharing it with another child.

*Recorded by Jane Martin.

In the first episode we see Davie carefully looking through a book. Did he have some special picture in mind? At last he calls his teacher's attention to a picture, "Look what I found here, teacher!" She answers with a question, "What is it, Davie?"

There is an opportunity here to extend the conversation and encourage Davie's verbal communication. Why did Davie pick out the train as something important enough to call to his teacher's attention? What does he already know about trains? What does he want to know?

In this situation the teacher replied by asking a question, "Where do you think the train is going?" to which the child replied, "Don't know." The teacher's question is limiting. It does not enable her to discover a reason for his interest. The teacher might have said, "Tell me about the train, Davie," or she might have asked him, "Have you had a ride on a train, Davie?" Her next question, "Is there another picture of a train in the book?" gave her no more help in discovering what Davie was thinking about.

We see a teacher making an effort to encourage conversation but her specific questions, asked at random, did not bring results. Open-ended questions or personal questions about experiences may be tremendously rewarding in what they bring out in response, while specific questions are often less fruitful.

The second episode begins as Shaylan, a two-and-a-half-year-old, sits down beside Davie and asks, "Train?" picking up his word, showing that she had been listening. He goes on to turn pages and to give her the correct name for each picture. When Shaylan begins to cry, Davie makes an effort to comfort her, pushing the book in front of her, using her name, but with no success. The child stops crying when a student enters the situation.

But what about Davie? He closes the book and leaves. What might the student have done to help *both* children? As well as reassuring Shaylan (which she did effectively), might she have supported Davie in his efforts to help Shaylan?

The student might have gone on to comment, "You and Davie have been looking at pictures together Shaylan. Davie, do you suppose that Shaylan might like to go to the homemaking corner with you and put the babies to bed or set the table?" She could use this suggestion because Davie had been looking toward that area. She could add, "I think Shaylan misses her big sister and feels sad. You can be her friend." The student could have gone with the children to help them get started playing together. Shaylan might have had a friendly experience with another child and perhaps become less dependent on the teacher. Davie would have been successful in his sympathetic role with a younger, lonely child. It might have been a constructive social experience for both.

Discussion

Asking Questions

Contrast open-ended questions with specific or closed-ended ones. When is one appropriate? When is the other? Make a list of possible open-ended questions. What clues can one use in asking a question?

Following Through in Guidance

Consider the needs of *each* child involved in a situation.
What are some clues to use in following through with guidance?

PROJECTS

1. In the school where you are observing or participating, check these points:
(a) The number of children in each group.
(b) The ratio of boys and girls in each group.
(c) The ratio of children and adults in each group.
(d) The training and the experience of the staff members.
What factors are considered in selecting the children?

2. Arrange to observe in a "family type" group, where ages are mixed; also observe in a group where the ages of the children are within about a year of each other. What differences are there between the two groups? What differences might be due to the difference in age range?

REFERENCES

Children

Burt, M.: The effect of a man teacher. Young Children, Vol. 21, 1965.
Cohen, Dorothy: Continuity from prekindergarten to kindergarten. Young Children, Vol. 26, No. 5, May, 1971.
Highberger, Ruth, and Teets, Sharon: Early schooling: Why not? Young Children, January, 1974.
Johnson, Harriett: Children in the Nursery School (1928). (Reissued.) New York, Agathon Press, Inc., 1972.

Evaluation and Certification

Bentley, R. J., Washington, Ernest, and Young, James: Judging the educational progress of young children: Some cautions. Young Children, November, 1973.
Stinnet, T. M., with Pershing, Geraldine: A Manual on Certification Requirements for School Personnel in the U.S.A., Washington, D.C., National Education Association, 1970.

Staff Aides

Aides to Teachers and Children. Washington, D.C., Association for Childhood Education, International, Bulletin 24, 1968.
Kendall, Earline: We have men on the staff. Young Children, Vol. 27, No. 6, 1972.
Klein, Jenny, and Weathersby, Rita: Child Development Associates: New professionals, new training strategies. Children Today Vol. 2, September-October, 1973.
List of capacities and of CDA competencies, available from Office of Child Development, P.O. Box 1182, Washington, D.C. 20013; and from CDA Consortium, 715 Wisconsin Avenue N.W., Washington, D.C. 20014.
Todd, Vivian Edminton, and Hunter, Georgennie: The Aide in Early Childhood Education. New York, Macmillan Publishing Co., Inc., 1973.

CHAPTER 5

My Play Yard (girl, 3 years 4 months)

THE BUILDING: THE EQUIPMENT: THE USE OF SPACE AND TIME

THE BUILDING

The nursery school building itself is an important factor in determining the learning possibilities within the school. A good deal of thought should be given in planning it, for it extends or limits the experiences children have there.

What should we look for in a building to be used as a school or a center for young children?

Amount of Space. The amount of play space per child recommended by

79

the National Association for the Education of Young Children is "at least 35 square feet of free space per child indoors and 75 square feet of space outdoors."

Exposure.   A south exposure is desirable for the playrooms so that they may be sunny and bright. There should be plenty of light coming in through low windows. Children want to be able to look out and see what is happening outside.

Parking Space.   Parking space near the entrance is not only convenient for parents but it also reduces the hazards of traffic for children.

Relation of Rooms to Each Other.   The entrance should be spacious enough to accommodate parents and children as they come and go. It should look attractive, and it should lead directly into the play areas. Outside doors should have child-proof latches. Space for individual lockers for the children should be near the entrance area. The toilet and washrooms should open off the playroom. The outdoor play area should open directly off the inside play space if possible. This arrangement permits a more flexible program and easier supervision of the group.

Playrooms.   The playrooms should be large. They should be arranged in centers bounded by low dividers that can be used for storage and for protecting the play from interference. Low room dividers also enable the teacher to see what is going on. She can supervise from strategic points. In addition to the large playroom, there should be a smaller room adjacent to the large room where individuals or small groups of children can go for special kinds of play or just to be alone. There should also be a staff room with an adjacent toilet and wash basin. The staff room can be used for conferences with parents. It should have a telephone and a locked file for records.

Storage Space.   As every teacher knows, adequate storage space is essential. Storage space where supplies and equipment can be conveniently stored is needed both inside and outside. Water should be available in both places, too. It is needed for mixing paints, for washing soiled clothes, for cleaning up after messy play, and for enriching children's play experiences. There should be provision for drying wet clothing and for a work space for making and repairing equipment.

Playground.   The playground should consist of sunny areas and shady areas and should have a variety of surfaces—grass, dirt and hard-surfaced areas for wheel toys and for play when the ground is wet. A covered outdoor shelter is desirable adjacent to the building so that children can play outdoors even on rainy, cold days. There should be a child-proof fence around the playground with adequate fastenings on any gates. Good landscaping will add interest and variety to the children's experiences. Different kinds of areas—such as a slope, a digging area, and garden space for the children—make different types of play possible.

Health.   Provisions for protecting health are important. The heating and ventilation should be adequate. Shades or blinds may be needed as a protection against glare. Floors should be easy to clean and should be thoroughly washed each day. They should be polished only with a nonslip polish to prevent falls.

Safety.   Hazards like open stairwells or open railings should be eliminated. An experienced teacher is soon able to estimate what may be a hazard and should take steps to remove these. Equipment must be well-maintained, with no loose steps or broken ladder rungs, no protruding nails, no sharp edges at child-height. Fire hazards should be eliminated and fire extinguishers provided as recommended by the fire authorities, with fire escapes as required. The safety and

Courtesy of Robert Overstreet.

Most important is space.

health of the children are a first responsibility for the school. It is wise for every school to carry accident insurance to cover children and staff.

Beauty.   In addition to being safe and functional, a school should be an attractive place where attention is given to color and pleasing lines and shapes—a graceful arrangement of flowers in a bowl, a picture on the wall, an interesting mobile. Children respond to beauty in their surroundings. Many schools must use space in existing buildings that do not have all of these desirable features. The school may have to adapt spaces in churches or schools that are far from ideal. Much can be done in remodeling, however, and in the organization of available space, to make the facilities serve adequately the needs of children.

EQUIPMENT

Equipping a center takes money, but it also takes resourcefulness and imagination. Some minimum essentials must be purchased; but many pieces of equipment can be made, and others can be found in junk shops or second-hand stores or in someone's backyard or attic.

Equipment that is purchased should be sturdy, safe, and capable of serving a variety of purposes. Some large equipment may be fixed, as a jungle gym, but most of it will be moveable. Moveable equipment can be arranged in different ways or set up in different places to suggest new activities or reawaken the children's interests. Sturdy boxes and boards, for example, can serve many purposes on a playground.

Minimum Essentials

The most valuable materials, and often the least costly, are the raw materials that can be used for many purposes, as sand and water, for example. A large sand area contained by a low ledge serves children from ages two through five. They can use it in many different ways, playing alone or in groups. Its possibilities are almost unlimited.

One resourceful mother reported giving her two-year-old rice to play with because she could not provide him with sand in their tiny apartment. She was Japanese and bought rice in twenty-five-pound sacks. She was rewarded by the delight he took in pouring it, piling it, making tracks in it—all the things that could be done in sand. As she said, she could still use the rice afterwards, for she always washed it well before she boiled it.

Play with water is important for young children. It should be provided for because of its great value for children. Tubs, pails, and shallow pans for floating things, washing things, or for just enjoying the feel of water should be part of the equipment of a school. Water, sand, and mud remain essential experiences in children's play today as they have been through the ages.

Another important minimum essential has, from the beginning, been blocks.* Every center should have a variety of blocks of different sizes and shapes. Large blocks promote motor development and encourage cooperative play and dramatic play. Small blocks offer many opportunities for children of all ages to construct and learn in areas such as mathematics, science and art. Blocks should include units, half units, double and quadruple units, as well as a variety of basic shapes

---

*See Hirsch, Elisabeth (ed.): The Block Book. Washington, D.C., National Association for the Education of Young Children, 1974.

A sandbox with accessory materials and water nearby.

Courtesy of Sam Hollander, San Diego State University.

and sizes. Blocks are useful in different ways to children at different stages of development. It has been estimated that about one-third of the floor space should be devoted to block building.

Other minimum essentials are blocks of different sizes, things to push and to pull, wagons and tricycles, old tires and a truck inner tube, and boards and boxes, as well as art materials and books and materials for a housekeeping center.

Materials for Dramatic Play

Among the important supplies in a nursery school are materials for dramatic play. Here the ingenuity of the teacher plays a big part. She will discover all kinds of "bits and pieces" that children can use: squares of cloth, a piece of hose and a firefighter's hat, a brush and a painter's cap, pans from the kitchen, old purses, dress-up clothes of all kinds. With the aid of such props the children can re-create the life around them.

Use of Materials

Some equipment may be used either indoors or outdoors, as the easels or doll carriages. The use of other materials is better restricted to one area. Balls, for example, should be used outdoors. One teacher found it desirable to restrict the use of toy guns to the dramatic play outside in order to prevent disruption of quiet play inside.

Not all materials will be put out for use at any one time. In the first weeks of a session it may be wise to have only a small amount of equipment available for use. Included here should be things likely to be familiar to the children, such as materials in a housekeeping center or blocks. Children can turn to these readily, using them for their own purposes or with others. Things that are easily identified with the cultural patterns of the community are important, such as items used in occupations followed by the fathers or mothers. Paints may not be familiar to the children, but they can be introduced early because of their appeal and the avenues they open for self-expression.

Adequate storage for materials is important. Some materials will be taken out only occasionally, for example, the materials used around Christmas time or for birthday celebrations. A storage area with boxes or cartons clearly labeled so that it will be easy to find them again is essential. The same area may be used to store supplies of paper, paints, crayons, or miscellaneous items ready to use in activities or projects as these develop.

Sometimes equipment seems dangerous at first glance, especially outdoor climbing equipment. But we should remember that children need adventure in play. Every child should have the chance to experience the thrill of climbing up high. Our concern should be with the *safe use* of equipment. Safe use means permitting the child to do as much as he can *by himself*. Giving him too much help may result in the child doing something that is beyond his level of skill. He is more likely to fall or to have an accident, then. Safe use means maintaining certain rules about the use of equipment, such as permitting only one child at a time on a ladder. Safe use may mean showing a child how to use a piece of equipment properly: placing a ladder in a secure way or carrying a sharp implement with the

Logs for active outdoor play.

point downward. Helping children use equipment safely is better than restricting its use. It is part of good teaching.

Children sometimes bring play materials of their own to school. Having something of one's own to hang on to may be an acceptable "security measure" in the beginning, but it is not a desirable practice in general. In nursery school the play equipment belongs to everyone, to be shared on an equal basis. Things are there for everyone to use. If children bring things from home, they should expect to let other children use these, or the article can be put away after the child has shown his possession to his friends, ready for him to take home at the end of the day.

Suggestions for Items to be Included

There are many lists of equipment and supplies for the teacher's reference. She can consult these with the needs of her group in mind. No one list is ever complete. Here we will suggest only some of the items that might be included in different centers of interest in a school.

General Items

Chairs that are sturdy and stack easily, of different heights to fit the varying heights of children, including some for adults.

Low tables that may be fitted together to make larger units when desired, with perhaps a round table for the book corner.

Low room dividers that have shelves for storage of materials such as blocks, puzzles, small trucks, and cars.

A large wall clock, bulletin boards at child-height for children and a higher one for parents, pictures, vases for flowers, or a large aquarium.

Housekeeping Center

Many of these items may be of the homemade variety.

Several dolls, doll beds sturdy enough to hold a child, and doll clothes.

Stove, sink, cupboard for dishes, small table and chairs, a rocking chair, storage unit for dress-up clothes, a mirror. The dress-up clothes should include neckties, belts, coats, caps for boys as well as the more feminine type of apparel, costume jewelry, scarves, hats.

Doll dishes for the table, and cooking pans. At least two doll buggies and two telephones.

Building Center

Blocks of different sizes and shapes, including some large, hollow blocks. It may be wise to purchase a set of unit blocks. If properly cared for, they last for years. Shelves for storage of blocks.

Supplementary materials such as small cars, trucks, cranes, airplanes, farm animals, small figures of people which stand upright. These can be added gradually.

Center for Quiet Play

Small blocks with colors or patterns, puzzles, other manipulative toys, nests of cubes, large beads to string, interlocking blocks.

Matching games (such as "lotto" games), sorting games of all kinds, collections of objects, boxes of materials for collages, and so forth.

Crayons, sheets of plain paper and colored paper, felt pens or marking pencils, paste, blunt scissors.

Center for Exploration and Experimentation

Such a center might include a magnifying glass, magnet, balance scales, egg timer, hourglass, abacus, measuring cups in sets, measuring spoons, steel tape, rule, compass.

It might also include "junk," such as an old clock, pipe fittings, and so forth.

Music Center

A piano, if possible, and a record player (a battery-run machine can be used outdoors), instruments such as a large drum made from a keg and an old drumhead, smaller drums, bells (large gong, if possible, and smaller wrist bells), xylophone, triangle, song books, and squares of colored gauze or scarves for use in dancing.

Art Center

Easel with space for two or four children.

Paint (all colors, including black), large sheets of paper stored adjacent to paints, and provision for drying paintings.

Crock with potter's clay, and a surface where clay can be used.

Paste, colored paper, scissors, collage materials.

Library Center

This center will have a table, some chairs, and a rack or shelves for books. Some books will be part of the school library, and others will be borrowed from the nearest children's library, selected in line with current interests. There may be attractive pictures on the wall, here.

"Messy Play" Center

Table with plain surface that can be washed to be used for fingerpainting or wet clay, perhaps a heavy piece of plastic to be used under the table to protect the floor. A tray for finger-paint jars and a pail in which to wash hands if there is no low sink nearby, containers for finger-paint, roll of butcher paper with cutter on shelf or wall nearby, potter's clay in tightly covered container.

Tub for water play, with small boats and articles to use in the water, plastic aprons for children.

Dramatic Play Materials for Use Indoors or Outdoors

This includes the housekeeping and dress-up materials mentioned earlier, as well as a long mirror. In addition there may be a stethoscope, nurses' caps, and doctor's kit for doctor and hospital play. For playing store, there may be empty cartons, cans, small boxes, paper sacks, string, cash register, telephone, and wagon. For fire-fighting play, there may be several short lengths of hose, small ladders, and hats. For playing service station, lengths of hose, an old hot-water tank with hose attached, painted to resemble a gas station pump. Large paint brushes, buckets, painters' caps for painters.

Other items that might be included: steering wheel from old car, truck inner tube, old tire pump, old faucets, elbow joints, ice cream churn, barrel with pump attached, pulleys.

Active Play Outdoors

Climbing equipment of all kinds such as a jungle gym, ladders, ladder boxes, large crates, barrels, rope ladders or commando nets, shapes and forms of

A suspension walk offers challenges to children.

Courtesy of Jean Berlfein.

cement. (Make sure that these latter objects are not designed only for appearance but that they also provide activities for children. They can be both attractive and functional.)

A slide, crawl barrels, perhaps a section of a large culvert, a tree trunk, rocking boat, balls, beanbags, old tires. On a large playground there may be room for an old car or an old boat. At least two swings with soft thongs for seats.

Building materials such as large hollow blocks, boards of different lengths, saw-horses, packing boxes, canvas to use as roof.

Sand area with accessories such as pans, spoons, strainers, small pails, cars.

Gardening tools such as small sturdy shovels, rakes, trowel.

Wheel toys, like tricycles, wheelbarrows, wagons, trucks.

Carpentry area with storage for tools, places marked with the shape of the tool so that tools can be returned to correct place. The area should have a solid workbench with a vise and tools such as a saw, two or three hammers, a screwdriver, nails of different sizes with large heads, some screws, a soft pencil for marking, a ruler, and plenty of soft wood in a big box or on shelves. (*Note:* Here it is important to limit the number of children using the workbench at one time to a number that can be supervised adequately. This can be done by limiting the tools available.)

Cages for pets—animals need proper housing if they are to be cared for adequately and conveniently.

HOUSEKEEPING

Just as a mother at home knows that order reduces needless frustration, the teacher in the nursery school finds that having a place for materials and equipment and keeping things in their place make for a smoother program. Students, assistants, or volunteer workers in the nursery school find it easier when they know where materials are kept. A neat label on a shelf indicating what is kept there helps those working in a nursery school to be clear about what to replace there. Children, too, gain from knowing that things have a place. They can expect to find them in this place and to take responsibility for putting them back in the right place.

A nursery school assistant will take time to restore order when she finds material scattered during the day. She will not do this in such a way that it interferes with children's play. She will do it in such a way that it adds to the play by giving a sense of new opportunities again. She will also be alert to wiping up spilled water or paint or cleaning a table that may need to be cleaned. It will be important to have mops, cleaning cloths and a broom and dustpan conveniently near. Good housekeeping is as important in a school as in a home.

The nursery should look well lived in, but it should also look attractive. Fresh flowers in a vase with a lovely shape, artistically arranged, bright-colored autumn foliage, perhaps a plant, the children's pictures mounted and carefully hung or fastened to a display board, an interesting mobile, perhaps a piece of fabric with lovely colors, pattern or texture as a wall hanging, an arrangement of forms and shapes which is pleasing—all these add to the charm of a room which should be full of life and color. Children are sensitive to beauty. It becomes part of them. Their attention is caught by the introduction of something lovely. They are aware of these things even though they make no comment on them. The playroom may often be in disorder while it is in use, but if there is an underlying sense of orderliness and of attention to beauty, we can feel it. All of us are influenced by the atmosphere of a room.

Another important aspect of housekeeping with which even the beginning student in the nursery school can assist is in making sure that material is available and that equipment is in working order. If the easel is set up, it needs checking to be sure that the paint jars still have plenty of paint in them, for example. A piece of broken equipment should always be removed, or repaired, if possible. It is discouraging to a child to struggle with a toy which is supposed to stand upright but does not because a part is gone. He may feel that something is wrong with him. He fails to learn what he might have learned through using the equipment. He may carry the frustration he feels into his next experience with things or people where it may interfere with good learning. We avoid difficulties when we keep materials in good condition. They can serve their purposes. Keeping equipment in good condition means keeping surfaces smooth to prevent splinters, for example, or renewing the paint on painted surfaces as it wears off. Equipment kept in order, freshly painted, and stored in a proper place is more likely to be treated with care. We encourage the child to treat equipment with care when we keep it in good order and respect its upkeep ourselves. We are setting a pattern for the child to follow.

THE USE OF SPACE

Arrangement of Equipment

The way equipment is placed in the space available for it influences the use that children will make of the equipment. A housekeeping center with plenty of room in it encourages more children to play there and reduces the amount of conflict. Two or more items of a kind, like two doll buggies, encourage more social play. Easels placed side by side give children a social experience as well as an art experience. Even the use made of wheel toys will depend in part on the amount and arrangement of the hard-surface space available. A broad walk that circles the playground will handle traffic in a way that an unbroken block of hard surfacing in one part of the playground cannot.

Storage space where the children themselves can reach the equipment and put it away easily offers opportunity for them to be independent and self-sufficient. These are all ways in which the arrangement of and for equipment influences the children's behavior. By providing materials that have been carefully selected and by offering adequate arrangements for their use, the nursery school helps ensure a rich environment for children.

The Need for Space

Young children need plenty of space, and the good nursery school will provide enough space for children. They need space for vigorous active play, space for social play, space for "messy" play, space to play alone and undisturbed. Space may be especially important to children who come from crowded homes and neighborhoods.

Courtesy of Marianne Hurlbut.

A commando net for climbing.

When one school* experimented with space arrangements, the teachers found that the children seemed to value "roominess and openness" most. When the children were given the chance to do what they liked with the furniture in the room, they dispensed with the tables, preferring to work on the floor. They left the room rather bare and open. The teachers reported that the children seemed more constructively occupied with materials in the room they had arranged themselves and needed less teacher help in solving conflicts.

Plenty of conveniently arranged storage space is important, space for collections, for "junk" of all kinds that may be of use in the future, things which can be taken apart and examined, and raw materials out of which things can be constructed.

In addition to open spaces there is a need for protected, private corners where children can play undisturbed.

The Contents of Space

Our concern must be with the quality of space as well as the quantity of space. In a pamphlet, "Planning Environments for Young Children: Physical Space,"†

*Pluger, L. W., and Zola, J. M.: A room planned by children. Young Children, Vol. 24, No. 6, September, 1969.

†Kritchevsky, Sybil, and Prescott, Elizabeth, with Walling, Lee S.: Planning Environments for Young Children: Physical Space. Copyright © 1969, National Association for the Education of Young Children, 1834 Connecticut Avenue N.W., Washington, D.C. 20009.

Kritchevsky, Prescott, and Walling present a useful analysis of play space, based on a three-year study made in day care centers. According to their analysis, quality depends on the content and the organization of the space. They classify contents into simple units, such as a swing or a wagon; complex units, such as a sand table with digging equipment; and super units consisting of three or more play materials combined, such as a sandbox with play materials and water. Complex and super units allow for more types of activities and for use by more children at one time.

Using such a classification, the teacher can check her play areas to see whether or not there are a sufficiently wide choice of activities and enough activity for each child. Is there a sufficiently wide choice of things in the units available, or are there a lot of tricycles and no wheelbarrows or wagons, for example? Are the number of play spaces sufficient to provide a place for every child to be doing something and also to permit a change of activity? For example, a housekeeping center equipped with a table and dishes, a stove and cooking utensils, dolls and doll bed, doll clothes and an iron and ironing board will accommodate four children at one time. If there are three children using this "super unit," they can shift activities or make room for another child to enter.

Organization of Space

A recent investigation of preschool programs* concludes that there are three main factors that seem to be related to the quality of the programs observed.

*Day, David, and Sheehan, Robert: Elements of a better preschool. Young Children, November, 1974.

Courtesy of Marianne Hurlbut.
Equipment that promotes large muscle activity.

These are (1) the organization and utilization of physical space, (2) the child's access to materials and the way in which these could be used, and (3) the amount and type of adult-child interaction. With two of the these factors relating to space and equipment, we can see how important these aspects of the environment are.

When space is well-organized, according to Kritchevsky and others cited earlier,* it will have (1) sufficient empty space, (2) a broad, easily visible path through it, (3) ease of supervision, and (4) efficient placement of storage units. Based on their observations, the authors conclude that not less than one-third, and not more than one-half, of the play space should be empty. The empty space should be capable of being used in different ways, such as for setting up a store or for building with blocks. It should be easy for a child to see how to get from one place to another without interfering with any activities. It should also be easy for the teacher to see what is going on in the room without having to walk through the room. Low room dividers that separate play centers make this possible.

The authors point out that the advantage of well-organized space is that the teacher has more "discretionary time" or "time to act out of her own choices made in terms of her knowledge, experience and sensitivities, just as the children are acting out of theirs. . . . It is not necessary for the staff to provide directed activities as a compensation for spatial inadequacy. . . .*

By proper organization of space, the teacher can make the available space serve the needs of the group most effectively. She can eliminate points where activity is likely to be unproductive or full of conflict. She will give herself more time to observe and to work with individuals or small groups. Using space well is an important aspect of good teaching.

USE OF TIME: A SCHEDULE

Every school will work out a schedule to fit its own needs. The schedule will depend on the purposes of the school; the needs of the children; the physical set-up and what it makes possible; and the number of staff, their experience, and their preferences.

There are some generalizations, however, that we can make about a schedule because all children have some needs in common. Any program lasting more than two hours should make provision for the following:

1. Active play outdoors.
2. Quiet play, indoors or outdoors.
3. Rest.
4. Toileting and washing.
5. Nourishment of some kind.

Children also need some order in the events of the day. Those children who have known little order in life at home may be especially in need of order in their school day. A fixed structure to parts of the program gives a child confidence because he knows what to expect. The order need not be rigid. It may be modified when necessary, as for a trip or a special event. Throughout much of

---

*Kritchevsky, Sybil, and Prescott, Elizabeth, with Walling, Lee S.: Planning Environments for Young Children: Physical Space. p. 25. Copyright © 1969, National Association for the Education of Young Children, 1834 Connecticut Avenue N.W., Washington, D.C. 20009.

the day, of course, there should be freedom for children to make choices within the structure. Here are suggestions for events in a schedule:

Arrival. Children like to know what to expect when they arrive at school. They like to know that the teacher will be there to greet them, that she is waiting for them to come, and that she expects them to greet her, too, and then go on to hang up their coats in their lockers or to proceed outdoors, as the case may be.

Snack Time. A mid-morning snack for a morning group, with a snack after rest for an all-day group.

Mealtime. A fixed point of time when the meal is served, preceded by washing and usually toileting and followed by washing, when necessary.

Rest or Nap. A short rest or quiet period before lunch, a longer rest period on cots after lunch in the all-day program (not over an hour if the child does not fall asleep).

Group Time. A time in the day when children are together in small groups under the guidance of a teacher. The activity may be (a) a music period, with singing and marching or other rhythmic activities; (b) a story period, with reading or storytelling; (c) a "work" period, with puzzles, "matching" games, lotto, Lincoln logs, small blocks, and so on, or investigations of some kind; (d) a discussion time, making plans, talking over a past experience, expressing ideas. Some groups will have more than one such period during the day.

Picking-up Time. A time for putting away materials at the end of the morning and at the end of the afternoon in the all-day program.

Departure. After preparations for ending the day are completed, the time comes to say "good-by" to the teacher, something to give a sense of an ending before welcoming the arrival of the parent.

Between these regularly occurring points in the program there should be large blocks of uninterrupted time for play. Someone has said, "No child has enough time for play." The nursery school should make sure that children have plenty of time for play, especially for dramatic play. The teacher will make some of her most significant contributions to children's development through extending and enriching their play, skillfully and unobtrusively, and through observing them as they play and thus coming to understand them better.

Over a period of days, experiences such as these will be part of every program, with children having the chance to participate according to their individual interests:

Music and Dance. Teachers should be ready to sing with children frequently, to play the piano or a record player, or to play for dancing.

Books. Teachers should be ready to read to a child or to small groups.

Art. A variety of art materials should be available for use through the week.

Exploration. Teachers should plan to introduce new materials and experiences for discovery in the school, as well as plan walks and excursions to broaden the children's experiences outside the school.

Language. Teachers should be ready to talk with children, answer questions, listen, and encourage children to create with words.

A flexible schedule for activities encourages initiative on the part of children and teachers. It sustains interest. It permits the group to develop projects over a period of time. But a schedule exists as a framework. It gives a sense of sureness and order to the day.

PROJECTS

1. Draw a diagram of the indoor space and a diagram of the outdoor space in the school where you are. Indicate where a teacher is needed if the areas are to be adequately supervised.

2. Considering the units of equipment as simple, complex, and super, check to see if the number of play units or "spaces" is adequate for the number of children who may be using them.

3. Comment on the variety in play materials available.

4. Comment on the organization of the play space. Are the pathways clearly visible? Does supervision appear to be easily given? Is there enough but not too much empty space?

REFERENCES

Buildings and Grounds

Berson, M. P., and Chase, W. W.: Planning preschool facilities. *In* Frost, J. L. (ed.): Early Childhood Education Rediscovered—Readings. New York, Holt, Rinehart and Winston, Inc., 1968.

Featherstone, Helen: The use of settings in a heterogeneous preschool. Young Children, Vol. 19, No. 3, 1974.

Friedberg, M. Paul: Playgrounds for City Children. Washington, D.C., Association for Childhood Education, International, Bulletin.

Housing for Early Childhood Education. Washington, D.C., Association for Childhood Education, International, Bulletin 22A, 1968.

Lady Allen of Hartwood: Design for Play. (Available from the National Association for the Education of Young Children, Publications Center, 1834 Connecticut Avenue N.W., Washington, D.C. 20009.)

Rudolph, Nancy: Work Yards: Playgrounds Planned for Adventure. New York, Teachers College, Columbia University Press, 1974.

Stanton, Jessie, and Rudolph, Marguerita: Planning a Nursery School Building. New York, Bank Street College of Education, 69 Bank Street, 1962.

Stone, Jeannette Galambos, and Rudolph, Nancy: Play and Playgrounds. Washington, D.C., National Association for the Education of Young Children, 1970.

Equipment

Croft, Doreen, and Hess, Robert: An Activities Handbook for Teachers of Young Children, 2nd ed. Boston, Houghton Mifflin Company, 1975.

Friedman, David, and Colodny, Dorothy: Water, Sand and Mud as Play Materials. (Revised edition.) Washington, D.C., National Association for the Education of Young Children.

Gross, Dorothy: Equipping a classroom. Young Children, December, 1968.

Hirsch, Elisabeth (ed.): The Block Book. Washington, D.C., National Association for the Education of Young Children, 1974.

Hirsch, Elisabeth: Block building—Practical considerations for the classroom. *In* Hirsch, Elisabeth (ed.): The Block Book. Washington, D.C., National Association for the Education of Young Children, 1974.

Play—Children's Business: A Guide to the Selection of Toys and Games. Washington, D.C., Association for Childhood Education, International Bulletin No. 7A.

Stanton, Jessie, Weinberg, Alma, and the faculty of the Bank Street School for Children: Play Equipment for the Nursery School. New York, Bank Street College of Education, 69 Bank Street.

Space and Time

Butler, Annie L.: Early Childhood Education: Planning and Administering the Program. New York, Van Nostrand Reinhold Company, 1974.

Carmichael, Viola, and others: Administration of Schools for Young Children. Sierra Madre, California, Southern California Association for Education of Young Children, 1972.

Day, David, and Sheehan, Robert: Elements of a better preschool. Young Children, November, 1974.

Hewes, Dorothy, and Hartman, B.: Early Childhood Education: A Workbook for Administrators. San Francisco, R. & E. Associates, 1972.

Hirsch, Elisabeth: Transition Periods, Stumbling Blocks of Education. New York, Early Childhood Education Council of New York City.

Kritchevsky, Sybil, and Prescott, Elizabeth, with Walling, Lee: Planning Environments for Young Children: Physical Space. Washington, D.C., National Association for the Education of Young Children, 1969.

Pluger, L. W., and Zola, J. M.: A room planned by children. Young Children, Vol. 24, No. 6, September, 1969.

Sanoff, Henry, Sanoff, Joan, and Hensley, Anderson: Learning Environments for Children (Physical Space and Its Effects). Raleigh, North Carolina, Learning Environments.

PART TWO

BASIC TEACHING SKILLS

CHAPTER 6

Trains (boy, 3 years 7 months)

INITIAL SUPPORT THROUGH GUIDES TO SPEECH AND ACTION

We have described the nursery school itself. Now we turn to the question of how we will fit into a nursery school as students. What guides are there to speech and action? How can we best meet the demands made on us by the school situation while we are increasing our understanding?

We Are Likely to Feel Inadequate at First

Each of us will respond somewhat differently to the experience of beginning to work with children. Some of these responses may interfere with what we do, while others may be helpful.

We discussed in an earlier chapter the necessity of accepting the fact that we may feel uncertain and uncomfortable in the nursery school at first. Too frequently we only increase these feelings by struggling against them, making it more difficult to develop constructive ways of acting. Sometimes we try to defend ourselves against feeling inadequate in a new situation by plunging into action as though to take our minds off the way we feel. In the nursery school we may do unnecessary things like talking to children when talking serves no useful purpose for the child. We may offer help which is not needed or try to start activities which have no real place at the moment in the child's pattern of play. Sometimes we may defend ourselves against feeling inadequate by withdrawing and taking no action at all. Sometimes we may fight against the necessity for direction at first by being very critical of the direction given; and at other times we may seek reassurance by trying to be completely dependent on instructions, insisting that these be specific and detailed so that there is no room for uncertainty.

These adjustments or defenses are part of a resistance to change which we all feel and which is sometimes a protection and often a limitation on growth. Growth is often an uncomfortable process. But growth is rewarding and satisfying when we have mobilized our resources and reduced the conflicts which interfere with our growth. Instead of spending energy trying to deny feelings, we can make constructive use of them.

Guides or Simple Rules Give Support

When one feels inadequate, one needs support of some kind. What are the supports available in the situation? In the nursery school, for example, what help can one get from the experienced teacher? What help can one find in one's own past experiences in related situations, in books, or from discussion? In any new experience we begin to gain confidence when we assemble the useful, appropriate supports and build a framework in which to operate.

In this chapter we will list some techniques and principles which can be depended on at first as guides to action in the nursery school. These can be applied in an increasingly individual way with added experience. The success of some of these techniques depends in part on the relationship built up with individual children. Time is required to build as well as to understand relationships, but during the process these "rules" will give clues to appropriate action. In time, with experience and increasing insight, each one of us will make her own generalizations and add new interpretations. There is always more than one "right" way.

Set down alone, these statements may seem somewhat like letters in an alphabet. Only when they are combined by experience into larger units will they have much meaning. At this point they must be accepted as part of the alphabet which goes to make a "language" used in guiding behavior.

These fifteen points can serve as guides to speech and action in the beginning when the nursery school situation is an unfamiliar one. Here they are.

GUIDES

In Speech

1. State suggestions or directions in a positive rather than a negative form.
2. Give the child a choice only when you intend to leave the choice up to him.

3. Your voice is a teaching tool. Use words and a tone of voice which will help the child to feel confident and reassured.
4. Avoid trying to change behavior by methods which may lead to loss of self-respect, such as shaming or labeling behavior "naughty," "selfish."
5. Avoid motivating a child by making comparisons between one child and another or by encouraging competition.
6. Redirect the child by suggesting an activity that is related to his own purposes or interests whenever possible.
7. The effectiveness of a suggestion or a direction may depend largely on its timing.

In Action

8. Avoid making models in any art medium for the children to copy.
9. Give the child the minimum of help in order that he may have the maximum chance to grow in independence, but give help when the child needs it.
10. Make your directions effective by reinforcing them when necessary.
11. Forestalling is the most effective way of handling problems. Learn to foresee and prevent rather than mop-up after a difficulty.
12. When limits are necessary, they should be clearly defined and consistently maintained.
13. Be alert to the total situation. Use the most strategic positions for supervising.
14. The health and safety of the children are a primary concern at all times.
15. Observe and take notes; increase your own awareness of what goes on.

GUIDES IN SPEECH

1. State Suggestions or Directions in a Positive Form

A positive suggestion is one which tells a child what to do instead of pointing out what he is not to do. If a child has already done what he should not do or if we estimate that he is about to do this, he needs help in getting another, better idea. We give him this kind of help when we direct his attention to what we want him to do.

It has been demonstrated experimentally that directions stated in a positive way are more effective than the same directions given negatively. This can be subjected to proof informally in many situations. For example, a teacher in nursery school demonstrated it in this situation. She was finding it difficult to weigh the children because almost every child reached for support when he felt the unsteadiness of the scale platform. When the teacher asked them not to touch anything, she had very little success. She changed her negative direction to a positive one, "Keep your hands down at your sides," and the children did just that. Telling them what to do, instead of what not to do, brought results.

A question is *not* a statement. We may find ourselves putting something in the form of a question instead of a statement because of our own uncertainty. We may say, "Don't you want to pull the plug?" when we mean that we want the child to pull the plug, but we are not at all sure that we can persuade him to do it. What we should say is, "Pull the plug now and dry your hands. It's time for a story."

A positive direction is less likely to rouse resistance than a negative one. It makes help seem constructive rather than limiting and interfering. Perhaps the child is doing the thing because he thinks it annoys us. By emphasizing the positive we reduce the attention and thus the importance of the negative aspect of his behavior. We usually help rather than hinder when we make a positive suggestion.

In addition, when we make suggestions in a positive way we are giving the child a sound pattern to imitate when he himself directs his friends. He is likely to be more successful, to meet with less resistance, if he puts his suggestions in a positive form. We give him a good social tool to use. One can tell something about the kind of direction that a child has received as one listens to the kind of direction that he gives in play.

More important still, having clearly in mind what we want the child to do, we can steer him toward this behavior with more confidence and assurance — with more chance of success. Our goal is clear to us and to him. We are more likely to feel adequate and to act effectively when we put a statement positively.

To put directions positively represents a step in developing a more positive attitude toward children's behavior inside ourselves. Our annoyance often increases as we dwell on what the child should not be doing, but our feelings may be different when we turn our attention to what the child should be doing in the situation. We may have more sympathy for the child's problem as we try to figure out just what he could do under the circumstances. It helps us to appreciate the difficulties he may be having in figuring out a better solution.

An experienced teacher will often say, "Keep the book on the table, not on the floor," thus letting the child know what he should avoid doing, but her emphasis is on making it clear what he should do. At first, it may be wise to use only the positive part of the statement. It is easy to slip into old habits and rely on the negative. Making only positive suggestions is a hard exercise because most of us have depended heavily on negative suggestions in the past and have had them used on us. It is worth correcting oneself whenever one makes a negative statement in order to hasten the learning of this basic technique. Every direction should be given in a positive form.

For example, the teacher will say:

1. "Ride your tricycle around the bench," instead of, "Don't bump the bench."
2. "Throw your ball over here," instead of, "Don't hit the window."
3. "Leave the heavy blocks on the ground," instead of, "Don't put the heavy blocks on that high board."
4. "Give me the ball to hold while you're climbing," instead of, "Don't climb with that ball in your hand."
5. "Take a bite of your dinner now," instead of, "Don't play at the table."
6. "Take little bites and then it will all go in your mouth," instead of, "Don't take such big bites and then you won't spill."
7. "Play softly on the piano," instead of, "Don't bang on the piano."

2. Give the Child a Choice Only When You Intend to Leave the Situation Up to Him

Choices are legitimate. With increasing maturity one makes an increasing number of choices. We accept the fact that being able to make decisions helps to develop maturity. But there are decisions which a child is not ready to make because of his limited capacities and experience. We must be careful to avoid offering him a choice when we are not really willing to let him decide the question. Sometimes one hears a mother say to her child, "Do you want to go home now?" and when he replies, "No," she acts as though he were being disobedient because he did not answer the question in the way she wanted him to answer it. What she really meant to say was, "It's time to go home now."

Questions such as the one above are more likely to be used when a person feels uncertain or wishes to avoid raising an issue which he is not sure that he can handle. Sometimes using a question is only a habit of speaking. But it is confusing to the child to be asked a question when what is wanted is not information but only confirmation. It is important to guard against the tendency to use a question unless the circumstances make a question legitimate.

Circumstances differ, but usually the nursery school child is not free to choose such things as the time to go home or the time to eat or rest. He is not free to hurt others or to damage property. On the other hand, he is free to decide such things as whether he wants to play outside or inside, or what play materials he wants, or whether he needs to go to the toilet (except in the case of a very young child).

Sometimes a child may be offered a choice to clarify a situation for him. For example, he may be interfering with someone's sand pies and the teacher may ask, "Do you want to stay in the sandbox?" A response of "Yes" is defined further as, "Then you will need to play at this end of the box out of Bobby's way."

It is important to be clear in one's mind as to whether one is really offering the child a choice before one asks a question. Be sure that your questions are legitimate ones.

3. Your Voice Is a Teaching Tool. Use Words and a Tone of Voice Which Will Help the Child to Feel Confident and Reassured

All of us have known parents and teachers who seem to feel that the louder they speak, the greater their chances of controlling behavior. We may also have observed that these same people often have more problems than the parents and teachers who speak more quietly but are listened to. A quiet, firm manner of speaking conveys confidence and reassures the child.

It may be necessary to speak firmly, but it is never necessary to raise one's voice. The most effective speech is simple and direct and slow. Decreasing speed is more effective than raising pitch.

It is a good rule never to call or shout across any play area, inside or outside. It is always better to move nearer the person to whom you are speaking. Children as well as adults grow irritated when shouted at. Your words will get a better reception if they are spoken quietly, face to face.

Speech conveys feelings as well as ideas. Children are probably very sensitive to the tone quality, the tightness in a voice, for example, which reveals annoyance or unfriendliness or fear—no matter what the words may be. One can try for a pleasant tone of voice and one may find one's feelings improving along with one's voice.

The teacher sets a pattern, too, in her speech, as she does in other ways. Children are more likely to use their voices in loud harsh ways if the teacher uses her voice in these ways. Voice quality can be improved with training, and every one of us could probably profit from speech work to improve our voice. A well-modulated voice is an asset worth cultivating.

4. Avoid Trying to Change Behavior by Methods Which May Lead to Loss of Self-respect Such as Shaming a Child or Labeling His Behavior "Naughty," "Selfish"

We need to learn constructive ways of influencing behavior if we are to promote sound personality growth. Neither children nor adults are likely to develop desirable behavior patterns as the result of fear or shame or guilt. Improvement will be more apparent than real, and any change is likely to be accompanied by resentment and an underlying rejection of the behavior involved when these methods of control are used.

It takes time to learn constructive ways of guiding behavior. The first step is to eliminate the destructive patterns in use. We must discard the gestures, the expressions, the tones of voice as well as the words that convey the impression that the other person should feel ashamed of himself. In passing judgment on another, we make the other person feel that we do not respect him. It is hard for a person to change his behavior unless he feels some respect for himself. The young child is especially dependent on feeling that others respect him.

If we believe that there are reasons why a person behaves as he does, reasons why patterns of reacting are established, we will not blame the individual for his behavior. We may see it as undesirable or unacceptable. We may try to change it. But we accept and respect him. We will not add to his burden by passing judgment on him. Labeling behavior, as by calling it "selfish," means we are passing a judgment which is undiscriminating and fails to take circumstances into account. It often prevents us from observing closely. It does not build self-respect.

A child will be helped if we accept him as he is and try to make it possible for him to find some success rather than if we reprove him because he does not meet our standards. Here is an example.

Mark, an active child with a short attention span who often acts destructively, sits down and starts to put a puzzle together. He whines when a piece does not fit in the first place he tries and throws the piece on the floor.

The teacher says, "Does it make you mad when it doesn't fit right away?" She puts into words the feeling he appears to have, thus indicating her acceptance of it and him. This probably helps him to relax.

She reaches down and gets the piece and passes it to him and he completes the puzzle successfully. She says, "That's fine. You did it." She does not reprove him for throwing a piece on the floor or expect him to pick it up. He is not ready to meet such an expectation. It is more important for him to have some success. She helps him be successful and respects him for what he can do.

5. Avoid Motivating a Child by Making Comparisons Between One Child and Another or by Encouraging Competition

Comparing one child to another is a dangerous way to try to influence behavior. We may get results in changed behavior, but these changes may not all be improvements. Some of these results are sure to be damaging to the child's feeling of adequacy and his friendliness.

Competitive schemes for getting children to dress more quickly or to eat more of something may have some effects that are not what we want. Children who are encouraged to be competitive are very likely to quarrel more with one another. In any competition someone always loses, and he's likely to feel hurt and resentful. Even the winner may be afraid of failing next time, or he may feel an unjustified superiority if the contest was an unequal one. Competition does not build friendly, social feelings.

Competition not only handicaps smooth social relationships but also creates problems within the child himself. We live in a highly competitive society, it is true, but the young child is not ready to enter into much competition until his concept of himself as an adequate person has developed enough so that he can stand the strains and the inevitable failures that are part of competition. On the one hand, constant success is not a realistic experience and does not prepare a child well for what he will meet later. Too many failures, on the other hand, may make him feel weak and helpless. Both are poor preparation for a competitive world. For sound growth it is important to avoid competitive kinds of motivation until children have developed ego strength and can balance off failures with successes.

This raises a question about what is sound motivation, anyway. Do we really get dressed in order to set a speed record or to surpass someone else? Is it not true, rather, that we dress ourselves because there is satisfaction in being independent and that we complete dressing quickly in order to go on to another activity? There may be a point in spending time enjoying the process of dressing if there happens to be nothing of any greater importance coming next. We may be better off when we get pleasure out of the doing of a thing, not just in getting the thing done. It is wise to be sure that we are motivating children in a sound way even though we may seem to move more slowly. We ensure a sounder growth for them, and give them a better preparation for the years ahead.

Children should not feel that their only chances for getting attention and approval depend on being "first" or "beating" someone or being the "best." They should feel sure of acceptance whether they succeed or fail. One has only to listen to children on a playground to realize how disturbing highly competitive feelings are to them. Statements like "You can't beat me," or "I'm bigger than you," or "Mine is better than yours" increase friction and prevent children from getting along well together.

6. Redirection Is Most Effective When Consistent with the Child's Purposes or Interests

What does this mean? It simply means that we will be more successful in changing the child's behavior if we attempt to turn his attention to an act which has equal value as an interest or outlet for him. If he's throwing a ball dangerously near a window, for example, we can suggest a safer place to throw it. If he's throwing something dangerous because he's angry, we can suggest an acceptable way of draining off angry feelings—like throwing against a backstop or using a punching bag or pounding at the workbench. In the first case his interest is in throwing and in the second case it is in expressing his anger. Our suggestions for acting differently will take into account the different meaning in his behavior.

We will always try to suggest something which meets the needs he is expressing in his behavior.

Bobby, for example, stands up in the sand and throws a pan at Susan who is startled and cries. Bobby has been playing in the sandbox for some time. The teacher assumes that he has lost interest and needs a suggestion for doing something more active. She says, "Bobby, Susan didn't like that. If you want to throw something, there's a ball over there. Let's fix a place to throw." She turns a barrel on its side and suggests to Bobby that he try throwing the ball through the barrel. He tries it and is successful. They throw it back and forth. Another child joins and takes the teacher's place in the game. It involves a great deal of running and chasing, which both children enjoy.

If a group is running around wildly after a long period of quiet play, its members may need a suggestion about engaging in some vigorous and constructive play like raking leaves outside. Their needs will not be met by a suggestion about sitting quietly and listening to a story. The meaning of their behavior lies in a need for activity. The teacher's part is to help them to find some acceptable expression for this need. If they are running around wildly, on the other hand, because they are fatigued by too much activity and stimulation, a suggestion about listening to a story meets their need for rest.

Effective redirection often requires imagination, as in the following example where the teacher gave a suggestion which captured the interest of these particular children.

Donnie and Michael are at the top of the jungle gym and notice a teacher nearby who is busy writing. They shout at her, "We're going to tie you up and put you in jail." They have a rope with a heavy hook on it. Donnie climbs down with it saying, "I'm going to tie you up!" He flings it toward the teacher and stands looking at her. She says, "You don't quite know what I'm doing here, Donnie, do you? I'm writing down some things I want to remember," and she continues, "I wonder if you could use the hook to catch a fish from the jungle gym. It would take a strong man to catch a big fish from the top of that jungle gym." He picks up the rope and climbs up the jungle gym and the teacher ties a "fish" on to the hook. The boys have fun pulling it up and lowering if for a fresh catch.

Effective redirection faces the situation and does not avoid or divert. The teacher who sees a child going outdoors on a cold day without his coat does not give him help when she stops him by saying, "Stay inside and listen to the story now." She is avoiding the question of the need for a coat. She helps him by saying, "You'll need a coat on before you go outside." On the other hand, in another situation, suggesting a substitute activity may help the child, as in the case of two children wanting the same piece of equipment. The teacher helps when she says to one, "No, it's Bill's turn now. You might rake these leaves while you're waiting for your turn." Redirection should help the child face his problem by showing him how it can be met, not by diverting him.

7. Effectiveness of a Direction or Suggestion May Depend Largely on Its Timing

The timing of a suggestion may be as important as the suggestion itself. Through experience and insight one can increase one's skill in giving a suggestion at the moment when it will do the most good. When a suggestion fails to bring the desired response, it may be due to the "timing."

Advice given too soon deprives the child of a chance to try to work things out for himself. It deprives him of the satisfaction of solving his own problem. It may very well be resented. A suggestion made too late may have lost any chance of being successful. The child may be too discouraged or too irritated to be able to act on it.

Help at the right moment may mean a supporting hand *before* the child loses his balance. It may mean arbitration *before* two boys come to blows over a wagon, or the suggestion of a new activity *before* the group grows tired and disorganized. Effective guidance depends on knowing how to prevent trouble.

Douglas says to Robert, "There's Pam. Let's hit her." They run over and hit Pamela and run away. The teacher comforts Pamela and goes after the two boys. They are already interested in digging and appear resentful of her interfering with their digging. If the teacher could have stopped them firmly and quickly as they started toward Pamela, she might have made it clear to them that she expected them to control their impulse and that she was there to help them control it. She might have asked them what other possibilities there were for action. They were readier to learn the lesson before they hit rather than afterwards. Timing is important.

GUIDES IN ACTION

8. *Avoid Making Models in Any Art Medium for the Children to Copy*

This may seem like an arbitrary rule. We hope that it will seem justified later. Of course it takes away the fun of drawing a man or making little dogs or Santa Clauses out of clay for an admiring crowd of preschoolers. All this may seem like innocent fun, but we must remember that art is valuable because it is a means of self-expression. It is a language to express feelings—to drain off tension or to express well-being. The young child needs avenues of expression. His speech is limited. His feelings are strong. In clay or sand or mud, at the easel, through finger paints, he expresses feelings for which he has little other language. If he has models before him, he may be blocked in using art as a means of *self*-expression. He will be less likely to be creative and more likely to be limited to trying to copy. Art then becomes only another area where he strives to imitate the adult who can do things much better than he can.

Notice what happens to a group at the clay table when the adult makes something. The children watch and then ask, "Make one for me." It isn't much use to say, "You make one for yourself." They can't do it as well and they feel that the adult is uncooperative. Most of them drift away from the table, the meaning gone out of the experience. It is no longer art or self-expression.

You may see children cramped over a paper with a crayon trying to make a car like the one the adult made, or children who will not touch the paints because they are afraid that they can't "make something." They may well envy the joy of the freer child who splashes color at the easel, delighting in its lines and masses, and who is well content with what he's done. He has had no patterns to follow.

The need for help with techniques comes much later after the child has

The freedom to paint over large areas is satisfying to children.

explored the possibilities in different art media and discovered that these can be used as avenues of self-expression. Then the child will want to learn how to use the material to express better what *he* wants to express, but not to imitate better.

The skillful teacher will avoid getting entangled in "pattern making" under any guise. She may sit at the clay table, for example, feeling the clay, patting it and enjoying it as the children do, but she will not "make" anything. It is possible, of course, for children to watch adults who have found in art a means of self-expression as they work in their favorite medium, and for this to be a valuable experience for the children. Being with an adult who is expressing himself through an art medium is valuable for any child, but it is a very different experience from having an adult draw a man or a dog to amuse one. Avoid patterns!

9. Give the Child the Minimum of Help in Order That He May Have the Maximum Chance to Grow in Independence

There are all kinds of ways to help a child help himself if we take time to think about them, such as letting him help to turn the door knob with us, so that he will get the feel of how to handle a door knob and may be able to do it alone someday; or such as putting on his rubbers while he sits beside us instead of picking him up and holding him on our laps, a position which will make it hard for him ever to do the job himself someday. Too many times the child has to climb down from the adult's lap when he might have started in a more advantageous position in the first place on his trip to independence.

Giving the minimum of help may mean showing a child how to get a block or box to climb on when he wants to reach something rather than reaching it for him. It may mean giving him time enough to work out a problem rather than stepping in and solving it for him. Children like to solve problems, and it is hard to estimate how much their self-confidence is increased by independent solving of problems. To go out and gather a child into one's arms to bring him in for lunch may be an effective way of seeing that he gets there, but it deprives him of the chance to take any responsibility in getting himself inside. It is important to give a child the minimum of help in order to allow him to grow by himself as much as possible.

In leaving the child free to satisfy his strong growth impulse to be independent, we support his feeling of confidence in himself. "I can do this all by myself," or "Look what I can do," he says.

We must remember, however, that looking for opportunities to let the child do things for himself does not mean denying his requests for help. When a child says, "Help me" as he starts to take off his coat, he may be testing out the adult's willingness to help. The adult does not meet the test if she replies, "You can do it yourself." She reassures him if she gives help freely, with a full measure of willingness, or if she cannot, answers like this, "I'd like to help you but I'm busy just now," giving whatever real reason she has for not being in a position to help. A child may say "Swing me," and he may be wanting assurance that the teacher really values him enough to do extra, unnecessary things for him. He seeks a relationship with the teacher. It is important to offer him a friendly, giving type of relationship.

Confidence in self is based on a foundation of trust in others and a feeling of being valued by others. When a child *asks* for help, we listen to his request and answer it in a way that will make him less afraid of being helpless and dependent on us. This in no way interferes with our efforts to avoid giving unwanted help, with our efforts to leave the child free to act independently, and with our efforts to help the child find ways to move away from his dependency on us. We will give only the help which the child feels he needs.

10. Make Your Directions Effective by Reinforcing Them When Necessary

Sometimes it is necessary to add several techniques together in order to be effective. A verbal suggestion, even though given positively, may not be enough in itself. "It's time to come in for lunch," may need to be reinforced by another suggestion such as, "I'll help you park your wagon," if the child is reluctant to leave his play, and then reinforced by actual help in parking. A glance at the right moment, moving nearer a child, a verbal suggestion, actual physical help are all techniques, and one must judge when they are to be used. Give only the minimum help necessary but give as much help as may be necessary.

One teacher says quietly, "It's time to go inside now" and moves toward the house. The child moves with her. Another teacher says, "It's time to go inside" and stands as though waiting to see what the child will do. He stays where he is, for her behavior does not reinforce her words. Her behavior suggests something different.

When several children are playing together, some will accept suggestion more readily than others for different reasons. Success with one child will reinforce one's chances of success with others. It is wise to consider which child to approach first when one wishes to influence a group.

One of the most common faults of parents and teachers is that of using too many words, of giving two or three directions when one would have been sufficient. Anxiety and insecurity often take the form of oververbalizing, showering the child with directions. Children will develop a protective "deafness" to too many words. It is important to have confidence in the child's ability to hear and respond to one suggestion, given only once. It is better to add different techniques together until one is successful rather than to depend solely on words.

11. Forestalling Is the Most Effective Way of Handling Problems. Learn to Foresee and Prevent Rather Than Mop-up After a Difficulty

We are all aware that "an ounce of prevention is worth a pound of cure." This is true in working with children. The best strategy depends on foreseeing and forestalling rather than mopping-up operations. Success in forestalling problems comes with experience. It takes time to learn what to expect in certain types of situations or with particular children or combinations of children.

Learning to prevent problems is important because, in many cases, children do not profit from making mistakes. The child who approaches others by doing something annoying may only learn that people don't like him and this may become a reality. He may learn acceptable ways of approaching others if the teacher, observing that he is about to go up to a group and knowing what he did previously in a similar situation, says to him, "If you'd like to play with them, you might knock first or ask Michael if he needs another block," or some other suitable suggestion. She may move into the situation with him to give him more support or to interpret to the group what his intentions are or even to help him accept his failure and find another place where he might have a better chance of success. If she waits until he fails, he may be unable to learn anything constructive. He may only run away.

Learning from experience may not be possible for the child, too, because the consequences would be too serious. In some cases, also, even if the child does suffer consequences, he may interpret them incorrectly. He may not really understand what is involved. This is often true where responses of others or their values and standards are concerned.

Sometimes children tell us what they are going to do. In these cases we need to listen and prevent what may be undesirable, not wait until the damage is done and there is little chance to learn from the experience.

12. When Limits Are Necessary, They Should Be Clearly Defined and Consistently Maintained

There are some things which must not be done. There are limits beyond which a child cannot be allowed to go. The important thing is to be sure that the limits set are necessary limits and that they are clearly defined. Much of the difficulty between adults and children which is labeled "discipline" exists because of confusion about what the limits are. In a well-planned environment there will not be many "no's" but these "no's" will be clearly defined. The child will understand them, and the adult will maintain them.

The children are absorbed in observing a process and anticipating the results to come.

Courtesy of Myron Papiz.

We are very likely to overestimate the child's capacity to grasp the point of what we say. Our experience is much more extensive than his. Without realizing it we take many things for granted. The child lacks experience. If he is to understand what the limits are, these limits must be clearly and simply defined for him.

When we are sure that a limit is necessary and that the child understands it, we can maintain it with confidence. It is easy to feel unsure or even guilty about maintaining limits. We may not like to face a child's unhappiness or his anger. Our own feelings bother us here. We may be afraid to maintain limits because we were overcontrolled, and we turn away from the resentment and hostility that limits arouse in us. Because of our past experiences we may not want to take any responsibility for controlling behavior. Gradually we should learn to untangle our feelings and handle situations on their own merits with confidence and without hesitation.

The adult must be the one who is responsible for limiting children so that they do not come to harm or do not harm others or destroy property. Children will feel more secure with adults who can take this responsibility. They will feel freer because they can depend on the adult to stop them before they do things that they would be sorry about later.

13. Use the Most Strategic Positions for Supervising

Sometimes one will observe an inexperienced teacher with her back to most of the children as she watches one child. On the other hand, the experienced teacher, even when she is working with one child, will be in a position to observe at a glance what the other children are doing. She is always alert to the total situation.

Turning one's back on the group may represent, consciously or unconsciously, an attempt to limit one's experience to a simple situation. It is quite natural that one should feel like withdrawing from the more complex situations at first, or that one should take an interest in one particular child because other children seem more difficult to understand. It is a natural tendency, but one should guard against it. It is important to develop skill extending one's horizons. Observation of the total situation is essential to effective guidance. It is essential if the children are to be safe.

Safety requires teachers who are alert to see that all areas are supervised and not just one area. Enrichment of experience also will come when a teacher is observing all the children and their interest, not just one child. The teacher who is reading to children, for example, may encourage a shy child to join the reading group by a smile, or she may forestall trouble by noticing a child who is ready for a change in activity and encouraging him to join the group before his lack of interest disrupts the play of others.

Sitting rather than standing is another technique for improving the effectiveness of one's supervision. One is often in a better position to help a child when one is at the child's level, and children may feel freer to approach the adult who is sitting. It also makes possible more unobtrusive observation.

In a nursery school where there may be many adults, it is important that the adults avoid gathering in groups, such as near the entrance or in the locker room or around the sandbox. Grouping calls attention to the number of adults present. It may limit the children's feeling of freedom and may increase any tendency they have to feel self-conscious or to play for attention. Too many adults in one place may also mean that other areas are being left unsupervised.

Where one stands or sits is important in forestalling or preventing difficulties. A teacher standing between two groups engaged in different activities can make sure that one group does not interfere with the other and so can forestall trouble.

"Remote control" is ineffective control in the nursery school. Stepping between two children who are growing irritated with each other may prevent an attack, but it cannot be done if one is on the other side of the playroom. Trouble in the doll corner, for example, may be avoided by a teacher moving quietly near as tension mounts in the "family" and suggesting some solution. Her suggestion is more likely to be acceptable if her presence reinforces it. Trouble is seldom avoided by a suggestion given at a distance.

Depending on the physical plan of the school, certain spots will be more strategic for supervision than others. If the teacher is standing near the entrance to the coat room, it will be easy for her to see that a child hangs up his coat before he goes on to play. If she is standing on the far side of the room, she is not in a position to act effectively if he chooses to disregard her reminder. Some places are favorable because it is possible to observe many corners, and others are "blind spots" as far as much observation goes.

Choose the position for standing or sitting which will best serve your purposes. Study a diagram of the school where you are teaching and check the spots which are strategically good for supervision. List places where close supervision is needed for safety, such as at the workbench.

14. The Health and Safety of the Children Are a Primary Concern

The good teacher must be constantly alert to the things which affect health, such as seeing that drinking cups are not used in common, that towels are kept separate, that toys which have been in a child's mouth are washed, that the window is closed if there is a draft, that wraps are adjusted to changes in temperature or activity.

The good teacher must also be alert to things which concern the safety of children. Being alert to safety means observing and removing sources of danger such as protruding nails, unsteady ladders, or boards not properly supported. It means giving close supervision to children who are playing together on high places, or to children who are using such potentially dangerous things as hammers, saws, and shovels. The point is familiar but clear-cut and important. The skillful teacher never relaxes her watchfulness.

15. Observe and Take Notes; Increase Your Own Awareness

Underlying all these guides is the assumption that teaching is based on ability to observe behavior objectively and to evaluate its meaning. As in any science, conclusions are based on accurate observations. Jot down notes frequently, statements of what happens, the exact words that a child uses, the exact sequence of events. Make the note at the time or as soon after the event as possible, always

Courtesy of Pat Schroeder, Bakersfield Community College.

A child squeezes paint from a tube into the water while teacher and other children watch and wonder what will happen.

dating each note. Reread these notes later and make interpretations. Skill in observing and recording is essential in building understanding. Improve your ability to select significant incidents and make meaningful records.

SITUATION FOR DISCUSSION

Play of Younger Children in a Group*

10:26   Shaylan (3–1) is playing, washing dishes in the sink in the homemaking area.

10:28   Shanna Dee (2–7), a blue-eyed little girl with soft blond hair, enters the area, climbs into the cradle, and lies down. Shaylan takes the blanket, shakes it and puts it over Shanna Dee. Shanna smiles at Shaylan. Her eyes sparkle as she says, "Baby, me baby." Shaylan bends over the cradle, nods her head and gives Shanna a hard pat, saying "Baby." She turns and leaves the homemaking corner.

Shanna Dee stays in the cradle. She sits up, rearranges the blanket, rolls over, and pretends to be asleep. Natalie (2–2) appears, leans over the cradle and looks at Shanna Dee. Shanna rolls over and looks at Natalie. Natalie then pushes her with both hands, saying "Out, out." Shanna gets out, clinging to the blanket. With a determined look, lips tight together, Natalie pushes Shanna away and steps into the cradle. Shanna, still holding the blanket, grabs Natalie's dress and tries to pull her out. Natalie yells, "No, no," pushes Shanna with both hands, and then hits her on the chin. Shanna Dee's eyes open wide, and she gives a surprised gasp.

The teacher steps into the homemaking corner. She stoops down, putting one arm around Shanna while with her other arm she gently but firmly helps Natalie out of the cradle. She says, "Natalie, it is not good to hit people. It hurt Shanna when you hit her." Shanna leans against the teacher while Natalie listens with a serious expression on her face. The teacher continues, "Shanna was playing in the cradle first. When she is through, you may have a turn. While you are waiting, would you like to go with me and see what book Lena is looking at?"

Natalie frowns as she watches Shanna get back into the cradle. Then she slips her hand into the teacher's hand saying, "See Lena." The teacher says, "Have a good nap, Shanna Dee. Then Natalie can have her turn." Natalie looks up and smiles. She says, "Read a story." They leave and Shanna Dee snuggles down in the cradle, pulling the blanket up to her chin. She closes her eyes. *10:36*

Comment

The teacher's guidance is well adapted to the age level of these children. She accepts the fact that they are only beginning to learn about property rights and possessions, that they have limited language and social skills. She explains and enforces a standard but attempts to make it easy to accept with her suggestion to Natalie of another activity. Feelings remain good. Natalie is eager for another social experience.

---

*Recorded by Jane Martin.

PROJECTS

1. Observe and record ten directions stated positively which you heard a teacher use in the nursery school. Contrast each with the corresponding negative statement. Indicate the effectiveness of each statement you recorded, giving the reasons why the statement seemed effective, or did not.

2. Observe and record five questions asked by the teacher. Classify the reason for asking a question as (1) to get information about a fact, (2) to discover an opinion or preference, (3) to suggest a possibility, (4) to clarify a situation, (5) another purpose. How effective was the question in each case?

3. Listen to the quality of the voices around you. What feelings do the tones seem to express when one pays no attention to the words spoken? Note the differences in pitch, in rate, and in volume in the voices of the teachers. Report a situation in which you feel that the tone of voice was more important than the words in influencing the child's behavior.

4. Report a situation in which the suggestion or help given was well-timed. Why? Report a situation in which the suggestion or help given failed, apparently because of poor timing. Why?

5. List ways in which you have observed a teacher protecting the health and safety of the children in the nursery school.

REFERENCES

Cohen, Dorothy: Learning to observe—Observing to learn. *In* Engstrom, Georgianna (ed.): The Significance of the Young Child's Motor Development. Washington, D.C., National Association for the Education of Young Children, 1971.

Cohen, Dorothy, and Stern, Virginia: Observing and Recording the Behavior of Young Children. New York, Bureau of Publications, Teachers College, Columbia University, 1958.

Pratt, Caroline: I Learn From Children. New York, Simon & Schuster, Inc., 1948.

Rowen, Betty: The Children We See: An Observational Approach to Child Study. New York, Holt, Rinehart and Winston, Inc., 1973.

CHAPTER 7

Three Naughty Girls (girl, 3 years 6 months)

USING DISCIPLINE

No subject is likely to seem more important to a parent or a teacher than the subject of discipline. Normal, healthy children misbehave at times, and their behavior must be controlled when it gets "out of bounds," for their own good as well as for the good of those around them. How should one discipline a child? What is the difference between discipline and punishment?

We will try to develop here a point of view about discipline and about ways of exercising authority. Later we will discuss other aspects of the subject in the chapter on setting limits (Chap. 18).

Most people have strong feelings on the subject of discipline. Many of these feelings come from childhood experiences with discipline. We hear a person say, "Behavior like that should be nipped in the bud," or we may see a cartoon picturing a father with a small boy over his knee, administering a spanking while saying, "I'll teach you not to hit your little sister." Too few people consider the important question, "How can I best help the child do what I think he should be doing?"

Healthy Children "Test Out" the Environment Through Disruptive Behavior

The sources of misbehavior lie within the child and within the environment. In infancy and early childhood, normal, healthy children "test out" the world with all kinds of disruptive behavior. They need to discover how the framework of their world will stand up to what they can do to it. They need to find firmness and strength and love in the adults around them. Not all homes can stand up under such testing out. Many homes are only partially successful. A home that refuses to allow *any* testing-out behavior keeps a child in swaddling clothes, in a sense, giving him little chance to discover what will happen as a result of misbehavior. The child may become timid and anxious, afraid of misbehavior, yet attracted by it. A home that lets the child do anything he pleases gives him no chance to learn, either, and leaves him anxious and disturbed about himself and the world. Some homes punish the testing-out behavior of children harshly. Unloving parents cannot help the child deal with his urges to destroy and hurt. Where there is love and firmness and the tolerance that comes with confidence, children are helped to master their impulses and to accept the realities of a world of which they are part.

A Permissive Attitude

The word "permissive" is sometimes used to describe the type of guidance that permits a child to do anything he or she wants to do. We know that few sensible people would follow such a course. Letting the child do whatever he wants is not guidance. It is an indication of indifference or irresponsibility or perhaps ignorance. It is not realistic. Neither is it fair to the child.

If we are loving people who care about the child, we are glad to see him doing what he wants to as often as possible, but we accept our responsibility for stopping him when he starts to do what is harmful to himself or to others or what will result in damage. The *way* we stop him or set a limit for his behavior will be important, but we will not hesitate to act with firmness. We are concerned and we are responsible. Sometimes, out of ignorance, a person will stop a child when the child might very well be allowed to do an act from which he could learn much and have much pleasure.

A permissive attitude, as we will use the word, refers to an attitude of permitting, freely and generously, all legitimate activity for the child at his stage of development. It reflects a "giving" attitude and a feeling of being glad that the child can do the things he wants to do. A young child profits from living in a permissive environment when limits are also enforced as they are needed, by someone who really cares about him. Discipline is usually more consistent in this kind of environment.

With adolescents other factors enter into the subject of discipline. Sensible discipline* in childhood tends to reduce the strains in adolescence and lay the foundation for self-discipline.

Testing-out Behavior Needs to Be Met with Sympathetic Firmness

Most healthy children will still be doing some testing out of their environment when they enter nursery school. A few will be doing a great deal because of

---

*See Chap. 11, Contemporary concerns of adolescent development and their implications for higher education. *In* Winnicott, D. W.: Playing and Reality. New York, Basic Books, Inc., Publishers, 1972.

"unfinished business" left from their previous experiences. All children will tend to misbehave, not just in the beginning, but as they feel freer and have developed some confidence in the new environment. They need to find teachers who can meet their behavior with sympathetic firmness. They need to find teachers who are responsible and confident and who care about them as well as for them.

Our feelings probably matter more than the methods we use in our discipline. If we expect that children will misbehave sometimes, disrupt a story period or the play of other children, or destroy and defy, we are not surprised by their actions. We find it easier to respond to their behavior in ways that help the child. We are helped, too, if we understand that it is often not our failure that has brought about the behavior, but that it is a result of the ordinary conflicts in growing.

Growing-up is a complicated process. It takes a long time. Children have a right to a certain level of irresponsibility during the process. But they can only be free to enjoy this irresponsibility if the adults around them are loving and firm and permit only what does no real harm and produces no real anxiety or rejection. We must have confidence in the child and in ourselves, knowing that in time, with our help, he will learn to master his impulses and aggressive urges "without losing the ability to be aggressive at appropriate moments, whether in loving or hating."* If we lack this confidence, we may respond to the child's misbehavior in a punishing way that can be very damaging to him.

A Distinction Between Discipline and Punishment

It is important to make a distinction between discipline and punishment. When we talk about discipline, we are talking about helping a child change random, impulsive, testing-out behavior into controlled, purposeful, informed behavior. Doing this is a long, slow process. Punishment emphasizes what the child should not do. It depends on fear. It seldom helps the young child learn how to harness the energy and desire within him. It may even interfere with the process of learning because of the fear and resentment engendered. Punishment may play a part, but it is never enough by itself. What the child needs most is help in the direction of doing what he should. He wants to be an acceptable person, and he must have a reasonable hope of becoming just this.

We Help the Child

By Setting an Example

The word "discipline" goes back to the word "disciple," or follower. It suggests an important element in discipline, that of following an example. The child wants to be like us. He follows our example. What he sees us doing tends to

---

*Winnicott, D. W.: The Child and the Outside World. New York, Basic Books, Inc., Publishers, 1957. Part III, No. 6.

become part of his own behavior. One of our responsibilities in discipline is the example we set.

By Being Clear and Reasonable

We also help him when we make it clear what we expect. We put our directions to him simply and clearly. We are reasonable in what we expect, reducing the difficulties that confront him when we can.

By Accepting His Need to Assert Himself

The young child is in the process of becoming an independent person. He has an urge to assert himself and thus prove that he is independent. In *not* doing what he is told, he asserts his independence at times. He is testing out what it is like to be a separate person, a person in his own right. Earlier, with his mother, he may have closed his mouth tightly, refusing the food she offered; or he may have resisted putting his arm into a sleeve when she was dressing him. Instead of looking on this behavior as defiance, the wise mother waited, giving him time to be a separate person, to assert his independence, knowing that he would soon be ready to please her again.

The urge to assert oneself is an important and necessary urge. Few of us would want a child to grow up always doing what he was told. A child needs to feel that it is possible to assert himself safely just as he also needs to find that he can live with restrictions and limitations. The kind of discipline that he receives will determine how well he learns both lessons.

Self-respect Is Necessary for Self-control

The ultimate goal of discipline is self-control, making it possible to direct one's own behavior in the end, realistically and with integrity. As we work with young children, we try to help them take steps toward responsible self-direction, as they are ready.

Most important for this goal is the child's feeling about himself. No child will try to control and direct his behavior if he sees himself as a worthless, unimportant person. He must respect himself if he is to make the effort to control his behavior and respect the rights of others. In disciplining, we need to be careful that we do nothing that will shake a child's respect for himself. We will not depend on methods that humiliate him or make him feel ashamed or lower his self-esteem. We do not label him "bad" or use threats. We will try to show him that we have confidence that he can behave acceptably, whatever he may have done earlier. We expect only what we think he is capable of doing, so that he can be successful most of the time. We want him to feel himself to be an acceptable, successful person.

The Reasons for Prohibitions

The framework of the environment in nursery school has only a few don'ts, but these prohibitions are enforced. We usually prohibit acts (1) for the child's safety and welfare and (2) to protect the rights of others. Let us look at how these purposes can be accomplished.

Prohibition for the Child's Safety and Welfare

There are things the child must do and things he must not do, if he is to be safe and well. He cannot leave the playground on his own, for example, if he is to be safe. If he does, he meets disapproval and suffers some consequence, such as not being allowed to play outside for a time. We will explain the reason to him, but we know that his understanding is too limited and his control over his own behavior is too uncertain to be depended on. We must take responsibility and watch him. He usually obeys us because he doesn't want to bear the consequences and also because he has an underlying trust that we are setting limits because we truly care about what happens to him. He needs our limits.

Prohibition to Protect the Rights of Others

The child often needs help in learning to respect the rights of others. For example, two young three-year-olds may be playing in the sandbox when the first one hits the second and takes his spoon. The second hits back, and there are tears on both sides. What happens? If the teacher has been observing the play, she reaches the spot quickly, and immediately and firmly takes the spoon and returns

Courtesy of Jean Berlfein.

There is a conflict of interests over possession of a cap.

it to the second child, putting her arm around the first, saying, "No, it belongs to him. Ask him, if you want it. You must not hit him. Hitting hurts." If the second child still seems upset, she may say, "I'm sorry. These things happen. It is all right now. It is your spoon. You didn't need to let him have it." Then she may say to the first child, "I wonder what you wanted to do with the spoon?" and she may help him find another spoon to carry out his purpose. If all goes well, the two will soon be playing together happily, with more chance of settling their own difficulties another time because of the teacher's help.

The teacher may also help a child by explaining and interpreting how others feel when something happens. "He doesn't want to play with you now because you knocked over his tower," or, "He hit you because he didn't like what you did," or, "I can see he is making faces, but you don't need to let that bother you." Understanding why people behave as they do is important at all ages.

Sometimes a child is helped if the teacher changes the situation—separating two children who are in conflict, helping a child move his building to a more protected spot, protecting a group from intruders—making it easier for them to behave acceptably.

Learning to control impulses and feelings in constructive ways is a complex area of learning. Guiding a child requires insight and understanding. It requires time spent in observing children's play to build this kind of understanding. Too often the adult has to intervene without having first observed. Overdirection may distort development; so may lack of direction. The chld needs time to learn through suitable experiences. He is sure to make some mistakes in the process of learning.

We Help the Child When We Act Confidently

We help the child most when we act with certainty and confidence in stopping him or in maintaining the standards of the school. A child must not hurt others, for example, or disturb or tease or take things from others. The teacher acts with firmness and certainty when she stops such behavior. She does not scold the child or blame him or use a lot of words. She acts matter-of-factly and even sympathetically. She is sure that this behavior should be stopped and that she can do it. If she feels all this "in her bones" in a sense, she communicates this sureness to the child. He knows she means it by the tone of her voice, the feel of her hand on his, and her movements. She is being responsible, and he can relax.

Jeff comes from a home where his mother constantly nags him but never troubles to insist on anything. When the teacher does expect something of him, she puts it in simple words with an explanation, and puts herself in a position to enforce it. She may direct him to hang up his coat, and she stands blocking the door until he does it even if she has to help him by holding the coat with him. She repeats this each time until he has accepted the necessity, and she praises him and gives him a hug when he does it, for they really are friends. If it is a matter of putting blocks on the shelf, they work together; but she insists that he put some on the shelf, holding him if necessary while she talks with him casually, perhaps making up a song about a boy putting blocks on the shelf until he takes the role in reality.

The teacher restrains an angry boy and explains while he listens somewhat reluctantly.

Courtesy of Jean Berlfein.

Everyone Has a Right to Feel, but Not to Act, Unacceptably

A child may be angry in response to a restriction or interference. This is natural and to be expected. He may call his teacher names or make threats, but it is important to face calmly the child's angry response to discipline. He has a right to his anger and he should not have to deny it. Verbal insults are an acceptable way to drain off strong feeling at his stage of development. We do not have to take his words personally or respond with anger. We know we are right to stop his act. It cannot be permitted, but we can understand how he feels. His feelings will change; meanwhile, we are firm.

We Need to Acknowledge Our Feelings

Sometimes we are angry ourselves. We must deal with our own anger, accepting the feelings we have. In the nursery school the teacher may say to the child, "You make me very cross when you do that." Bringing feeling out into the open makes it more manageable. The child can understand how we feel. He is learning about behavior, and he is less bewildered by it when feelings are identified directly. Both teacher and child may be helped by pursuing the question, "Now what do we do about it?"

If we face our own feelings, if we deal calmly and confidently with unacceptable behavior, we will create the kind of climate in which the child is helped to master his impulses and to direct his own behavior. We will be using authority in constructive ways.

Guides for Action

Here are some additional "guides for action" that apply particularly in situations where discipline is involved.

1. Act with confidence and sympathetic firmness in disciplining.

2. Good timing of action is essential in discipline.

3. Use simple, clear statements about what is acceptable behavior, with choices when possible, adding a statement about what is not acceptable if this will clarify the situation.

4. The consequences for misbehavior should be immediate, of short duration, and without humiliation for the child. They should bear some relation to the act, if possible, and should be consistently applied and maintained.

5. Effective consequences are restrictions in space, such as where the child can play or be, and restrictions in use, such as what he can use. Consequences should not be restrictions in activity, such as being made to sit on a chair. A child's thoughts during the time he is sitting are likely to be of questionable value.

6. Respect the child's feeling of guilt, but do not try to add to it. Accept any restitution he may wish to make, and then leave the incident behind.

7. Forestalling and preventing misbehavior reduce the necessity for discipline.

Erikson sums it up in these words: "Be firm and tolerant with the child at this age, and he will be firm and tolerant with himself. He will feel pride in being an autonomous person. He will grant autonomy to others; and now and again he may even let himself get away with something."*

SITUATION FOR DISCUSSION

Nels in the Homemaking Corner†

9:00   Three-year-old Nels, alone in the homemaking corner, leans against the sink. With both hands he grabs the faucet handle and moves it back and forth. His lips move slightly as he makes a soft zum-zum-zum sound. Smiling, he puts his right hand into the sink and swishes it around and around. Leaning down, he opens the cupboard doors under the sink and quickly takes out a plate and

---

*Erikson, Erik: Identity and the Life Cycle. New York, International Universities Press, 1959. Vol. 1, No. 1, p. 70.

†Recorded by Jane Martin.

spoon. He sets them on the table, pulls up a chair and sits down. He pretends to eat, puts the spoon into his mouth and rolls it around with his tongue. He gets up, walks around the table, and pulls the doll's high chair up to the table across from his own place. He goes back to his seat and starts "eating" again. Then he stops to watch the children across the room, putting up stars on the attendance chart. He stands up, pushes the chair back with a quick movement of his legs, and quickly runs across the room to put up his star.

9:15 Smiling, Nels returns to the homemaking corner followed by Davie. Nels climbs into his chair and pretends to eat again. Davie goes to the stove (which is behind this chair) grabs the handle of a pot and begins to stir vigorously. Bobbie, a four-year-old, walks into the kitchen, bumping the table as he goes to the sink. Reaching for the faucet, Bobby tips over a stack of plates which fall into the sink. "Splat, splat," he shouts with glee. Putting both hands into the sink he swishes the plates around, making a loud clatter. With a determined look, Davie turns and grabs for Nels' plate. Nels, eyes wide with surprise, grabs it back. Davie, his face flushed, tries to move Nels' chair to upset him. Nels stands up and holds the plate high out of Davie's reach. Davie says, "Bobbie, plate."

9:18 Bobby, who is taller than Nels, tries to take the plate and pushes Nels down into the chair. Nels holds tightly to the plate and does not allow Bobby to take it from him. Davie watches, frowning. Bobby shrugs his shoulders, turns back to the sink and continues to stack the dishes. Without a word Nels puts the plate on the table. He claps his hands on top of his head and walks out of the homemaking corner. Davie quickly picks up the plate, takes it to the sink and adds it to the stack of dishes there. Davie and Bobby both leave. (These two boys appear to be close companions.)

Comment

Here is a well-recorded observation in which some teacher guidance might have been given, enabling the children to learn more about resolving conflict over purposes.

In this situation we see a delightful example of three-year-old Nels, exploring equipment in the homemaking area in the playschool. His soft "zum-zum" shows his pleasure. He pretends, and he also remains responsive to what is going on around him. Bobby and Davie also enjoy the equipment, each in his own way.

A clue to Nel's behavior in the incident may be that he is the youngest child in a large family. He is used to playing with children who are older than he and against whom he cannot assert himself too openly. At home his mother reports that he is a "handful." He may need to act this way in order to get much attention at home. He may especially enjoy some independent play in nursery school. Nels seems to play actively and imaginatively, but he may need some help in understanding his position as an equal in the group and some support for his efforts to maintain his purposes in play.

In this record an interesting succession of purposes appear. The timing of any help given seems important. The first chance to offer help occurs when Davie struggles to take Nels' plate and Nels asserts his right to keep it. Davie's words, "Bobby, plate," suggest that he may want Bobby to have *all* the plates to pile in the sink.

An adult approaching at this point might say, "Tell Nels why you want the plate, Davie." She would probably need to put her arm around Davie to restrain him from taking the plate. She might need to put it into words for him, "I think you want Bobby to have all the plates in his pile. Ask Nels to put his plate on Bobby's pile when he finishes using it." She would give Nels support in possessing the plate until he was through with it, but she would reassure Davie that there was a way to achieve his purpose by putting it into words. Nels, too, needs to be encouraged to use words to help make clear his wants.

If the boys had responded favorably, the adult might have gone on to suggest something that they could all do together with the dishes, such as pretending to eat with Nels or to wash and put away the dishes with Bobby. Children often need help at this age in getting started playing together and in the techniques of making contact. These children seem friendly enough, but their purposes are in conflict. A completely successful solution would have seen all three boys developing a play in the homemaking corner together. Encouraging children to verbalize about their purposes generally helps clarify a conflict and improves the chances for cooperation.

Another chance to help Nels comes as he starts to walk away, his hands on his head (an unusual gesture for a young child). The adult might have explained, "It was all right to keep the plate, Nels. The boys want to stack the plates, and you can help if you wish. I think they would like it." Reassurance and a simple explanation about what he might do could help Nels understand more about other people's purposes and his own place with them. Play with equals is not quite the same thing as playing in a family as the youngest member. Nels seems to be purposeful and to have the strength to assert himself, but he seems to need help in seeing himself as an equal in the give and take of play.

Discussion Topics

Giving explanations and interpretations of behavior.
Encouraging verbalization of purposes.
Timing of help.

PROJECTS

1. Observe and report a situation in which a limit was set for a child's behavior. How did the adult define the limit? How did the adult maintain it? What was the child's response? What were the values for the child in the situation? How do you think he felt about himself in the end?

2. Report a situation in which the statement of a limit was well-timed. Why did you feel the timing was good? What was the result? Report a situation in which the timing was poor or the teacher failed to maintain the limit set. What was the result?

REFERENCES

Becker, Wesley C.: Consequences of different kinds of parental discipline. *In* Hoffman, M., and Hoffman, L. M. (eds.): Review of Child Development Research. New York, Russell Sage Foundation, 1964. Vol. 1, pp. 169–204.
Fraiberg, Selma: The Magic Years. New York, Charles Scribner's Sons, 1959. Chap. 8.
Galambos, Jeanette W.: A Guide to Discipline. Washington, D.C., National Association for the Education of Young Children, 1969.
Redl, Fritz: The nature and nurture of prejudice. Childhood Education, January, 1969.

CHAPTER 8

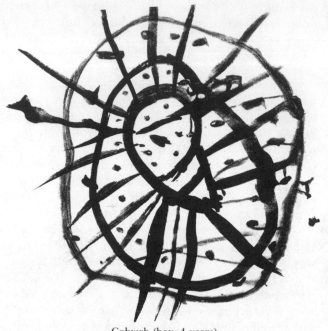

Cobweb (boy, 4 years)

MAKING OBSERVATIONS

OBSERVING IS A WAY OF LEARNING

All teachers need to develop skill as observers. They need to see and record as accurately and as objectively as possible what is happening in situations. Teachers learn most about children by studying their behavior directly. By learning to observe with objectivity, to make careful notes, and to go over these thoughtfully, a teacher increases her understanding of a child's behavior.

The teacher as an observer is someone who is, herself, part of the situation. She is an "involved observer" or "participant observer." Hers is not an easy task. She is looking for facts and looking for understanding. She is interested in the meanings that lie behind the behavior. To achieve even a measure of objectivity takes practice and self-discipline. When the teacher is successful, she can make a valuable contribution through her records of children's behavior.

Objectivity means seeing what is actually taking place. It means observing without being influenced by value judgments like "bad" or "good" or "right" or "wrong." It means trying to reduce the distortions that are the result of biases or defenses or preconceptions.

Students need to develop their skill in making observations before they undertake the role of "participant observers." As a part of their training for teaching they need to spend a great deal of time observing and recording their observations of young children.

Teachers need to continue making observations as a part of their teaching. They need to make notes and keep records. The teacher can carry a pad and pencil with her in a pocket and then jot down notes about situations as they occur and complete these later when there is time. She will jot down the words said by the child, for these are hard to recall exactly later, and she will note the date and add a word or two about the circumstances. Such notes are valuable. They are the "raw material" out of which understanding grows. When written up more completely, later, and filed, notes make up a record about a child. This record can be reviewed and summarized at intervals and can be used in evaluating a child's progress and in making plans for him. It can be used in a conference with his parents.

Every teacher should try to manage time during the week when she can step aside and do more sustained observing. She may have a special purpose in mind, such as trying to discover how a certain child approaches other children, or why there is trouble so frequently in the block-building corner, or how the setup for fingerpainting might be improved. If the staff feels that a particular child has problems, they may all try to observe him through a week, making notes on what they observe. One of them may take time to do a longer observation in order to

Courtesy of Marcy Hull.

Success in blowing bubbles.

add still more information. Pooling these records, they can discuss his problems in a staff meeting. They will have more accurate information on which to base their understanding of his problems and to plan for him.

TYPES OF RECORDS

There are many types of observational records. The *informal, random notes* that a teacher makes are of value in understanding a child's behavior. They usually record characteristic behavior, or significant behavior, or examples of a particular type of behavior. The *diary record* or *running record* is an observational record covering a period of time, including all that can be recorded in that time interval. *Sampling records* are observational records repeated at intervals. *Selected observations* may be made of certain types of activity, such as observations of a rest period or of children's behavior in the housekeeping corner or on the first day at school.

A useful reference on the subject is the monograph by Cohen and Stern, "Observing and Recording the Behavior of Young Children."* Two books by Susan Isaacs, *Intellectual Growth in Young Children* and *Social Development in Young Children,*† contain a wealth of examples of situations involving children individually and in groups, recorded with interpretive comments.

A good teacher will spend time observing and making records, and using these to increase her understanding of young children and their behavior. Here are some examples of different kinds of records.

Informal Notes

5–12 Bruce, constructing a building, tried to enlist the help of Marvin, saying, "You can be a roof helper," and then turned to me, "You are so tall you can help with the roof"—example of reasoning and social skill. *K. R.*

Report of a Single Incident

10–6 As I came out onto the playground, Joe ran up and asked me to tie his shoe, which was untied. I bent over and did it for him. Off he ran, and then Betsy, who had been sitting on the step said, "Wait." She reached down and carefully untied her shoelace and stuck her foot out, asking me to tie her shoelace. I smiled at her, tied it, and patted her; and off she went. *K. H.*

Comment and Interpretation

In this record one is struck by the *un*self-conscious way in which Betsy asked for a share of the teacher's attention. The teacher seemed well able to accept her

---

*Cohen, Dorothy, and Stern, Virginia: Observing and Recording the Behavior of Young Children. New York, Bureau of Publications, Teachers College, Columbia University, 1958.

†New York, Schocken Books Inc., 1966 and 1972, respectively.

request and give her an extra bit of attention. It appeared to satisfy Betsy, and she moved away into activity rather than just sitting. It would be worth observing Betsy further to see whether she may be an "easy" child who is not getting much attention, or whether she has a real problem with jealousy or with finding her place in the group. At least she is showing that she has ways of coping with the situation.

Ten Minute Running Record — An Observation of Billy, a Four-Year-Old

10:30 Billy is kneeling in front of a low blackboard, carefully drawing diagonal lines of scallops across the board, pursing his lips as he draws. Kim comes up, kneels beside him, and draws a heavy dark line through his scallops; and then she sits back with a pleased expression. Billy looks at her in surprise and then back at the board. He picks up the eraser and erases both lines carefully. He appears to ignore Kim and begins to draw scallops again, tracing the lines of the previous scallops, which are still faintly visible. As he draws the fourth scallop, Kim reaches out and draws another dark line intersecting the scallops. Billy sits back on his heels and looks at the board, but not at Kim, frowning slightly. Then he reaches forward and erases the board, glancing at Kim. He begins to draw the scallops again, this time looking at Kim each time he makes a scallop. Just as he begins the fourth one, again Kim reaches out and scribbles over his drawing. Billy turns to her, raises his hand with the eraser over his head, and then lets it fall. He turns back and uses the eraser to erase the board very thoroughly.

10:35 Then he draws a line down the center, saying as he finishes, "There." and, pointing to the side nearest Kim, "Use your own spot." He sits quietly back on his heels and says in a determined-sounding way, "I'm going to be a good boy." Kim, bringing her eraser across the entire board, says, "Now we got to race." Billy says, as though to himself, "I don't care." Then he says to Kim, "Do you want to erase your name?" "OK," Kim answers. Billy draws a "B" on the board.

10:39 Just then a teacher calls to Kim to tell her that it is her turn to have the swing. She jumps up and runs off. Billy goes back to work on his scallops, and when he finishes he leans back on his heels and says, "There's my monster."

Comment and Interpretation

The observation seems complete, giving details that enable us to reconstruct what has taken place. The descriptive phrases that are used, such as "looking at the board but not at Kim" and "a diagonal line of scallops," are clear. It is objective, free of interpretation. The impressions are clearly labeled, as "in a determined-sounding way" or "with apparent satisfaction." We have an objective picture of Kim's and Billy's behavior, relatively unclouded by what the observer thought.

Billy seems wholeheartedly involved in his own purpose. He copes with the problem of Kim's interference in an unusual way. First, he tries to ignore it. He almost seems to want to pretend she isn't there. As she persists, he repeats his attempt until it obviously is unsuccessful. He feels like hitting her with the eraser,

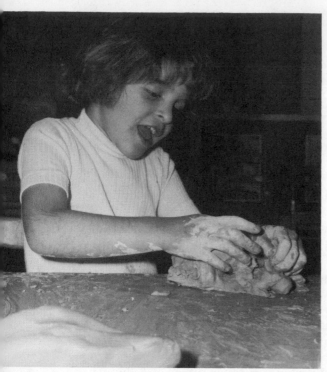

One can easily see how this child feels.

Courtesy of Sam Hollander, San Diego State University.

but he controls the impulse. Perhaps he feels better after he drains off some of this feeling by erasing the board vigorously—as he would like to have wiped her out.

Then Billy moves on to another level of coping. He divides the space, one side for Kim and one for himself where he probably hopes he will be undisturbed. His internalized adult conscience comes out in the words, "I'm going to be a good boy." He is trying to exorcise the monster with these often-heard words. But Kim is operating on a different level. She feels aggressive and competitive. She suggests a race. At this point Billy tries the device of persuading himself that he doesn't care. This doesn't seem to work, and then he comes up with a remarkable solution. He decides to give her something to erase, her own name, a wonderfully positive suggestion with significant overtones. It is in line with her interests at the moment, and the "B" he draws is the first letter of his own name, probably the only name he knows how to write. As she has been intent on destroying his product, erasing the "B" seems significant. When Kim leaves at this point and Billy is able to finish his drawing, it becomes a "monster," probably carrying the load of frustration and resentment that he feels. It seems to satisfy him.

Billy's control over his impulses seems to be very strong. His strengths lie in his ability to put his feelings into words and finally to express them in his drawing. One might wonder whether or not this control is almost too great for a four-year-old boy and may interfere with his standing up for himself with other four-year-olds. "I'm going to be a good boy" is not an easy thing when one is with others who have not "internalized" this concept. But it does lead him into some unusual problem-solving actions: dividing the board with Kim, giving her something to erase. These show his capacity to cope with a situation on a high level and, later, his capacity to use the drawing as an avenue for finally expressing the feeling that he has not allowed to come out more directly.

How effective his defenses are, where they will lead him, what they really mean to him, can only be understood after further observations of Billy. Billy is the third child in a family of four children. One suspects that Billy has had a lot of help in coping with the interferences of a younger sibling in a family where standards are high standards and relationships are good. What help does he need in the nursery school? We see that he is a child well worth studying.

We also meet Kim in this record, the minor character in the drama, at a moment when she has been thwarted in carrying out a purpose. She wants to swing and she has had to wait for a turn. She begins to frustrate someone else, teasing and annoying Billy, but not in an unfriendly way. She is apparently an active child. She does something rather than wait. She is also sociable. She turns to another child rather than to an object. She tries actively to get Billy's attention. In making a line through his drawing, she is also probably draining off some of *her* frustration. She is persistent, but she is not concerned with trying to be a "good girl." She, too, can make a suggestion. Her suggestion, "We got to race" is a vigorous, competitive one, but she is flexible. She accepts Billy's different suggestion about erasing her name instead. She quickly returns to carry out her original purpose when the teacher calls her. She seems to be a normal, healthy four-year-old.

Kim's behavior is a reminder to us that any child who has to "wait" may need some teacher help. To be left at loose ends, frustrated in the immediate carrying out of a purpose, is not easy for a child. As teachers, we need to be alert to the child's need for a suggestion about what to do while waiting. Perhaps the waiting time can be used for a conversation with the child. At least we need to keep an eye on what the child does in the waiting period. Kim needed some help in coping with her problem. She put a burden on Billy in this case.

SITUATION FOR DISCUSSION

*An Incident in the Homemaking Area in a Play Group**

Background Information

Alicia (3–2) is the youngest of ten children in a warm, loving Mexican-American family. Her mother takes care of Davie and Donald during the day, so the three children are well acquainted.

Davie (3–0) is also Mexican-American. He lives with his mother, who works outside the home, and with his grandparents

Donald (3–1) has parents who are in the process of getting divorced.

Situation

Davie walked into the homemaking corner where Alicia was sitting at the table pretending to eat eggs. She scraped her spoon across the plate, put it into her mouth, smacking her lips. With her eyes sparkling, she said, "Davie, have

---

*Recorded by Jane Martin.

some eggs!" Davie pulls a chair away from the table and sits down. Alicia, pushing her plate towards him, says, "Come closer to the table, Davie, and eat your breakfast." Davie pulls his chair nearer to the table and very seriously begins to "eat."

Donald who has been curled up in the cradle in the corner gets out and comes to the table. He starts picking up the dishes. With two already in his hands he grabs for Davie's plate. Davie frowns and in a positive tone says, "No, you have two plates. This is mine." He grabs his plate and holds it firmly, raising his hand to hit Donald. Alicia immediately says, "Don't hit Donald, Davie." Without a word Donald turns and walks out of the homemaking corner. Alicia starts clearing the table, putting the dishes in the sink. Davie remains at the table, a frown on his face, his lips set tight, still holding his plate.

Comment

What May the Behavior of These Children Suggest to an Observer?

Alicia is revealed as a friendly, secure child, with imagination. She enjoys pretending and takes the maternal role in this sociodramatic play. She appears to identify with her mother. She seems to have good patterns in family relationships to imitate. She uses positive statements, "Come closer to the table, Davie." She defines limits, "Don't hit Donald, Davie." She seems social, alert, practical.

Donald is in a "baby" role in the cradle when the incident begins, but he changes this, apparently somewhat jealous of the role Davie is taking with Alicia. He acts aggressively toward Davie, but Davie defends himself. Alicia is looking out for Donald and forestalls Davie's retaliation. Donald, apparently sure that Alicia is not neglecting him, leaves the situation. He has not spoken a word. He seems less free to be creative in his play than the others and less sure about relationships. Curling up in the cradle may signify his wish for greater security and more babying than he has known.

Davie appears friendly and social. He enters easily into the imaginative play suggested by Alicia. When Donald interferes, Davie stands up for himself. He makes an excellent positive statement, "No, you have two plates. This is mine." He is ready to be aggressive but does not hit Donald when Alicia warns him not to. He has control over his impulses. But he seems puzzled in the end, holding firm when it is not longer necessary. Is he more upset than we might think?

Individual differences are already evident in these three children. They will need guidance of different types from the teacher.

What Help Could These Children Use?

Davie may need to have an adult clarify or explain to him by commenting quietly, "You wanted to keep your plate. That was right. Donald didn't need it. It was good to tell him and I think he understood." The adult might then have continued, "I wonder if Alicia would like someone to help her with the dishes," thus suggesting another step in the play to help Davie get started again. He may need help in recovering from situations, leaving them behind, becoming less concerned with the "right" and "wrong" of behavior. As a little boy he may be finding it difficult to try to live up to the standards and expectations of three older people.

Discussion Topics

What sociodramatic play may reveal about individual differences.
The values of pretending or of imagination as an aspect of development.

Equipment that tends to foster sociodramatic play.

Guidance techniques.

PROJECTS

1. Observe and record three incidents of behavior that seem to be characteristic of the particular child you are observing or that illustrate behavior characteristic of most children of this age. Comment on the significance of each, briefly.

2. Observe one child for a ten-minute period, keeping a record of what the child does and says in this time. Comment on what you have learned about the child or what questions the observation has raised.

3. Select a piece of equipment and observe and record which children make use of it through a period of twenty minutes. Summarize your observations. Of what value is this equipment?

REFERENCES

Cohen, Dorothy: Learning to observe—Observing to learn. *In* Engstrom, Georgianna (ed.): The Significance of the Young Child's Motor Development. Washington, D.C., National Association for the Education of Young Children, 1971.

Cohen, Dorothy, and Stern, Virginia: Observing and Recording the Behavior of Young Children. New York, Bureau of Publications, Teachers College, Columbia University, 1958.

A Guide for Teacher Recording in Day Care Agencies. Child Welfare League of America, Bulletin, 1964.

Isaacs, Susan: Intellectual Growth in Young Children. New York, Schocken Books Inc., 1966. Chaps. 1 and 2.

Isaacs, Susan: Social Development in Young Children. New York, Schocken Books Inc., 1972.

Rowen, Betty: The Children We See: An Observational Approach to Child Study. New York, Holt, Rinehart and Winston, Inc., 1973.

Schulman, Ann S.: Absorbed in Living, Children Learn. Washington, D.C., National Association for the Education of Young Children, 1966.

Wright, H. F.: Recording and Analyzing Child Behavior. New York, Harper and Row, Publishers, 1967.

PART THREE

GUIDANCE IN EXPERIENCES COMMON TO EVERYONE

CHAPTER 9

Fun to Go to the Store (boy, 4 years)

HELPING CHILDREN ADJUST TO NEW EXPERIENCES

We All Know What It Is Like to Be in a New Situation

We suggested earlier that one of the first steps for us to take in the nursery school was to accept the feelings which we had because we were new and strange there. These feelings probably included feelings of inadequacy which led us to defend ourselves in some way against the inadequacy we felt. Some of our

135

defenses may have been handicapping to further learning. We had to learn to feel comfortable about being new and strange.

Each Child Has Characteristic Patterns of Response to New Experience

The child faces the same problem when he meets new situations such as entering nursery school or accepting the approaches of strange people. He may defend himself against the uncertainty and inadequacy he feels by inappropriate behavior or by rejecting the experience. Because we know what it is like to feel strange, without skills and inadequate, we will find it easier to understand the child's behavior. We may be able to recognize the meaning which lies behind what the child does. We may be better able to help him as he goes through a new experience because we ourselves know what it is like.

For the child, as for the adult, new experiences call forth defenses, tendencies to retreat or, on the other hand, to explore and find satisfactions. What the child or the adult will do depends on his individual makeup and his past experiences.

What kind of adjustment is a "good adjustment" in a new situation? Obviously fear is very limiting. An uncritical acceptance sometimes reveals a lack of awareness which may lead to undesirable consequences. What we might consider most desirable is a readiness to accept differences, an ability to pick out familiar elements and relate the unknown to the known.

There Are Reasons for Differences in Adjustment

What lies behind differences in children in adjustment to the same situation?

For one thing, we can be sure that it is not the same situation to all children. Demonstrable differences in responsiveness to stimulation are present at birth or soon after birth. One child, for example, will be more disturbed than another by a sudden, loud noise or a difference in the intensity of light. Experiences will have different meanings for each, depending on the sensitivity which is part of his native equipment.

Each child also brings to a new experience his own past experiences. These have prepared him differently. It does not matter if we do not know specifically what these past experiences have been as long as we accept the child's present behavior *as having some meaning*. Being taken to a new place may mean pleasant possibilities to one child and disturbing possibilities to another. We can expect and accept different behavior in different children. Each child is a different organism. Each has had different past experiences.

The many daily experiences which a child has are probably of more importance in influencing his adjustments than single traumatic events. In other words, the sum total of the child's experience is usually more important than any single experience. It is desirable, therefore, to have each experience contribute to making the child feel more secure and more adequate. We are not likely to gain strength by being hurt; we are sure to acquire scars.

Children who are forced into making adjustments for which they are not ready are less prepared for further adjustment. They may try to conceal their feeling, as is sometimes the case with the child whose mother declares, "He doesn't mind being left anywhere." The damage they suffer may be evident only in indirect ways, as in a loss in creativity, greater dependence, or increased irritability. But many experiences of feeling strange or frightened, however small and seemingly insignificant, add up to a total which may be disastrous for sound adjustment.

ENTERING NURSERY SCHOOL IS AN IMPORTANT EXPERIENCE

The experience of entering nursery school is an important new experience for the child. It means leaving his familiar home and depending on adults other than his parents. It means finding a place for himself in a group of other children of about his own age. There are new toys, different toilet arrangements, a strange play area. He meets a variety of responses from the other children, some of them apparently unreasonable responses. He must trust the teachers to understand him and keep him safe through these new experiences.

The child's feeling of confidence in himself will be strengthened if he can meet these new experiences successfully. He may be able to recover to some extent from the fear and uncertainty left by earlier experience. For many children there are valuable opportunities at this point to "work through" problems and take steps in rebuilding a shaken sense of trust.

Courtesy of Myron Papiz.

A separation experience: saying good-bye at school.

Readiness for Nursery School

What makes a child ready for nursery school? Why do some children enter eagerly and others hold back from the new experience? What can we do to reduce the difficulties to manageable proportions for all children?

Here we will refer to the concept of developmental tasks as outlined by Erikson. According to this concept, the development of a sense of trust is the first and basic task for a healthy personality. The sense of trust grows out of experiences of being cared for by loving parents. Feeling safe with his parents, he can proceed to feel safe with other people. There are many reasons why one child may not feel so safe or secure as another. Many moves, leaving little in the way of familiar physical surroundings to tie to, may make it harder for a child's sense of trust to develop. Frequent separations from parents or separations coming at critical times in development may be another reason.

Because feeling secure contributes significantly to healthy personality development, it is important to reduce the difficulty of the new experience of entering a school, so that this experience may add to, rather than threaten, the child's feeling of being safe. Safeguards include avoiding starting a child in nursery school shortly after a new baby has arrived, or after the family has just moved, or after there has been some upsetting change in the family such as his mother starting to work outside the home. If it is necessary for the child to start school under circumstances like these, he should be given much more time to make the adjustment.

The Significance of the Experience for the Child

Because the experience of entering nursery school may contribute to growth in important ways, let us try to understand its significance for the child and his parents, and then outline steps to follow which will promote healthy growth through the experience.

The tasks facing the child in entering nursery school are twofold. First, he must go out to meet a new experience, rich with possibilities for growth and for sensory and social contacts, but full of the unknown for him. The second and perhaps the more significant task which the child faces is that inherent in growth itself. He must resolve the conflict inevitably felt in leaving something behind in order to go on to something else.

The conflict to be resolved in this case is lessening the close dependency on his mother in order to live in the world the nursery school offers and to find the new satisfactions it makes possible for him. In going forward, he must leave behind a measure of dependency in order to take a step in the direction of independence. He must resist his desire to cling to the relationship with his mother which has been the main source of his satisfaction and security up until now. He must act on the wish to separate himself from her and be ready to explore new relationships which may also prove to be sources of satisfying experience.

For some children who may have found their sources of satisfaction in a number of other people, as with children from large families, there may be less conflict. These children have already found security in a variety of relationships and have less need to hold on to dependency. There are children, too, who have not known closeness to any one person and who do not appear to need any sup-

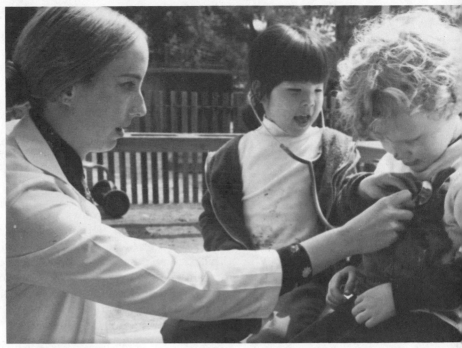

Courtesy of Jean Berlfein.

A new experience: listening to a heart beating. A mother who is a physician brings her stethoscope to school.

port. They have other needs which are likely to come out later in other ways. For the child from the ordinary small family with good relationships, there will usually be some degree of conflict to resolve, a step to take in growing up as he enters nursery school and leaves his family for even a short time.

Each Child Comes Differently Equipped

In meeting these tasks each child brings different equipment with him. His own constitutional endowment will differ, the senses with which he perceives, his tempo of living, and the intensity of his response. One child may delight in sounds, another in color, another in movement. One child may respond quickly, reacting to a variety of stimuli; another may be content to experience slowly. What each child has known in the past will differ even more, although affected to some extent by the differing endowments of each. Some children will come to nursery school having had limited opportunities for sensory experience, while others may have had many opportunities to touch, taste, smell, and hear. Some children will come having known much uncertainty and fear. Others will have known more often the familiar and the safe.

Relationships with His Mother and His Teacher Are Important

The quality and variety of relationships with people which each child has known will also differ. Of these relationships, the one with his mother will probably have the most effect on the way the child proceeds toward independence. If his mother has been able to give him a basic experience in trust, she will have satisfied in large measure his pressing infantile dependency needs. He is now free to move on to include new relationships which will meet new needs. The conflict he feels in separating himself from her is more easily resolved when he does not carry a heavy burden of "unfinished business" in the way of infantile dependency.

The teacher plays a significant role because of the help she gives the mother as well as the child. They both face a new kind of separation experience. The teacher can give support to the child's desire to move toward independence as well as to the mother's desire to leave the child free. The teacher will do this best when she sees clearly the significance of what the experience of entering nursery school may contribute to growth for both child and parent.

It is not simple for the teacher to move with certainty, for each child and each parent differ in what he or she brings to the situation and in what he or she needs to find in it. In addition, the teacher herself may be handicapped by set patterns of the way school entrance is handled, or handicapped by her own fears, by her own need to control, or by the way her own dependency needs have been met. But as she develops sensitivity and skill she will find satisfaction in working out this problem, for it is here that the nursery school makes one of its most significant contributions. If it can help the child and the parent here, it has given them help which will be of value in future separation experiences.

THE PROCESS OF HELPING THE CHILD AND HIS PARENTS

How does the teacher proceed in helping the child and his parents? How may the philosophy of nursery education be translated into action in this particular experience?

We will suggest a series of steps which may be taken in helping a child enter nursery school. Our goal in these steps will be to use the experience of entering nursery school so that it may contribute to the child's satisfaction in the world around him and his growth in confidence and adequacy.

In outlining these steps we need to recognize that, in many situations, the steps will necessarily have to be condensed, as in the case of a mother who is employed. Attending school for an hour with his mother or father or other relative or care-giver may be all that can be managed as a first step for the child. But it should be emphasized that *no* young child should *ever* be "dumped" at a school without any preparation. He should have someone staying with him on his first day, and the first day should never be a long one. The mental health of a child is too important to put it at risk in this way. Attending for only part of the time for the first week saves time in the end because the child is less likely to be overtired and to succumb to an infection.

We will discuss here the steps in entering school with their implications for teacher and child as these steps might be carried out under optimal conditions.

One Step in the Process Is a Conference

The first specific step is a conference between the teacher and one or both parents. In this conference the teacher explains to the parents the policies of the school, makes clear the matter of fees, health regulations, hours, and steps in admission. She tells them something of the program, of their part in it, and tries to answer the questions they have. She learns something of the child's past experiences and the parents' expectations. She may ask them to fill out a home information record to be kept by the school.

One of the important parts of the conference will be the discussion of the steps to be taken in entering the child in the nursery school. These steps will need to be clarified in subsequent conferences, but it is essential for the parent to understand, especially for the mother who may be employed or have other obligations, that someone from the family must participate with the child in the first days of school.

In discussing the kind of help the child will need from the parent the teacher will point out that the child needs to feel that his parent is glad to have him go to nursery school, and that nursery school is a good place to be. The child also needs to feel, not that the parent is leaving him, but that the parent is letting him leave and will always be glad when he returns.

Another Step Is Visiting the School

The next step is to give the child some concept of what nursery school is like through a visit to the school. The child needs a picture in his mind when he hears the word "nursery school." He needs to be anticipating what lies ahead in as realistic a way as possible.

Visting the school when other children are not present keeps the situation simple and manageable for him. There are not so many new and unknown factors. He can become familiar with aspects of the physical setup, discovering areas where he feels secure. He is protected against the unpredictableness of other children's behavior. He has an opportunity to enter into a relationship with the teacher without the competition of other children dividing her attention. She has a chance to become acquainted with him and to take a step in understanding what his needs are likely to be and what role she may play as his teacher.

Attending for a Short Session

The third step, following this visit, is for the child to visit with his mother at the nursery school when school is in session. School as a place where children are present is added to the concept he is forming about a nursery school. He can watch, make the contacts he wishes and participate only as he is ready.

Children will differ in the way they use experiences in this visit. Some will make many contacts with children. Others will follow, watching from a distance. Still others will return to the play materials which they enjoyed on the earlier visit, seeming to pay little attention to the other children around them.

The teacher will add to her understanding of a particular child by observing him in this new situation. She also has many opportunities to help him. Seeing his interest in something, she may place this material near him, bringing it easily within his reach. If he looks at a child painting at the easel, she may walk nearer with him, and say a few words about the paint, the colors, and so forth. She does not push him into activity. She only moves with him if she feels this makes him feel more secure. He may find the piano and together they may share some music, with other children joining them, perhaps. If he is most interested in watching what other children are doing, she may comment on what is going on, mentioning the children's names. Some children may be made anxious by much attention from the teacher until they feel more at home. The teacher can limit her help to a reassuring smile when such a child looks in her direction and be ready with more active help later.

When a new child enters a group, he holds a special place as a visitor. Other children have a chance to become aware of him as a "new" child. They may become aware of "newness" and the fact that there are steps in proceeding from being "new" to feeling familiar and at home in a group.

A wise teacher may use the opportunity to support growth in individual children already in the group. "Remember when you were new and visited?" perhaps recalling some special incident and adding, "Now you know where things go and what we do. You have friends." In this way she points out and strengthens the movement this child has made toward independence and greater security.

There Must Be Opportunities to Develop a Relationship with the Teacher

Through experiences with the child during his visits, the teacher makes an effort to establish a relationship with the new child which he can accept. Her task is to help him discover a teacher as a person who is there to be depended on, who cares for and about him, before he can let his mother go with confidence. For this reason it is important for the teacher to have time to spend with the child or to be available to him. He may need the same person to whom he can turn if he is to make the separation in a constructive way.

In order to make the best use developmentally of the experience for the child, the teacher will bring only *one* new child at a time into the group. It is difficult to be able to give the needed reassurance to more than one new child at a time. We are speaking here of bringing children into a group. If a group is just forming, it represents a different situation. The teacher may then plan to bring perhaps four children together for an hour with their mothers. Four new children are not likely to enter into sustained relationships with each other or to demand a great deal from the adult immediately. She can be available to them all as she introduces the possibilities of the school environment to them. Another group can come at another hour to go through the same process and, in a few days, the groups may come together to become a school to which another group of four or five children who have been together are added. In this way, each child begins in a small group first. He is with children he knows when he enters the larger group.

A Clear Understanding About the Length of Time the Child Is to Stay Helps in the Adjustment

The wise teacher will have a clear understanding with the parent as to the length of time the child will be staying on his first day at the school. More than an hour spent in an environment which calls for as much responsiveness as the nursery school is fatiguing for most children. The child needs to be protected from fatigue. Some children can, of course, stay longer and many children will wish to do so, but there are advantages in setting a definite length of time for the first visit and maintaining it.

The teacher will decide with the mother on the best time in the day for the child to come. It is important to give consideration to the family schedule in planning here. The child is not helped if the running of the home is disrupted by the demands made by the school. The needs of other members in the family must be considered.

During these first days it is usually important for the child that his mother come without bringing other children in the family with her, if possible. Entering nursery school is a significant event in the life of the child and his mother. If she is free to give him all her attention, she may reaffirm for him his sense of being valued by her. This may be especially important to him if there is a baby at home who has necessarily been taking much of her attention. It may help him realize that she cares for him at this moment of approaching separation.

One of the reasons for a clear understanding about the length of time for staying is that it helps the mother to feel sure about what is expected of her. If she knows that she is to bring the child and stay with him for an hour and then they are to leave, it reduces her uncertainty. She may be better able to relax and use the time to add to *her* picture of what nursery school is like.

Here, too, the teacher has a chance to gain some understanding through the way the mother reacts to this time limit. Does she find it difficult to accept? Does she try to change it, saying as the time for departure approaches, "He's getting along so well. I think he might as well stay on, don't you?" Is she afraid she may not be able to get the child to leave? Does she comment anxiously, "I'm afraid he won't want to go. What do you do about that?" Does she needlessly disturb the child with warnings, "You haven't much time left. It's almost time to go." Is she comfortable with the time limit set?

The Mother's Feelings Influence the Child in His Adjustment

The way the mother really feels about sending the child to nursery school will have a profound effect on the way the child adjusts there. If she feels reluctant or unsure or overanxious about his attending, she hinders his accomplishment of the task of meeting the new experience and growing more independent. It is sometimes hard for both parent and teacher to realize how completely a child senses what the adults who are close to him may be feeling.

There are many reasons why a mother can feel uncertain. She inevitably feels some conflict between wanting to hold on to the child, to prolong his dependence, and wanting the child to be strong and independent. The teacher needs to stand ready with reassurance. She needs to strengthen the mother's acceptance of the reality of what nursery school really is and the mother's confidence in her child's readiness for it. A parent may want very much to have a child in nursery school and yet still not want him there. She may be afraid of the disapproval of people. She may be afraid of her own feeling of not wanting him home all the time. It is for the teacher to encourage those feelings in the mother which will support the growth of the child toward independence and reduce the conflict for them both.

The mother helps a timid child by saying, "I will be right here. I am staying with you. I won't leave." She may find a chair where she can see and be seen easily by the child and stay there. She does not push him away from her with words like, "Why won't you go play with the blocks or with that little boy over there."

It is the teacher's responsibility to encourage the child to move away from his mother, not the mother's responsibility. The mother may show him by a smile that she is glad to see him when he returns to her side, but she indicates her pleasure in what he has done on his own. If he is hurt or is rebuffed by another child, she gives him the comfort he seeks, but she accepts the incident as part of the reality of existence with others, trying to look at it in the way she hopes that he will. She shows confidence in his ability not to be upset just as she will not be unnecessarily upset.

The Teacher Finds Ways to Help Both the Child and the Mother

The teacher is also the one to take the responsibility for helping the child to participate when he is ready. Always she is alert to the need to give him support in the efforts he makes to move toward greater independence. When he does leave his mother, she stays near him to give him the protection he needs at first. Things are more upsetting to someone who is already feeling uncertain. By staying near him she is also demonstrating to both him and his mother that she is there, looking after him. She makes it easier for the mother not to interfere but to leave the child free.

Some children are helped to make the adjustment if they bring something from home to keep with them at first. While it may not be the usual practice of the school to encourage children to bring their own toys to school, it may be desirable to permit it during the initial adjustment period. It is unlikely that the child will be able to "share" this possession if he is depending on it for support, and he should be protected against having to share it. A simple explanation by the teacher such as, "Mary is new at school and needs to keep her doll. Later when she knows us better, she'll let us play with it, too," will serve to deepen understanding all around.

Some mothers find time spent at nursery school full of interest. Others are restless, seeing little to interest them. If a mother is interested, she will find it easy to respond to the child's request to come and look at things, but she also needs to make him feel that it is *his* school. She looks at what he shows her, but she will avoid trying to point out many things to him. The teacher, for her part, will look for ways to help the mother appreciate the significance of what is occurring. As she has time, she can sit with the mother, pointing out and explaining things that are going on. Many people have had little background for understanding the development of children. They lack interest in it because they know little about it. Parents are almost sure to be interested if they are helped to see the significance of the play experiences children are having. The teacher and the school may open up possibilities to parents for growing in understanding which will be valuable through the years.

Regular Attendance for Part of the Session Without His Mother Comes Next

The fourth step for the child in entering nursery school is to attend regularly for part of the session and to begin the process of having his mother leave him at school. The point to keep in mind is that a relationship of trust in the teacher and interest in the school program itself are the sources of support which will enable the child to be successful in staying at school by himself with confidence and a sense of achievement. The first visits have been steps in preparation for the separation. Most children will need their mothers with them for a few days until they feel at home in the school and with the teacher.

One mother reported to the teacher on the second day that her three-year-old son had told her on the way to school, "I want you to go home today, Mummy." Wisely, they decided to follow his request. She went home for a short time and then returned. He was telling them clearly that he felt ready to be left for awhile, and they showed him that they had confidence in him. He did not need her the next day. He was ready.

It is interesting to note that most mothers overestimate their children's capacity to adjust. One cannot depend on a parent's assurance that "He'll be all right without me; I've left him lots of times." He may be a child who stands quiet and withdrawn, the very child who needs his mother most because he cannot express his insecurities. He may have had too many experiences of being left! Entering nursery school with his mother may mean the chance to overcome some of the past, to reassure himself by this present situation that his mother really will stay with him when he needs her. This may be the feeling that he needs if he is to be free to explore and enjoy the new.

The tendency on the part of most parents to expect too much of their children in the way of adjustment probably indicates how universally we fail to perceive what is involved in an experience for a child. We are not accustomed to observing behavior for clues to feelings. We look for what we want to see and not for what is really there.

The Teacher Plays an Active Part in Helping the Child Separate Himself from His Parent

It is usually necessary for the teacher to take an active part in the process of separation. The teacher is the one who must actively give support to the child as he shows signs of readiness to leave his mother. If the teacher plays a passive role and leaves the responsibility up to him by saying, "Do you want your mother to go now?" or "Is it all right for her to leave?" she may be asking for an answer which he is not ready to give, in most cases. This is the very question to which the nursery school experience will give him the answer in the end. As a result of his experiences, he should be readier to answer it later with, "It is all right. I know I am safe. I am an independent person."

Some sensitive teachers today, concerned about the danger of forcing a separation, lose sight of the growth potentials in the child. They fail to pick up the clues he offers as to his readiness to move toward independence provided he can get help. Prolonging his dependency in the new situation may interfere with his growth toward independence, which is the task at hand developmentally. The skillful, experienced teacher will help the child reach this goal in the shortest time possible.

During this fourth step in the process of entering nursery school, the child will come for only part of the session. Until he has successfully completed the stage of separating from his mother, it is better for him not to stay for the full program. For one reason, it will probably make too long a day for him. For another reason, postponing the full session will be an incentive for him to make the effort of staying without his mother in order to achieve the goal of full-time attendance. If he can have his mother and the nursery school, too, he has less incentive to become independent.

The Mother Helps with Her Understanding

As soon as the mother and teacher agree that the child is feeling comfortable at nursery school and is able to accept help from the teacher, they will plan for the mother to leave the child by himself for a short time.

The mother will find an opportunity to prepare the child for her leaving, saying perhaps, "Today, I am going to do some errands while you are playing at nursery school. I will be gone a little while, and when I get back, I'll see what you are doing." If his response is, "I don't want you to go," she may answer, "I won't go

Courtesy of Santa Monica College.

One of the children is not sure that she can do it.

for a while after we get to nursery school, not until you are having fun and I know you are ready. I will tell you and I'll only be gone a very little while."

The teacher can prepare the child for what he already expects by saying quietly, "Your mother is going now, John. She will be back very soon." With the teacher there, the mother can say good-by to the child and leave for a short time. If they have estimated the child's readiness correctly, the teacher will be able to help the child handle the anxiety he feels until his mother returns. She will be careful to stay near him.

The first separation should be a very short one if the child is finding it difficult to let his mother leave. Even fifteen minutes may seem a long time when one feels unsure of oneself and under some strain. When the mother returns, she will speak to him and then stay for a while, giving the child time to enjoy his play before they go home together. In this way his mother is showing him the pattern which she will follow. She goes but she comes back. He is discovering the satisfaction of feeling more and more comfortable about being able to stay at school without his mother.

The Child Is Ready for Full-Time Attendance Without His Mother

When the mother is able to leave the child almost as soon as they arrive at school and stay away for as long as two hours without his becoming uneasy, the child is ready for the fifth and last step—that of full-time attendance by himself including lunch and perhaps an all-day program.

Few three-year-old children reach this in less than a week. Others take much longer. Sleep disturbances, toilet accidents, and increased irritability may be the result of trying to move faster than the child is ready. Good adjustment requires time, and there are less likely to be relapses if the adjustment has not been either hurried or prolonged unduly.

The four-year-old child will probably be able to feel safe at school more quickly than the three-year-old. He has had more experience and more time to develop confidence in his own resources. Sometimes the struggle to make the separation may be unduly prolonged, often because the mother finds it hard to leave the child. She may lack confidence in herself or the child or the school. It is important that the teacher be aware of the point at which the separating has "bogged down" and the child wants to stay but cannot, for some reason, manage it without more help. The teacher needs to take positive steps in this case to resolve the conflict. She will talk with the mother, indicating her feeling that the child is ready to stay by himself, and they will plan together about how this is to be done. The teacher will act with firmness and confidence in carrying through the steps, sometimes holding the child in her arms when the mother goes, giving him time to cry, putting into words the fact that she knows he wants his mother, that his mother will be back. Then she will help him to find his place in the nursery school, sitting with him watching, or finding him a familiar toy or perhaps taking him to visit the homelike kitchen which he enjoyed earlier. While his mother is gone, she will make sure that she is always available if he needs her. She will try to see that the first separation is a successful one. Through it, the child gains confidence to continue separating himself from his dependency on his parents.

It often happens that a child who is disturbed by some event at home or at

Courtesy of Sam Hollander, San Diego State University.

Getting acquainted with a guinea pig.

school will revert to an earlier level of dependency, wanting his mother again. Again, it is important that his real needs be accepted and met. If his adjustment is sound, he is usually quickly reassured by his parent's willingness to stay with him for a time, and it does not take long for him to become independent. Again, the teacher helps him by accepting him but by giving all the support she can to his desire to be more self-sufficient.

TO SUMMARIZE

We may summarize the steps in entering nursery school in this way:

1. The teacher has a conference with the parents in which, among other things, the procedures to be followed as the child enters school are defined.

2. The child and his parent or parents visit the school when it is not in session to become acquainted with the physical setup and to establish a relationship with the teacher in the school.

3. The child and his parent visit during the regular session of the school for a limited, specified time.

4. The child begins attending school regularly for part of the session and begins the process of separating himself from his parent as soon as he feels comfortable there. The teacher takes the responsibility for planning with the parent

the time and method of separation. She may visit in the child's home so that he and she can become better acquainted.

5. The child attends school without his parent for increasingly longer periods until he is coming for the full session.

If the step of moving toward independence and away from the dependency on his mother is taken so that it does not produce more anxiety than the child can manage easily, he is free to enjoy and profit from the new experience. He gains in self-confidence. We may wonder whether children who have had this kind of help in a significant experience in separation will be as likely later to suffer from panic in strange situations or to be disorganized by feelings of homesickness.

Here are some examples of the ways in which different children make the adjustment to entering nursery school.

Mikey, Who Was Ready to Stay by Himself

Mikey's grandmother brought him on the first day. He was the next to the youngest in a family of six children and one of the youngest children entering the nursery school. His reaction that day seemed to be one of complete amazement. He darted from area to area and toy to toy, touching everything and exclaiming, "Oh, no! Oh, no! Look at all these toys. All kinds of toys. So many toys!" He could hardly bear to leave when the time came but wanted to touch everything all over again even though the teacher explained that he could come back the next day. Finally he was persuaded to go and he left saying, "Goodbye, I hope I can come back some day."

On arriving with his grandmother the second day, he made a check to see if everything was still there. He spent most of the time dashing from place to place and exclaiming with wonder at all the things for children. He commented on the fact that there were "little tables and little chairs just for children." When his grandmother tried to leave for a short time, Mikey stated emphatically that she was to stay at nursery school. On Mikey's third day he asked why he had to go while some of the other children could stay. The teacher explained that when he could let his grandmother go and stay at nursery school by himself, he could stay with the others for lunch. The next day he told his grandmother that he was ready to stay with "his teacher" now and she was to go home and come back after lunch. His first lunch period showed the same pattern of amazement and delight. He seemed entirely comfortable with the teacher. At the end of the day he said, "I hope I can stay for lunch again someday."

Here we see a child who manages his dependency needs easily but who is almost overwhelmed by the wealth of impressions. Incidentally, Mikey made an excellent adjustment. His friendliness, lack of defensiveness, and his delight in new experiences were a source of help to many children less sure of themselves.

Ralph, Whose Mother Could Give Him Time to Grow in Feeling Secure

Ralph was an only child, a little over three years of age, with a father and mother who were very fond of him. Although they were gentle and kind, they were very anxious to have Ralph come up to all expectations, perhaps because they were not too secure themselves.

On his visit to the school before he entered, Ralph enjoyed playing with the cars and blocks, but he called his mother's attention to everything and referred to her constantly. It was apparent that he depended on her and would not be ready to have her leave for some time even though he was eager for school and friendly with the teacher.

When he came on the first day of school, he held his mother's hand tightly. She went into the playroom with him and sat down near the block corner. Ralph immediately began playing. When other children approached, he seemed pleased and made attempts to join their play. One of the boys took a block from him in spite of his mild protest. Tears came into his eyes as he relinquished his hold on the block. He turned toward his mother but did not go to her. She smiled sympathetically and encouragingly, not quite sure what to do, and the teacher quietly reassured him, "That was your block, wasn't it? I'll ask Bill to give it back. There are other blocks for him. There are plenty for both of you to build with." It was easy to get Bill to return the block, and under the teacher's watchful eye the two had a satisfactory play, side by side. Ralph returned to his mother's side finally, flushed and happy.

Ralph was inclined to stutter when he got excited. This was further evidence that it was especially important to proceed slowly in introducing him to experiences. The stuttering showed that he was sensitive to strain. It was also apparent that there would be some strain for him in adjusting to the realities of three-year-old behavior because of the somewhat "adult" standards to which he had been accustomed. But he had shown a capacity to enjoy not only the play materials, but also the other children on that first day, and to accept help from someone other than his mother.

Ralph and his mother went home at the end of an hour and a half to return the next day, both eager for more. Ralph's mother watched with interest the things that went on in school. After Ralph and his mother had been coming to school for a week for two hours each, both his mother and teacher agreed that Ralph no longer needed his mother, but that he still needed a short day at school. He came happily the next morning, knowing that his mother was not staying. When she started to leave, however, he asked her to go to the store and not to go home without him. Apparently he could not quite bear to think of his mother at home without him. She went shopping and he had a good morning at school. It was nearly a week later that he decided he would like to stay for lunch like the other children, and did. His adjustment had proceeded smoothly. His mother smilingly remarked one day that she missed being at nursery school, adding, "It was such fun and I learned so much. They're all different, aren't they?" The days had been worth almost as much to Ralph's mother as to Ralph. She had gained confidence in the school, too.

Not long after this as Ralph was leaving one day he ran back and threw his arms around the teacher's neck and gave her a kiss. It probably showed that he felt he belonged to the school and to the adults who helped him feel comfortable there as his mother did at home. As the result of this experience in adjustment he had probably grown less tense and felt himself to be a more adequate person, more secure because he knew he could handle an experience at his own rate.

ADJUSTING TO OTHER NEW EXPERIENCES

All New Experiences Need to Be Handled Carefully to Build Greater Confidence in the Child

Entering nursery school is a big adjustment, but it is not the only new experience which the child may face. Any moment during the day may bring something new. When the children go on walks, for example, they may see unfamiliar or even frightening things. New experiences, wherever they are found, need to be handled carefully. They serve to build confidence or to destroy it. A visit to the fire station may mean strange noises, unfamiliar people, as well as the sight of the huge fire engine itself. Some children will need to proceed slowly. One child may be able to watch the fire engine comfortably if he holds the hand of the adult. Another may need the safety of being held in the adult's arms. Others may need the reassurance of knowing that they can leave the situation whenever they want.

The necessity of keeping each experience within the level of the child's ability to take part in it without anxiety means that at least two adults must go with any group from nursery school to all but the most familiar places. On a walk to the barns, for example, a child may show signs of fear about going inside. An adult will need to stay outside with him, accepting the fact that for some reason he is not ready for the experience of going inside. They both can have a pleasant experience outside a barn. Later the child may want to go inside or he may want to return. With his fear accepted and with time to proceed at his own rate, a child will gain confidence in himself as he succeeds in handling the fear. If he is pushed into entering the barn when he is still afraid, he may only learn to conceal his fear or to depend on adult support. In such a case if anything happens which startles him while he is in the barn, such as a cow mooing, he may be thrown into a panic because of the feelings of fear inside him which are released by the sudden noise. He becomes more afraid and loses confidence.

The Adult's Feelings Influence the Child's

The attitude of the adult influences the child, and in any emergency it is imperative that the adult meet the situation calmly for the sake of the child. A group of four-year-olds were visting the fire station one day when the fire alarm sounded. One of the firefighters directed them calmly, "You all stand right against the wall and watch this fire engine go out." His composure steadied the teachers and in a matter of seconds everyone was against the wall and the fire engine pulled out before the eyes of the thrilled line of four-year-olds. It was the best trip to the fire station they had ever had. The reports of experiences during the bombings of the last war showed that children reacted in the way the adults they were with reacted. If they were with calm people, they were not likely to be upset even when the situations were terrifying. They grew hysterical for much less cause when they were with hysterical people.

In planning any experience for the children the teacher must always be familiar with it herself. She must have made the trip so that she can prepare the children for what they may expect. What will it be like? What will they do? What will they see? Will they hear a noise? If there is much that is unfamiliar, it helps to go over it in words so that the children have some framework into which to fit the situation. Often a lively review on the way home of what each one saw will help to place the experiences among the "known" things.

It is usually important to talk to the non-nursery school adults about what will help the children enjoy the experience more. Not all adults understand the needs of young children. Some adults think it is fun to startle children by blowing a whistle unexpectedly or ringing a bell. If the adults are not helpful, it may be better not to visit the fire station, or at least to be very careful to take only the children for whom such possibilities will not be frightening. People who work with animals can usually be counted on to be gentle and quiet and to help rather than hinder the children's sound adjustment to the experiences they are having.

Watching Children Meet New Experiences Gives One Insight into the Way They Feel

Observing the way children explore the world outside nursery school is one way to become aware of the different patterns of adjustment which children already have. Some children go out to meet new experiences with confidence. There are others whose areas of confidence are limited, and there are others who are disturbed by the smallest departure from the familiar. Experiences offered to children must be adapted to what they are ready to accept.

When a child stops to watch something, the wise adult will wait. It is a sign that the child is absorbed in the new, attempting to relate it to what he can understand. He may ask questions or he may not. Moving on before he is ready will only mean leaving behind unresolved ideas. The habit of exploring an experience fully is a sound one and builds feelings of adequacy.

Most children in the first few months at nursery school need to have their experiences limited to the school itself, to have plenty of time at school before going on any trips. There are many new experiences inside the school. By watching, questioning, participating, the child digests the new, whether it be a wasp's nest brought in by the teacher, or a visitor in a foreign costume, or just a new toy. When he repeats an activity over and over, he is assimilating it, making it his own. He is adding to his feeling of being an adequate person by making it an "easy" experience.

Children Have Defenses When They Feel Unsure

Children, like adults, have defenses that they are likely to use when they feel uncertain because the situation they are in is new and strange. When children feel unsure of themselves, they may withdraw or retreat from any action and play safe by doing nothing and thus run no risk of doing the wrong thing. This is a type of denial of the situation—like turning one's back on something.

For example, Helen came to nursery school and made no protest at her mother's leaving her. She simply stood immobile on the spot where she had been left. If an adult took her hand and led her somewhere, as to the piano, she went passively. She had had many new situations to meet in her short life and much unfriendliness. A frail child, she had protected herself in the only way she could—by being passive. She was not far from being a "dummy" in one sense of that word. The teachers made no attempt to push her into any activity but gave her friendly smiles, often sat near her, and sometimes took her to the piano or the finger-painting table. Very slowly she began to show some responsiveness.

It was interesting to observe that only after Helen had been in nursery school some months did she begin to make a fuss over her mother's leaving and beg her to stay. It seemed likely that only then was she feeling free enough to dare to make some demands on her mother—to indicate how she really felt. Unfortunately, her mother could not accept her demands and refused to "baby" her, so Helen stopped this behavior; but in spite of her mother's denial she continued to progress at school, making some demands on the teachers and joining an occasional child in play. When the situation changed in any way, as when there were visitors, she became quite passive again. One wonders whether Helen would have been less passive if her mother could have accepted the child's demand that she stay. Would she have felt less helpless? Would she have been less likely to retreat into passive behavior?

Sometimes a child who feels strange and uncomfortable will suddenly begin to play for a lot of attention or act "silly" as though seeking reassurance by surrounding himself with attentive adults. Another child will be aggressive and try to bully others as though to prove to himself that he is really big and strong and not weak and helpless as he fears. This child is doing something actively about his problem. He gives us a chance to help him.

Steven, on the second day of school, appeared disturbed by all the strange children and teachers. He suddenly picked up a toy horse and said, "This horse is going to kill all these many bad people around here." His teacher replied quietly, "I think you don't like finding so many people here. They will be your friends someday." Because they were strange to him, they seemed bad. He was actively trying to cope with his anxiety through projecting onto the horse the wish that he could dispose of them all. He was also communicating to an understanding teacher his need for reassurance.

Children Need Help When They Act Defensively

It is not unusual to see a child, who has been frightened by something startling or unusual, turn and hit a companion on almost no provocation. In this way he drains off the feeling of fear which is uncomfortable. The adult's role is to help him face the feeling and find some acceptable outlet for it. Fear is a less uncomfortable feeling when one is not ashamed of it. It may help if the teacher can say, "That noise made you feel afraid, didn't it? Lots of people feel afraid when they hear a big noise like that. It's all right. Take hold of my hand and let's walk farther away and then it won't sound so loud. There's no need to hit Billy. He may be afraid, too." And Billy will need some help with, "I think he hit you because he felt afraid. I'm sorry." This kind of handling will help them both in understanding why people behave as they do.

Often children will actively reject a situation or some part of it because they feel strange and insecure. In the laboratory nursery school the large number of adults may increase any difficulty a child has in accepting adults. Frequently he will meet a friendly advance with the words, "Go 'way, I don't like you." It's like getting in the first blow when you're expecting the worst. For the child's sake, it's important to recognize the real feeling back of these words, to understand its meaning as "Go 'way. I'm afraid of you." It usually *is* better to go away until the child has had more time to make an adjustment. It is sometimes possible for a teacher whom the child does know to interpret his feelings to him in such a case, saying, for example, "I think that you don't like her and want her to go away because you don't know her yet. When you know her, you will like her. Her name is _____. She might help you find a shovel for digging."

It is important to be able to identify children's defenses and to help them make adjustments which are really appropriate to the situation or to help them discover how to drain off their disturbed feelings in acceptable ways. It is equally important to see that children have experiences in which they feel adequate so that they will have less need for defenses. When adults can do these things, they offer real help to the child.

SITUATIONS FOR DISCUSSION

A New Experience*

Situation

Susie, a student, came into the play school carrying a fat glass jar. Inside were two small mice nestled in a bed of yellow straw and grass. Pam (4–11) and Bobby (4–5) were sitting on a rug looking at a book. Susie walked over and joined them. As she sat down, she placed the jar in front of her. "Hi, Pam and Bobby. See what I have," Susie said.

"Mices," exclaimed Pam. Bobby threw his book aside. He lay on his stomach with his hands folded in front of him. "Now I can see better," he said. Jason (4–9), Alicia (3–2), and Ritchie (5–1) joined the group. Jason squatted down while Alicia bent over with her hands on her knees, her eyes wide with anticipation. Ritchie and Pam sat cross-legged. All eyes were on the jar with the mice.

Susie turned the jar around, and the white mouse stretched, yawned, and snuggled back down into the straw. The other mouse walked around the inside of the jar on its hind legs, stood on the white mouse, and climbed out! Bobby said excitedly to the group, "Get back!" as he pushed himself back. "They don't bite, do they?" he asked. "No, Bobby," Susie answered, "when we are careful with them, they don't bite. What color do you think he is?" Pam said quickly, "Brown. It's got white spots."

Comment

Here we see an example of the interest young children show in animals and the sustained attention they give when they are interested. We may wonder what preparation for the experience the children may have had beforehand. From the lack of questions asked throughout the experience, we suspect that there had not been much preparation.

Bobby's response to the mouse climbing out of the jar is interesting. He

---

*Recorded by Jane Martin.

seems to feel responsibility for the other children when he says, "Get back." His next words express some anxiety, "They don't bite, do they?" Susie tries to reassure him, "No," but adds a warning, "When we are careful with them, they don't bite." Then she immediately changed the subject, without waiting to see whether this satisfied him. By this answer she may have been trying to forestall any rough handling of the mice. Perhaps she herself was anxious. But her answer to his question probably does not completely answer what the child is asking. Does he know what "being careful" means in this situation? Has he had experiences with animals that bite? Bobby either doesn't know or is still wondering about biting.

What might the teacher have answered here? She might have acknowledged his fear, saying, "Do you think he might bite us?" thus facing it openly. It is natural to feel anxious in strange situations. She might have added, "No, he won't bite unless he is afraid or hurt. He has sharp teeth but he uses them to bite his food. We can handle him gently and he won't bite." She might have continued by saying, "I wonder what he is going to do next?" thus encouraging more observation and some speculation on the children's part, and preparing them for the mouse's movements.

Instead the teacher immediately asked a question changing the subject. "What color do you think he is?" A better phrasing would have been "What color is he?" The question doesn't lead into any discussion.

Children are often anxious or fearful in new or unexpected situations. These feelings can best be managed by allowing time for discussion, for ventilating the feeling thoroughly. Bobbie *was* a bit afraid that the mice might bite. He took a good step in managing the feeling by turning to the teacher with his question. Susie might have acknowledged his fear by saying, "Why you think he might bite?" She might have allowed more time for facing the question here instead of changing the subject. Other children may have felt uncertain, too. Are they sure how one is "careful" with mice? Watching, handling gently, moving slowly so as not to startle an animal, taking time to get acquainted, discovering what the animal likes, these are all part of the new experience. One can also accept the reality — and the benefits — of some anxiety and fear. Susie changes the subject and misses this opportunity.

Situation

Alicia, sitting on the rug across from Susie, puts out her hand, declaring, "I want it." Susie carefully puts the mouse in Alicia's outstretched hand, saying, "Hold it gently. It is just a baby. How does it feel?" Alicia giggles, "It's fuzzy." All the children want to hold the mouse and each has a turn. Then Susie takes the mouse and lets it run over her hand and up her arm. Jason (4–9) arrives and yells to his friends in the block corner, "Come, see the mouses."

Gilbert (3–0) joins the group. He sits down on his knees and watches intently. Susie asks, "Would you like to hold the mouse?" He looks apprehensively and shakes his head. Then he puts out one finger to touch it. The mouse moved suddenly and Gilbert hastily drew back. Susie reassured him, "It's OK, Gilbert. Not everyone likes to pet mice." She puts the mouse back in the jar, saying, "The mouse needs a rest. Let's put the jar on the table and you can all see it if you wish."

Comment

Susie is reassuring and accepting of Gilbert's timidity, but she does not help him manage it. She avoids it. Instead of saying, "Not everyone likes to pet mice," which confirms his negative feelings, Susie might have said, "The mouse moved quickly and surprised you didn't he! I'll hold him, so he won't move, and then you can touch him if you wish. He is so tiny. He feels so soft. I think he is a little afraid because he doesn't know us. He'll feel at home soon." The mouse's feelings may be something like Gilbert's!

Encouraging Gilbert to talk about the mouse even if he did not want to touch it might have helped him. Has he ever seen a mouse before? What do mice like to eat? One doesn't have to pet mice to be interested in them! Susie left him with his fear. She took him out of the situation by putting the mouse back in the jar. One wonders how long Gilbert may think of himself as someone who "doesn't like to pet mice." With a child of four or five it is often desirable to discuss fear directly and how we are all likely to feel afraid of the strange or unexpected.

Situation

Pam and Bobby follow Susie to the table to watch the mice and Nels (3–6) joins them. They watch as the little brown and white mouse crawls out of the jar again. Nels leans against the table with his arms folded in front of him. He smiles as the mouse tries to get back into the jar. Pam, elbows on the table and chin in her hands, watches closely. She asked, "When will the mouse grow up?" "In about two weeks," replied Susie. "Mice grow very fast."

Comment

Pam's question is a thoughtful, interesting one. Her interest has been sustained longer than any other child's. What is she really wondering about? Is Susie's answer enough to satisfy Pam? We will discuss questions and answers at more length in another section.

Then the class bell rings. Susie puts the mouse back into the jar and picks it up. "I must go now. Goodby, kids," she says. Pam follows her to the door and the boys go back to the rug.

Discussion

Note the behavior or language which reveals differences in developmental level such as attention span. Note individual differences such as the approach to experience of Alicia and Gilbert who are approximately the same age.

Language: Note the logic of child language in the plurals used here and the emergence of the correct terms with usage and without correction.

Contrast the approach of Alicia to the mice with that of Gilbert and discuss the different guidance needed by children who are eager for an experience and those who are hesitant or fearful.

Discuss the value of letting a child take the initiative in moving into a new situation.

Discuss both preparation for and follow-up of an experience to increase its value for learning. Consider also the amount and kind of participation by the adult. How much participation? The timing? Kinds of questions to ask? Explanations? Evaluation afterwards?

PROJECTS

1. Record a situation in which a child was faced with a new experience in the nursery school. Summarize your observation, noting the child's significant reactions and the help given by the adult (if any). Estimate what the experience may have meant to the child.

2. Observe a child anywhere, as in a Sunday church school or on a playground, and note the degree to which he seems to feel safe in the situation. How does he show his feeling? What defenses does he seem to use against the feeling of being strange and unsure? Is the experience building up or breaking down the degree of security the child feels?

REFERENCES

Baratz, S., and Baratz, J.: Negro ghetto children and urban education: A cultural solution. Social Education, Vol. 33, No. 4, 1969.

Berger, Allan: Anxiety in young children. Young Children, Vol. 27, 1971.

Bowlby, John: Attachment and Loss. Vol. 1 Attachment. London, Hogarth Press Ltd., 1969.

Furman, Robert: Experiences in nursery school consultations. Young Children, Vol. 22, No. 2, November 1, 1966.

Gross, Dorothy: On separation and school entrance. Childhood Education, Vol. 46, 1970.

Heinicke, Christoph, and Westheimer, I. J.: Brief Separations. New York, International Universities Press, Inc.; 1965.

Johnson, Beverly: Before hospitalization: A preparation program for the child and his family. Children Today, November-December, 1974.

Jones, Marjorie Graham: A Two Year Old Goes to Nursery School: A Case Study of Separation Anxiety. Washington, D.C., National Association for the Education of Young Children, 1964.

Murphy, Lois B.: The Widening World of Childhood. Part 1. The New and the Strange. New York, Basic Books, Inc., Publishers, 1962.

Plank, Emma: Working with Children in Hospitals, 2nd ed. Cleveland, The Press of Case Western Reserve University, 1971.

Robertson, James: Hospitals and Children: A Parent's-Eye View. New York, International Universities Press, Inc., 1962.

Speers, R. W., et al.: Recapitulation of separation-individuation processes when the normal three-year-old enters nursery school. In McDevitt, John, and Settlage, Calvin (eds.): Recapitulation-Individuation: Essays in Honor of Margaret Mahler. New York, International Universities Press, Inc., 1971.

Yarrow, Leon J., and Pederson, Frank: Attachment: Its origin and course. In Hartrup, W. W. (ed.): The Young Child, Vol. 2. Washington, D.C., National Association for the Education of Young Children, 1972.

CHAPTER 10

Street (girl, 3 years 6 months)

HELPING CHILDREN IN ROUTINE SITUATIONS

Understanding Is Important in Everyday Experiences

We have seen how new experiences can contribute to building confidence and security in a child. Having new experiences such as going to nursery school, visiting a fire station, taking a walk, even hearing a strange noise, will help a child to develop more confidence if we accept and respect the child's level of readiness for each experience. If we fail to do this, we may find that these experiences only increase his feelings of being little and helpless.

The need to understand and accept the child's readiness for an experience is as important with everyday experience as with new experiences. Experiences which occur daily may pile up feelings and set patterns in a way that influences growth even more significantly than do unusual or new experiences. Teaching which includes an awareness of the child's level of readiness is needed here, too. If we are to achieve the goal of developing secure people, free to make use of all

This is the way a zipper works.

Courtesy of Jean Berlfein.

their capacities, we will do this kind of teaching wherever children are having experiences, either new or everyday ones.

Routines such as toileting, resting, and eating are everyday experiences. They serve as a framework around which the child's day is organized. It probably gives the child assurance to know that there are familiar aspects of the day which he can anticipate and understand. It enables him to get a sense of the passage of time.

TOILETING

Experiences in the Toilet Room Offer Opportunities for Teaching

Some of the best opportunities for teaching in the nursery school occur in the toileting situation, for toileting is a significant experience in the young child's life.

It is one about which his feelings are sure to be strong. It offers the chance for a great deal of growth.

For the child, toileting is associated with many intimate experiences with his mother, with her care of him, with his efforts to please her, perhaps with conflicts over her attempts to train him. Toileting may even be tied up in his mind with ideas about "good" and "bad" behavior. One parent used to leave her child at nursery school with the admonition, "Be a good girl today." What she really meant by these words was, "Stay dry today." Morality such as this is confusing.

When the child is ready for nursery school, about the age of three years, he has probably only recently been through a period of toilet training. He is not likely to have emerged from this training period completely unscathed. His behavior will tell us something of what the experiences have meant to him.

Training for Toilet Control Has an Effect on Many Areas of Behavior

Excessive negativism is perhaps the most common result of toilet training which is not based on a child's readiness. The child who says "no" to everything, who looks on any contacts with adults as a possible source of interference and restriction, may have acquired this attitude during his training period. One of the most resistant, hostile children in one nursery school had been subjected to an early, rigid period of toilet training. She defied adult suggestions and could not share with children. The quality of the relationship she had with her earnest parents can be pictured in the note which her mother sent to school one day, "Ruth has *refused* to have a bowel movement for four days."

Inhibitions of many types may stem from the same source. If the child has been forced to achieve bowel and bladder control before he is able to comprehend and differentiate patterns, his "control" may include the inhibition of spontaneity and creativity in many areas. We see children who were trained early to stay "dry and clean" who are unable to use play materials in ways that are creative. They cannot get dirty in other situations, play in mud, or savor the ordinary joys of childhood and the social contacts that occur in the society of the sandbox crowd.

Loss of self-confidence may also characterize the child who has been subjected to early and rigid toilet training. In his experience the products of his body have been rejected and his natural impulses denied expression. He loses confidence in his impulses in other directions. His inevitable failures in the training process do not help him feel like an adequate person, either. Because he has had to give up too early the pleasure of eliminating as he wants, he is likely to "give up" easily in other ways—unless he goes to the other extreme of asserting himself to compensate for his loss.

The child whose parents have treated the acquiring of toilet control in the same manner as any other development step such as learning to walk or talk is likely to be a more comfortable child. The child who is left free to proceed at his own rate is likely to learn rather easily sometime after he has started walking. He will show an interest in the toilet and in imitating the behavior of the people he observes. Parents can make it easy for him to do this and can show the same satisfactions in his successes here as they do in his other developmental accomplishments. They should accept resistance as a sign that he has lost interest and is not ready, and drop for a time efforts they may be making to train him. They should not make an issue out of learning toilet control any more than they would out of learning to walk or talk. When there is no pressure, the child himself usually begins to take on the patterns of the adult in regard to toileting sometime between the ages of fifteen and thirty months.

Adult Attitudes and Standards May Complicate the Toilet Problem

Toileting is sometimes complicated for the child by parental anxieties. A parent may give a great deal of anxious attention to the child's elimination. It then becomes unduly important to the child, and even disturbs him. He feels anxiety, and this interferes with his behavior.

A mother may express her anxiety in this way if she is not sure of her ability to be a "good" mother. She tries to find reassurance by seeing that her child eliminates properly. She may use this means of expressing anxiety if she is having some difficulty in accepting the changes she has had to make in her life because of the child. She may wish that she could do the things she used to do, but she tries to hide her feelings, even from herself, by concern over the child's elimination. Mothers who have these feelings are likely, too, to undertake training early, in a determined way, as part of their efforts to prove themselves "good" mothers. Thus, they complicate further the problem for the child. The child, in turn, may use the withholding of his stools as an unconscious means of "punishing" his parents for withholding acceptance from him. It becomes hard for healthy attitudes to develop under these circumstances.

More confusion for the child is added by the standards about toilet behavior which adults sometimes impose before the child can understand them. Separation of the sexes, demands for privacy, disapproval of many kinds of behavior in relation to the toilet situation can have little meaning for the child except to confuse him. These standards add feelings of uncertainty or fear or guilt to the situation. Today these standards are becoming more relaxed and better adapted to the child's level of readiness.

Children Gain from Sound Handling of Toilet Experience at Nursery School

The important thing for us to remember as students in the nursery school or child care center is that children come from many different backgrounds. Some will have healthy, matter-of-fact attitudes, with no doubts about their ability to handle the toileting situation and expecting to meet friendly, accepting adults. They will not be disturbed about toilet accidents. Other children will be confused and insecure. They will resent attempts by the adult to help them and will be upset by their failures to control their elimination. Some will use the toilet situation to express their anxiety or their resentments or their defiance. Some will not be able to use the toilet at nursery school until they feel comfortable there. According to their different needs they must be helped. All of them, no matter what their background, will gain from a sound handling of the toilet experience at the nursery school.

The toilet room should be a comfortable, friendly place.

Courtesy of Myron Papiz.

If the handling is to be sound, the children must meet adults in the school who are themselves comfortable in the situation. This is not always easy, for many of us have had experiences in our past which have included being ashamed or confused about the subject of toileting. Being with children who have matter-of-fact attitudes will often help us to free ourselves from the conflicts generated by our own past experiences.

The interest that children show in the subject of toileting can be seen in the frequency with which it appears in their dramatic play. Again and again they will act out with their dolls what is for them the drama of the toilet. This is a desirable way of expressing any conflicts they may feel and making these conflicts seem more manageable. The good nursery school will supply equipment in the doll corner which can be used to represent the toilet room.

Be Alert to the Meaning of What the Child Does at Toilet Time

Toilet accidents, for example, are likely to be common in the first weeks at nursery school and are indications of the strain that the child is feeling in the new situation. They should be treated as a symptom, and the strains should be reduced for the child in every way possible. The child will be reassured when he realizes that he does not need to be afraid of having a toilet accident. This removes one possible strain. He will gain confidence if he finds friendly, accepting adults to help him when he is wet.

Some children, on the other hand, will react to the new situation of being in nursery school by holding back from the experience. They will be unable to use the toilet. This will be one symptom of the way they feel. It is hardly necessary to say that no pressure should be put on a child to use the toilet until he is ready. He may need to go home after a short stay, or he may be more comfortable after he has wet himself.

Sometimes a child who has been attending nursery school will suddenly have a series of toilet accidents. These accidents are a sign of emotional strain and should be regarded as a significant symptom. It is our job to make every effort to discover and remove the sources of the strain. We should not increase the strain by disapproval. The child's behavior gives us a clue as to how the situation is affecting him.

A Child is Reassured by the Casual Attitude of the Adult

It cannot be emphasized too strongly that a matter-of-fact attitude about toilet accidents on the part of adults is exceedingly important. If a child knows that toilet accidents are not condemned, he feels much freer and safer. He can proceed to acquire control at his own rate, and toilet accidents do not lessen his confidence in himself.

While we can show pleasure in his successes, we must not value success too highly. An undue emphasis on success may rouse anxiety in the child. If success is valued too highly, the child may find it hard to meet the inevitable failures. We can help him succeed without feeling anxiety. Under no condition should a child ever be made to feel disapproval or be shamed for his failure to stay dry and clean. Shame is not a healthy feeling. It does not contribute to the development of the confidence we all need.

When the child does have a toilet accident, we can try to make the experience a comfortable one for him. We can give him any help he may need in changing his clothes. The type of clothing the child wears becomes an important factor here. Small buttons, complicated belt buckles, fastenings in the back, or tight clothes make it hard for a child to take responsibility.

Acceptance of Children's Interest in Each Other at Toilet Time
Promotes Healthy Adjustment

Sound handling of toileting also includes a matter-of-fact attitude in meeting situations in which the children show an interest in each other in the toilet room. Children need a chance to satisfy their curiosity without becoming confused. Girls will be interested in the fact that boys have a penis and stand when they urinate. The way this interest is received by the adult will influence the development of their later attitudes toward sex. At this stage their interest is not very different from their interest in anything new in the school experience. A girl who has no brothers at home may not notice sex differences the first time that she uses a toilet beside a boy, but when she does, she will usually want to watch boys frequently as they urinate until her interest is satisfied. She may comment and ask questions. If she does, she will be helped by the teacher's casual acceptance of her comments. It may help her to have the teacher verbalize in some way as, "Bill has a penis. He stands up at the toilet. Boys stand up and girls sit down there."

Psychiatrists tell us that an important factor in later sex adjustment is the acceptance of one's sex. In this situation it is usually easier for the boys to feel acceptance because they possess a penis. Many times a girl will try to imitate the boy by attempting to stand—with not very satisfactory results! She learns from the experience and no particular comment is needed. But some girls may need help in feeling that being a girl is desirable. The teacher may remark, "Mothers sit down, too."

Procedures That Are Constructive

What are specific procedures in regard to toileting?

The physical setup plays a part in building positive feelings. If the toilet room is a pleasant place, light and attractive, the child is more likely to feel that it is a safe room in which to be. Just ordinary, pleasant conversation on any topic will help make a child more relaxed and comfortable. Some children, of course, who already possess a comfortable feeling, will not need such distraction, but conversation may help some children whose feelings may be mixed.

Interest in the plumbing usually rises to a peak around the age of four, and observation of the inside of the toilet while it is being flushed and discussions about water pipes and sewer systems are of absorbing interest. These have values. Any attempt to hurry the child out of the situation or to discourage his curiosity will make it harder for him to develop and maintain a healthy attitude. The wise adult will be prepared to spend time and feel comfortable in the toilet room with the child.

The easier it is for the child to manage independently, the more he will gain. Small-size toilets are desirable. If they cannot be obtained, a step can be made to fit in front of the toilet seat. A hinged seat to make the opening smaller may be desirable, too. A door to the room is a handicap and it is usually easy to have one removed if one is there. Doors present hazards for fingers and interfere with the casual matter-of-factness of the situation as well as with the ease of supervision.

Children at the nursery school level can be expected to be independent about their clothing at toilet time if they are properly dressed. Girls can pull down their panties and boys can use a fly. There are well-designed coverall suits with drop seats for both boys and girls. Boys can be reminded to raise the toilet seat before urinating. Both boys and girls can be reminded to flush the toilet after they have used it. When an occasional child refuses to flush the toilet, we can safely assume, as we can with any refusal, that there is some meaning behind it. Children are sometimes frightened by the noise and movement of water in a flushing toilet. They will be reassured in time as they watch others and as they gain more confidence in other places. Their refusal should be respected.

Handwashing should be encouraged after toileting. It is a desirable habit and a child usually enjoys the washing process. Handwashing is necessary before eating. Its value should be stressed.

In the nursery school, boys and girls use the toilets freely together while adults are present. Occasionally a child may find this difficult and the teacher can explain. "Here in nursery school we all use the toilet room together." Standards do differ in different places. Because it is customary to do a thing one way in one place does not make another practice in a different place wrong. Adults sometimes ask, "But won't this make it harder for a child when he has to learn a different custom, as in a public school?" We must remember that the important

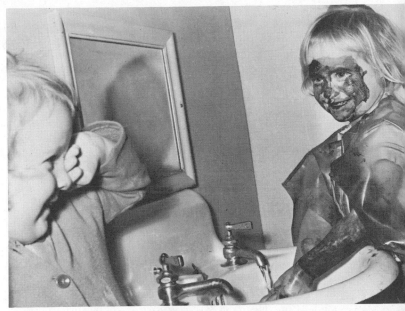

Paint can be washed off at nursery school.

Courtesy of Myron Papiz.

Children wash before eating and enjoy the process.

thing is to be able to accept the customs that are in use. Toileting on a picnic differs from that done at home. Boys accompany their mothers into public restrooms when they are young but learn to make a distinction when they are older. Patterns of behavior differ with age, place, and society. The child learns to accept differences as he begins to understand them.

Establishing a Schedule for Toileting

When a child starts nursery school, the teacher can soon discover how frequently he needs to go to the toilet by talking with his mother and by observing what happens in the school.

For the younger child she can establish a schedule to fit his rhythm. She will take most of the responsibility herself, saying to him, "Time to go to the toilet now," and attempting to time her interruptions to a shift in his activity. In this way she will avoid building resistances in him. If she is pleasant and friendly, he will welcome this opportunity for adult contact and attention. Going to the toilet will bring him satisfactions.

A new child usually adjusts more easily if he has the same adult helping him each time. He feels secure more quickly and may begin to come to her when he needs to go to the toilet.

As a next step the teacher may ask the child, "Do you need to go to the toilet now?" rather than simply telling him that it is time to go. This begins to shift the responsibility onto him where it will belong entirely in the end. If the number of toilet accidents show that the child is not ready to take this much responsibility, the teacher can drop back to the earlier stage. Many factors change a child's rhythm, such as cold weather, or excitement, or drinking more liquids than usual. Even older children will not always remain dry under unusual conditions.

A set schedule for going to the toilet has the disadvantage of not meeting individual needs, or not meeting changing needs in the same individual. Nevertheless, as children's needs are likely to follow a similar pattern, it is possible to have a framework within which to expect toileting, and this simplifies management. If we remember that the goal of any schedule is to help the child go to the toilet when he needs to go—and not any oftener—we can work out a schedule which will be flexible. For example, some children may need to use the toilet when they first come to school, depending on their last toilet period at home. The next logical time for an interruption is around juice or snack time, which is usually in the middle of the morning. A toilet period before lunch ensures a lunch period less likely to be interrupted by a trip to the toilet. The more mature children, those who have taken over responsibility for their toileting, will follow their own schedule, but the teacher will find it wise to suggest toileting before lunch for them all.

Examples of Problems in the Toilet Situation

Let us consider some specific problems which may arise.

Mary was a delightfully imaginative child with a fine sense of rhythm. She loved music and often played and sang at the piano or danced when music was played. She was friendly with other children and enjoyed "homemaking" play in the doll corner. She was curious about many things, played actively outdoors, and enjoyed expeditions outside the school. Toward adults she responded in a very negative way. She resisted suggestions and was likely to become self-conscious and "show-off." She found rest difficult and at the table seemed to concentrate on behavior that she felt might not be acceptable, putting her fingers in the food, throwing it, or running away from the table. She was wet several times a day, and consistently refused to go to the toilet. She always changed her panties immediately, leaving the wet ones on the floor in the toilet room. Her mother reported that she had been toilet trained early and then had suddenly begun wetting again within the last year. They had "tried everything" to make her stop, even to shaming her and making her wear diapers. At first she would stay wet, but they had succeeded in impressing on her how "dirty" that was and now she wouldn't stay wet a minute.

It was easy to see where Mary's negativism came from. It seemed likely that here was an able little girl trying to assert herself. The methods of training and disciplining that her parents had used with her more docile older brother had only increased her resistance. She was defiantly insisting on being independent.

Since she was out to defeat "bossing," it was evident that pressure for conforming to standards, no matter how desirable the standards, needed to be reduced before she could be expected to change her behavior. The whole matter of toileting was dropped in nursery school, and no comment was made on her wetting. There was no insistence put on her to use the toilet. It was hard for her parents to see that before she could accept adult standards she must be convinced that she was a "free agent" and that they could convince her of this only by accepting her right to wet as she pleased. They themselves valued conformity. However, they were friendly, intelligent people and very fond of their small daughter. Somewhat reluctantly they followed the suggestion of saying nothing, perhaps because there was nothing left for them to do. It was several months before Mary began using the toilet at nursery school. It might have happened sooner if her parents could have been more wholehearted in turning the responsibility completely over to her. Whenever she was subjected to domination, Mary would revert to a series of wet pants. It was the area in which she felt she could win in the battle to assert her independence. When left to accept things at her own rate, she was an unusually social and capable child with a wholehearted enjoyment of experience.

A child does not always express his resistance to pressure as directly as Mary. In a less friendly and understanding home a child may have to conceal his feelings of resistance and resentment.

Sam was a child whose mother reported that she had felt that "the sooner I started him on regular toilet habits the better." She began when he was six months old and he responded "perfectly." He now says to his younger brother, "I never got my panties wet when I was little." But he chews on his blanket, sucks his finger, and is very inactive. He often sits passively instead of playing. His mother reports, "He doesn't enjoy anything that I can see." This child, with perhaps more against him, has not felt strong enough to protest in a direct way as Mary has been able to do. With many other strains added to the pressure to be clean, his position is far less favorable. He is dry but not free! Spontaneity and creativeness have been sacrificed to conformity.

Alice was a child whose toilet training had begun at six months and had proceeded smoothly and quickly. Her mother felt that the early training was successful, and it certainly had made matters easier for her. Alice had no toilet accidents at the nursery school, and she was not a resistant child. In fact she was anxious to please. She was lacking in confidence in herself and somewhat tense and easily disturbed by new experiences. She needed reassurance and support from the teachers.

Alice enjoyed nursery school and was friendly with both adults and children—friendly with children who did not get wet, that is. If a child had a toilet accident, Alice avoided him or even actively rejected him in play. One day, for example, Alice was in the toilet room when Gary happened to come in. Gary was thoroughly wet, having had one of his not infrequent toilet accidents. Gary was one of the youngest children in the group, but he managed well in spite of the short time he had been in school. He was friendly and eager to play with the other children. Alice watched the teacher help Gary get into dry clothes, but she kept as far away as possible and made her disapproval evident. "He's a bad boy," she remarked to the other children. Throughout the rest of the morning she refused to play with Gary. When he approached her, she would say, "We don't like you," although usually she found it easy to include other children in her play.

Alice had succeeded in staying dry herself because of the way her mother felt about wetting, but she was not able to accept people who failed to keep dry. How will she feel about her own children someday? Will she impose dryness on them, together with tenseness and fear and a rejection of those who do not meet her standards?

MEALTIME

Strong Feelings Also Exist in the Eating Situation

Eating is another area which is important in the development of feelings and behavior. When children enter nursery school, they enter with a long past as far as eating goes. They have had many previous experiences with food. These experiences have been satisfying or unsatisfying in varying degrees. The child's attitude may consequently be favorable or unfavorable toward the meal situation.

Like the toileting situation, the meal situation is highly charged with feeling. "The way to a man's heart is through his stomach" is true in more ways than one. The child's earliest feelings of comfort or discomfort, satisfaction or deprivation, helplessness or adequacy have come from what happened to him when he felt hungry.

Adult Behavior and Attitudes Influence the Child

From the very beginning the child is affected by the way the adults act and feel about his eating. While his toileting functions are not interfered with during the first months of his life, he is at the mercy of adults from birth on, as far as eating goes.

If his first days are spent in a hospital nursery, the infant is probably fed at a three- or four-hour interval because this schedule is part of the routine in most hospitals, not because he necessarily feels hungry then. He is expected to adapt himself to the hospital schedule even though he is adapting himself at the same time to the extreme changes which birth itself has brought. The generations of babies who were fed when they were hungry and cried, and who were kept close to their mothers, probably had an easier time developing positive feelings of trust than babies under modern conditions. The infant's hunger pangs are an individual matter and usually do not fit into a regular schedule. They are acute and distressing to him. If they are not relieved by food, he is miserable, and he is helpless to meet his own needs.

Some hospitals have a "rooming-in" plan whereby mother and baby are together, and shortly after his birth the mother can begin taking some care of her baby and can feed him according to his needs. She can thus not only meet the baby's needs for food and for comfort and reassurance but also satisfy her own need to be close to her child and to care for it. The enthusiastic reports of parents who have been able to follow this plan, especially parents of first babies, make us hope that someday more children will be protected by this kind of start in life.

The more experienced a parent is, the more likely she is to trust her child and feed him when he indicates he is hungry. This may account in part for the easier adjustment which is frequently seen in later children in families. Even being awakened to be fed constitutes an interference which may be annoying to a baby.

Parents today are more likely to feed their babies on a "self-regulating" schedule in the first weeks than they were a generation ago. They try to follow the child's rhythm rather than feed him by the clock. Sometimes, of course, an overanxious mother may interpret every cry as a demand for food until she learns to know her baby. Parents who follow the child's rhythm instead of imposing a rhythm on him usually find that he wants frequent feedings at first, at somewhat irregular intervals, but that he gradually establishes a regular pattern of his own which slowly shifts with his growth changes. After a few months it is not difficult to adjust the child's feedings to a schedule suitable both for him and for the family.

Basic Attitudes Appear in the Feeding Situation

From the child's behavior in the meal situation at nursery school we can get clues to his feelings, to the kind of adjustment he is making. Appetite is a sensitive index to emotional adjustment. Mary who resisted efforts at training over toileting also defied every convention at the table. This behavior was part of her effort to assert her right to be an independent person. When Alice made progress toward becoming a freer, less inhibited individual, she used her fingers more as she ate. She began to dabble them in her melting ice cream in a deliciously relaxed way at about the same time that she began playing more freely with the other children. It is important, not only nutritionally but also from the standpoint of personality development, that the child's behavior at mealtime be managed with understanding.

Eating with Others at School

The ordinary, healthy child enjoys eating. Unless he had had unpleasant experiences in connection with food, he enters school ready to enjoy the mealtime there. He usually has a conservative attitude about food, however, preferring those foods he already knows. He has his likes and dislikes, and he has not done much eating with groups outside his family. At first he may be distracted from eating by having other children around him. The implements, the dishes, even the chairs, may be different from those he has used at home. He is likely to meet quite a few unfamiliar foods. The expectations of the adults may be different, too. There is a great deal for him to adapt to in the new situation.

Methods and Goals at Mealtime

We set some goals for him in the group situation. We want him to continue to enjoy his food. We want him to learn to like a variety of nutritionally desirable foods. We want him to practice acceptable ways of eating and of behaving at the table. Achieving these things may take time. Pushing or forcing him will not help and is almost sure to lead to problems.

The teacher will start by making sure that he can enjoy his meal at school. She will find out from his mother about the child's likes and dislikes, and she will try to make sure that some of his familiar well-liked foods are served. She will suggest that he try a taste of all the foods but she will not insist on this. She will also consult his mother about the mealtime arrangements at home, so that she can explain to him about the differences at school, if there are any. She may invite his mother to have a meal or at least to observe a meal at school, so that the mother is in a better position to help her child understand the differences.

The teacher will expect the child to stay at the table at school until he has finished all that he wants to eat that day. She will try to make it easy for him to eat, talking with him and feeding him a bite if he wishes. She may put an arm around him. She acts responsibly but she avoids issues. She does not insist on a "clean plate."

Incidentally, children should not be expected to sit at the table until everyone is finished. They should be able to leave when they have finished their meal. There are slow eaters and fast eaters. No one should be hurried. It is another example of how individual difference can be accepted and provided for. Sitting at the table when one has finished eating leads to problems.

In addition to staying at the table during the meal, children of three and four can be expected to pour their own milk or juice if it is in small pitchers on the table. They can use a fork as well as a spoon and later a knife. They can serve themselves to "seconds" in most cases, with the teacher's help. They can be expected to wipe up any spilled milk or food if a wiping-up cloth is readily available. They may need a little help, but all these things promote their growth in independence and responsibility. They are ready to learn these skills.

There Will Be Individual Differences in Amounts of Food Eaten

There are individual differences, too, in the amount of food which children eat. Some children eat much more than others. The same child will eat different amounts on different days, or he may eat a great deal of one food and very little of another. It is a good thing if we avoid any preconceived notions about what or how much a child needs; then we will find it easier to accept the fluctuations in appetite which are common among all children.

The best practice is to serve very *small* helpings and leave the child free to take as much more as he wants. A child is likely to eat more when he is served small helpings rather than large ones.

Children should have the right to refuse a food and to make choices, but the main meal should precede dessert and at least some of the main meal should be eaten before the dessert. Drinking milk should be encouraged. With a good meal-time atmosphere a skillfull teacher helps the child live up to her expectation, most of the time.

Finger Foods

Finger foods, such as toast sticks, carrot sticks, and so on, should be served often. Green beans, for example, are often more popular than peas because of the ease with which they can be eaten as finger food. We are primarily interested in nutrition and only secondarily interested in table manners at this point, although table manners are not neglected. The teacher "models" good manners and gives approval to the child who says, "Please," or uses his implements properly.

A child will usually continue to use his fingers at times long after he has begun to use a spoon. It will be easier and he will drop back to the easier level when he is tired. If we believe that it is important for him to enjoy his food, we will not interfere. Gradually he will depend more and more on a spoon and fork. The kind of manners he will acquire in the end will depend on the example set by the adults around him and not on how much pressure they have exerted on him to meet their standards. On the other hand, his interest in food will be adversely affected by their pressure. We need confidence that the child will acquire the eating patterns of those around him *as he is ready,* just as he acquires their speech.

If we move too fast in teaching manners, we may interfere with the child's appetite. At this age the child is in the developmental stage where touch experiences are important. Having had plenty of "touch" experiences, he will be readier to move on to more mature behavior. Being "messy" with food normally precedes being neat in eating. I remember a three-year-old who ate like an adult, but who ate practically nothing at the table. She did eat between meals when she did not have to conform to the very high standards expected of her at home and the pressures to eat more than she wanted.

Introducing New Foods Gradually

We should not expect the child to learn to like too many foods at one time. We should move slowly in introducing new foods into his diet or we may meet resistance. Extending food horizons too rapidly does not bring good results in most cases. As he watches others enjoy different kinds of foods, he will be ready to try them himself. Giving him a chance to help with the preparation of food in the kitchen may be a very desirable activity. It may help the child take more interest in the food at the table.

Children have a tendency, in common with the rest of us, to resist the new

The feel of food: maybe this isn't finger food.

Courtesy of Jim Fisher, Bakersfield Community College.

and unfamiliar. A child often tends to reject a food because it is new. He may spit it out or make a face. But this may be the first step in learning to eat it. This kind of behavior does not constitute a real rejection. The child will gradually overcome his initial resistance to the food if his behavior does not receive a lot of attention. He will try the food again and, as he acquires familiarity with it, he will probably learn to like it.

Feelings Influence Appetite

There are important emotional factors and emotional consequences to what we do in the eating situation. A secure child, for example, may be able to accept a variety of new foods more easily than a less secure child who may need to cling longer to the familiar in food, as in other things, to gain reassurance. The emotional balance of the insecure child may be threatened if he is pushed into eating too many new foods. Feelings of security and confidence will influence the child's ability to accept new foods.

What the child eats will often depend on who is offering him the food. Infants seem to be sensitive to the likes and dislikes of the person feeding them. They are also sensitive to other feelings in the person feeding them. A baby may take his bottle well or accept his cereal when the person who gives it to him is relaxed and enjoys feeding him. He may refuse the same food if it is offered by someone who dislikes the "messiness" of his eating and is tense and uncertain in her relationship with him. Some children eat very little when there is a new teacher at the table, for example, but will taste new foods or eat everything on the plate when the familiar teacher is there with whom they feel safe.

Because feeling and appetite are so closely related, we must recognize that any emotional disturbance will affect the appetite. Probably we all know what this means. We have at some time had the experience of losing interest in food for a time because of strong feeling. We turn away from food until we have recovered our emotional balance. The child who is suffering from anxiety or some other emotion may have little appetite even though he may be physically well. When the emotional problem is solved, his appetite will respond to the normal demands of a growing organism.

Attacking the loss of appetite directly may do a great deal of harm. Try making yourself eat a big dinner when you have no appetite! The immediate effect on the child may be vomiting or at least regurgitation or storing of food in the mouth. The more serious and lasting result may be a strong conditioning against food. Being made to eat when one is not hungry is a very unpleasant thing. If eating is to be a pleasant experience for the child, we will avoid forcing him in any way.

Frequent demands to be fed should be regarded as a symptom, and may be part of a pattern of dependence. Perhaps the standards for eating behavior have been set too high. Often a child will ask to be fed when he grows tired because of the demand on his coordination that eating makes. As his motor skill improves, he will need less help. Sometimes a child asks to be fed because he wants to find out if the adult is willing to help, to be reassured about his ability to get help when he wants it.

There Are Ways in Which We Can Help

There are many indirect ways to help a child enjoy eating. An attractive-looking table appeals to children. Bright-colored dishes, flowers, a neatly laid table, all add to the child's pleasure and interest in food. Food that "looks good," with a contrast in color, is important. Colored junket, for example, usually disappears faster than plain white junket.

Children's tastes differ from adults' in that children usually do not care for very hot or very cold foods. They do not like mixed flavors, either. A casserole or loaf may be unpopular even though each individual flavor in it may be relished separately. They care less for creamed foods or sauces over foods than adults do. All this makes cooking simpler and should be a welcome advantage to a busy homemaker. Strong flavors or unusual textures in a food are usually less acceptable to a child.

A child will enjoy eating more if he is comfortable at the table. He needs a chair which will permit his feet to rest on the floor and a table that is the right height for him. He needs implements that are easy to grasp. A salad fork rather than a large fork, a spoon with a round bowl, and a small glass add to his comfort and his pleasure. He is more comfortable if he is not crowded too close to others at the table.

Midmorning snack is a social experience.

If there is a marker at his place at the table so that he feels no uncertainty about where he is going to sit, he may feel surer of himself. If he can put on his own bib, he will be happier. Even the youngest child can pull on a bright-colored wash cloth with an elastic across the end and such a bib is absorbent and easily laundered. The child will also enjoy getting up and down without help, clearing away his own dishes, and getting his dessert. If he can wait on himself, he may be less restless, too.

Companions can be distracting at times. Eating with other children is fun and one good eater will influence others, but sociability may need to be kept within bounds by proper spacing and placement of the children. The main business at the table is eating, although conversation has its place.

The teacher may need to help children by influencing the amount of conversation taking place. Conversation sometimes interferes with eating, for children have not mastered the art of talking and eating. In his enthusiasm for communicating with others, a child may forget about eating. If he is a child for whom the teacher estimates that talking to others has more value at the moment than eating, she may give him time to finish later or feed him herself, as in the case of a shy, withdrawn child who is just "blossoming out" and needs to be encouraged to continue. A different child who is already socially adequate may need to be reminded at some point to "eat now and talk later."

Length of Time for the Meal

There may be practical limitations inherent in the situation which determine how much time a child can be permitted to spend at the table. But eating should

Courtesy of Jean Berlfein.

Special friends enjoy each other's company at the table.

not proceed by a clock. Just as a "set" toilet schedule does not meet the needs of children, so a "set" length of time to eat cannot mean the same thing to all children. Some are deliberate and some are quick. These differences are reflected in the time they take for their meals. Meals are served because we need food and we enjoy eating. There is no special virtue in eating to get through a meal.

REST

Rest is something children need but often resist, both at home and at school. Many children find it hard to settle down for a rest. A rest period or a nap comes as an interruption to play. It may hold special difficulties when children are in a group and distract each other. The teacher herself must feel very sure that resting is a good thing if she wishes to communicate this conviction to the children.

Some alternation of quiet play and vigorous play is usually necessary if children are to avoid getting overtired. Every program should include some kind of short rest period. If the program is an all-day program, it will also include a nap period after lunch when most children will sleep but everyone will rest for a time. Sometimes a child will need an extra rest. There should be a quiet corner with a cot in it for use whenever a child wishes.

The morning rest is usually short, about fifteen minutes. The children relax on cots or on rugs on the floor while the teacher reads or tells a story or the children themselves look at books. There may be music to listen to. The rest period is a change from the activity of the morning.

A Rest or Nap Period

In the full-day program a nap period will follow the lunch period. The children may be expected to go directly to rest as each leaves the table, or they may have a period of quiet play until the whole group is ready for rest. The schedule will depend on the physical arrangements of space and on the number of staff available. It is desirable but not always possible for children to rest in a room other than the room where they have played actively. Whatever the arrangements, the children should be sleeping or resting on comfortable cots with a fitted undersheet and with adequate covers over them.

The teacher can set the stage for the nap period by seeing that the room is in order and everything is ready for rest, with shades pulled down. She will create an atmosphere which suggests rest. She will move quietly herself and speak in a low voice. She will make her expectations clear—that is, she will *expect* the children to come in quietly, remove their shoes and perhaps other garments, and settle down without disturbing others. Her expectations will be reasonable ones. She will give each child time to settle down, with perhaps a whispered word to his neighbor. A child may bring a favorite toy, perhaps, or a picture book to help him relax. The child who does not fall asleep can rest quietly for at least half an hour or more before getting up.

A rest period usually proceeds most smoothly when the children know the teacher well and have confidence in her. The children are more likely to be restless if the adult is new and strange to them or if there are too many adults present. A new teacher must accept the situation and not let it disturb her unduly. The experienced teacher is more confident and gives the children time to settle down in their own ways. Teachers are often tired by the time a rest period comes, and are eager to get the children settled. They may find themselves pushing the children into resting. The more experienced teacher tends to be more relaxed.

Dependency Needs Are Greater at Rest Time

One can expect the child to make demands on the teacher at rest time because resting is closely associated with experiences with his mother and her care. His need for her may come closer to the conscious level. He reverts to earlier dependencies. He wants the teacher's attention. He may want to have a blanket straightened just to have some contact with her. Failing in this, he may be noisy, which is another way of getting attention. He may be less able to bear her disapproval at rest time than when he is feeling more independent.

At rest time children are likely to be jealous when the teacher's attention goes to other children. The teacher must be able to make each of them feel that there is enough attention for all. If an individual child needs an extra amount of attention, she will remove him from the room so as not to make the others unduly anxious. The confident, maternal person will be most successful in helping the children grow through the nap room experience.

Individual Needs Differ

There are individual differences in the amount of rest children need, and these differences should be respected. Children who fall asleep will probably sleep for varying lengths of time. As each one awakes, he can get up quietly and put on the clothes he removed. Here is an opportunity for children to grow in independence, with the teacher giving only the help which is really needed and approving of what the child has done on his own.

After resting, some of the older children who do not take naps have an opportunity for play in small groups before the younger children are up. The teacher may use the period to give these children more advanced experiences and more individual attention. There may be chances for trips which are not geared to younger children or for games and "work" periods at a more advanced level.

The teacher will want to consult with the mother about the child's patterns for resting and for naps at home. Knowing what is customary for him at home will help her adapt the schedule at school to his needs, as she tries to help him develop good patterns for rest and relaxation in his group experience.

THE RELATION OF ROUTINES AND THE DEVELOPMENT OF INDEPENDENCE

We have discussed some of the meanings which toileting, eating, and rest may have for children. We have indicated some of the problems which arise in connection with these routine activities.

Problems Occur at "Transition Points"

From the standpoint of the teacher, many of the difficulties she faces in managing these routines exist at "transition points," or the points at which she interrupts the child's own activity to direct him into the routine. He delays. He resists. He defies. He asserts himself, in other words, and such behavior is appropriate to his developmental level. He needs and wants to direct his own activities, or to assert himself against others in order to test himself. Is he really an independent person? How much independence does he have?

If the teacher keeps the child's needs in mind, she will find it easier to meet his resistance without adding to it. For example, if the child is refusing to accede to a necessary request such as, "It is time to come in and get ready for lunch," the teacher may agree to wait until some part is completed rather than insisting on his coming immediately. She may get the child to tell her when he will be finished and ready. They may compromise and thus cooperate. He will be party to the bargain. She will need to see that the child carries out his agreement, although she can express sympathy for his wishing that he did not need to do so, "I know you would like to stay, but it really is time now. You remember we agreed." Then she may be able to suggest an important job he can carry out in helping with the serving. She tries, in other words, to help him move toward accepting the necessity of meeting reasonable demands without feeling a loss of self-esteem.

The teacher can value the fact that he is working at growing into a more autonomous, independent person. She can respect his right to assert himself and his desire to do it. But she should also recognize her responsibility to maintain certain reasonable demands. The child cannot do just as he likes all the time even though he grows best if he can do what he wishes a good deal of the time when he is young.

The child needs the experience of finding that he does not lose his independence just because he accepts some restrictions and meets some demands. It is important for him that his teacher feel clear about what she expects him to do and sure about her right to expect this of him. If she acts with confidence, she makes it easier for him. Acting confidently, she is likely to give him more definite and specific directions, to show less impatience and be more imaginative in the kind of help she gives him in making the transition. He may be able, in the end, to turn his desire to be independent into satisfaction in being able to work with an adult in a cooperative way. We all must do necessary things which, at the moment, we may not really want to do. Transition points from free play to routine activities can be growth points, but this takes time.

Clean-up time is another transition point which often presents difficulty. Children do not always feel ready to put materials away and help with straightening the play room. It is a challenge to the teacher to devise ways of helping them feel and act like independent, responsible people at this point. The teacher sets an example with her own actions. She reinforces whatever steps they take in helping by her attention and approval. They can talk as they work together about what they are doing or about the day's events. Sometimes singing together or making up games will help lighten the task. Some children will give more help than others, but the teacher makes no comparisons here.

Changes Can Be Made

Some of the problems which arise in connection with routines may be related to the physical setup of the school. A crowded locker room creates problems when children are pulling on their wraps. Cots set up in the playroom may make resting more difficult. A change in the situation may be possible. Sometimes making a change in the schedule itself, the time or the sequence, as well as the physical arrangements, may reduce the difficulties which have been arising.

Our Own Need to Help May Interfere with the Child's Need to Be Independent

Children find great satisfaction in doing a thing unaided. Shoes laced in irregular ways, a shirt on backwards, hands only partly clean may be sources of pride to a child because these things were achieved independently.

But the drive to be independent, which every healthy child feels, may come up against one of our own needs, the need to help. This need is especially strong when we feel least sure that we can help. By helping, by doing things for a child, we try to prove to ourselves that we are in fact competent and able. The child's dependency on us reassures us that we have a place in the school.

Watch what happens in the coatroom. The inexperienced teacher is the one who steps in and expertly buttons the button that the child has been fumbling with intently. She takes the child's coat from its low hook and holds it for him and then may be surprised that he runs away instead of putting it on. She puts in the plug when he is ready to wash his hands, pushes up his sleeves and hands him the soap. She deprives him of many chances to do things that he can do for himself.

Courtesy of Jean Berlfein.

Courtesy of Jean Berlfein.

Finger-painting on the table top encourages large, sweeping movements. After finger-painting comes clean-up time. Everyone helps.

She herself needs to help and she acts out of her own need. If she is to handle her strong feeling about wanting to help, she must be aware of this feeling as well as of the values for the child in being independent. Keeping his need in mind, she will plan the situation so that he has a maximum chance to do things for himself. She will keep from helping him needlessly.

The Child Reverts to Dependency at Times

When we have recognized the importance of the child's need to be independent, as well as the likelihood that we will feel a need to offer help unnecessarily at times, we must still be ready to accept the fact that there are times when the child does need to be dependent on us. Erikson makes it clear that no development is completed at any one stage. This means that we carry on to the next stage the uncompleted tasks of earlier stages. A child may ask for unnecessary help because he wants reassurance that he can still be dependent if he wishes. It may be important to help him with his coat if he asks us, as we mentioned earlier. In routines we must be sure only that we do not deprive the child of the chance to be independent when he is ready.

PROJECTS

1. Observe during a period in the toilet room, noting the different responses to the experiences shown by the children. Discuss the possible meaning of the responses you observed.

2. Observe during a meal period, recording the behavior of the children at one table during the mealtime. What differences in individual needs did you observe? What help did the teacher give? What goals did she seem to have in mind?

REFERENCES

Arnstein, Helene, with the staff of the Child Study Association of America: Your Growing Child and Sex — A Parent's Guide. Indianapolis, The Bobbs-Merrill Co., Inc., 1967.
Dayton, Delbert: Early malnutrition and human development. Children, Vol. 16, No. 6, November-December, 1969.
Food for the Pre-School Child 13 Months to 6 Years. Washington, D.C.., Department of Health, Education, and Welfare, Children's Bureau SRS, 1969.
Fraiberg, Selma: The Magic Years. New York, Charles Scribner's Sons, 1959. Chap. 7.
Levine, Milton: Early sex education. Young Children, October, 1966.
Murphy, Lois B.: The Widening World of Childhood (Part 4). New York, Basic Books, Inc., Publishers, 1962.
Nutrition and Intellectual Growth in Children. Washington, D.C., Association for Childhood Education, Bulletin No. 25A, 1969.

PART FOUR

THE PROGRAM

CHAPTER 11

Miss Annie in School (girl, 2 years 6 months)

THE ROLE OF THE TEACHER

The role of the teacher in a nursery school or child care center is to provide the setting, the experiences, and the guidance which will promote optimum development of children. The teacher's goal for each child is to help him or her grow as a person, able to enjoy and profit from opportunities for all kinds of learning, able to achieve and develop his or her potential as an individual and as a group member.

THE TEACHER AS A PERSON

Let us first look at the teacher as a person, because what she is like as a person may be more important than what she does. What she is determines to some extent what the child will learn under her guidance.

183

Every teacher serves in many ways as a "model" for the children in her group. They are influenced by her and imitate not only her actions but also her attitudes. Young children are likely to identify with their teacher in a positive way, following the examples she sets.

Qualities of the Good Teacher

The teacher of young children needs to be interested in *understanding* people, experiences, events, rather than passing judgment on them. The teacher also needs to be *sensitive* and *responsive,* able to "listen with the third ear" to what the child may be trying to say through his behavior. The teacher should know the satisfactions of learning and be able to *appreciate the child's accomplishments* as he masters each stage in development. With the help of such a person the child can grow, comfortably, as a whole person.

Courtesy of Jean Berlfein.

This child knows the excitement of discovery.

The child also needs a teacher who can *communicate* with him, both in language and in expression and gesture, with a smile or a nod, as well as an approving word. He needs a teacher who is aware of his or her own feelings and is able to *express feelings* as well as ideas in constructive and clear ways. The child needs a teacher who *values spontaneity* and yet is able to maintain an *orderliness* in activities and in the setting. In addition, the child needs a teacher who is *imaginative* and *resourceful* and who has a *sense of humor.* These qualities will influence him to reassure and stimulate him. Few of us show all these qualities in all situations, or all the time. We have our weaknesses as well as our strengths, but we grow and change with experience.

Attitudes Are Important

The teacher's attitudes are important to the young child, not only because they influence the way she deals with him, but also because they become part of him. There are changes taking place today in some of our attitudes. We are becoming more aware of the effect of discrimination on people. The old inequalities of sex, of class, of race, and of economic condition are no longer accepted. It is important that we help children to look at the world around them as free from bias and prejudice as possible.

There are many kinds of bias which affect the child. A teacher may find herself responding negatively or expecting little achievement from a child because he does not speak correct English, by her standards, or does not have the manners which she expects. It may not be easy to accept the fact that these differences do not reflect a child's innate capacities. Many so-called deficiencies in children are simply differences in background or experience. The teacher may misunderstand the meaning of the child's behavior just as he does hers.

When the values in the classroom are different from those in the home, the child can hardly be expected to adjust easily. It is the obligation of the teacher to understand as much as possible about a child's cultural-social background and to accept him in this context. Children are very sensitive to the "climate" of feeling around them. The teacher who accepts a child with understanding is better able to help him make use of the school experience and to make his own choice, when he is ready, as to where he will find his place.

Accepting Differences in Cultural Patterns

We are a multiracial culture rather than a homogeneous one, and we can profit from our mixture of peoples. It becomes a strength if we use the opportunities it offers. Some nursery schools consist largely of minority culture children. As teachers we must be aware of the particular strengths these children have. We must value and use their contributions, making life richer for everyone. We must also interpret the "mainstream" culture to them and help each one find a place for himself or herself, bringing about change as it is needed. Diversity enriches everyone when it is accepted and acceptable.

In accepting differences the teacher must accept and respect the cultural differences of parents as well as children and understand what parents' expectations are for their children. One of her important tasks, of course, will be to help *all* parents understand better what good early childhood education is. On many occasions the teacher needs to present the reasons for what she does in the school, and what she hopes will be achieved. She will also listen to the parents. She may modify what she does to accommodate their expectations, without sacrificing the fundamental principles in which she believes. Good education can take many forms if the feeling of respect for individuals is present.

Relations Between Teacher and Child

The teacher's first task is to build a relationship of trust and confidence with the child. Children develop within a framework of a personal relationship. Learning is personal for the child. Once the teacher has established a good relationship with the child, she should be careful to let nothing destroy it.

Courtesy of Jean Berlfein.

The teacher helps the child repair his rake.

A good relationship between child and teacher will make it easier for the teacher to discipline in constructive ways and easier for the child to respond in desirable ways. The teacher can be firm when it is necessary but still friendly. She can help the child face the consequences of his behavior, without resorting to punishments that stir resentments but not repentance.

The significance for the child in having a teacher whom he likes and who he feels likes him is tremendous. Every child, regardless of family background, will develop best if he has the feeling that he is liked and valued. Young children see the world in very personal ways and are influenced by their relationships with people even more than adults are.

The child is also influenced by his teacher's expectations about his abilities. He tends to behave and achieve accordingly. He needs to have a teacher who not only respects and values him as a person but also believes in his capacities and expects a good performance from him.

We must remind ourselves that the environment from which a child comes has some favorable and some unfavorable factors in it. Deprivations of some kind exist in every background. One child may have experienced poverty in material things, but he may be rich in the quality of personal relationships he has known; whereas another child may have known only poverty in his personal relationships, even though he has always lived with material riches. It is important that a teacher respect and make use of the strengths that children have as she helps them develop their individual capacities.

We are responsible, as teachers, for accepting and respecting each individual child as another human being who is trying to cope with difficulties, to find satisfactions, and to learn. Every child is worthy of all that we have to give him.

TEACHING SKILLS WHICH PROMOTE CHILDREN'S LEARNING

The teacher as a person is important, but her skills as a professional person are also important. What are the teaching skills or competencies needed to promote the optimum development of young children, whether they are at home or in a school group?

We have already discussed aspects of teaching skills in *Guides to Speech and Action* in Chapter 6 and given a list of competencies considered important for the teacher of young children on pages 71–73. Here we will discuss in more detail some skills of special importance to the child.

1. SKILL IN USING POSITIVE METHODS OF GUIDANCE

An important reason for the use of positive methods in guiding young children is that these methods tend to increase the child's self-confidence. They help him build a positive self-concept. Positive methods make it easier for him to grow and learn in healthy ways.

The competent teacher trains herself to give suggestions and directions in a positive way. She tells the child what he can do and emphasizes how he can be successful, whether he is climbing a ladder or pounding a nail or getting along with other children or trying to solve any other kind of problem.

Courtesy of Jean Berlfein.

Sometimes the teacher helps by participating in play.

There is no more important skill than the simple one of making statements or giving suggestions in a positive rather than a negative way. Everyone working with children, at home or at school, needs to practice this skill and become more aware of how directions may be phrased positively. Practice is often needed, but the effort is worthwhile.

Rules, too, can be defined in positive rather than negative ways. In helping a child complete a task, for example, the teacher may say, "Finish this puzzle first, then you can take out a new one," rather than saying, "You can't have a new puzzle until you finish the one you have."

Helping Children Be Successful

The teacher will always try to help children succeed in what they undertake. A child, or any of us, needs a large measure of success if he is to develop the capacity to bear the inevitable failures. Occasionally we see people who are so afraid of making mistakes that they have stopped attempting anything difficult. These people have had too few successes, or their failures have seemed too important to them. The teacher of young children will make sure that mistakes are not serious, and she will encourage the efforts that lead to success.

Positive Reinforcement

Positive reinforcement of behavior is an effective means of making sure that behavior is repeated. The reinforcement may be an approving nod or verbal encouragement. The teacher may say, "That's fine. Another step and you will be at the top," to the timid child who is making an effort to climb up high. The teacher, on the other hand, who tries to help the child by saying, "Don't be afraid," is calling attention to his fear. Her reinforcement is not positive.

When the teacher approves with a smile or nod, she will want to be sure that the child is clear about what it is that she approves, and the approval she gives should be as immediate as possible to ensure this.

A teacher is generous in the attention or approval she gives for effort as well as for success. Too often we give approval only when the child succeeds and do not reward his efforts even if they do not achieve the expected results. We are sometimes more likely to reward unacceptable behavior by our attention than effort and acceptable behavior. Give attention to successful and desirable behavior.

Helping the Child Face Failure in a Positive Way

The teacher gives approval and attention to the child when he achieves or behaves acceptably, but she also can accept his failures and try to turn these to constructive use. She may say to the child at the work bench, "Next time hold the hammer this way, and it may be easier to make the nail go in straight." In saying this the teacher helps the child look for causes, consider what has happened, and improve his performance. His errors become a means of learning and not just a failure. He gains a new perspective and uses his experience more positively.

Sometimes the teacher will say, "I wonder why that happened," if she thinks the child is ready to discover by himself the remedy or reason. In doing this she is helping him take a "problem-solving" attitude, one which is very necessary in learning. He gains new confidence in his own capacities if he is successful in finding out. The tower he built falls over because the base was not broad enough perhaps, or was not on even ground. It is easy for a child to want to blame someone or to blame himself when something will not work. He can learn to take a less personal view of matters.

Serving As a Good "Model" in the Way She Meets Frustration

In the way the teacher meets the frustrations which are an inevitable part of teaching, she sets an example for the children to follow in facing their frustrations. The teacher is not always successful. Her best efforts are rejected at times. If she can accept this state of affairs, she helps them build a concept of how one can live with frustration. One does not need to lose faith in oneself or in others. One can have patience and confidence that the next time will be better.

If the teacher can leave the children free to doubt and question, and sometimes *not* respond to her suggestions, she helps them, too. There is uncertainty and there is flexibility and it can serve purposes which can be constructive. The children can build more trust in themselves as well as in the teacher in a favorable climate like this.

Refraining from Using Competitive Methods for Motivating Children

The teacher does not use competitive methods to motivate children if she is using a positive approach. Most young children have not yet built up enough confidence in themselves to gain anything constructive by competing with each other. They are not ready to deal with the results of competition. They are not ready to make use of failure as a spur to further effort. They only see themselves as nonwinners and often cease to try. Cooperation is more important to children and brings more rewards.

Some people feel that it is necessary to introduce children to competition early. But if we think about stages in development, we can see the fallacy in this logic. The child advances stage by stage. Because our culture is competitive, it is all the more important to protect children from having to face competitive situations until they have progressed through the stages of developing a sense of trust, of acquiring independence, and of finding the rewards of individual initiative. It is more important to begin by learning to cooperate and help others than to compete with them.

Reassuring Children About Aggressive Behavior in Others

Some children, especially those who have lived mainly with adults, are timid about dealing with an aggressive child and retreat. The teacher can give reassurance, "It is all right to hold on to the pail. It is yours. You don't need to let him take it. Tell him it is yours." She can try to be on hand to help him when he makes the attempt to assert his rights. In another situation she may say, "He feels angry. Everyone gets angry sometimes. It is all right to feel angry, but it is not all right to hurt anyone. I will stop him." She will reassure all children by firmly keeping aggression within acceptable limits as well as not getting upset by it.

2. SKILL IN CREATING A CLIMATE FOR DISCOVERY AND THUS EXTENDING AND ENRICHING CHILDREN'S INTERESTS AND THEIR HORIZONS

By the way the teacher sets the stage for exploring, by the questions she asks, by her own zest for finding out about things, by her support, and by her encouragement to the children in their efforts, the teacher creates an environment that invites learning through exploration and discovery. Erikson has helped us become more aware of this stage in children's development, the stage he has called that of developing a sense of initiative. It is the stage in which we find our nursery school children. It is the time for encouraging individual initiative, reinforcing the excitement of discovering things which begins in early childhood and should be preserved through life.

Here is an example of learning by discovery in a group of four-year-olds. It

Courtesy of Myron Papiz.

The children play "store" with materials supplied by the teacher.

would not have taken place without guidance from the teacher. What might have led to conflict became a "social studies" investigation with the teacher's help.

In a block scheme, a boy had build a fish store.... Every time [a girl] went to his store to buy fish, he closed it. Finally, in great irritation, she yelled at him, "You can't do that. A store has to sell—that's what it's for, stupid." The teacher approached the children and entered the conversation, first by listening and then by asking, "Can you go shopping in a store any time you feel like it?" Discussion led to the following conclusions: (1) you do not shop late at night because you have to sleep; (2) stores do have hours for shopping to which people must pay attention.... It was decided that the boy and the girl plus two other children who had joined the discussion would take a walk around the block with the teacher in order to find the answer to her question, "How do you know when a store opens and when it closes?"

They returned from their trip and as they entered the classroom, their newly gained information exploded; "It's on the door," "It's not the same for all the days," "They have a sign." Information was explored and shared. Signs went up on several buildings posting store hours. One child posted times for visits to her house, fixing the hours around the baby's sleeping schedule.*

It is worth noting the way in which the teacher guided this experience. She "entered the conversation, first by listening and then by asking." She took time to find out what the argument was about and then asked the right question. She guided the discussion and supplied information which the children did not have by making a suggestion about how to find out. The children returned, excited by their discovery. The results of what they learned appeared in many forms, even the imaginative one of posting a schedule for visiting. It was a reading readiness

---

*Cuffaro, Harriet: Dramatic play—The experience of block building. p. 28. *In* Hirsch, Elisabeth (ed.) The Block Book. Copyright © 1974, National Association for the Education of Young Children, 1834 Connecticut Avenue N.W. Washington, D.C. 20009.

experience with meaning. The children gained information and, more importantly, they had patterns for problem solving and answering questions. One talks over a problem. One investigates. Learning can be exciting.

Providing Blocks of Uninterrupted Time

If the teacher is to make the most of children's spontaneous interests, she needs to allow long blocks of *uninterrupted time* in the schedule for the children to develop and carry through projects while she takes the time to observe the play. She will become more aware of when and how to make suggestions when she has observed and made notes.

It is important for a child to have some chance for a completed experience, one in which he feels he has done all he wants with it and has brought it to an end. It may be an experience completed in one session or an experience completed after several weeks of continual returning to repeat it again. But from any completed experience the child gets a feeling about a beginning and an ending and a going on to something else that helps him with learning to "let go" and leave behind satisfying things because he can be through with them. We may hear an adult say to a child, "You have painted enough pictures today," or "You played long enough with this," instead of saying, "There is no more time today for painting or for doing this." The child is being deprived of a chance to know the true meaning of "enough" in the first case. Sometimes there may not be enough time for a completed experience and then the child must be left unsatisfied, but it is good when there can be time in the program for *completed* experiences.

Teacher-Initiated Activity

There is a place for some teacher-initiated and teacher-directed activity in a program, although the teacher should respect the child's right not to participate. Teacher-initiated activities may be important for those children who have lived in unstimulating environments, environments unfavorable for learning. They may need the support of periods of work with a teacher if they are to learn to give attention and to develop the skills they need to make progress in learning. Not all children will need such help. But the teacher will accept responsibility for finding a way to get every child interested and involved in discovery and the "excitement of learning."

Some children may need a good deal of individual help from the teacher. Sammy, for example, is an active, distractible child from a large family. He has nothing of his own at home. No one has expected much of him. He teases other children, interferes with their play, and runs wild. He needs time alone with a friendly but firm teacher who will help him give attention to simple games and will expect him to finish what he undertakes. She will praise him for his success, and she will support his efforts. Nettie, described earlier, is another child who needs individual attention if she is to begin to see herself as a learner. The teacher will take time to work with her, helping her to gain skill and to complete activities.

Group activities that are teacher-directed should be of short duration. In one group, a young man, a volunteer, came in with his guitar to sing with the

Courtesy of Jean Berlfein.

The child plays with balance scales, trying them out.

The teacher explains how the balance scales work.

children. They were delighted and almost all of them gathered around him. The experience of having a man in the teaching role was new to them. He adapted his songs well to their level, and they participated eagerly as he taught them the words. He continued with song after song, enjoying their eager attention. By the time he stopped, many of the children were very tired although only a few had left the group. The children could not settle down for a while. There was crying and a good deal of disorganized behavior before they could carry on with other activities. Several short music sessions would have benefited the children much more than did the one long session.

3. SKILL IN ENCOURAGING EXPRESSION OF THOUGHT AND FEELING THROUGH LANGUAGE AND THROUGH OTHER AVENUES OF EXPRESSION

An important part of teaching young children is helping them become competent in expressing thought and feeling. Language is an important means of expression. A child needs to be able to put his thoughts and his feelings into words if he is to have satisfying social relationships. He needs competency in language if he is to learn in complex ways at higher levels. Teachers need to be aware of the ways in which this competency is developed.

There are other avenues of expression. For the young child art media offer important avenues for expressing feelings and also for communication. He uses

Courtesy of Jean Berlfein.

The teacher is sympathetic to the child's grief.

these freely when they are available, paint, clay, pencils, and crayons. Construction with blocks or at the workbench is a form of expression of ideas and concepts. Body movements are also a form of expression. Children enjoy dancing. They enjoy marching when the situation calls for this kind of expression. They enjoy music. Singing is a natural expression of feeling for young children.

These are all avenues which should be developed in a program for young children. We will discuss the skills needed by the teacher to encourage expression of thought and feeling in Chapter 14 and in Part Five.

PROJECTS

1. Observe the teacher in a nursery school group and record incidents in which she did any of the following:
 (a) Created a climate for discovery.
 (b) Extended and enriched an interest or purpose initiated by a child.
 (c) Allowed time for a child to have a completed experience.
 (d) Reinforced in a positive way a child's learning.
 (e) Played a supportive role in building a child's self-confidence.
 (f) Helped a child to face reality or to take a "problem-solving" attitude in a situation.

REFERENCES

Almy, Millie: The Work of the Early Childhood Educator. New York, McGraw-Hill Book Company, 1975.
Ashton-Warner, Sylvia: Teacher. New York, Simon & Schuster, Inc., 1963.
Beyer, Evelyn: Teaching Young Children. New York, Pegasus, 1968.
Bowman, Barbara: Teacher training: Where and how. *In* Spodek, Bernard (ed.): Teacher-Education, of the Teacher, by the Teacher, for the Child. Washington, D.C., National Association for the Education of Young Children, 1974.
Castillo, Max, and Cruz, Josue: Special competencies for the teachers of preschool Chicano children: Rationale, content and assessment. Young Children, Vol. 29, No. 6, September, 1974.
Child Development Associates: New Professionals, New Training Strategies. Washington, D.C., Department of Health, Education, and Welfare, Office of Child Development, 1974.
Ekstein, Rudolph: The child, the teacher and the learning. Young Children, March, 1967.
Hess, Robert, and Croft, Doreen: Teachers of Young Children. Boston, Houghton Mifflin Company, 1975.
Omwake, Eveline: What children and parents are expecting from teacher education. *In* Spodek, Bernard (ed.): Teacher Education. Washington, D.C. National Association for the Education of Young Children, 1974.
Spodek, Bernard: Teaching in the Early Years. Englewood Cliffs, New Jersey, Prentice-Hall, Inc., 1972.
Webster, Patricia R.: The teacher structure checklist: A possible tool for communication. Young Children, Vol 27, No. 3, February, 1972.

CHAPTER 12

Peter in an Apple Tree (boy, 3 years 7 months)

THE ROLE OF PLAY

Play Lies at the Heart of the Program

Susan, not quite three, was in the kitchen with her mother who was preparing for a tea party. "You may put the cup cakes on this big plate," said the mother in answer to Susan's wish to "help." Pleased at the task, Susan carefully placed the cakes one by one on the plate until it was covered. Then she faced a dilemma. There were several cup cakes left but there was no space left on the plate. She stood looking, uncertain and thoughtful, and then she began placing each remaining cup cake exactly on top of one of those already on the plate. They fit, and Susan exclaimed with delight, "Look, caps!"

The incident shows how a young child can use an experience in a playful way and in the process solve a problem imaginatively and enjoy her achievement.

196

Play lies at the heart of the nursery school program. It makes a major contribution to the physical, social, emotional, and intellectual development of children. In a good nursery school learning is promoted largely through play, supported by a variety of materials and a wide range of experiences, under the guidance of teachers who understand and value play as an avenue for learning.

Values of Play

In discussing the value of play in meeting educational needs, Biber comments:

The whole panorama of life is lived over again in the play of children. If there is any way of gaining knowledge particularly suitable to this stage of development, it is in the play which they spontaneously devise but which needs nevertheless an attentive teacher for its support and nourishment.*

In our somewhat compulsive society play is often not respected because it does not seem directly productive. Yet the creative achievements of scientific thought involve sustained attention and imaginative ways of perceiving and dealing with reality. These are characteristics nurtured through play. Play is essentially creative, involving the child as a person with all his capacities.

A healthy child in a favorable environment spends a great deal of his waking time in play. In play he learns about the external world and the forces that operate in it. In play he practices skills which help him develop physically and enable him to carry out his purposes. He establishes individual patterns of approaching experience and working out problems. He makes friends through play and takes a step in learning how to live with others and enjoy them. We need to appreciate the tremendous significance of play for the child if we are to guide his development.

Play is important for young children because it is a way of recreating experience, clarifying it and making it more understandable, a way of organizing perceptions, of testing out capacities, of managing feelings, and of discovering more about oneself and one's place in the world. Play is the business of childhood. It remains a source of relaxation for us throughout our lives.

The preschool child is in the stage described by Piaget as preoperational, the stage when sensory perceptions, representation and action, are of foremost importance. Piaget suggests that play is essential to cognitive development at this stage. The child is also in the stage in personality development which Erikson has described as a critical period for the development of a sense of initiative. Play encourages initiative. We will keep these values in mind as we consider the subject of play.

Beginnings of Play

The beginnings of play appear in infancy when the baby starts to be aware of people and of objects. The baby plays with his fingers, moving them and staring

---

*Biber, Barbara: Young Deprived Children and Their Educational Needs. Washington, D.C., Association for Childhood Education, International, Bulletin J, 1967. p. 6.

Courtesy of Santa Monica College.

The children are playing a "game."

intently at them. He plays with his toes later, and we notice the concentration that goes with any satisfying play activity. As his coordination improves he fingers an object, bangs it, grasps it tightly only to let go when another attractive object presents itself. He is learning about the "me" and the "not me," about objects and their qualities and what he can do with them. He smiles and his mother gives a response. There is mutual play between them as she cares for him. He is learning about relationships.

The playful modes of knowing begin early in the games parents play with infants, such things as smiling, repeating sounds, peek-a-boo, dropping and picking up objects, bouncing on the knee. These are games that have no rules. They are forms of relating to people, of finding mutual responses, of playing together. These kinds of responses will later be elaborated in play with other children.

Playful Behavior Depends on a Capacity to Trust

Being able to play freely implies a sense of trust. Building up a sense of trust, as Erikson points out, is the first and most basic task in healthy personality development. Its foundation is laid in the child's early experience in being cared for by a loving, responsive care-giver.

A mother or care-giver who is reliably present when the infant needs her and who can regulate her giving to his needs, who sees and responds to him as an individual, enables him to move into spontaneous playfulness. He can test out and discover his enlarging world. He can become involved in relationships with other people. Playing is a sign of health, made possible by a favorable environment.

As a toddler the child still plays best in the presence of his mother because he feels secure. In nursery school children continue to need a responsible person nearby and readily available when they are playing together, someone on whom they depend but not someone in a "managerial" capacity. The teacher's role is to provide the setting and to assist by enriching and extending the play as she observes a need, giving guidance and the techniques for play with others when these are lacking.

Transitional Objects

Sometime during the first year most young children find a favorite object. It may be a cuddly toy or a blanket to which they become attached. It becomes their first possession and serves as a comforter, a defense against anxiety. It seems to represent the early security of contact with the mother or care-giver. It stands in place of the mother as a symbol to tide the child over when she is not present or when he is under strain. Winnicott calls it a "transitional object." It has properties for the child that ordinary objects do not have, standing as it does between his inner world of feeling and fantasy and the outer world of realities to be faced. Possessing this object, he is freer to proceed with playing. We see the use made of such a symbol by children who bring an object from home in order to make the adjustment easier as they enter a group. We, for our part, need to respect the special qualities with which such an object is endowed. The attachment weakens as the child becomes more secure and is involved in a wider variety of play experiences.

Settings for Play

What settings offer the best provisions for play?

We discussed some of the equipment and materials needed for a favorable play environment in Chapter 5. We also considered the adequacy and use of space and time provided for play. There should be spaces where one child or a small group of children can play without being disturbed, open spaces for activities like block building where buildings can be left and worked on over a period of time, outdoor space that is full of variety and interest. Every group can use supplementary "bits and pieces" or "junk" as well as the standard equipment and the raw materials which have many uses. A schedule should provide both flexibility and a framework for ordered activities. These are all considerations which promote a rich play experience.

The teacher's "ingenuity and resourcefulness in providing the necessary equipment must be combined with understanding of the value of different forms of play, e.g., dramatic, creative, free, organized, constructional, etc."* All these forms of play have a place in the nursery school.

---

*Winnicott, D. W.: The Child and the Outside World. New York, Basic Books, Inc., Publishers, 1957.

Children Play to Learn

One of the reasons children play is to explore, discover, learn. From the beginning, play is essentially satisfying to a child. The healthy child is motivated and absorbed in the activity he himself has initiated. Play brings its own reinforcement, and the child puts wholehearted effort into it. He repeats and repeats until he masters the skill required to carry out his purposes. This is the behavior of a good learner. These characteristics are promoted by play.

Children need to play often with materials in what appears to be random play, "messing about," before they can use the materials to the best advantage in problem solving. It is a kind of "as if" or "what if" exploration of the materials in play to discover what their possibilities are before they can make use of them. Watch a child at play and observe how he tries out possibilities, finds new uses for objects, arranges, combines, pretends, and through these activities comes to understand more about the materials.

Language is important in learning. One has only to listen to a group playing in the homemaking corner or building a structure on the playground to realize that their language here is more extensive and highly structured than it is likely to be in an adult-controlled situation. They give themselves a lot of practice in talking as they play.

Make-believe play makes a contribution to the learning process. Cohen points

Courtesy of Jean Berlfein.

Children play with water in many different ways.

out, "This capacity for pretending is at the heart of symbolic learning."* Children say, "Let's pretend that . . ." and play out situations about what a firefighter does or what they imagine goes on in a school.

There will, of course, be activities planned and structured by the teacher in a good nursery school, but the largest amount of time will be devoted to play initiated by the children. The teacher who understands and values children's play will nurture the child's normal curiosity and drive to explore and discover. She will be ready to provide the materials and suggestions needed to enable him to solve the problems he meets in his play. In doing this she is contributing to the development of skills he will need in other learning situations, and she may be protecting him from the inhibiting effects of poor school experiences later.

Children Play to Make Contact with Others

In playing together, children share ideas and extend the range of one another's experience. They make friends through play. In their dramatic play they re-create and rehearse roles and seek to understand better their common problems in family life. Play with other children seems to be essential to healthy growth.

Dramatic play probably has great value for all children. As they take different roles, they are trying to discover more about what these roles are really like. Family dramas are the ones most frequently enacted. Relationships of fathers and mothers and of mothers and children are an almost universal theme in dramatic play. Cooking, setting the table, washing, ironing, caring for the baby, going to the store, carrying on telephone conversations, disciplining children, entertaining friends, dressing up, and going to the doctor are activities that are carried on day after day as children strive to clarify for themselves the grown-up world. Firefighter, gas station attendant, or any other occupation with which the children are familiar will also be included. All these activities have an absorbing interest for children. They enjoy themselves in important ways in dramatic play.

Through play with others a child begins to be aware of the feelings of other children. He is better able to understand that others may be sad or happy, or afraid, or frustrated, or that they may want to possess or be first. These feelings are not his alone but belong to others as well. They can be dealt with in an outer world and managed with help.

Children Play to Master Feelings

Children use play as a way of reducing and gaining mastery over their fears and anxieties. They have many fears, the fear of being left or deserted, the fear of being hurt and helpless, and sometimes the fear of their own violent impulses. As we watch children at play we observe how often they take the role of the one who punishes and controls and who does the going away and leaving. By revers-

---

*Cohen, Dorothy: Is TV a Pied Piper? Young Children, November, 1974. p. 11. Copyright © 1974, National Association for the Education of Young Children, 1834 Connecticut Avenue, N.W., Washington, D.C. 20009.

ing roles in play they are helped to deal with their feelings in such situations. They grow in confidence.

Some children handle the problem of being little by using gun play to help them feel big and powerful. Whatever we ourselves may feel about the use of guns, we accept the fact that this kind of play may meet a need for the child. We will discuss this later in the chapter on dramatic play.

Children are often helped by playing out situations that have aroused fears in them. We see this in the frequency with which "doctor-nurse" play appears. It is especially absorbing to those children who have had painful experiences with doctors and hospitals. Through playing out a frightening, painful experience they work their way toward healing the psychological wounds of the experience, as in the case of Ellen described earlier. Freer of fear and anxiety, children can then go on to master other problems with more confidence.

It is important that children have outlets for reducing fears and anger and aggression by draining them off in play. Without such opportunities healthy development may be blocked. It is important, too, that the play materials they use are not broken or unworkable. The child needs to be successful in his play with the thing-world if he is to gain the confidence that comes with mastery.

Winnicott believes that, "In the pre-school years play is the child's principal means of solving the emotional problems that belong to development."*

*Winnicott, D. W.: The Child and the Outside World. New York, Basic Books, Inc., Publishers, 1957. p. 22.

Playing "doctor" may help reduce a child's anxieties about visiting his physician.

Courtesy of Myron Papiz.

Play Leads to the Integration of Personality

The feelings that young children have are very strong feelings. They are not only terrified at times, but they are also filled with rage. They may feel helpless to control these angry feelings. They must have help from the adults in managing these feelings, but they also are helped by reducing these feelings in play. Here they can "pretend," and take the role of lions or soldiers or firemen fighting a fire. By expressing aggressive feelings in dramatic form, under their own control, children are helped to feel that they can manage such feelings. Even throwing objects at a target or banging on big drums are forms of play that may be useful to children who need to feel that they can express strong feelings in ways that do no damage. Play helps to keep feelings within manageable proportions.

Play brings the inner world of feeling in touch with the outer world of "shared reality." Play leads to an integration of the personality.

Playing is a creative experience, an act of the imagination in part, but one based in a reality that can be shared with others. Spontaneous, playful behavior is a part of creative experience on any level and wherever it is found, whether in the arts or in scientific research. Winnicott writes, "It is in playing and only in playing that the individual child or adult is able to be creative and to use the whole personality and it is only in being creative that the individual discovers the self."*

Winnicott connects playing with our cultural heritage, "the common pool of humanity." In his words, "There is a direct development from transitional phenomena to playing, and from playing to shared playing, and from this to cultural experiences."* The child painting at the easel is a child who has been engaged in playing and imagining. Winnicott adds, "Playing leads on naturally to cultural experience and indeed forms its foundation."*

Television Is Likely to Impoverish Play

Most children today do a lot of television viewing, but many early childhood educators feel that young children are exposed to television too soon and in too big doses. The exposure limits the child's time for play, which is his natural avenue for learning. Play is an active process in which the child is doing and imagining. Television viewing is a passive process. It may reduce the child's capacity for self-initiated activities.

Teachers in some schools have reported an impoverishment in children's play and an increase in nervous activity after extensive television viewing. A recent study at the University of Southern California† reported that children's creativity dropped after three weeks of intensive television viewing, especially that of the younger children.

Television is a mass media. It cannot be adapted to the individual needs of children and their individual readiness for an experience. Misconceptions cannot be discovered and cleared up. Amassing facts, partially understood, does not promote sound learning. For older children television can and does offer material

---

*Winnicott, D. W.: Playing and Reality. New York, Basic Books, Inc., Publishers, 1972. London, Tavistock Publications Ltd., 1972. pp. 54, 51, 106.

†Education U.S.A., October 29, 1973.

that broadens their horizons just as reading does, with television adding the vividness of pictures and movement. For young children, however, the excitement, speed, noise, and constantly changing stimuli are probably bewildering and overwhelming. Children lack the background for interpreting the rapidly changing sequence of events. Children need actual, concrete experiences that they can deal with in some way, "the world presented in small enough doses," which is not what television offers them. Young children believe what they see on television. They are still trying to sort out what is actual from what is fantasy or fiction, and television does not make this easier for them. The personal element so necessary for the young child is lacking.

Violence is often what children see as they watch television. Violence on television may give older children and adults some release and a chance for draining off some hostile, aggressive feelings, but young children are still in an "acting out" stage. They have not developed much "inner control" as yet. They tend to hit or bite or kick and their impulses are strong. They are not sure of the difference between acceptable and unacceptable behavior. Television does not offer young children much in the way of control of impulse or of limits in acting out feelings. These are very necessary in draining off negative feelings. They are part of what the good nursery school offers when it stops aggressive behavior and helps the child find constructive outlets for hostile feelings in words or activities. One may well wonder how much of the teen-age violence we see today is due to television watching, begun at an early age. Little distinction is made between acceptable and unacceptable behavior. One must conclude that television does not belong in a good nursery school experience.

Educational Television

There are a number of educational programs designed for young children, such as the well-publicized "Sesame Street." Cohen* points out, however, that these educational programs did not start from concern about the best development of children but from adult anxiety and adult politics. They do not truly fit what we know about young children's growth and development, their need for concrete, actual experience with objects and people as a basis for concept formation, their need to strengthen the feelings of autonomy and of initiative as a basis for sound personality development. Even language competency is best developed by dialogue with actual people for one's own purposes. Distorted images and values are inevitably part of television viewing even in present day educational programs.

Since most homes have a television, it would seem desirable to have good programs for young children to view at home. Cohen suggests that it might be possible to have "a few special programs for the very young, carefully edited in accordance with their stage of development, simple, short, attractive and entertaining. It could be fun, or it could be 'educational' in the truest sense—broadening the mind, not the rote learning of skills, sharing with adults, not being manipulated by them."*

---

*Cohen, Dorothy: Is TV a Pied Piper? Young Children, November, 1974. p. 13. Copyright © 1974, National Association for the Education of Young Children, 1834 Connecticut Avenue N.W., Washington, D.C. 20009.

Observing Play Behavior

Perhaps in no other area will the parent or teacher find more clues to help her understand individual children than in their play. By careful observation of play she can evaluate the progress a child is making in reaching his potential as a functioning human being. She can become more aware of what materials or experiences she may provide to meet his needs. Observing and recording the child's behavior in play situations increases the adult's insights. It is time well spent. The teacher can build her program on these observations of play.

Valuing Play Activities

There will, of course, be activities planned and structured by the teacher. Many of these will be the result of observations of the children in their spontaneous play, extending and enlarging the children's observed interests. In the activities she plans, the teacher will often make use of games, simple ones, suitable to the children's level of understanding. Games help create a "climate for learning."

Some children need a more structured situation than others. They may not trust themselves enough to play freely in an unstructured situation. They may prefer order, being more familiar with an orderly routine at home. Children differ in their play needs as they do in other ways. In providing for play, the teacher makes it possible for children to satisfy different styles of playing behavior.

Our role as adults is to provide a rich variety of play materials and adequate space well arranged for use, so that children have opportunities for play which promote growth in all areas. In the discussion of areas in the program we will consider ways in which the teacher fosters growth in each area. Some of these will be through activities initiated by the teacher. Most of these will center around extending and enriching the play which children themselves have initiated. All those who work with young children will respect and value their play and allow plenty of time and space for it. Play is important for physical, intellectual, social, and personality development.

It takes independence, imagination and fantasy, initiative, adjustment, accommodation, and wholehearted interest to learn and to develop one's capacities. These qualities are not likely to be nurtured by drill or by adult directions. They are qualities that the child uses in an environment with rich possibilities for play with materials and with other children.

The personalities of children develop through play just as those of adults develop through experiences in living. Play offers an effective avenue for growth.

SITUATION FOR DISCUSSION

*An Incident in the Play Group**

Nels, a red-headed three-year-old, came into the playroom and walked straight to the rocking horse. Walking around the horse, he leaned down, patted

---

*Recorded by Jane Martin.

the rocker with his right hand and then climbed on. As he rocked back and forth, he smiled to himself. A passing student said, "Hello, Nels," but Nels made no reply. His rocking became more vigorous. The teacher approached him, "Good morning, Nels. It is a good day to ride the horse." Nels smiled, wrinkled up his nose, and nodded his head. He continued his rocking at a slower pace.

Mary, a student, placed several puzzles on the rug. Two children immediately joined her. Nels watched from the rocking horse for several minutes. Then he quickly slipped off the horse and went directly to a puzzle. Without speaking to anyone, he sat down and dumped the puzzle pieces out onto the rug. He stretched out on his stomach and lifted his feet into the air, waving them back and forth, as as he started to put the pieces of the puzzle back. Then he got up on his knees, looked at Mary and held out a piece as though for help. Mary smiled, "Try to put the piece near the bear's head, Nels." Nels quickly put the piece into place, not looking at Mary again. He sat up and looked around the room. Alicia was on the rocking horse. Nels watched her intently. When she climbed down, Nels left the puzzles immediately and ran back to the rocking horse and climbed on it.

Comment

What Does This Observation Tell Us About Nels?

Nels enjoys rhythmic activities. He is interested in what goes on around him. His interests seem sustained. He acts quickly when he makes a decision. He seems more interested in materials and activities than in people. He controls his impulses. He waited until Alicia finished riding the rocking horse before going to it himself. He used no speech during the observation.

What Guidance Does Nels Seem to Need?

He needs encouragement in using language. The adult might try to ask questions that really *need* a verbal reply, give approval when he does put something into words (reinforcement), read to him, and encourage him to talk about pictures and stories and experiences. To illustrate, when Nels held up a piece of the puzzle, Mary might have said, "Tell me what you want, Nels." If he had not answered, she might have put it into words, "Do you want to know where the piece belongs?"

PROJECTS

1. Observe a group of children playing and record an incident:
   (a) In which a child seems to be discovering something about the nature of the world through his play.
   (b) In which the child seems to use play as a way of mastering an anxiety or a fear or a conflict that he may be feeling.
   (c) In which the child is re-creating a role in the world around him.
   (d) In which he is discovering what other people are like.

REFERENCES

Almy, Millie: Spontaneous Play: Early Childhood Play: Selected Readings. New York, Selected Academic Readings, 1968.

Athey, Irene: Piaget, Play and Problem Solving. *In* Sponseller, Doris (ed.): Play as a Learning Medium. Washington, D.C., National Association for the Education of Young Children, 1974.

Axline, Virginia: Play Therapy. New York, Ballantine Books, Inc., 1969.

Biber, Barbara: Play as a Growth Process. Pub No. 4. New York, Bank Street Publications.

Curry, Nancy, and Arnauld, Sara (coordinators): Play: The Child Strives Toward Self-Realization: Proceedings of a Conference. Washington, D.C., National Association for the Education of Young Children, 1971.

Erikson, Erik: Identity and the Life Cycle. New York, International Universities Press, Vol. 1, No. 1, pp. 82–86.

Fowler, William: On the value of both play and structure in early education. Young Children, Vol. 27, No. 1, October, 1971.

Hartley, Ruth, Frank, Lawrence, and Goldenson, Robert: Understanding Children's Play. New York, Columbia University Press.

Herron, R. E., and Sutton-Smith, Brian (eds.): Child's Play. New York, John Wiley & Sons, Inc., 1971.

Lowenfield, Margaret: Play in Childhood. New York, John Wiley & Sons, Inc., 1967.

Millar, Suzanne: The Psychology of Play. Baltimore, Pelican Books, 1968.

Piaget, Jean: Play, Dreams and Imitation in Childhood. New York, W. W. Norton & Company, Inc., 1962.

Play: Children's Business. (Revised.) Washington, D.C., Association for Childhood Education, International, 1974.

Riley, Sue Spayth: Some reflections on the value of children's play. Young Children, February, 1973.

Smilansky, Sara: Can adults facilitate play in children? Theoretical and practical considerations. *In* Curry, Nancy, and Arnaud, Sara (coordinators): Play: The Child Strives Towards Self-Realization: Proceedings of a Conference, Washington, D.C., National Association for the Education of Young Children, 1971.

Sponseller, Doris (ed.): Play as a Learning Medium. Washington, D.C., National Association for the Education of Young Children, 1974.

Stern, V.: The Role of Play in Cognitive Development. Final Report, Research Division. New York, Bank Street College of Education, 1973.

Sutton-Smith, Brian: The playful modes of knowing. *In* Curry, Nancy, and Arnaud, Sara (coordinators): Play: The Child Strives Towards Self-Realization: Proceedings of a Conference. Washington, D.C., National Association for the Education of Young Children, 1971.

Sutton-Smith, Brian: Play as novelty training. *In* Andrews, J. D. (ed.): One Child Indivisible. Washington, D.C., National Association for the Education of Young Children, 1975.

The Value of Play for Learning. Theory into Practice, Columbus, Ohio, College of Education, Ohio State University, October, 1974.

Winnicott, D. W.: The Child and the Outside World. New York, Basic Books, Inc., Publishers, 1957. pp. 149–152.

Winnicott, D. W.: Playing and Reality. New York, Basic Books, Inc., Publishers, 1972.

Winsor, Charlotte: Blocks as a material for learning through play—the contribution of Caroline Pratt. *In* Hirsch, Elisabeth (ed.): The Block Book. Washington, D.C., National Association for the Education of Young Children, 1974.

Television

Cohen, Dorothy: Is TV a Pied Piper? Young Children, November, 1974.

Melody, Williams: Children's Television: The Economics of Exploitation. New Haven, Yale University Press, 1973.

Mukerji, Rose.: Why not feelings and values in instructional television? Young Children, May, 1971.

Mujerki, Rose, Akers, Milton, Campbell, Bertha, and Liddle, E. A.: Television Guidelines for Early Childhood Education. Bloomington, Illinois, National Instructional TV, 1969.

Springle, Herbert A.: Can poverty children live on Sesame Street? Young Children, March, 1971.

Springle, Herbert A · Who wants to live on Sesame Street? Young Children, December, 1972.

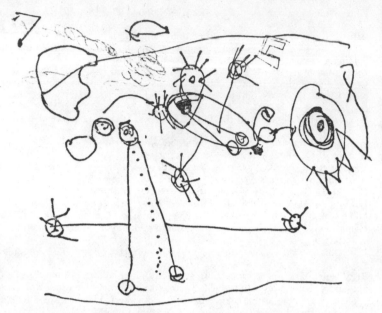

CHAPTER 13

Man and Airplane (boy, 3 years 3 months)

THE PROCESS OF LEARNING
IN EARLY CHILDHOOD

We have looked at the role of the teacher in fostering development. We have considered play and its values in learning. Now we will look more closely at the learning process itself and how young children are helped to develop sound strategies for thinking and reasoning. We are concerned with the "nature of the knower and of the knowledge-getting process."

The Nature of Intelligence

Intelligence is considered something that grows through nurture by the environment, rather than something fixed at birth. It develops in a series of stages. Its growth depends on the quantity and quality of the nurturing experiences. Without the input of stimulation from the environment and the encouragement of attentive adults, the child's more complex intellectual skills and competencies may fail to develop or may develop only in restricted ways. Too much inappropriate stimulation may be as damaging as lack of stimulation. Intellectual and personality developments are closely related. All the evidence we have suggests that the process of learning is exceedingly complex.

The development of knowledge in the early stages in growth is personal. It depends on personal relationships between learner and teacher. Learning is done by individuals, not by groups. Children who have shared experiences together may enjoy listening to stories in a small group or to music or to poetry, but they do most of their learning as individuals, in different ways, at different rates, about things of immediate and personal interest. Just as they play first as individuals, then in parallel play, and only slowly in groups, so they grow through these same cycles in cognitive activities.

The Nursery School Child as Learner or "Knower"

The nursery school child, the "knower" we are concerned with, is still engaged in building a balance of trust in himself and others that will free him from too great mistrust and enable him to use his capacities. He is also still engaged in moving beyond his infantile dependency and in achieving a greater measure of independence. This will enable him to assert himself actively in the learning process. Above all, he is engaged in using his initiative, in exploring, discovering, imagining, going on to the new and untried. These three personality tasks, building a sense of trust, a sense of autonomy, and a sense of initiative, are critical at this stage.

As a learner, the nursery-school-age child continues to use all his senses as he did in the sensorimotor stage, gathering impressions of the world around him and acting on these impressions. But he has also moved into the preoperational stage described by Piaget. He is doing more organizing and classifying of these impressions. He sees similarities and differences, develops systems in his thinking, and tests out his conclusions. He is developing concepts. In water play, for example, he is no longer content just to splash, enjoying the feel and sight of water, but he fills containers, pours the water, and watches what happens. He may put various objects in the water; he finds an object that sinks and then tries to make others sink. He imagines and uses symbols in his play. After he has seen a boat on the lake, he pretends a box is a boat as he rocks it or "fishes" from it. He rehearses and clarifies concepts in dramatic play. He accommodates to what he has assimilated in more complex ways. His play reveals his progress. He makes things happen. If one block is not long enough for bridging a distance, he turns to the one that fits the space.

The nursery-school-age child is increasing his competence in language expressions as well, and this ability makes possible greater complexity in thought. Words help him recall experience and organize and classify perceptions. He can communicate better with others and share in their ideas. He asks questions and understands the answers better than when he was younger. Verbal expression helps him clarify his own ideas.

In nursery school the child also learns from being with other children and with the adults there. He finds out more about how other children respond to his approaches and what he can and cannot do with them. He identifies with the

Watching to see where the water goes.

Courtesy of Jean Berlfein.

teacher and learns from her. He "accommodates" to a greater range of social experiences.

An Example of Learning About the Properties of Water

We said earlier that understanding is based on implicit knowledge gained through sensorimotor experiences. The teacher helps the child extend his experiences and use these in ways that lead to more explicit knowledge on which he can later build an understanding of general principles.

Let us use as an example the implicit knowledge and the possible explicit learnings that come from experiences with water. It takes many years, for example, to reach an understanding of such a complex subject as the laws of floating bodies, but children begin to gain some of the necessary implicit knowledge through the experiences they may have with water from infancy on. Children love to play in water. They are well motivated for learning here. What are some possible experiences with water? What explicit teaching may be done in this, or in any other area of experience?

Here Are Some Possible Experiences with Water

Bathing in water.

Washing one's face and hands, using soap, using water of different temperatures.

Turning the faucet on and off.

Pulling the plug in the basin, letting the water out, filling the basin.

Washing other things: doll clothes, a variety of fabrics or objects that change in feel when wet, fabrics that are colorfast and those that are not.

Drying wet objects in sun, in shade, over heater.

Painting with water on different surfaces, seeing it dry in sun and shade.

Scrubbing table or floor, using wet cloth, mop, sponge.

Wringing out cloth, sponge, or mop.

Watching water being absorbed by blotter or sponge.

Flushing the toilet.

Pouring water, filling containers.

Using a hose to water plants, squirting streams of water.

Using a watering can with a nozzle or spray.

Feeling the spray of water, feeling the force of a stream of water.

Playing in water in a pool, swirling with stick, using a strainer.

Dropping objects in water, watching patterns made.

Floating different objects: light ones and heavy ones that sink or float; wading, swimming.

Blowing soap bubbles, indoors and outdoors in sunshine and in wind.

Mixing substances with water: paint powder, powdered clay, flour, dry bread crumbs, salt, sugar, oil.

Dissolving substances like jello, and watching them set.

Watching kettle boil and steam condense.

Observing dew on grass, on cobwebs, on branches.

Observing frost patterns on windows.

Experiences with rain: watching it fall, feeling it on face, seeing it flow down slopes and in gutters, stepping in puddles.

Experiences with snow and hail: playing in snow, watching snow or hail melt, tasting snow, compressing it into balls, piling it, observing drifts and icicles hanging or melting.

Making ice cubes in refrigerator, and using them.

Making ice cream.

Caring for animals that live in water: fish, pollywogs, frogs, turtles.

Playing in water with sand and mud, digging channels for the water, putting all kinds of objects in the water, observing properties of water.

Out of these experiences, and many more, the child builds an implicit knowledge of some of the properties of water. He can begin to predict what will happen when he does certain things. He knows that water doesn't run uphill, for example. He can dig channels to lead the water where he wants it to go. He can begin to estimate what will float and what will sink.

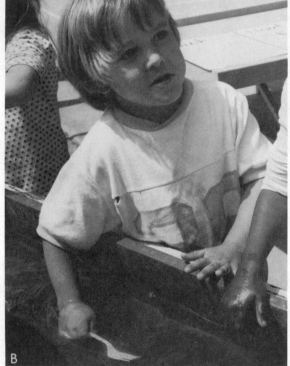

Courtesy of Jean Berlfein.

The group experiments with floating and sinking objects. A child wonders if the fork will sink or float.

She finds out and places it in the column marked "sink."

How Does the Teacher Use These Experiences for Explicit Teaching?

In addition to providing these experiences for the child, the teacher may call the child's attention in explicit ways to how water behaves. She may ask questions. She may make suggestions to extend the child's experimentation. She may describe what is happening and encourage him to describe it. She may give explanations in answer to his questions and help him explore.

The teacher may call a child's attention to the way his water paint evaporates in the sun in contrast to what happens in the shade. She may point out the way the water acts on the dry sand in contrast to the wet sand. She may point out the steam on the windows in the kitchen.

The teacher may ask questions as the child plays with water in a tub. "Do you think that big piece of wood will float?" and when he tries it she may ask, "What did happen?" In other situations she may ask, "What will happen when you add water to the clay powder?" or, "Where do you think the steam comes from?" or, "What makes the frost on our window?"

Through these experiences the child acquires some implicit knowledge about buoyancy, resistance, gravity, wave motion, and other principles. The teacher guides children in these steps towards "organizing facts already internalized about the real world," so that these will be useful to them in the concepts they are building.

Developing Concepts Involves Clearing Up Misconceptions

The child begins early to reason, but his conclusions often reveal the limitations on which his reasoning is based. Four-year-old Maria, for example, was full of excitement about the birth of a baby to an older sister. When she arrived at school, she told her teacher all about it. The teacher smiled as she remarked, "Now your mother is a grandmother." Maria stopped, her eyes wide with surprise. Then she shook her head very positively. "Oh, no," she said, "My mother still lives with us." One gets an insight into what her concept of "grandmother" is based on as well as the different viewpoints of child and adult. The incident also shows us the difficulty a child has in thinking about relationships among people.

In helping the child gradually clear up misconceptions, we may ask questions such as, "Why do you think that?" or, "How can you tell?" In doing this we are helping him examine his premises. There are probably few subjects about which the child has more curiosity and more misconception than the subject of where he came from, how he was conceived, how he was born, and how he grew. We can answer his questions by asking, "What do you think?", following the suggestions given by Fraiberg in her excellent discussion, "Education for Love," in *The Magic Years*. We can use books such as Marie Ets' *The Story of a Baby*. We can give him information in simple words, giving only as much as he can understand or wants to know about at the moment. We should give only accurate, true information. The subject will need repeated clarification, but, bit by bit, his concepts will come closer to the facts.

In spite of explanations, children's misconceptions will persist until there is readiness to understand. Francis said to his mother, "You're going to have to blow up your tummy, so we can have a baby." Francis was eager for a baby to arrive. The child keeps assimilating information in his personal ways, weaving it into the fabric of his experience. We do not always know what the meaning of it is to him.

Other questions likely to arise are in connection with toileting, as boys and girls use the toilets together. Here we have opportunities to make clearer the physical differences in the sexes and discuss the male and female roles. Changes in the roles of men and women in society are taking place and children can begin to understand these changing roles.

The Teacher Helps the Child Distinguish Between the Real World and the World of Fantasy

The thinking of children at this stage is largely personally oriented. Charles, described in an earlier chapter, could exclaim, "It doesn't wait for me," when he saw the water flowing away from him. This kind of perception of the world is revealed in the drawings of young children where the head or face is usually very large, because it is the part that is important for the child.

Fantasy and reality are often confused in children's thinking at this stage. What they think seems true to them whether it corresponds to reality or not. Children need help and time to make this distinction between reality and fantasy without having to reject their fantasies. They have a right to imagine and to create fantasies as well as a need to learn to identify reality.

It is sometimes a struggle for children to get the real world and the world of magic into their proper places. A child is fortunate when he has help from a parent or a teacher in this learning. His imaginative tales can be valued for what they are, delightful figments of the imagination, a method of escape that we can all use at times. It is fun to make up stories, but one should be clear about the differences between the "pretend" and the factual.

Francis, a four-year-old, tended to turn away from difficulties and deny unpleasant realities. He often tried to make his world be what he wanted it to be. He teased and was successful in manipulating the succession of "baby sitters" who cared for him when he was not in nursery school while his mother worked. His teacher watched for opportunities to help him enjoy reality without distorting it. It was not difficult, for he was a friendly child, eager to please and to find a place for himself in the group.

Francis is playing with dough at the table, patting, squeezing and folding it. He suddenly looks down and exclaims, "Hey! Hey, I made a turtle. I made a turtle!" He smiles a big smile and is obviously pleased with this discovery. With his hands he carefully forms the legs and head so they are more prominent. The other children start making turtles too. Francis exclaims to an approaching teacher, "Hey, look at my turtle!" He jumps off his chair. Jamie joins in excitedly, "Turtle, turtle, see my turtle." The teacher admires the turtles.

Francis says, "I didn't know I could make a turtle, but I did. I made a turtle." He then puts his hand behind the turtle and gives it a shove. The turtle sticks to the table and changes form slightly. Francis frowns and carefully unsticks it and shoves it again. This time it slides on the table but changes shape. He looks up at the teacher with a distraught expression and says, "My turtle can't walk."

Teacher: "Do you know why your turtle can't walk?"

Francis: "No—oh ya, because he is play-dough instead of real."

Teacher: "Yes, you know why."

Here we see Francis pleased with himself for making a turtle and then finding that the turtle does not fit in with his dream of a turtle. The teacher helps him return to a satisfying reality.

The Teacher Encourages the Use of Imagination

The teacher does not discourage the use of imagination by children. She encourages it. Imagination is valuable. We know that "hunches" and "brain storming" often produce worthwhile ideas with adults. Children are naturally good at using their imaginations, or "taking them out for a run," as someone has called it. As they become clearer about reality and fantasy, they have fun making up stories as well as describing real experiences. They play games of pretending as, "Wouldn't it be funny if. . ." or, "This looks like a. . . ."

Thinking of alternatives or possibilities is an exercise for the intellect and the imagination. The teacher may ask, "How many ways are there to go to the store?" or, "What do you think we will see when we get to the top of the hill?" or, "What would you do if you found you were lost on the street?" or, "What do you think we could make out of this?" Guessing and risking a guess are often valuable aids in problem solving when one can check on the results. Imaginative solutions are worth cultivating.

How Are Young Children Motivated to Learn?

As we observe children, we see that they are most absorbed when they are most interested. They concentrate and they persist when they are really interested just as we ourselves do. If we are to teach effectively, we need to understand the *interests* children are likely to have and the particular interests of the individual child. Only as we make available materials and experiences in which the child is truly interested can we facilitate his learning.

Purposeful activity grows out of interests and it is this kind of activity which generates the energy that learning demands. Brearley puts it this way, "Teaching is a cultural task and our business is to gear these natural curiosities and interests to the traditional skills which the culture has built up and valued...," adding that in teaching we need "the energy of his [the child's] willingness on our side."*

One interest of young children is *activity,* all kinds of physical movement, large and small muscle activities, indoor and outdoor play which gives a chance to explore the possibilities of what can be done with movement. Children find great satisfaction in physical achievement, and there are many opportunities for cognitive learning in most of these activities. There are problems to be dealt with, things to be observed and compared.

Curiosity is a motivating force in children in the sensorimotor and preoperational stage of development. We need to provide a rich variety of firsthand experiences to be explored and acted upon. The curious child can use his experiences in "structured thinking" as he is ready. The teacher can supply words, ask questions, call attention to aspects of the experience and extend it. She can "deepen the interest into knowledge."

The *desire for love and appreciation* is also a strong motivating force in young children. It is a need that can easily be exploited unless we keep clearly in mind the child's purposes and his level of development. Too often we may be more concerned with our own purposes than with his. If we give the child approval for being "good" by our standards or for doing what *we* think is best, we may be limiting his development as an individual in his own right. We need to make sure that we acknowledge with approval the effort that went into constructing an airplane that satisfied *him,* or the control he exercised in not acting on the impulse to hit an offending companion, or the spontaneous sharing done among friends, or the imaginative observation, rather than giving approval only for achievements that satisfy us.

The supportive role of the adult is an important one. He or she gives support to the child by showing an interest in what the child does, by treating the child's questions with respect, by giving more attention to the positive than to the negative aspects of his performance, by generous giving of approval for real accomplishments.

---

*Brearley, M. (ed.), Bott, R., Danes, M. P., Glynne-Jones, M. L., Huchfield, E. M., Johnson, J. E. L., and Tamburrini, J. R.: The Teaching of Young Children: Some Applications of Piaget's Learning Theory. New York, Schocken Books Inc., 1970. Reprinted by permission of Schocken Books Inc. Copyright © 1969 by Basil Blackwell, Oxford.

Group watching pollywogs swimming in the jar.

Courtesy of Jean Berlfein.

A teacher extends the experience by showing them a book about pollywogs.

The Urge Toward Mastery

Motivation depends on many factors. One of the strongest of these is the urge toward mastery of a problem and the satisfaction which all of us feel from performing with skill. We see this in a young child as he persists in working on a fastening until he succeeds in opening it and then turns to fresh fields of endeavor.

This urge toward competency, as R. W. White has called it, is a strong motivating force as long as we feel that there is a hope of success. The strength of the urge diminishes if our efforts are continually blocked. The child who has lost hope of any success is not motivated to try. He has lost this powerful urge. When a child has lived in an environment that is largely unfavorable for successful learning, the teacher must work to reawaken his curiosity and zest for exploring and discovering. Above all she must help him rediscover his faith in his own competence. He must believe that he *can* succeed, if he tries. He must see himself as someone who is able to achieve. If the teacher is to help him, she must herself believe that the child can learn. She must believe in him and his capacities.

Under favorable conditions, the child's natural curiosity and his urge toward competency motivate him. He wants to learn and to gain skills. The teacher does not need to depend on extrinsic forms of motivation. The child wants to grow to be like the important adults around him. When these adults present themselves as "models" who work and achieve, they give direction to the child's efforts. He can work and become competent.

Bruner comments: "The will to learn is an intrinsic motive, one that finds its source and its reward in its own exercise."* He points out that the most lasting

---

*Bruner, Jerome S.: Toward a Theory of Instruction. Cambridge, The Belknap Press of Harvard University, 1966. p. 127.

Mastery of a tool: making the saw work.

satisfactions lie in learning itself, not in extrinsic rewards. These do not give reliable nourishment "over the long course of learning." The urge toward competence is strong in a healthy child. He needs little else except encouragement to sustain his learning.

The teacher has a responsibility to guard this precious "will to learn" that motivates the child, or to reawaken it in children who may have lost it. She needs to help these children find "the confidence to try and to make mistakes, and the confidence to know that it is worth doing for its own sake. *And the daring to like yourself and trust your product."**

Readiness for Learning

The child learns most easily those things that he is developmentally ready to learn, but readiness, too, must be nurtured. Bruner points out that readiness may be a half truth if one depends on readiness alone. He comments that "one *teaches* readiness or provides opportunities for its nurture, one does not simply wait for it. . . ."†

A good teacher is continually nurturing the child's readiness to move forward to more complex activities. When the child is able to pound short nails into a board, she provides him with longer nails so that he can move on to making more

---

*Carroll, Vinnette, as quoted in Christian Science Monitor, November 29, 1969.

†Bruner, Jerome S.: Toward a Theory of Instruction. Cambridge, The Belknap Press of Harvard University, 1966. p. 29.

Mastery of a skill: cutting takes concentration.

Courtesy of Robert Overstreet.

complicated things out of wood. She encourages his mastery of new skills. The teacher gives the child choices in order to develop his capacity to make decisions. As his capacities increase, she expects more of him. His readiness for new activities has grown.

Nurturing readiness for formal learning does not imply pressures for earlier formal learning, however. Most educators are opposed to these kinds of pressures. Members of a colloquy held at the Childhood Education Center in Washington, D.C., in 1962, declared themselves "unreservedly opposed to pressures on children for earlier formal learning," and stated:

....formal learning tasks may displace the informal play-type learning which involves imagination, fantasy, creative activities and the other higher mental processes, and in that way deprive the child of the very activities so necessary for his development. What every child needs is much opportunity to experiment with materials and tools, much experience learning, much opportunity for exchange between children and between a child and his teacher, much opportunity for para-language, that subtle interpretation of one's self through one's manner, stance, feeling, tone, and all the ways of communicating without speaking. A gread deal can be done in these ways to build a rich background for later symbolic learning.*

Reading Readiness

There are many experiences at the preschool level which prepare a child for learning to read. One of the most important of these is a "reading atmosphere" fostered by people who are themselves interested in and enjoy books and who enjoy reading to the child from suitably selected books. Books become an important part of his world, too. As he sits with the adult, he observes her eye movements and becomes aware of the way she follows the line of print. She may use her finger to indicate where the words she is reading are appearing on the page and when she is ready for the page to be turned.

There are many opportunities to call the child's attention to words and their meaning. A "stop" sign on the street or a "stop" sign on the playground to indicate where the wagons and tricycles must stop, or a sign "store" on a block construction, or the sentence "This is a store" makes the child more aware of the written word (as the group were after a trip to the store). His name can be printed over his locker or cubby, or on his paintings, or at the table where he sits for lunch. Later he may copy the teacher's lettering and make his own name. There may be discussion of the letters and comparisons with other people's names with the recognition of letters that are the same or different. Lotto games give the child practice in discriminating lines and forms, a skill needed in reading.

Handling tools, using scissors, drawing, and painting are activities (in addition to many others) which promote the neuromuscular development which is required for reading and writing. Equally necessary is a wide variety of experiences with objects and people and situations which enable the child to understand what he will be reading later. All this is part of nurturing reading readiness.

_____

*Basic Human Values for Childhood Education. Report of Colloquy. Washington, D.C., Association for Childhood Education, International, 1962.

Adult Anxiety About a Child's Learning to Read

Adult anxiety often centers around children's reading. We see this in educational television programs for young children. Learning to recognize and write the letters of the alphabet is not an appropriate activity for most three-year-olds, but it is often included in these programs. Far more important as a basis for reading are the experiences we have mentioned.

When children have lacked this background, we give them help by providing what they have lacked rather than by working with them to master skills for which they lack the preparation. Skipping a stage does not promote optimum development in the end. Beginning too soon, without enough background, may mean that the child struggles for months to achieve a level of skill he could reach with very little effort later. Parents and sometimes teachers of young children grow anxious and attempt to push the child toward reading, not trusting him to learn, and thus not building his trust in himself. There is little point in learning to read before one has the background for understanding what one may read. Partial comprehension may become a habit. One only reads words. There will be individual differences in the age at which children are ready to begin reading, of course, and these differences can be respected.

In one nursery school a three-and-a-half-year-old child was able to read quite well. His parents loved books and were pleased with his precocious development. The child was ready to demonstrate his skill on every occasion, but the other children were not interested. He lacked skill in riding a tricycle. He did not know how to use blocks or climb in the jungle gym. He did not know how to play. It was some weeks before he could make contact on his own with the children. He was full of fears and had wild fantasies. He was a child who needed nursery school experience.

When he left the group more than a year later, he was a much more relaxed child, eating and sleeping better at home. While his motor skills were still below average for his age, he had made a great deal of progress in developing these as well as in developing his social skills. He was taking part in active, group play in a more childlike way. His parents had revised their goals for him. They were pleased with his development, for they could see that he was a happier child. He will do well in school, but he also has a good chance of becoming a well-developed human being. He is sure to be less handicapped socially, emotionally, and even intellectually.

The Characteristics of a Good Thinker

An important characteristic of a good thinker is a *feeling of confidence in himself.* Experiences in being successful encourage the child to persist and to believe in his own success. His teacher's belief in him and her expectations for him also give him confidence. This confidence enables him to face frustrations and failures and to use them, as the scientist does, for learning what does not work.

An ability to pay attention or concentrate is a characteristic of a good thinker. Providing what is of real interest to the child and allowing him time to complete an activity that interests him is one part of the teacher's contribution. She will note the materials which call forth the longest attention spans in children and supply more of these. She avoids interrupting purposeful activities when possible, keeping the schedule flexible to allow for concentration. A teacher reported that one four-year-old in her group worked for a full hour at the work bench making an airplane, using the tools and materials on hand there.

A good thinker makes a practice of *estimating* and *planning*. A child may say, "I need three pieces of wood to finish this." Afterwards the teacher may say, if this is the case, "You thought you needed three pieces. Now you know you only needed two." Learning to estimate approximately what will be needed, or how far it is around the playground, or how long it will take, and then finding out are characteristics of a thinker which the teacher can encourage. She can also help the child check on results and *reflect*. As he sees similarities and differences, she can ask him, "Why?" or "How do you know?"

A good thinker uses his *imagination*. He is creative. Children often pretend in their play. "Pretend I'm the mother or the father or the baby" and proceed to imagine and act the role. Or they say, "Pretend I'm a lion and I'm going to eat you." They exercise their imaginations more actively than most adults do and deal, in fantasy, with all kinds of realities. Using imagination about personal relationships increases children's awareness of aspects of relationships. Here, too, the teacher can give direction to the thinking. "What would you have done if you had been this little boy?", she can say as they read a story together. Or she can ask, "What would you do if you found you were lost and didn't know your way home?" Thinking can take place in these discussions and a pattern for solving difficulties can evolve as thinking begins to find its place along with action. Dramatic play of all kinds stimulates cognitive growth. Symbolic thinking depends on being able to imagine.

The good thinker needs to be able to *communicate* his thoughts. Language plays an important role in the development of the intellect. It is a means of clarifying thought as well as a means of communication. It nourishes the growth of the capacity to reason. We will discuss this further in the section on language.

Blocks in Learning

A child may be blocked in learning because of fears that he may bring to the learning situation. Fear of making a mistake or of failing is one of the common fears here. This fear is serious because it may prevent him from daring to take necessary risks.

Blocks in learning may result from the child's attitude toward authority and authority figures. If the child is continually resisting authority, he is blocked in learning because there is inevitably a measure of authority and discipline necessary in a learning situation. He must in the end be able to discipline himself. The child needs to come to terms with his feelings about authority before he is free to learn as he might otherwise do. Discriminations of many kinds may inhibit learning. Meeting attitudes of discrimination or holding these attitudes is a block to learning in the areas involved.

Cognitive learning is best carried on under relatively conflict-free conditions. There should be an element of surprise or uncertainty or some disequilibrium, as an unanswered question, but not an element of conflict, for the best use of capacities. As part of her teaching role the teacher will try to help the child with any blocks that may hinder his learning.

In summary we might say that the conditions that favor intellectual growth are those in which the child feels secure and relatively free from conflicts, and has confidence in himself and in his ability to cope with the problems presented. He does not learn readily when he is discouraged and sees little hope of success or when he feels alienated from others.

PROJECT

Select an area and list all the possible ways in which children may be able to have experiences here. Indicate also what some of the explicit learnings might be. In what way might these be valuable for later learning? For example, what are possible experiences with colors, or with sounds?

REFERENCES

The Process of Learning

Almy, Millie: Young Children's Thinking. New York, Teachers College Press, 1966.

Andrews, J. D. (ed.): One Child Indivisible. Washington, D.C., National Association for the Education of Young Children, 1975.

Bailey, Nancy: Development of mental abilities. *In* Mussen, Paul (ed.): Carmichael's Manual of Child Psychology, Vol. 1. New York, John Wiley & Sons, Inc., 1970.

Beck, Helen: Viewpoint, pressures in the nursery. Children Today, September-October, 1972.

Biber, Barbara, Shapiro, Edna, and Wickens, David: Promoting Cognitive Growth: A Developmental-Interaction Point of View. Washington, D.C., National Association for the Education of Young Children, 1971.

Blank, Marion: Teaching Learning in the Preschool: A Dialogue Approach. Columbus, Ohio, Charles E. Merrill Publishing Company.

Brearley, Molly (ed.): The Teaching of Young Children: Some Applications of Piaget's Learning Theory. New York, Schocken Books Inc., 1970.

Dowley, Edith, and Bromwitch, Rose: The role of curriculum in early childhood development programs. *In* McFaddon, Dennis (ed.): Early Childhood Development Programs and Services: Planning for Action. Washington, D.C., National Association for the Education of Young Children, 1972.

Gallagher, James J.: Productive thinking. *In* Hoffman, M., and Hoffman, L. N. (eds.): Review of Child Development Research, Vol. 1. New York, Russell Sage Foundation, 1964. pp. 349–378.

Hammerman, Ann, and Morse, Susan: Open teaching: Piaget in the classroom. Young Children, October, 1972.

Isaacs, Nathan: A Brief Introduction to Piaget. New York, Schocken Books Inc., 1972.

Isaacs, Susan: Intellectual Growth in Young Children. New York, Schocken Books Inc., 1966.

Kamii, Constance: One intelligence indivisible. Young Children, May, 1975.

Kohlberg, Lawrence: Early education. A cognitive developmental view. Child Development, Vol. 39, No. 4, 1968.

Landreth, Catherine: Preschool Learning and Teaching. New York, Harper & Row, Publishers, 1972.

Streissguth, Ann, and Bee, Helen: Mother-child interactions and cognitive development in children. *In* Hartrup (ed.): The Young Child, Reviews of Research. Washington, D.C., National Association for the Education of Young Children, 1972.

Suchman, J. R.: The child and the inquiry process. *In* Passow, A. H., and Leeper, R. R. (eds.): Intellectual Development: Another Look. Washington, D.C., Association for Supervision and Curriculum Development, 1964.

Tulkin, Steven.: An analysis of the concept of cultural deprivation. Developmental Psychology, Vol. 6, No. 2, 1972.

White, R. W.: Motivation reconsidered: The concept of competence. Psychological Review, Vol. 66, 1959.

CHAPTER 14

Bay Bridge and Ship (boy, 4 years 7 months)

AREAS OF LEARNING IN THE PROGRAM

In all the areas for learning in any program for young children, teaching begins where the child is in his competencies and his understanding.

We must remember that the child has learned a great deal before he enters the group. He has had many experiences and has developed strategies in thinking and solving problems. He has what has been termed a "cognitive unconscious." He "knows" implicitly a great deal. Our teaching must be based on this knowledge. It is important not to skip any stages in his intellectual development.

These comments apply with special force to those children whom we have labeled "deprived" or "underprivileged." They are children who have missed important experiences in earlier stages. Their need is to go back and experience what was lacking rather than push for learning at a higher level. Some of these children may need more firsthand experiences on which to build the concepts they need for understanding number work or reading or any of the other traditional skills which the culture requires. They need this before they attempt to acquire the skills themselves. Some of the children may need a chance to develop more trust in adults and in themselves before they can learn. Learning depends on a measure of trust.

Our task, then, is to find out where the child is in his competencies, in his understanding, and in his feeling. We need to observe children, consult with the parents who have guided their earlier learning, and build a good relationship with each child. On this basis we are ready to guide the child's learning in the group.

We will discuss areas in turn, beginning with sensorimotor aspects of learning.

SENSORIMOTOR EXPERIENCES: CONCEPT FORMATION

DEVELOPING MOTOR SKILLS: PATTERNS OF RESPONSE

Acquiring skill in using body muscles is important for the young child. He gains confidence when he is able to control his muscles and he can feel "in tune"

Courtesy of Sam Hollander, Bakersfield Community College.

These children have implicit knowledge of space and stance and of their own bodies.

with his own body, able to use it freely, following his own rhythms. His posture and the way he uses his body reveal attitudes he holds about himself. The child with good motor skills can do more about what he perceives. He has more confidence as he plays with other children and copes with situations.

A healthy child enjoys practicing until he masters a skill. The toddler goes up and down stairs or climbs over objects until he can do it easily. The nursery-school-age child will try out many methods of riding a tricycle after he has mastered the art of riding. He goes fast on it, cuts corners, rides close to objects. He enjoys his competency. It gives him confidence.

Skills in using large muscles develop through vigorous, active play. This kind of play usually takes place outdoors. Some of the activities that develop *large muscle* skills are:

Lifting and piling large hollow blocks, boxes, or short boards.
Pulling a loaded wagon or using a wheelbarrow for carrying objects.
Digging with shovel or spade.
Climbing on a jungle gym, rope ladder, or in a tree or over a box.
Swinging in a swing, or on the rungs of a bar or a horizontal ladder.
Riding wheel toys.
Pounding nails, sawing, and using other carpentry tools.
Balancing by walking on low boards or on bouncing boards or on the trampoline.
Running, sometimes barefoot, on sand or grass.
Throwing balls through a hoop or throwing beanbags at a target, or just throwing.
Rhythmic activities to music.

Some of the activities that develop coordination in the use of *small muscles* are:

Activities in connection with dressing, buttoning, lacing shoes, pulling on boots, hanging up coat or towel.
Activies in connection with eating, such as using a spoon and fork, pouring juice or milk from a small pitcher into a cup or glass.
Play with all kinds of manipulative toys like trucks, cars, interlocking blocks, puzzles.
Using a paintbrush or large crayons or felt pen, or cutting with scissors.
Finger plays.

Good posture is important, too. It is encouraged by active play. It is also encouraged by making sure that chairs are of the proper height so that a child's feet are on the floor when he is seated and by making sure that a child sits only for short periods of time. Good posture may also be developed by dancing and games such as balancing a beanbag or a basket with a pad on one's head when marching.

Motor activites form an important part of the curriculum for young children. As the teacher observes the play, she may extend the range of experience by introducing a game of throwing beanbags at a target or of balancing on a walking board. She may rearrange the boards and boxes in new patterns to encourage more climbing. Part of her teaching will consist in making sure that children have a range of activities to develop coordination of large and small muscles.

With opportunity children can develop surprising skill. One four-year-old boy had extraordinary skill with tools. He could hammer a nail with accuracy, saw through boards, use a screwdriver. His father had a workshop in their basement, and he had provided a small one for his son with proper tools. They often worked there together. This boy took the lead in the construction of a play house at nursery school. The project lasted several weeks, and he continued his interest in the project throughout the time, helping sustain the interest of other children in it.

There are many implicit cognitive learnings in motor activities. The child who has balanced on a walking board, built a high tower of blocks, bounced on a springing surface, swung on a set of rings or the horizontal ladder, rolled down an incline, or ridden his tricycle fast around corners knows implicitly some of the principles of physics which will later be the basis for explicit learning. His understanding of the abstract principles will be based on his own body experience with them in his play.

SKILLS IN SENSORY PERCEPTION: FOUNDATION FOR CONCEPTS

The child learns about the world around him through his senses, seeing, hearing, feeling, tasting, and smelling, and through his kinesthetic sense. The greater the input of sensory impressions, the more material he has out of which to build concepts of what the world is like. He improves his tools for understanding the world as he improves the keenness of his sensory perception. The teacher provides for a wide variety of sensory experiences and encourages their use. Her role is an important one here.

A child with a sensory defect, such as a partially sighted child or a hard-of-hearing child, is handicapped because he takes in less complete or less accurate impressions. He must make more effort to learn because of his sensory limitation.

Kinesthetic Sense

A child's kinesthetic impressions come through using his body, through knowing what it feels like to lift a weight, to roll down a slope, or to throw something, for example. As he jumps from a box, he experiences distances and depths. There is evidence that perception of depth is present early in life, but this can be developed and tested out in many, varied ways. Reaching out and touching, jumping, climbing, and rolling over play a part in refining kinesthetic perception.

Smelling

There are many different kinds of smells—the smell of food or of flowers, the smell of clay or paint or soap, the smell of freshly washed towels or wool when it is wet, the smell of new shoes. Some smells are pleasant; some are unpleasant. The smell of food is good when one is hungry. It is easily identified. Some flowers have a strong fragrance; some have a delicate fragrance. The teacher will comment on different odors or respond with appreciation when a child comments. She may help the child develop more awareness of odors by asking, "Do you smell

Does wet sand have a smell?

Courtesy of Jean Berlfein.

something? What does it smell like? Where does it come from, I wonder? Can you find it?"

The teacher can supply a variety of experiences and can reinforce the child's learning by her interest and attention.

Tasting

The most likely place for children to be interested in taste discrimination is at the table when they are eating. They often comment on differences in taste, saying, "It tastes bad," or, "good." But there are other ways to discriminate, and the teacher can introduce them to "sweet" and "sour" and "bitter," with samples. Things that look the same do not always taste the same, as pineapple juice and grapefruit juice, or a pinch of sugar and a pinch of salt, for example.

Describing these tastes not only increases the children's awareness but also challenges their ability to express their perceptions. Enjoying taste perceptions increases enjoyment in eating.

Hearing

Sounds are important to children. Interest in sounds and the capacity to listen and to discriminate sounds contributes to the development of speech. Pleasure in sounds is the basis for the enjoyment of music.

At this stage of learning normal hearing is important for good development of language as well as for sensory impressions. The teacher is in a position to detect deficiency early. A child may seem inattentive because of a hearing defect. The teacher can make a simple test such as speaking to the child in a normal tone when his back is turned, or moving a ticking clock toward him and noting when he pays attention. If she suspects any hearing loss, she can consult with his parents. Many children have been handicapped in school because of an undetected hearing loss.

The teacher provides many experiences in sound for children and encourages their exploration of sounds. She helps them discriminate differences in sound and pitch. Children today may live in such a confusion of noises that they fail to learn to identify individual sounds or to learn to listen. The teacher helps children listen to sounds—bird songs, the sound of an airplane, the eggbeater in the kitchen, the clock, a whisper, the rumble of a truck, the swish of feet in the leaves. She helps them make different sounds—hitting two things together, ringing a bell, making musical sounds by using a variety of instruments. She helps them learn to discriminate sounds—soft and loud, high and low, and the music made by different musical instruments. She gives them opportunities to listen to music and to speech in stories and poems.

Children discover many sounds on their own as they explore materials. The teacher can reinforce these experiences and extend them by her comments: "You made a different sound when you hit the spoon against the cask," or "What does it sound like to you?" or "Is it higher or lower this time?"

Children often play with words and make up nonsense lines. They like the sounds of some phrases. The teacher can select stories and poems in which the words make music, or she can call attention to sounds. A keen ear is a help to children as they go on learning and enjoying experiences.

We will comment further on some of these experiences when we discuss the place of music and language in the curriculum.

Feel or Touch

Children are very responsive to the feel of things. They learn from touching and need a wide variety of experiences with touching in order to develop adequate concepts about the world around them. They need help in making discriminations and in using the correct descriptive words. A teacher can exercise ingenuity in providing children with touch experiences and encouraging their personal descriptions of the feel of things.

Objects feel hard or soft, rough or smooth, firm or spongy, for example. A "feel box" with different objects hidden in it gives a child the chance to try to identify objects by their feel. Sorting games based on the feel of materials of different textures, or on shapes or sizes or forms may interest children. Children enjoy collecting different things that have special "feels," as stones and shells

The feel and look of fingerpaint on a smooth surface.

made smooth by the water, smooth beechnuts, or other objects that are smooth and hard. They enjoy the sensory delights of feeling things.

The teacher can provide a variety of materials of different textures in the "dress-up" area, such as squares of filmy gauze or chiffon, velvet, silk or soft wool or cotton, along with synthetic fibers. In each case the teacher uses the correct designation as she talks about the different materials.

The same object feels different at different temperatures, as the handlebars of a tricycle in the sun or the shade. Water feels different when it has turned to ice. The feel of a leaf when it is green and when it is dry is different, as is the feel of bark on different trees or the feel of different animals—a worm, a baby chick, a kitten. There is the feel of food as well as its taste to identify it. Some foods are soft and some are crunchy. The feel of clay when it is dry is different from its feel when wet and "gooshy." The child experiences these things, but the teacher reinforces and extends the experience by her comments or descriptive words. She may share the experience with him, describing it without asking any response from him. Children learn by touching and feeling.

Seeing

The teacher should be alert to the possibility of visual handicap in individual children in the group. It is easy to misjudge the cause of behavior. The child with poor vision may be distractible or clumsy. It is important to correct visual defects at an early age because defective vision handicaps learning, especially in the sensorimotor stage of development. The teacher can make a simple test of vision such as asking the child to identify objects at a distance or to describe a picture held at a distance where most children can see it. She can consult with the parents if there seems any likelihood of a defect.

Visual impressions are one of the most constant and valuable sources of learning for most children. A bottle-fed infant responds in an excited way to the sight of a bottle being brought near him. The older infant experiences an object as completely as possible by touching it, rolling it, pulling and twisting it, chewing on it, looking at it from all angles, and finally dropping it when he "understands" it. Winnicott, in his chapter on "Further Thoughts on Babies As Persons," has given us a delightful description of a ten-month-old baby "coming to know an object," a spoon, by playing with it.* The preschool child continues to learn by looking at, feeling, and doing something with the objects around him.

In favorable environments young children have many opportunities to see and come to know many objects. In unfavorable environments young children may have fewer of these experiences. The effect is to decrease the input of impressions and to discourage their curiosity and urge to explore.

In a program for children who were failing in their early school experiences, Bank Street College of Education, in New York City, found that some of these children were helped when they were given cameras and taken in small groups for trips through their own neighborhoods to photograph, and thus become again interested in looking. Earlier they had often been actively discouraged from trying to "come to know" the world around them. Encouraged to look and discover and find meaning in experiences, they began to respond to what was offered them in school and to learn there.

*Winnicott, D. W.: Mother and Child. New York, Basic Books, Inc., Publishers, 1957.

The child learns from experiences with everyday objects.

Beauty in line and form and color are important for children. They are helped to become more aware of beauty by having some lovely things to look at in the nursery school—a bowl of flowers or of autumn leaves, a beautiful picture in the entrance hall, a lovely print hanging on the wall, some of their own paintings attractively mounted and hung and changed frequently, pleasing lines in furniture design, pleasing colors, orderly surroundings.

Shapes and forms interest children. The teacher can help make these differences more explicit. Blocks can be stacked according to shapes and sizes. Big and small, long and short, wide and narrow are terms to learn in relation to objects seen as well as felt. There are different textures and patterns to be looked at as well as felt—the bark on trees, the tracks in sand or mud, or ripples made by waves. Experimenting with shadows, children can change shapes and sizes.

Every teacher will build on what is available around her to broaden the children's visual experiences and give them more material for developing concepts through looking and examining what they see.

ORGANIZING SENSORY IMPRESSIONS: FORMING CONCEPTS

✓ As children use their senses, they are storing up a multitude of impressions. In the course of doing this they begin to classify these impressions and to make distinctions. All furry animals are not kittens. An animal can be a kitty or a dog. Other children have mothers and fathers. Some children are bigger than others.

Courtesy of Jean Berlfein.

Discovering shadows.

When does tomorrow really come? It is often a confusing matter and there is an endless amount to learn. We can help children to organize, classify, and discriminate.

Identifying, associating, organizing, classifying, and perceiving relationships are important aspects of learning in the nursery school years. Children do much of this in their play, but some of this is done through games and experiences devised to focus on developing these skills. They are learning to perceive basic relationships involving objects and space and time relationships, and cause and effect relationships.

To organize impressions, a child must be able to identify and label objects. All objects have *names*. The teacher will use the names of things in speaking to a child. She will call the child's attention to names, his own name on his locker or on his painting. She may point out signs when they are walking, the name of a street or a "stop" sign. She will give the child the name of any new object he meets.

Objects have *characteristics* by which they can also be identified. They may differ in color. They may be heavy or light or large or small. As she talks with

The child matches the block to the pattern on the paper.

Courtesy of Jean Berlfein.

children, the teacher will use descriptive words. The cup he is using is green. The box is large, but it is also light. Another box may be large and heavy. The teacher makes sure that the child has a chance to have experiences with many objects having different characteristics. She may introduce games that depend on identifying characteristics, such as what can you find that is heavy or what can you find that is light or what can you find that is blue?

It is important for the child to know about the *uses* and *functions* of objects as a way of learning about them. For example, the child paints with a brush, and he cuts with scissors. The teacher may ask, "What do you need when you want to cut the paper?" Some things have more than one use. We use water for several purposes. The teacher may ask, "What do we use water for?" In conversations the teacher and the children can talk about what things are used for, or what they might be used for.

Objects are *related* in many different ways. They may be the same, or they may be different. They may be similar, as are plates and saucers. They may belong together in sets, as do cups and saucers. There are size relationships. Some objects are large and some are small. There may be an order in size, from smallest to biggest. There are relationships in quantity, too, from a few to a lot. There are relationships in qualities. Some objects may be the same because they are soft or hard, or they may be different in these ways. They may be rough or smooth.

Making explicit the way in which things are alike or different is important. Things may be alike because of their function or their color or their size, for example. They may both be used for drinking but be different in color. Through

Courtesy of Jean Berlfein.

A game of sorting into categories with the teacher.

many experiences with objects the teacher tries to help the child sharpen his ability to perceive, to make distinctions, and to classify. Matching and sorting games are useful here.

Even simple experiences, like deciding where an object belongs, involves a decision about the *class* of objects to which it belongs. In an article entitled "It Pays to Organize," Cauman has pointed out how a teacher can arrange boxes or tins for the storage of "bits and pieces" to make them readily available for use and thus give the children a valuable experience in analysis in "the process of deciding where to look for a needed object or where to put away a contributed object just brought from home. . . . "* The young child will often need help because the classifying concept is new and difficult, but a discussion of "why" it belongs in this or that box helps a child build his own concepts.

There are labels that refer to *position* in space, too, such as under, over, inside, outside, beside, on top of, below. The teacher can use these words as she gives directions: "Put the block on top of the box beside the truck." She can encourage the children to use specific words in describing where a thing belongs. She may introduce games in which children follow directions about placing or hiding objects.

---

*Cauman, Judith: It pays to organize. *In* Bits and Pieces — Imaginative Uses for Children's Learning. Washington, D.C., Association for Childhood Education, International, Bulletin 20–A, 1967. p. 58.

Courtesy of Jean Berlfein.

The teacher sometimes works with an individual child. Can the child make his string on the table match the shape on the board?

The teacher will also help the child become more aware of *time* and the place of events in time. There is a time for lunch and a time for rest. One event comes before another event, or after it. There are days for school and days at home. There is a long time and a short time, and even a beginning and an end to an experience.

Things *change,* and some of the changes relate to time. A child is three, and then he is four. After the day time comes the night time. Other changes are not related to time. Water freezes when it is put into the freezer or when it is very cold outdoors. A child is cold, and he gets warm when he runs. The teacher calls attention to these things, making them more explicit for the child, helping him to build concepts and to clear up misconceptions as he organizes his impressions.

Recalling and *remembering* involve making associations. Children enjoy recalling what they did once or what they saw then they were on a walk or trip. "Remember the fire engine...." or, "Remember the baby colt and how he looked...." It is good to be able to think about what one has experienced. It helps one learn and it helps one solve problems sometimes. "Remember when you..." may help the child find a solution to the problem of how to make an airplane. Deciding what he needs to finish his airplane or boat may necessitate recalling what materials he used before and where he found them. He begins to do planning this way.

Recalling will depend on *giving attention* in the first place. The teacher may introduce games that depend on paying attention and remembering, such as a game in which the child first looks carefully at some objects placed in front of him, then closes his eyes while one of these is removed, and, when he looks again, tries to remember the name of the missing object.

Many times children will suprise us by the new patterns they see or the associations they make. Seeing patterns in relationships is a high order of thinking. Children often have a fresh approach that can be nurtured by our appreciation.

LANGUAGE

Increasing the child's competence in the use of language is an important part of any program for young children. Social relations of all kinds are extended and improved as speech develops. Language is necessary for higher forms of thought processes.

Early Stages in Language Learning

Learning to talk is a complex learning and parents rightfully feel that the baby's first words mark a milestone in his development. A great deal of cognitive growth has taken place to make it possible. Yet it is worth noting that the ordinary, healthy child learns to talk without any formal teaching if he is in an environment where he hears plenty of speech.

The infant communicates by crying and by body movements, including mouth movements. He wriggles all over with delight when he is pleased. He stretches out his arms for what he wants and later he will point. He vocalizes and blows bubbles. His mouth movements and his other body movements tend to resemble those of his mother as she talks with him. He pays attention to sounds and uses visual cues in understanding meanings. He begins to understand that a word stands for an object long before he himself uses the word. His mother has used the word "bottle" as she brings it to him, and he understands.

As he moves into the stage in which he is becoming aware of the permanence of objects, the fact that something exists even when he cannot see it, he recalls the bottle when he hears the word. The word calls up the image, an important function of language. Without the experience the word is of no use to him. When he comes to the stage of using words, he can communicate the idea of "bottle" by using the word himself or some reasonable attempt at the word, another significant achievement. It is interesting to note that for a long time the gesture is still the preferred method of communication if the object is in sight.

In the early stages a word often stands for a whole object or an experience. The word "hot," for example, may mean the stove as well as the heat it gives off and the warning given to control action. With more experience the child will discover that the word refers to only one attribute of a stove and can be applied to other objects.

In this sensorimotor stage of development nothing takes the place of a wide variety of appropriate firsthand experiences with an object if the child is to develop concepts about it. The child needs to see, to touch, to taste, and to do something with the object if he is to understand its nature and the meaning of the label attached to it. If, for example, he can roll a ball, sit on it, bounce it, watch it float in water or sink, and bite it, and if he can use several different types of balls, he stores up impressions which make up a more complete concept of "ball." He *knows* about balls. As adults we still learn in this firsthand way although we have added other ways of knowing.

Individual Differences in Use of Speech

In any group of three-year-old children we observe great individual differences in the children's competence with language and their verbal "styles." Some children are always talking as they play. They sing or talk to themselves. When they are with other children, they chatter with them, describing what they are doing, giving directions, agreeing and disagreeing. Other children use very few words in the same situations, going quietly about the business of play although they show that they understand and are listening to what is being said. They give themselves less practice with speech. They may have other interests at the moment.

We can appreciate how much children are influenced by the speech they hear when we listen to the telephone conversations carried on during play in the housekeeping corner in a nursery school. Some children carry on long conversations about going to work, caring for babies, arranging parties. Other children, probably from homes where language use is restricted, tend to be monosyllabic in their telephone conversations. They are the children who may need some help in the nursery school if they are to develop competence with language.

We know that the child needs (1) variety and richness in experience, adapted to his level of understanding, (2) many experiences with speech, hearing speech and trying out the forms of speech, if he is to develop competence in the use of speech. Mothers and teachers encourage children's speech by talking with them, by paying attention when the child speaks and by responding appropriately, so that the communication is rewarding for them both.

The Young Child Develops Competence Without Being Corrected

An interesting finding in one recent study on language is that at home mothers do very little correcting of a young child's speech. They may correct errors of fact, but they tend to ignore errors in speech. Cazden, who has done extensive research on how children learn to speak, considers that the commonsense view that holds that children learn a language by imitation and by having errors corrected is a myth. Learning by imitation and by correction is true only in a general sense, according to Cazden. Children appear to imitate some people and not others, depending on the affectional ties. They pick their own speech models, and correction does not occur often enough at home to be an important factor in speech development.

The Logic of Children's Speech

Each child goes through stages in learning to talk which are strikingly similar from child to child and quite different from the adult speech that they hear. Children themselves are actively discovering language and trying to make some sense out of its structure. In this effort they apply their own logic to the structure. At one stage, for example, almost all children will say "foots," or "mouses." These are not words they are likely to have heard, but it shows that they have observed that an "s" is used with plurals. They try applying this rule, a logical operation, only later to discover that there are exceptions. The same thing happens when they reach the conclusion that past tense is indicated by "-ed" and they begin saying "comed," "goed," "teached."

In the situation given on pages 154–156 we have an example. We see how some of these children corrected their own mistakes. Pam, seeing the mice, called excitedly to the others, "Look, mices." Jason ran over to see and called to his companions, "Come and see the mouses." Later Pam, sitting with her elbows on the table while she watched the mice closely, suddenly asked, "When will the mice grow up?" In phrasing her question Pam shows us that she had become aware of the correct singular and plural forms and had corrected her own usage. She had taken this step on her own, adding to her confidence in herself as an independent learner. Jason remained at the "mouses" stage, not yet ready for this discovery in language structure.

The attempt to construct a logical grammar is evidence of an advance in thinking, although it may seem more like a regression. It drops out as the child adds to his observations. All this goes on, not in any conscious way, of course, but as a formulation out of tacit knowledge from experience such as we all continue to do through life in the attempt to make sense out of things.

Coming to a conclusion by one's own efforts sets a constructive pattern for learning in the future. The child is more likely to remember what he himself has discovered. Correcting the child and calling attention to his errors tends to put him on the defensive unless he is a very confident child. It may take away from the excitement of learning. The healthy child is an eager learner unless he is corrected too often and discouraged in making the effort.

Cognitive Skills Developed by the Need to Master Language

There is some evidence, as a result of recent studies in early language development, that "certain cognitive skills are exercised and thereby developed solely because of the need to master language."* While it is enough for the child to use his senses to discover the meaning of many words, he begins to meet words which he cannot understand by this method. He must deal with words like "how" and "why" by some other means. He uses the word in order to get enough "feedback" to build a concept of its meaning. As Blank has put it, the child must "engage in a concentrated course of hypothesis testing." To do this he keeps asking a lot of "why" and "how" types of questions. From the answers he gets, he begins to attach some meaning to abstract terms about relationships or purposes.

The Importance of Questions

It is worth noting that mastering the question form is an evidence of intellectual growth. The question itself gives us clues as to the child's level of thinking. All this makes question-answering an important matter, deserving thought and attention. Pam's interesting question in the situation with the mice, "When will they grow up?", reveals that she is working on the aspect of time. The teacher's answer in this case was, "In about two weeks. Mice grow very fast." The answer was correct but probably very inadequate for Pam's concerns. How long is two weeks? Evidently it is connected with "fast." She will go on searching. Pam is nearly five and will be going to kindergarten soon. The teacher might have asked, "Are you thinking about growing up and going to a new school?" This might have led to a discussion on a subject important to Pam.

Examples of areas in which understanding is limited at first until a level of language and of cognitive development has been reached are those relating to time and relationships. Pam had difficulty comprehending "short time." Young children are often confused about time intervals, days of the week, years, phrases like "a little while ago." Until children have asked questions, tested out the answers, corrected and refined their understanding, they cannot appreciate the meaning of these concepts. Maria, mentioned on page 214, did not understand in any general way a term about a relationship. She reasoned from her own experience about the word "grandmother." A grandmother is someone who cares about you but does not live with you.

When the Language at Home is Different

A special situation exists in any group where some of the children speak a language other than English as their first language, or speak a dialect other than

---

*Blank, Marion: Cognitive functions of language in the preschool years. Developmental Psychology, Vol. 10, No. 2, 1974.

standard English. These children are faced with the necessity of becoming competent in understanding a second language, or another dialect.

Gone are the days, we hope, when children were not allowed to use their home language in school. All children should be encouraged to use all the speech they have. When a child does not speak English, it is important that the child or children have someone in the school who speaks their language. If the language of the minority group happens to be Spanish, for example, there should be a Spanish-speaking teacher to talk with them, help with explanations, and encourage them in learning to become able to use English. If there is no Spanish-speaking teacher there may be a volunteer who speaks the language and can spend some time in the group.

Using some Spanish, in this case, in the school or center will help the English-speaking children learn about language differences and begin learning some Spanish themselves. Songs and games and stories in Spanish along with ones in English open the door for more language learning, an opportunity much needed by American children whose experience with other languages is usually limited. Children learn readily at this age if all languages are respected and valued. A school with a mixture of nationalities has a chance to broaden the experience of all its children.

When the whole group consists of Spanish-speaking children they adjust more readily if the language of the school is Spanish at first and if English is introduced as a second language. There is considerable information about teaching English as a second language which may be helpful to the teacher in this situation. The teacher herself must be bilingual.

Other countries have problems with mixture of languages. In Malaysia, for example, there are three "official" school languages. For the first three years in school the children are taught in the language of their home, with Malay as a second language. After the third year all the teaching is in Malay, but the children are still free to talk as they wish outside of lessons.*

Question of Dialects

Other questions arise when there are children in the group who speak a dialect other than standard English. Here again, it is important to respect the child's home dialect. Our attitudes are changing today because of recent studies in the area of language. These studies seem to indicate that all dialects are "systematic, highly structured language codes," different from but not inferior to one another. "The language variety one learns simply reflects where and with whom one lives, not the intelligence with which one is endowed."† Black dialect itself arose out of the culture of black people when this culture came in contact with white, western culture. Dialects have developed in some American Indian groups in the same way.

---

*Cynthia Parsons: Christian Science Monitor, November 25, 1974.

†Cazden, Courtney, Baratz, Joan, Labov, William, and Palmer, Francis: Language development in day-care programs. *In*, Cazden, Courteny (ed.): Language in Early Childhood Education. Copyright © 1972, National Association for the Education of Young Children, 1834 Connecticut Avenue N.W., Washington, D.C. 20009.

Since it may be important for children to be able to speak standard English if they are to compete in an English-speaking country, the nursery school should help a child toward competency in speaking standard English, while he remains comfortable with his home language or dialect.

There are choices open in language teaching, and the parents and the community itself should understand what these choices are. They should have a part in deciding what kind of emphasis they want in the education of both minority and majority groups in respect to language in the schools.

There are many specific kinds of language programs on the market today with diverse methods as well as objectives.* The teacher needs to inform herself and offer what seems most suitable to the needs and desires of her group.

An Environment that Facilitates Language Learning

We feel sure of some points: 1. Children learn the words they put to use, so we encourage speech and give children a great deal to talk about. For example, at lunch the teacher may encourage children to recall their experiences, saying, "Do you remember when . . . " and encourage each one to recount his version, or to make plans for the future. 2. Talking with other children in play tends to stimulate more extensive and more sustained speech than talk with adults, in most cases, so we provide plenty of opportunity for play, especially for sociodramatic play among children. 3. One-to-one conversation between a child and an adult on a subject of real interest to the child advances development in more complex forms of speech, so the teacher takes time for conversation with individual children.

Ways in Which the Teacher Promotes Language Competence

The teacher is a "model" for the children in speech. They identify with her, and her warmth and responsiveness encourages their speech expression. Frequent staff changes hinder this identification. Continuity in contact is essential for speech growth as well as for personality growth.

The teacher stimulates children's growth in language competence in many ways:

1. The teacher herself uses *complete sentences* with *explicit words*, as "Please bring me the red truck on the top shelf," rather than "Please bring that truck over there." The child has a pattern of exact speech in the first but not in the second example. A good reference here is an article "The Right Words" by McAfee.†

2. The teacher uses *variety* in her own speech, saying the same thing in different ways, or using new words as she talks. She *expands* the ideas being discussed, bringing in new but related ideas.

---

*Bartlett, Elsa: Selecting preschool language programs. *In* Cazden, Courtney (ed.): Language in Early Childhood Education. Washington, D.C., National Association for the Education of Young Children, 1972.

†McAfee, Oralie: The right words. Young Children, November, 1967.

3. She asks *open-ended* questions as, "What do you think will happen now?" instead of, "Do you think it will melt?"

4. Above all, she *listens* to the child's speech, responding relevantly. Meeting with indifference when one speaks is discouraging to anyone.

5. She *"monitors"* her conversations with the children occasionally to find out who does the most talking, she or the child, and to become aware of any tendencies to talk more to the verbal child who responds than to the quiet child who may be more in need of speech stimulation.

6. She provides the learning opportunities but she *encourages* the children to do the *talking* and *questioning* themselves. Children learn most from active participating and not from being talked to. She may call their attention to things they may have overlooked, or clear up misconceptions, but she does not give out information where there is no interest. There is a difference between saying, "When we mix yellow and blue, we get green," and saying "I wonder what is going to happen when we mix these two colors, yellow and blue" or saying, "Water runs downhill" as opposed to saying, "Where did the water go when you poured it?"

7. She avoids being "an agent for social improvement" by passing judgment with remarks such as, "That's not nice," which serve to leave the child speechless. Instead she may say, "What's the trouble?", which helps the child verbalize and look at what really has happened.

8. The teacher takes *time for conversation* with individual children on subjects of interest to them. In doing this she gives added experience with speech. "While the quality of (verbal) interaction is far more important than the quantity, still prolonged back and forth interaction contributes to the growth of language complexity, particularly if it is varied and rich."*

9. Above all, the teacher plans *activities* which promote language. These will include such things as providing plenty of time, space, and props for dramatic play. Sociodramatic play is an excellent stimulus to speech production, as are small-group projects such as cooking or a major construction project. The teacher uses games such as guessing games, describing objects, finishing a story. Puppet play necessitates language as simple role playing does for older children. *Excursions* to places of interest stimulate conversation, as do *reading* stories and poems and *telling stories* to children. The child can talk about the pictures in a book. The teacher can question, "What do you suppose she is doing?" Interruptions while reading are welcomed for their language values. The teacher will develop skill in knowing the point at which she must turn back and continue the reading.

Feelings Can Be Expressed in Words

Feelings as well as thoughts can be expressed in words. The child takes an important step in controlling his feelings when he can put them into words rather than expressing them through action only. He can ask for what he wants rather

---

*Mattick, Ilse: The teacher's role in helping young children develop language competency. *In* Cazden, Courtney (ed.): Language in Early Childhood Education. Copyright © 1972, National Association for the Education of Young Children. 1834 Connecticut Avenue N.W., Washington, D.C. 20009.

than grab. He can express his anger in words rather than blows. He can express sorrow and pleasure.

Good feelings can be described, too. A mother who was sensitive to feelings and communicated well told this story about her small son. He loved apricots and felt bad when the apricot season was over. He often asked for an apricot, and each time she told him, "There will be some apricots next spring. When spring comes, we will have more apricots." One day she found apricots in the market and picked out a delicious ripe apricot. When she got home, she said to her little boy, "Close your eyes and open your mouth. I have a surprise," and as he did so she popped a juicy, ripe apricot into his mouth. He took a bite and exclaimed with delight, "Now I know what spring tastes like!"

We will discuss more about language as an avenue for self-expression in a section to follow on *The Arts*.

The verbal child has an advantage over the less verbal child. We clarify our ideas and our feelings when we express them. Young children who are reproved for talking, whatever the circumstances, may get into the habit of avoiding expressing themselves verbally. We should think carefully before we say to a child, "Keep still." It may be better to say, "Talk later."

In addition to all that the teacher does, she may help the child by what she does *not* do. Although she tries to promote his language development, she does not push it. Too much emphasis on verbal skill at first may discourage expression. The teacher enriches the child's language environment, but she does not overemphasize it or emphasize it at the expense of playfulness and spontaneity in approaching experience.

Special Problems with Speech

Some children may withdraw from trying to communicate because they are afraid or resentful or disturbed in different ways. The teacher's task here is that of building a relationship of trust with the child before doing anything direct about his speech.

Some children may stutter or stammer in speaking. Stuttering is a common occurrence in young children. They are eager to communicate, but they have not developed enough control of the speech muscles to get the words out rapidly. The teacher helps this child by giving her undivided attention when he is speaking so that he feels less need to hurry. She will speak slowly when she herself talks to him. The child may come from a home where the parents speak rapidly, setting a pattern that is hard for him to imitate. The teacher will also try to make sure that any strains or pressures on the child are reduced. Frequent stuttering is a sign of strain in the child. A real problem in speech may develop if too many pressures continue. Every young child does some stuttering in the proces of learning to use speech. Nothing should be done about it directly. Calling the child's attention to the stuttering by asking him to speak more slowly may make him conscious of it. He becomes afraid of stuttering and more likely to continue it. The child who is free of undue pressures will stop stuttering as he becomes better able to control his speech muscles.

There are children, too, who have defects of articulation in speech. They may have difficulty in saying letters like "r" or "th." The teacher helps these children by pronouncing the letter very clearly herself, repeating the word the child has said rather than asking him to repeat it. She wants him to hear the correct pronunciation and, in time, to imitate it without interfering with his spontaneity in verbal communication.

The whole nursery school curriculum plays a part in increasing the child's competence with language by offering him experiences to talk about and people to talk with. Speech is an important tool for expression, communication, and thought.

LITERATURE

✓ Experiences with books are part of the daily program in a good nursery school. A variety of well-chosen books should always be available under conditions that will encourage their proper use./

In selecting books the teacher will find the *Horn Book* magazine a source of help in becoming acquainted with the new books being published for children, and with children's literature in general. The children's librarian in the local public library is an important source of help to use in selecting books. Most schools will depend on the library for many of their books. The books can be selected with the interests of individual children in mind, and the books can be changed frequently.

Bookshelves or a rack for books with plenty of table space and chairs adjacent make it possible for a child to look at books comfortably. A heap of picture books piled on a small table can only lead to misuse of the books. Children cannot be expected to handle books carefully if the space is crowded; nor can they be expected to be interested in them for long if they are not comfortable as they use them.

A few colorful books laid out on a table near the bookshelf may serve to attract the children's attention to the books. Adding a new book or changing the selection available stimulates interest. Reading groups should be small, for the child likes to be close to the teacher and the book. He is easily distracted in a large group where he does not have this closeness. Reading need not be confined to one story period. Some children will want many opportunities to listen to stories, while others may not. Small informal groups formed when there is an interest meet these needs. In pleasant weather, reading can be done outdoors in a shady spot, and the new location creates new interest.

Books Should Fit the Interests of the Children

Variety in the books selected for the nursery school library is important, for children differ in their interests just as we do. I remember one little boy who showed no interest in books. He had evidently had few experiences with books at home, or else his experiences had been with books that were not suited to his level of development. But he did like cars, and one day he found a small book about cars. He looked at it carefully for a long time and then asked the teacher to read it to him while he listened attentively. For days he carried this book around. Sometimes he would stop and find someone to read it to him again. Then he

Discovering books.

Courtesy of Marianne Hurlbut.

began enjoying other books and joining the group when they listened to stories. Through the one book which was related to his interest, he had begun to discover the world of books.

This case illustrates the importance of having books that are related to the children's individual interests. Each nursery school group will enjoy a somewhat different selection of books, depending on their particular environment and the experiences they have had. Books about trains will be popular in one place, and books about boats in another. Everywhere, children will enjoy books about boys and girls and animal pets, for they are all familiar with these subjects.

Books Should Present the Familiar World

In selecting books we must remember that the function of books for the young child is not to present new information, but to re-create for him the world he knows and by re-creation to strengthen his understanding of it. New knowledge should come from firsthand experiences and not from the printed page. We will find many city children thinking of milk as coming from a bottle no matter how many stories they have heard about the cow and her contribution to the bottle. Stories about cows have more meaning after a trip to the barn. Books like *Let's Go Outside* present information that can be used in connection with experiences in the garden. It is fun for the children to find the pictures of earthworms and read about them after having discovered worms in their digging, or to find the picture of tadpoles when there are some tadpoles swimming in the bowl at school. Whatever the children's experiences, they can be broadened and enriched through books related to those experiences.

In the past there have been many books which presented an unrealistic picture of the world. All the children in the stories were white, for example; all mothers worked at home. Today we have more books for children which present the world that the child is likely to be experiencing. Bernstein, in an article, "Books for Young Children,"* lists some examples.† There are other books for children which picture men and boys in care-giving roles.‡

Poetry Has an Important Place

Books of poetry are important in the nursery school library. Children can appreciate the beauty and imagery of good poetry. They need to be introduced to it early and hear it read with expression. They love the rhythmic quality of words, the alliteration and repetition that are all part of poetry, beginning with the Mother Goose rhymes and going on to the delightful verse of A. A. Milne or John Ciardi. Children who are familiar with good poetry will often go on to create beauty with words themselves. Poetry may become a lifelong source of enjoyment for them.

Books Should Be Attractive and Interestingly Presented

Books which are desirable for the nursery school not only are about familiar, everyday subjects, but also are short and written in simple, correct English with many clear illustrations in color. There are many books which are reputedly for young children but which fail to hold their interest because they are not attractive in appearance and their vocabulary is above the child's level. The child who has these books will be less likely to develop an interest in them. He will be handicapped, for there are advantages in liking books. Much of what we learn later in life will be through books.

When we present stories to children, we should read slowly so that children have no difficulty in understanding. Anyone who has tried to follow a conversation in a foreign language with which he is not too familiar will understand how difficult even the ordinary rate of speech may be for the child who is listening to reading. As we read, we need to remember that children are still in the process of learning the language. We must read slowly and with inflections that will clarify the meaning as well as add interest and variety. In telling stories one has the ad-

---

*Bernstein, Joanne: Books for young children. Young Children, September, 1974.

†Adoff, Arnold: Black Is Brown Is Tan. (Emily McCully, illus.) New York, Harper & Row, Publishers, 1973; Wells, Rosemary: Noisy Nora. New York, Dial Press, 1973; Lasker, Joe: He's My Brother. New York, Albert Whitman, 1974; Rockwell, Harlow: My Doctor. New York, Macmillan Publishing Co., Inc., 1973.

‡Zoloton, Charlotte: A Father Like That. (Ben Schecter, illus.) New York, Harper & Row, Publishers, 1971; Zoloton, Charlotte: William's Doll. (W. P. Dubri, illus.) New York, Harper & Row, Publishers, 1972.

Courtesy of Jean Berlfein.

The group is absorbed in listening to a story.

vantage of being able to keep closer to the audience. Telling as well as reading stories is an ability which every teacher should work to develop.

Effect of the Story on the Child Deserves to Be Considered

We have mentioned realistic stories as suitable for nursery school. The suitability of "fairy tales" and imaginative tales in general may well be raised here. Folk and fairy tales formerly constituted almost the entire literary fare available to children, along with the moralistic tale. If one has a chance to look at samples of early literature for children, one will realize how much change there has been in books for children in the last hundred years. John Newberry, the so-called father of children's literature, who first took advantage of the market in children's books, published the pocket books of the eighteenth century. He was obliged to throw in sonnets from Shakespeare along with his Mother Goose to make it acceptable to the buying public of those days.

In selecting books today we are helped by the fact that we know more about children's development, including such facts as that rousing fear in them is damaging, that there is a readiness factor in learning, that children need help in understanding the world around them rather than in having it confused by things that are fanciful. These facts have changed our ideas about what constitute suitable books for children. We now feel that it is better to omit frightening elements from stories until the child has had time to develop secure feelings and confidence in his ability to meet the real world and to distinguish the possible from the impossible. This doesn't mean that stories for the child should lack action and suspense, but that terrifying elements should be left out. This, of course, precludes the use of stories like "Jack and the Bean Stalk" or "Little Red Riding Hood" with most nursery school children. Some children will, of course, be readier at an earlier age than others for folk tales, depending on their level of emotional development. The price of introducing such stories too early may be disturbed sleep and a child more timid than he need be in facing the new and unknown.

Fanciful, unreal stories are better left until the child has had time to form a sound concept of what the real world is like. Imagination is fun when it is a play between the real and the unreal. Listen to the children's "jokes" to gain some concept of what is real and unreal to them. "How would you like to eat a horse?" draws a big laugh because they can perceive how impossible such a thing could be. They laugh at things like this because they know that they are not true, but what do they know about wolves and giants and what they might or might not do?

There are many unreal stories on bookshelves which make poor reading material for children. There are many stories of animals dressing and talking like people which are decidedly not among the best in books for children. As one child remarked, "I wonder why they make them talk like that."

Many imaginative stories are on the young child's level. "Karl's Wooden Horse" is an example of a delightful, first fairy tale with a wish fulfillment element and a safe ending of being welcomed home after an adventure that will be appreciated by most four-year-olds. It constitutes a good beginning in the realm of the unreal where the child is still on "safe" ground. Perhaps we do not need to be too eager to offer fanciful stories to children. The real world is certainly sufficiently wonderful to stimulate the imagination of any preschool child. It is important that it be understood and that the child feel related to it. We need to look for books which will help him to understand it better and which will do this with artistry and humor.

THE SCIENCES: MATHEMATICS, PHYSICAL AND BIOLOGICAL SCIENCE, SOCIAL STUDIES, AND TRIPS

"I wonder what's wrong with this puzzle. I'll have to figure this out." Mike has discovered some puzzles in nursery school. They are new to him, but he has learned that there are ways of mastering problems. He has confidence that he can figure things out. He uses a scientific approach.

Children in favorable environments come in contact with many science experiences. The young child runs downhill and falls. He tries to pull a loaded wagon up the hill. He watches snow melt in the sun. He discovers a worm as he digs. He feeds a leaf of lettuce to the bunny. He watches a bulb sprout and finally blossom. He becomes aware of numbers, too. He has three candles on his birthday cake when he is three years old. He needs two blocks to finish his building.

Out of all these experiences the child develops ideas about the nature of the world. The teacher in nursery school helps him extend these ideas, not only the

A magnet fascinates this boy.

Courtesy of Jean Berlfein.

opportunities she provides for added experiences, but also by her comments and questions that give more meaning to what he is experiencing. We will look at each area in turn in this section.

MATHEMATICS

As children play, they handle objects and become aware of quantity. They store up impressions of amounts and relationships that are essential for later stages in understanding mathematical concepts. Piaget has made it very clear through his observations that learning to count does not mean that the child has an understanding of the numbers. He gains this from his experiences. He "knows" two from having had many different experiences with two. He has two hands and two feet. At the table there is a chair for him and one for his friend. The teacher says, "Here are two chairs for two boys." Later she may say, "How many chairs do we need?" or, "How many cups?" The teacher may count the number of cups as the child puts them on the table. Learning to count is a tool for organizing impressions about quantity. It is of value when it is related to a concrete experience.

As the child plays with blocks, he finds that he can fill the space with one large block or two small ones. Two small blocks are equal to one large one. He may use many blocks. When he goes to the shelf for more, he estimates what he will need for the building. He "knows" this in an implicit way because he has done a lot of building in the past. The teacher may make it more explicit, saying, "You needed four blocks that time to finish."

The child playing in the doll corner selects the biggest doll. Then she sorts the doll clothes and finds the ones that fit this doll, discarding the smaller sizes. Children playing at the clay table want a lot of clay. They try to divide it, and one says, "You have more," or "Yours is the biggest." They are having experiences which are part of understanding in mathematics.

In the sand area a child arranges containers in a row on the ledge, filling them with sand. As he fills them, he perceives that they need different amounts. It takes much more sand to fill the big container than it does to fill the little one. The teacher may comment on these differences and on the relation of size and amount. He may line the containers up in order from the biggest to the smallest.

In the housekeeping corner a child may line up the doll dishes and survey them with satisfaction. There are a lot! In contrast there are only a few cooking utensils. He may match the cups and saucers. He may fit the lids on the cooking dishes. Things sometimes come in sets. The teacher may comment, "There are four pans and four lids, a lid for each pan."

The teacher weighs each child and measures his height. How many pounds does he weigh? How many inches high is each one? With a balance scale available, the child has a chance to weigh things and to compare weights. The teacher helps him put into words what he is discovering.

Courtesy of Jean Berlfein.

How long is the space?

The teacher provides measuring cups—one-cup, two-cup, or four-cup sizes—and measuring spoons. There are measurements to be made in cooking. It takes a cup of water to soften this much jello. A teaspoonful of salt is needed here, and two tablespoonfuls of sugar. The child at the workbench uses a ruler to measure the length of the piece he needs to complete his airplane. He measures it and saws the piece to measure.

There are many other situations in which the child makes estimates of quantity, the number of crayons the box will hold as he puts away the crayons, the amount of juice to pour into the cup, or the size of the serving on his plate. With the guidance of an alert teacher the nursery school offers many experiences that give children a basis for understanding mathematical concepts.

PHYSICAL SCIENCE

Every child is interested in how things happen and where things come from. There are many opportunities in the simple, daily experiences of children to build up a fund of knowledge about the nature of the physical world around them. A child tries to pull a heavy load in his wagon, and the teacher says, "It is too heavy. It will be lighter and easier to pull if you take off the big block." He begins to know what "heavy" means and something about weight and bulk.

He explores many aspects of a wheel, for example. He rides the wheel toys and discovers differences in the ease of riding wheel toys of different sizes. He pulls and pushes toys on wheels. He steers with the wheel. He turns the wagon upside down and tries the wheel, watching it rotate freely. He slows it down. He uses a pulley, pulling objects up and lowering them.

He wonders about many aspects of nature, the snow falling, hail bouncing on the roof or sidewalk, the rain evaporating in the sun and staying on the damp grass under the shade of the tree, the force of the wind that blew off the top of his shelter. He may blow soap bubbles outdoors and watch their colors and the direction they take as they float and burst. The teacher will give him simple explanations and suggest ways to find out more about the things that interest him. She will raise other questions.

BIOLOGICAL SCIENCE

Children are interested in all living things. They enjoy watching growth and the changes it brings. In an earlier chapter we saw how teachers helped children in a city nursery school extend their knowledge of seasonal changes.

A garden offers rich opportunities for learning and extending concepts about plant life. Children enjoy digging and planting seeds. There are many kinds of seeds, from the tiny carrot seed to the big, wrinkled nasturtium seed. They find seeds in pods as they gather nuts, peas, or beans. Picking fruit from a low tree and gathering the products of a garden are satisfying experiences when they are possible for children. But beans can be sprouted in a jar, and children can watch the unfolding of seeds kept moist in a dish. Bulbs will grow and flower in a window. The teacher and the children can talk about what they have planted and what will happen. Some children will participate eagerly, with a sustained interest. Others will show only a casual interest, but all will gain something.

There are seasonal changes to be noted in the garden. The leaves fall and can be gathered or heaped into piles for play. The children discover roots as they dig in the ground. They pick flowers or sprays of berries in the fall. At Christmas time there is a tree to decorate and to dance around and they can enjoy its fragrance and beauty.

Watching pets and caring for them gives children a chance to learn more about animals, how they eat, how they sleep, eliminate, and reproduce. The child is curious about many things. He can observe and discuss these things with other children and with the teacher. Fish need to be fed only occasionally, while the rabbit and the chickens are hungry many times a day. The bird splashes in his bath, but the baby ducks go right into the water. The turtle moves very slowly, and the bird has to be kept in his cage because he flies away so fast and so far. Tadpoles slowly change into frogs. The baby chick is fluffy at first, but it finally grows feathers like the hen. There are many similarities and many differences among the animals children observe. These experiences make up a background for understanding.

In one school it was usually possible each spring to have a lamb for a few weeks. The children loved to give the lamb his bottle of milk in the morning. He would play with them and often managed to slip in an unguarded door and make straight for the kitchen, the direction from which his bottle appeared, to the delight of the children. A young kid one spring proved as adept as the children

Courtesy of Jean Berlfein.

Friends share easily and take turns.

on the walking boards and in jumping over boxes. The children enjoyed his companionship.

When there are pets in a nursery school, it is important to have adequate provisions for caring for them, a proper shelter, pens that can be cleaned easily and thoroughly. This, too, is part of what children need to learn about animals.

Trips to a farm to see other animals are sometimes possible, a cow with a calf, or sheep and pigs. It is sometimes possible to visit a hatchery at a time when chicks are hatching in the incubators. All these things extend the children's experiences.

Children in the city may extend their experiences with animals through visits to the zoo. Many zoos today have an area, planned for children, in which there are barnyard animals and other animals that can be petted and played with. City gardens may be limited to window boxes, but the feel and the smell of earth and the growing plants can still be there; only the space is restricted.

Where Children Are Having Experiences with Animals, They Come in Contact with the Fact of Death

If the children are having many experiences with animals, they are sure on some occasion to come into contact with the fact of death. The baby rats sometimes die, or a dog may get in and kill a chicken. The children may see a dead lamb when they visit the barn during lambing season, or they may discover a dead bird in the yard.

In their response to these experiences the children will reflect the attitudes of the adults with them. There is no need to hide the fact of death from children, or to try to escape from facing it with them. It is a mystery, like life, and sometimes far less of a tragedy. The children will want to understand why the animal died, and they may be helped in their acceptance of the reality of death by touching and feeling to see how the dead animal differs from the living ones they have known. They will not be greatly disturbed if the adult with them does not feel the need to dramatize or distort or escape from the fact of death herself. If the children can be helped to have sound, reassuring experiences in this area, they will be helped to face life as well as death with less fear.

Questions about Babies

All children are interested in the subject of where babies come from and how they grow. They are really interested in how they themselves were born. They are trying to develop concepts about where they came from and how they got here. They need simple, factual information on the subject. Occasions for giving this may arise when the pets in the school reproduce, and the children follow the sequence of events.

Children need to feel that it is all right to be interested and to ask questions on the subject of birth. The teacher needs to answer questions freely and with appreciation for the great significance of the subject for children. She will not burden them with more information than they want at any one point, but she will make sure that they are given information when they want it. The information is needed in small doses, with time to digest it, and with many repetitions. The teacher will listen to conversations among the children on the subject and will be ready to clear up misconceptions. She will give simple information, "Babies start growing from an egg inside the mother. The father starts the egg growing."

If the female rabbit is expecting babies, the children can help care for her. "We will take care of her while the babies are growing inside her. We don't know how many babies there will be. The mother rabbit will pull out some of her fur to make a nest when it is time for the babies to be born." This will lead to other discussions and speculation about other babies. Discussions about where they came from and how they were born will follow—how each one of them grew from an egg inside their mother, fertilized or started growing by the father and protected inside the mother until they were big enough to be on their own outside.

Before offering information in answer to questions here, the wise teacher will herself ask the child, "What do you think happens?"* When the teacher understands what the child is imagining or how he is interpreting matters, she is in a better position to clear up his misconceptions and to give him the information he really is seeking at the moment. The teacher may comment to clear up points, but she will understand that it takes time to build correct concepts, and she will not discourage thinking. We need only remember the richness of myth and legend that has come from attempts in the past to account for the wonder of creation.

Watching a mother nurse a baby is a fascinating experience for children who have not had baby brothers or sisters, as we can see in the pictures. The group of children watching the mother nursing her baby are absorbed in what they see. It

---

*Refer to Selma Fraiberg's chapter on "Education for Love" in her book, The Magic Years. New York, Charles Scribner's Sons, 1959.

A

All children are interested in babies. *A*, Seeing a baby nursing is a new experience for this child.

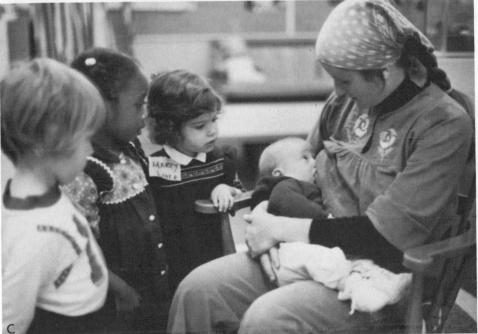

Courtesy of Jean Berlfein.

B, The mother understands. She explains to the group and they listen. The mother is a trustworthy source of information. *C*, They have accurate information. All watch the baby nursing.

seems apparent that the child in the first picture has never seen an infant nursing before. Her response is one of astonishment. The mother explains, and all the children look at her intently. The mother is a trustworthy source of information. This mother seems "in tune" with the children and is enjoying their interest. After the explanation all quietly watch the baby nursing, completely wrapped up in the wonder of the experience. Attitudes are being formed. The children are getting accurate information.

A few children who are interested may enjoy looking at pictures of prenatal growth in a book such as *The Story of a Baby,* by Marie Ets. There are other books with stories about babies, which all children will enjoy hearing. Conversations about babies are very important for young children. There may be negative feelings expressed. The teacher should listen with respect, without discouraging such expressions, but she can suggest other interpretations or aspects, for there are both positive and negative sides to any experience.

Gaining some understanding about reproduction is an important part of learning in the nursery school years.

SOCIAL STUDIES

Children live in a community, and they want to understand it. We see how often they work on trying to understand the roles of different people as they play. In dramatic play they include not only the family roles but also those of firemen, policemen, bus drivers, taxi drivers, service station attendants, garage mechanics, airplane pilots, astronauts, and the milkman or the postman. The teacher helps them by talking over questions of interest such as where daddies or mothers work, or what policemen or firemen do. She has books and stories and pictures, and she also tries to give them real experiences with these people as a basis for better understanding the roles of people in a society.

Children's experiences may be enriched by having visitors come to the school, or by trips. The person who delivers the milk or the groceries may be willing to stop and talk with interested children. A friendly police officer may be able to stop by for a visit so that children can ask him questions, learn his name, and show him their school. He can help them build a positive concept about the role of the police officer. The mail carrier, the taxi driver, the service station attendant, the checker in a grocery shop are people whom we take for granted, but they are new people to children. Meeting them, talking to them, watching them carry out their work, will serve to make community services better understood by the children.

Children see these people at work as they go on walks or trips outside the school. They can talk about what they see and reenact these roles in their play, later. When visits to a fire station are not possible, the fire chief may be willing to come to the school and bring some of his equipment to show the children. A father or mother may bring the tools he or she uses or a product he or she makes so that children will have clearer ideas of what people do at work. It may be possible to arrange a trip to places where parents work, such as a store or packing house or bottling plant.

Understanding Cultural Differences

Another aspect of the social studies curriculum is that of helping the children become acquainted with differences among people. America is especially rich in the variety of races and nationalities living within its borders. We have white Americans and black Americans and yellow Americans. Our ancestors came from many countries. Our children need to be aware of their American heritage and to feel pride in it. Accepting these differences and helping to maintain the different cultural traditions here is a way of strengthening the nation and the individuals in it.

Some nursery schools are fortunate in having children of different racial origins within the group. Children in these schools "know" that all people do not have the same color of skin or hair, that they do not all dress or eat or even respond in the same way, but that they do all go to the same school and make friends with people there. If every child feels that his differences are accepted, he can readily accept differences in others. They can all enjoy what these differences may offer. They may enjoy eating different "ethnic" foods and thus become more aware of differences in eating patterns among peoples. They may have a piñata party with the help of the Mexican children and their parents. They may have the experience of lighting the candles for Hanukkah, along with an explanation given by parents of the Jewish children. They can celebrate Christmas in many ways and make presents for their parents.

In schools that do not have children with different cultural backgrounds, the teacher can broaden the children's experience by bringing in visitors. There may be someone from Japan or from India who will come in her native costume and share stories or songs or games from his or her childhood. Foods from these countries can perhaps be prepared by a visitor and the children. If the school does not have children with different skin colors, a black American or an American Indian may visit to sing or play an instrument or tell stories and share a meal with the children.

It is important to give children the opportunity to know from their own experience that people are different. The children themselves are different, but they are all growing up in the same country in one world.

Festivals and Holidays

In helping the children understand the meaning of festivals and holidays, the teacher must first be familiar with the cultural patterns of the area. In a neighborhood with a mixture of cultural customs there may be a variety of celebrations.

Children enjoy participating in celebrations, provided the celebrating is suited to the child's pace and not the adult's and that it does not intrude on what the child himself is concerned with doing. The teacher should be sure the child is left free to enter into the activity or ignore it, as he wishes, in the school.

Christmas is the important festival in the Christian calendar and Hanukkah in the Jewish. Children enjoy making decorations for the Christmas tree. They can do this without the introduction of commercial decorations. With paste, a roll of cotton, colored paper, boxes of glitter, paints, scissors, an assortment of things to string, and materials for collages a great variety of decorations can be produced to the satisfaction of the children. They can sing the simple traditional songs connected with Christmas and listen to the Christmas stories. They may have the experience of the lighting of candles on successive days with an explanation given by one of the Jewish teachers or parents. They can produce gifts for their parents, but the gift should be something they have planned and created rather than an assembly-line product.

Too often children are overstimulated by the hustle and bustle of grown-up preparations. School can be a haven for them at this time, free from pressures. They create their own versions of the celebration if they have the opportunity. One group was satisfied to play out the "Santa Claus" theme day after day, both before and after Christmas. Several of them would gather blocks, or objects from the shelves or the housekeeping corner, stuff these into sacks or baskets which they carried from place to place, depositing an article occasionally beside another child. Clean-up time was a chance to repeat the activity.

Halloween means making a pumpkin and wearing a mask. Much is added to the experience if the children can take a trip to get the pumpkin from a garden. This leads to planting some pumpkin seeds later. Valentine's Day has little meaning for three- and four-year-olds unless they are pushed by adults. Thanksgiving and Fourth of July, two traditional holidays, are holidays for the family. Much will depend here on what families do for these celebrations.

Localities have different traditions depending on their different backgrounds. In a Mexican-American community, for example, piñatas are part of many celebrations. With the help of a parent the children can enjoy a piñata party. The teacher can explain, in simple ways, what is being celebrated and help the children feel a part of what goes on.

Birthdays are an important celebration for children. They can be shared with friends in the nursery school and can add to the child's feeling of being an important and valued person. The celebration is best when it is simple such as a birthday greeting by the teacher as the child comes in the morning; at lunch or at snack time a birthday cake with candles, with the child cutting the cake and serving it with any help that may be necessary; singing "Happy Birthday." The children may make special cookies that day in honor of the birthday child, with one specially decorated for him or her. Often the mother enjoys bringing the cake and sharing in the celebration, and the father, too, if that is possible. It is probably wise to establish a policy of no presents or favors brought in by parents for the celebrations. Such a policy maintains equality in the parties and prevents problems which can arise otherwise for some parents. The nursery school birthday party need not be like a party at home.

TRIPS OUTSIDE THE SCHOOL

We have been referring to trips as a way of learning more about the world in which children live. In making a trip, the children may themselves use some of the community services. They may go by bus to a park or a zoo.

Trips may be made to some of the places that offer community services, such as a fire station. There they will have a chance to examine the fire engine, observe the long hoses and the ladders, perhaps try on a hat, or even sit on the seat of the truck. They will meet the people whose business it is to give fire protection to their community. There are many such opportunities for children to extend the range of their experiences about the role of workers. The teacher can make use of the experiences that her community offers, visiting industries that are within the range of the children's comprehension.

In planning trips the teacher should always visit the place herself before she takes the children there. In this way she can make sure that it is a suitable place for learning. She will know what hazards there may be and how to guard against them. Above all she will know how to prepare the children for the experience. Preparation for a trip is important. The children need to know what they are going to see, what to look for, and what to expect. They can be prepared for any unusual or unexpected events such as loud noises or sudden changes like a crane overhead. They are less likely to be startled. They can enjoy and profit more from the experience. In her visit beforehand, the teacher can also prepare the people there by making sure they know what to expect from young children. They are more likely to be able to do their part in making the experience a good one for the children.

Any instructions or prohibitions should be clearly stated before the children start. They should know what is expected of them, what they can do, and what is not permitted in the situation. They can enjoy being responsible people if they understand what fits this role. The adults who are accompanying the children should also understand clearly what the rules are. There should be enough adults to enable each child to feel secure and free to explore at his own pace.

In planning trips the teacher will keep in mind that children learn most when there are familiar elements in the experience and when they can relate the unfamiliar to something they know. A child is likely to enjoy watching a cement mixer and men at work putting in a new driveway more than he will enjoy a trip to a factory with a lot of big machinery, the function of which he can hardly grasp. A hatchery with incubators full of eggs and tiny chicks is of great interest because he already knows something about eggs and chicks. He gets the most satisfaction out of simple experiences in which he can see clearly and, if possible, touch the things he sees.

On most trips there will be some children who will want to spend more time than others to satisfy their special curiosity about some aspect of the experience. Susan, for example, was most interested when the group visited the sheep barns one day, arriving just after a ewe had given birth to a lamb by cesarean section. Susan had recently been in the hospital for emergency surgery and had many questions. When the group moved on, she stayed behind with an assistant teacher who helped answer some of her questions and talked with her about how one feels about operations. It was important for Susan to have time to explore the subject thoroughly. It probably helped to reduce some of the anxieties that remained from her recent hospital experience. The rest of the children did not need this much time there.

Four- and five-year old children profit from many trips outside the school. The teacher will go often with them, taking small groups to places of interest. When the group is small, it is easier for her to be sure of the experience each child is having and to interpret for him what may need interpreting. There should always be two adults on every trip when there are more than three or four children. Emergencies arise, such as having to find a toilet for one child, or maintaining a limit and taking a child back to the school when necessary. Many times parents are able and eager to help with trips and with transportation on trips. It may be of real value for a parent and a teacher to share such an experience.

Courtesy of Myron Papiz.

A trip to the barns offers many new experiences.

THE ARTS

Art media offer both child and adult an avenue for the discovery of self and for the expression of feeling. Creative expression through the arts, whether in language, in music or dance, or in the graphic or plastic arts, has an important place in the nursery school curriculum.

For the young child art also serves as a means of communication. He is telling us something by what he paints on the paper, and he is sometimes disappointed when we do not seem to understand. He is expressing ideas and thoughts, as well as feelings. Later as he becomes more competent with words he depends less on art for communication. Looking at a collection of one child's paintings, one can often see a theme running through most of the pictures. It is interesting to wonder about what the child who painted the picture on the cover was conveying.

We are interested in creative expression through art because of the satisfactions that this kind of expression brings. There is fulfillment and increased awareness in expression of feeling. We are happier when we are creative. All of us have within us warm, loving feelings, a responsiveness to beauty, to laughter, and to the richness of life itself. These are feelings that are good to express. With expression, we grow as people. Art is an important avenue for this kind of growth. When expression through art is blocked, the blocking limits personality growth.

We are also interested in opportunities for creative expression because such expression can serve as a safety valve, draining off destructive feelings that might otherwise pile up to disturb us in unrecognized ways. As strains and tensions mount, it becomes more important to have avenues for draining off these feelings.

We appreciate the art products of the child, too, not because of the talent shown but because we can truly appreciate the effort that lies behind any achievement in controlling and expressing feeling in an art form.

Because of these values, it is essential that children have opportunities for creative expression through art media and that we recognize and protect the spontaneity of their expressions. By keeping many avenues of expression open in language, in movement, in the arts, we leave the child freer to grow as a person. We protect him against the effects of blocking and inhibitions which result when few avenues of expression are open. We help him to find the satisfactions which come from expressing himself freely as a person, without fear and with confidence.

As we watch children in the nursery school, we may become more aware of the avenues of expression through art which are open to us as adults. In the nursery school we see children expressing a feeling through an art medium. But the need for expression and the values of expression may be as great for us as adults. The kind of adjustments that we are making may depend in part on whether avenues for creative expression have been blocked for us or kept open. We may need to seek ways in which we can express ourselves creatively.

Here we will only suggest some of the ways in which children express themselves in language, in music and rhythm, and in the graphic and plastic arts.

LANGUAGE AS SELF-EXPRESSION

Ruth Expresses Her Feeling Through Language

Ruth is a delightfully verbal four-year-old whose spontaneity seems a gift from two accepting parents. Ruth welcomes approaches by others as gestures of friendliness. She disarms the most aggressive children by her own friendliness. She expresses her feelings freely in language which is fun to listen to.

"Wouldn't it be funny if I were an egg, or if I were a tomato and someone picked me in the garden?" she laughs as the group is returning from a trip to the farm.

She feels a part of whatevever she sees and identifies closely with the world around her. "I'd like to have a comb like that," she says as she looks at the rooster. Patting the setting hen she exclaims, "I'd like to be a chicken and have someone pat me like this!"

Her imagination seizes on many things and weaves them into fascinating patterns. In the spring the nursery school had two ducks and a white rabbit. Ruth gave this verion of the legend of the Easter Bunny when she came to school one morning: "When this bunny and the ducks grow up, we can teach them to paint eggs, can't we? The ducks will have the eggs, and the bunny will paint them, and when we come to nursery school there will be painted eggs all over, won't there?"

Ruth's feelings tumble out in words, and she finds these feelings easy to handle as she creates pictures of her world through language.

Language Is More Than an Avenue of Communication

Not all children use language as freely as Ruth, but for most children language is an important avenue of self-expression, not just an avenue of communication. They use it to express the delight they feel as well as the anger and resentment. They use it without regard to any listener. A young child will chatter to himself as he plays, or he will accompany his more rhythmic activities with singing.

Cindy is swinging and she talks to herself. "I'm going to ride a horsey, a horsey, a horsey. It's going to be a real big one. I'll be big, too, 'cause I ate my breakfast this morning."

When a group of children are happy and satisfied, they talk and sing as they play, even though they are not communicating with each other. Sometimes their singing is in the form of a chant, repeating sounds or words together in a rhythmic pattern. Sometimes their chanting is an expression of their delight in companionship as well as in sounds. Often these chants have an element of humor, as when Terry sang to the group, "Would you like to eat a hammer?" and the three other children replied together, "No." He continued the song with "Would you like to eat a tongue?" and they chorused, "No," and so on through a long list of nonsensical questions with the group replying "No" in great delight. This is not only language expression but it is a form of group game which is beginning to make its appearance with four-year-olds, as we have noted earlier.

Teachers or parents should jot down these language expressions for the light they throw on the feelings or ideas and concepts of the child, as well as for their literary interest.

Children are helped by putting experiences into words when the experiences have an element of fear or of discomfort. Lynn, aged four years, nine months, reminisces pleasantly, as he is swinging, about an experience which was not entirely pleasant.

> Last night my Daddy got a needle,
> A needle, needle, needle, needle,
> He took the silver out of my hand,
> And it didn't hurt one bit,
> And it didn't hurt one bit,
> And I didn't cry at all.
> It didn't hurt at all.
> Last night my Daddy got a needle,
> And he stuck it in my hand
> Took the sliver out,
> And it didn't hurt one bit.
> And I didn't cry one bit,
> No, I didn't, 'cause it didn't hurt,
> Because he did it with a needle.
> Needle, needle, needle, needle.

Linda climbs high on the jungle gym and says: "I can climb right up here. Now look what I can do. I'm higher than Mommy now. She can't catch me. Now she can, now she can't."

She expresses her delight in being up high, out of her mother's reach but not really out of touch. She reveals the ambivalence of her feelings.

Children who use language as an avenue of self-expression are not likely to be children who have been taught to recite the words of poems or songs. As in any art experience, especially in the early stages, self-expression is blocked by "patterning." The young child who speaks "pieces" may never discover the creative possibilities of speech. He may continue to depend on learning the words of others and never perceive the possibilities which language may hold as an avenue for expressing his own feelings.

Self-Expression Through the Use of Language Can Be Encouraged

By Hearing Poetry and Prose

There are ways in which we can encourage self-expression through language, on the other hand, by giving children many opportunities to hear language which expresses thoughts and feelings that are within the level of their comprehension. Simple, well-written stories about everyday experiences with which they are familiar, and imaginative stories such as they themselves might create, bring the medium of language expression within their grasp and yet leave them free to find their own way. Understanding and enjoying these stories, children are more ready to tell their own stories which grow from similar experiences. Careful selection and a generous number of books with stories and poems available for children encourage a growing interest in language expression.

Many children are attracted by the rhythm of poems, beginning with the nursery rhymes, and repeat these. They enjoy poems about everyday experiences, as in *Poems for You.** These may encourage expressions of their own.

By a Teacher Who Has Time to Listen

Equally important in encouraging this form of expression is the fact that the teacher must be ready to listen to what the children say. She must listen, and she must show that she appreciates the children's expressions. Sometimes a child comes with a "story" to tell and finds his teacher's attention divided, with more of it going to her work of straightening up the equipment than to listening to his words. He realizes that his story has no great value for the busy teacher. He does not bring another one to her. If we are to encourage the use of language as a means of self-expression, we must listen to what the children create, and value it.

Baruch outlines some steps to take in encouraging language expression in the chapter "When Children's Words Make Poems," in her book *Parents and Children Go to School.* She points out that jotting down the expressions one hears and later reading them back to the child help him grow aware of the possibilities of creating with words. The bits of poetry or story can be read when the child asks for a story and he will gain a sense that he, too, can create things that have value. Baruch warns against requesting the child to "tell a story," for then we are likely to get products aimed to please us rather than true expressions of self.

By Satisfying Activities

There will be more language expression in groups where the children can participate freely in many activities. Large muscle activities which are rhythmic, such as swinging and bouncing, stimulate language. In fact, almost any satisfying

*Martin, Ruth: Poems for You. New York, Vantage Press, 1973.

experience may find expression in language. The dramatic play which centers around housekeeping materials is often rich in its output of song and story. The teacher who sits quietly near this area with pencil and paper will record much interesting material which will give her an insight into what the children are feeling, as well as how they are using language as a means of expression.

Children are conscious of word sounds, too, and enjoy using them. As Connie uses the crayons, she talks. Holding up a red crayon, she says to Judy, "Red, red, wet your bed." They both repeat this several times, giggling together. Then Connie adds, "Rain, rain, what's your name?" They repeat this several times with obvious pleasure. Judy leaves and Connie continues,"Know what this is? A baby bat on his back!" She goes on, "Know what this is? Camel with a hammer in his hand. I saw a camel at the zoo. Camel, pamel." Connie likes words and the way they sound.

When we encourage the use of language as a means of self-expression, we help keep open for the child an important avenue through which he can drain off feeling, or share it with others, or find creative delight for himself. We also have for ourselves a valuable means of gaining insight into what experiences mean to the child as we listen to what he expresses through his words.

MUSIC AND DANCE

Music offers another avenue of expression to children which is closely related to that of language. It is an avenue which is used by children everywhere. There is significance back of the concept of a mother as a person who rocks and sings to her child. The sound of a mother's voice, the feeling tones expressed in it, the rhythm of rocking are important to a child very early in his life.

The Tones of the Human Voice Tell Us a Great Deal

The child in nursery school will respond to the tone of the teacher's voice as much as to the words she uses. He will be reassured if her tone is confident and friendly, without regard to what she says. The "music" of the voice is an important medium for communicating feeling. As teachers and parents we need to be aware of the effect that the tones of our voices have on children. We need to use with effectiveness the important tool of voice quality as we work with children.

Just as the child senses meanings through the tone quality of adult voices, so we can be alert to what the child is communicating through the tones of his voice. The high-pitched tight, rapid speech of one child, the low, only half-articulated speech of another, the strong full tones of a third, tell us a great deal about each of these children and what they are feeling. We can learn to identify more and more accurately what the voices of children reveal as we listen and observe.

Satisfying Activities Stimulate Singing and Dancing

When children are happy and content, when they are engaged in satisfying activities, especially rhythmic activities, they will sing. We can encourage musical expression when we help them find satisfactions and see that they have plenty of opportunity for rhythmic activities such as swinging, bouncing, pounding, running, or pedaling a tricycle. Two swings side by side make companionship possible under simple circumstances, so that the joy of having a friend may find expression along with the joy of movement through space. Swinging and singing go together. One school used a large truck inner tube for many rhythmic activities. Two or three children would sit on it and bounce, or the group would use it for a drum, pounding on it with their hands as they listened to music, or set their own rhythmic patterns. When a long board is placed between two low sawhorses, bouncing may take a rhythmic pattern, too. In fact there are endless ways in which rhythm can be introduced into the experience of children, bringing singing with it.

The teacher who can sing "on the spot" and move freely to music will encourage spontaneous responses in the children. Parents may be glad to bring musical instruments they can play to nursery school, so that the children will have a chance to see and hear wind, string, and percussion instruments. Activity and music go together. Singing around the piano may be fun, but it does not take the place of singing in connection with activities. There should be plenty of singing by the children and the teachers on the playground and through all the areas of play activity in the nursery school. There should be the opportunity for dancing wherever there is space and music.

The Ability to Keep Time Improves with Maturity Rather Than Practice

There is evidence that ability to keep time is not improved by practice but that it depends on maturity and innate ability. At four, a child keeps more accurate time than he did at three—whether or not he has had training. One four-year-old will keep better time than another, regardless of experience, because of innate differences in ability. But if a child has been subjected to pressure to "keep time with the music," he may find less enjoyment in music experience than he might, and he may feel less adequate in this area. There are individual differences in the rate at which a child develops a sense of time, but all children enjoy rhythmic experiences—if this enjoyment has not been interfered with. The more opportunity they have to move freely, either with music or without it, the more pleasure they will find and the more release for their feelings in this form of expression.

The Ability to Sing Improves with Practice

Ability to "carry a tune" responds to training, according to what we know at present. Singing with the teacher gives a child practice, but the teacher must value singing as a means of self-expression rather than as a skill, especially with the young child. She can help him enjoy this avenue of self-expression by bringing songs within the measure of his ability to sing them rather than setting him difficult patterns. Children's singing voices as a rule are not high-pitched. Children usually pitch their own songs below rather than above middle A, for example. Many of their own songs are sung in a minor key, quite different from the songs that we often give them to sing. Simple, childlike songs, used in connection with activities, build skill and enjoyment of singing in the children.

The teacher with a musical background can encourage creative expression in singing in the children by jotting down the songs that the children themselves sing in their play and then playing and singing these songs back to them later, in the same way that she encourages their stories and poems. Her interest will heighten their awareness of the creative possibilities of music.

Listening Is Important

Another important experience that the nursery school can offer is that of listening to good music through records or music played on the piano, the violin, the flute, or any other instrument. If the teacher herself is not a musician, she can often find someone who likes children and who will enjoy sharing music with them. This adds to the variety of the children's experience with music and increases their interest. Not all children may wish to listen each time such a music experience is offered. There should be no compulsion about listening, for this does not build desirable attitudes toward music. The child who does not wish to listen can respect the needs of the listening group for quiet by playing at the other end of the room himself or playing outside. Many times curiosity about a new instrument will bring even a nonlistener into the group for a time.

When a record player is used, it needs to be played where children can listen undisturbed by others. Some children will want to listen far more often than others, and they should be free to listen without interfering with the play of other children or being interfered with themselves as they listen. With the proper physical setup, listening to music may form a large part of the curriculum at nursery school for some children at some period. There should be a place for listening, as well as for responding to music, in the program of the school.

Sometimes we find a child who spends a great deal of time listening to music—or listening to stories. He may be doing this as a form of escape from facing difficulties, such as attempting to adjust to other children in play situations. The teacher needs to recognize this situation and to take steps to encourage the child to extend his interests, giving him more support in his group relations and building up his confidence, when she meets such a case. It is important that the total pattern of the child's adjustment be understood. Music should *not* serve only as an escape.

Children Enjoy Using Many Instruments

Most children love to play the piano and many of them will go often to the piano to play and sing there, turning the pages of a favorite song book, perhaps with a friend beside them. With very little supervision, children can use and enjoy the piano by themselves. Drums of all kinds, and bells, are fun, too. They should be freely available. Wind instruments may have only restricted use because children cannot be expected to keep from passing them from mouth to mouth. But every nursery school should have plenty of all types of sound instruments, and the children should experiment freely with sound, both indoors and outdoors.

Setting Patterns Should Be Avoided

We must keep in mind through all these experiences that the values that we seek are those which come with creativity. Music and dance have their greatest value for young children as avenues of self-expression. Children will use them in this way unless adults block them by offering patterns or defining limits for their use.

Setting patterns for musical expression will serve to block the use of music as a means of self-expression. If the teacher sets a pattern for a rhythmic activity by directing, "This is the way leaves blow in the wind," or, "big tall elephants," or anything else, she is interfering with the creative possibilities of the experience for the child. If she endeavors to show the child how to keep time, to fit his response into the pattern of the music she is playing, she is blocking him in the expression of his own feeling in response to the time. The skillful teacher will, instead, adapt the music to the child's own rhythm. She will give the children many opportunities to respond to music, but she will not attempt to dictate what their responses will be.

Dancing Is a Natural Outlet for the Expression of Feeling

Dancing as well as singing will occur in many areas when children are free to act spontaneously. Running in the wind through falling leaves, crunching dry leaves underfoot in a marching rhythm, rolling down a grassy slope on the first warm spring day when space and sunshine seem to make everything burst into song and movement, and imitating the movements and the splashing of the swimmers seen in the pool, may all be experiences in dance for children. The children who danced the unfolding of a baby leaf were expressing their concepts and feelings about spring.

One of the most natural and spontaneous forms of expression for a young child is expression through body movements. When these become rhythmic and are used for the expression of feeling that he wishes to communicate, they form a creative outlet that he can use easily and develop with time. With opportunity and encouragement and increasing skill in using his body, he can translate many emotions into dance patterns. He has taken a step in control and enrichment of feeling.

All children take delight in large, free body movements when there is plenty of space. A gymnasium or a large room equipped with full-length mirrors for modern dance practice, for example, inspires joyful and graceful experimentation with movements, especially if there is music to accompany the movement. Incidentally, it seems likely that opportunities to dance and play in front of full-length mirrors may add a dimension to the child's concept of himself as a person, especially for a child who has had little or no opportunity to see himself in a mirror.

To be in tune with one's body helps free a child from doubt about himself. It gives him confidence. For young children, simple actions like rolling over and over, getting up very slowly or very quickly, or pretending to lift something heavy

Courtesy of Robert Overstreet.

Children enjoy a variety of instruments as they move to music.

help them to learn to control their movements and to have fun in doing this. Teachers, too, can discover the pleasure in free movement as they dance with the children in unpatterned ways. Expressing feeling through dance movements adds to one's capacity to enjoy experiences.

Elaborate settings are not necessary for rhythm and music. In one of the wartime child care centers a group of two-year-olds was playing in the limited area available to them. They had little in the way of play materials and less in the way of stable, continued contacts with reassuring adults. Their long day at school was followed by a home experience that offered little security to most of them. In the tiny court where they played, the wind was blowing one day. It picked up some stray pieces of toilet tissue (used to wipe drippy noses) and swirled them round and round in the corner of the cement courtyard. Observing this, one of the two-year-olds suddenly began turning and whirling with the bits of paper. Several children joined her, and in that bleak corner they did a graceful dance with the bits of tissue in the wind for a few brief minutes, and then ran off, laughing.

Children who are in groups in which there is plenty of expression through music have less need to drain off feeling in undesirable ways. They are likely to have fewer difficulties in working out relationships as they play together. When teachers are aware of the values which music and rhythm offer and the dangers of patterning these expressions, they can offer children many experiences in these areas, limited only by their own talent and resourcefulness and the limits imposed by the physical environment. The children will welcome these opportunities and profit from them. They will use them in creative ways.

PAINTING; DRAWING; MODELING

The Process Rather Than the Product is Important

Experiences in the graphic and plastic arts offer another avenue through which individuals release their feelings, find satisfactions and an avenue for communication. It is an avenue of expression which may serve as an outlet throughout the life of the individual. Too many of us have had this avenue blocked for us by the teaching we have received at home or at school. We are convinced that we can't draw a straight line, and we probably are right. Nothing that we are likely to do will ever rate as a "work of art." But we probably could have drawn much better than we think and, more important, we could have found pleasure and emotional release in the process if we had had sound teaching, or at least had been left alone. The anxious attention on the product rather than the process, the coloring books, and other "patterns" that were imposed on us have all served pretty effectively to prevent most of us from expressing ourselves through art. Yet art is an important means of expression and of draining off feeling as well as a source of satisfaction. No avenue could be less likely to do damage to others.

As we ourselves work with children, we must try to safeguard their use of art media as a means of self-expression. For every child, art can serve as an outlet for feeling if the process is emphasized more than the product. It does not matter that there are differences in ability just as there are in music. Given an easel, paper and paint, and no directions, every child will paint. For some children painting will remain an important avenue through which they can express feeling all through their lives.

We Avoid Patterning

How do we keep open the avenue of individual, creative expression? In the first place, as we have said before, we must avoid making or setting models to be copied. We must never say, "Do it this way," or "Do it that way." Even the drip from a full brush can make fascinating patterns on the paper. Some methodical children will wipe their brushes carefully because that is the way they want to make their pictures—no drips. Others may slop on the paint, expressing their own overflowing and as yet less well-controlled feeling; while others may drip the paint deliberately on the paper as they explore the possibilities of the medium. They do not all use the paint in the same way.

Greg puts on green paint in one big spot. Then he adds blue, then orange, and then red, smearing the red up to the top of the paper. He paints so that the colors overlap with only some of the pure color showing. He puts yellow in the middle of the red and then smears black over the yellow and part of the red. He paints in a serious, intent way and covers the whole paper before he is through

Betty picks up the brush from the jar with red paint and draws a circle. She puts red lines and dots inside the circle and then smears red paint in a few places outside the circle. "All done with this one," she says. On a fresh piece of paper she begins with paint from the orange jar and dabs the bright color on the paper in one spot, then uses broad, brisk strokes to paint with orange across the paper. She picks up the red brush and makes a few more strokes across the paper, covering very little of her previous work. She dabs a small amount of yellow in one spot near the corner of the paper and says again, "All done with this one."

Kay is a child for whom painting became a favorite medium for expression. When she first entered nursery school, she explored all the possible experiences with paint. The teacher watched her as she approached the easel with evident satisfaction on that first day. She painted on the paper with full strokes of brush, using all the colors. Then she touched the tip of the brush to her tongue, and stood relishing its taste. Next, she brushed it under her nose, getting its smell. Afterward she carefully painted the palm of her hand. She found out what paint felt like. She had enjoyed all the sensory experiences that paint offered, and she used it often during the time she attended nursery school.

Ginny is a child who delighted in the feel of paint on her skin. She usually ended a session at the easel by carefully painting her hands, arms, and face and then, just as carefully, washing off the paint, enjoying the sight of herself in the mirror all the while.

Large sheets of paper, an easel or wall board of suitable height, large brushes and rich colors, a location relatively free from distraction, with perhaps a covering on the floor to take care of the drips, give the child what he needs. For the rest we can show our interest and appreciation when the child wants these things, and refrain from asking questions about what he is painting.

The youngest nursery school children usually do not intend to represent anything when they use paints. They are using art as a means of expressing themselves, and paint as a medium whose possibilities they are beginning to explore. By the time they are three or four, they may name and describe what they are doing as they work; but we should be careful to avoid pushing them into naming their picture by asking questions. Again it is Kay who gives us a clue as she laughingly said when she put her painting away, "What is it? What is it?" The teacher asked her, "Is that what you think your mother will say when she sees your painting?" "Yes," replied Kay with a smile.

Left alone, children put down many of their experiences on paper, even though they may not add titles for our benefit. A large barn burned near one nursery school in a spectacular night fire witnessed by some of the children and described vividly to the others. Following that, there were many paintings of "barns burning." Most of them were splotches of dark paint covered by red color. These pictures appeared again and again, and many of the children were probably helped to drain off the fear which the fire had roused by expressing it in an art form, thus turning it into a more pleasant and manageable experience.

David was painting with a hard, circular movement. He talked as he painted. "I'm making a jungle. Look at my jungle. There's a lion. That's a trail and a river that the lion can't cross." With this painting David may have been expressing feelings about dangerous things that need to be controlled. They can be represented by lions in jungles with a river that sets a boundary. Through his painting he reduces his anxieties to more manageable proportions.

When we leave children free to use art media as avenues of self-expression, we gain a great deal of insight into what they are feeling as we observe what they paint and how they paint. It is worth reading some of the studies published in this area in order to understand better what we observe.

Finger-Paints Are Valuable

Finger-painting is another form of painting which allows for a great deal of valuable, spontaneous expression. The pressure to keep clean may be less damaging to a child if he has this acceptable outlet for sensory experience and for messiness. Being messy with finger-paints should reduce the need he feels to be messy in other places and times, and lessen the damage he may suffer from having to limit himself at these places and times.

We learn something about the kinds of control that a child has built up as we watch him approach the new experience of using finger-paints. Is his response wholehearted and immediate? Does he hesitate and withhold himself, finding participation difficult? In what ways does he enjoy the experience—by patting or squeezing or just poking the paint? Does he use a small bit of paint or a whole lot? Does he touch it with only one finger as though afraid of the sensation, or does he use his whole hand or even his arm?

Changes in the child's behavior at the finger-painting table will give us clues as to changes taking place in behavior in other areas, too. Finger-painting may help to free children for more creative activities in other areas. It offers a valuable avenue of release to children who have had too little chance for play with mud pies or for messy play at other times.

Crayons Versus Paints

For reasons of convenience, many preschool children are limited to crayons in their art experiences at home. Crayons are a much "tighter" medium than paints and are used with more cramped movements. They are, in fact, more suited to the level of representation which belongs at a later stage in development. All this makes it especially important to supply children at nursery school with a good setup for painting. When this is done, they usually turn to crayons for expression only occasionally. The child who continues to use crayons in preference to paints is often a tense, tight child. Richard, for example, had a very difficult time adjusting to nursery school, and during this period he used crayons frequently. After he had relaxed and become more comfortable, he turned to the easel where he painted freely, seldom touching crayons again.

Clay Is Another Desirable Medium

Clay is another medium which may have many of the same values for children as finger-painting. It offers a direct, sensory experience.

Children who have felt conflict over toilet training are especially likely to use it for release of feeling. The squeezing, the patting and pounding which they do with clay serves to drain off some of the resentment at interferences which they may have been unable to express in other ways. We often see a child make something out of clay and then destroy it by flattening it on the table. It is all right to smash clay, and one can get rid of hostile feelings in this way. It is a way of "acting out" feeling which does no harm and may have much value.

Because the sensory experiences offered by clay are important, it is wise to encourage handling it with the fingers rather than to introduce tools of any kind. We are less interested in products than in the process, and fingers are the best tools to achieve what we want. By making the clay wetter and thus messier, we may increase its value for some children. Some inhibited children, on the other hand, may be unable to touch clay at first if it is too wet and sticky. These children need to have clay that is only soft and moist until the barriers they have built up against messiness in any form are relaxed. The older preschool child who produces something that he values may find satisfaction in letting it dry, and later painting it. It may even be possible to fire the product to give it added value for the older child.

There is no art medium which seems more likely than clay to tempt the inexperienced adult into model making. The idea that one can play with clay, rolling it, patting it, feeling it without making anything, seems hard for even a well-intentioned adult to act on. Shades of past experiences in which it was necessary to "make" something operate against one's being content to play with the medium. We all need to be on our guard, or we will find ourselves making models that the children are only too prone to follow. Then we may have deprived them of the creative values in using clay.

Children Need "Messy" Play Experiences

Children need the "messy" play types of experiences which clay and finger-painting offer. These experiences help to lessen the burden imposed on children by the effort to be clean. Because they are sensory experiences, they are deeply satisfying to children. As teachers we must look at our own attitude toward the sensory satisfaction of messy play. We may have suffered from training experiences in our childhood so that it is hard for us to see children delighting in using sticky clay or gobs of finger-paint. Unless we can accept our own feelings, we may find ourselves avoiding the use of clay or finger-paint, preferring dough or plasticene. We may find ourselves depriving the child of a satisfying experience or, on the other hand, being unable to set limits when limitation is necessary because we are afraid of being too restrictive. We may need to take steps to handle our own feelings if we are to offer help to the children here.

It is probably important to mention here that mud and sand and water offer many of the same values to the child as clay. We might even consider clay and finger-paints as sophisticated substitutes for the mud hole or mud puddles that have brought joy to the hearts—and fingers—of many healthy children. Children who have been denied access to mud and water have more need of experiences with clay and finger-paints if they are to satisfy the desire for sensory experience which is strong in all young children. But children who use clay and finger-paints will have a richer experience if they also know the feel of sand, both dry and wet, through their fingers and have dabbled in mud, and explored the possibilities of water play. A good nursery school will supply these "down to earth" experiences, for they, too, are avenues of self-expression and among the most direct and satisfying open to a child.

PROJECTS

1. Observe and record five examples of questions asked by a child. Indicate the circumstances briefly. How was each question answered? How would you evaluate each as a learning experience for the child concerned?

Sensorimotor Experiences: Concept Formation

1. Observe and record incidents in which a child added to his store of sensory impressions in some area, as touch, sight, sound, smell, taste.
2. Observe and record incidents that give evidence of a child's learning:
(a) Perceiving characteristics of an object.
(b) Perceiving functions of an object.
(c) Perceiving relationships.
(d) Ability to recall or associate perceptions.

Language and Literature

1. Select a child and record his speech as completely as possible for three ten-minute periods during one hour. Summarize your record and characterize his speech, covering such points as these: Is his speech "restricted" or "elaborated" speech? Are there defects of articulation or defects in rhythm? How would you characterize his voice quality? For what purposes does he usually use speech? How many questions did he ask? What ideas and attitudes did he express in speech? Is his speech adequate for his purposes? How does his speech aid him in learning?
2. Select five books for this child on the basis of his interests and his stage of development, giving the name of the book, the author, and the reason for your selection.
3. Observe and record a situation in which the teacher made effective use of an experience to increase the child's language competence.

The Sciences

1. Outline a plan for introducing an experience in the school that will extend or enrich concepts or understandings in mathematics or in physical or biological science for some of the children in the group in which you are observing or participating. Indicate what concepts the children might gain from the experience, as well as the way in which you would plan for the experience.
2. Make a list of field trips that are desirable and possible for the children in your group, and that might help to extend their concepts about work done in the community or about community services.
3. Outline a plan for a field trip for these children, indicating what the purposes of the trip would be, what preparations would be made beforehand by the staff, how the children would be prepared, and what follow-up activities there might be.

The Arts

1. Children often use language as a means of self-expression as well as communication. Record a monologue or poem or song which you heard during an observation. Note the circumstances under which it was expressed.

2. Over a period of observation note (a) the kinds and amounts of experience which the children have with rhythm and music, and (b) the sounds that they appear to notice, and (c) their participation in group experiences which are musical or rhythmic. What differences do you observe in individual interest here and in ability?

3. Watch two children using paint or clay. Note the differences in the way they use the material. Record their behavior and conversation. Indicate what values the experiences seemed to have for each child.

4. Look at a series of paintings done by one child over a period of weeks. What seems to remain the same? What changes in his paintings over the period? How would you characterize this child from looking at his paintings? What meaning does painting seem to have for him? Discuss.

REFERENCES

Activities

Baker, Katherine (ed.): Ideas That Work with Young Children. Washington, D.C., National Association for the Education of Young Children, 1972.
Bersen, Minnie: Opening, Mixing, Matching. Washington, D.C., Association for Childhood Education, International, 1974.
Brearley, Molly (ed.): The Teaching of Young Children: Some Applications of Piaget's Learning Theory. New York, Schocken Books Inc., 1970.
Buschhoff, Lotte: Going on a trip. Young Children, Vol. 26, No. 4, March, 1971.
Cartwright, Sally: Blocks and learning. Young Children, Vol. 19. No. 3, 1974.
Croft, Doreen, and Hess, Robert: An Activity Handbook for Teachers of Young Children, 2nd ed. Boston, Houghton Mifflin Company, 1975.
Dittman, Laura: Curriculum Is What Happens. Washington, D.C., National Association for the Education of Young Children, 1970.
Estavan, Frank: Teaching the very young: Procedures for developing inquiry skills. In Anderson, R. H., and Shane, H. G. (eds.): As the Twig Is Bent: Readings in Early Childhood Education. Boston, Houghton Mifflin Company, 1971.
Hirsch, Elisabeth (ed.): The Block Book. Washington, D.C., National Association for the Education of Young Children, 1974.
McCarthy, Jan, and May, Charles R. (eds.): Providing the Best for Young Children. Washington, D.C., National Association for the Education of Young Children, 1974.
Ovitt, Jean: What about the school bus. Young Children, Vol. 25, No. 5, May, 1970.

Sensorimotor Experiences

Elder, Connie: Miniature sand environments: A new way to see and feel and explore. Young Children, June, 1973.
Friedman, David, and Colodny, Dorothy: Water, Sand and Mud as Play Materials. (Revised edition.) Washington, D.C., National Association for the Education of Young Children.
Gerhardt, Lydia. Moving and Knowing: The Young Child Orients Himself in Space. Englewood Cliffs, New Jersey, Prentice-Hall, Inc., 1973.
The Significance of the Young Child's Motor Development. Proceedings of Conference Sponsored by the American Association for Health, Physical Education and Recreation, the National Education Association and National Association for the Education of Young Children. Washington, D.C., National Association for the Education of Young Children, 1971.
West, Suzanne: A sense of wonder—Parents and children together. Young Children, Vol. 29, No. 6, 1974.

Language

Blank, Marion: Teaching Learning in the Preschool: A Dialogue Approach. Columbus, Ohio, Charles E. Merrill Publishing Company, 1973.
Blank, Marion: Cognitive functions of language in the preschool years. Developmental Psychology, Vol. 10, No. 2, 1974.
Brown, R.: A First Language: The Early Stages. Cambridge, Harvard University Press, 1973.
Cazden, Courtney B.: Child Language and Education. New York, Holt, Rinehart and Winston, Inc., 1972.
Cazden, Courtney B, Baratz, Joan, Labov, William and Palmer, Frances: Language development in day care programs. *In* Cazden, Courtney B. (ed.): Language in Early Childhood Education. Washington, D.C., National Association for the Education of Young Children, 1972.
Cazden, Courtney B. (ed.): Language in Early Childhood Education. Washington, D.C., National Association for the Education of Young Children, 1972.
Chomsky, Noam: Language and Mind. New York, Harcourt, Brace & World, Inc., 1968.
Greene, Margaret: Learning to Talk: A Parent's Guide for the First Five Years. New York, Harper & Row, Publishers, 1960.
Labov, W.: The logic of non-standard English *In* Williams, F. F. (ed.): Language and Poverty. Chicago, Markham Publishing Company, 1970.
McAfee, O.: The right words. Young Children, Vol. 23, 1967.
Mattick, Ilse: The teacher's role in helping young children develop language competence. Young Children, Vol. 27, No. 3, 1972.
Piaget, Jean: Language and Thought of the Child. New York, Humanities Press, Inc., 1959.
Sparling, Joseph, and Sparling, Marilyn: How to talk to a scribbler. Young Children, August, 1973.
Tizard, B., Cooperman, O., Joseph, A., and Tizard, J.: Environmental effects on language development: A study of young children in long-stay residential nurseries. Child Development, Vol. 43, June, 1972.
Weir, Ruth.: Language in the Crib. The Hague, Mouton, 1962.

Literature

Bernstein, Joanne: Books for young children. Young Children, Vol. 29, No. 6, September, 1974.
Fassler, Joan: Children's literature and early childhood separation experiences. Young Children, Vol. 19, No. 5, July, 1974.
Griffin, Louise: Multi-Ethnic Books for Young Children: An Annotated Bibliography for Parents and Teachers of Young Children. Washington, D.C., National Association for the Education of Young Children.
The Horn Book Magazine. (Reviews and discussions of Children's books). Boston, 585 Boylston Street.
Katz, and Akers, M.: Books in the Preschool. Washington, D.C., An Eric-National Association for the Education of Young Children Publication in Early Childhood Education, 1972.
Lewis, Claudia, and McPhee, Miriam: Books for young children. Young Children, Vol. 26, No. 6, August, 1971.
Lincoln, Robert.: Reading to young children. Children Today, May-June, 1974.
Stern, Virgina: The story reader as a teacher. Young Children, October, 1966.

The Sciences

Carmichael, Viola: Science Experiences for Young Children. Sierra Madres, California, Southern California Association for the Education of Young Children, 1972.
Croft, Doreen, and Hess, Robert: An Activities Handbook for Teachers of Young Children. Boston, Houghton Mifflin Company, 1975.
DeSchweinitz, Karl: Growing Up: The Story of How We Become Alive, Are Born and Grow Up. New York, The Macmillan Company, 1965.
Ets, Marie: The Story of a Baby. New York, The Viking Press, Inc., 1939.
Hochman, Vivienne, and Greenwalk, Mildred: Science Experiences in Early Childhood Education. New York, Bank Street College of Education Publications, Teacher's Handbook Series.
Hochman, Vivienne: Trips in Early Childhood. New York, Bank Street College of Education Publications, Teacher's Handbook Series.
Koocher, Gerald: "Why isn't the gerbil moving anymore?": Discussing death in the classroom—and at home. Children Today, January-February, 1975.

Plank, Emma: Young children and death. Young Children, Vol. 23, No. 6, September, 1968.

Wann, K., Dorn, N. E., and Liddle, E. A.: Fostering Intellectual Development in Young Children. New York, Bureau of Publications, Teachers' College, Columbia University, 1962.

Wolf, Anna: Helping Your Child to Understand Death. (Revised edition.) Child Study Association of America, 1973.

The Arts

Baker, K. R.: The nursery school fosters creativity. Education, Vol. 87, No. 8, April, 1967.

Biber, Barbara: Premature Structuring as a Deterrent to Creativity. New York, Bank Street College of Education, Publication No. 67.

Lark-Horovitz, Betty, Lewis, Hilda, and Luca, Mark: Understanding Children's Art for Better Teaching. Columbus. Ohio, Charles E. Merrill Publishing Co., 1973.

Lindstrom, Miriam: Children's Art. Berkeley, California, University of California Press, 1959.

Maynard, Olga: Children and Dance and Music. New York, Charles Scribner's Sons, 1968.

Osborn, Keith, and Haupt, Dorothy: Creative Activities for Young Children. (Revised edition.) Detroit, Merrill Palmer Institute.

Pile, Naomi: Art Experiences for Young Children, Vol. 5. Threshold Early Learning Library. New York, Macmillan Publishing Co., Inc., 1973.

Sheehy, Emma: Children Discover Music and Dance. New York, Holt, Rinehart and Winston, Inc., 1959.

Wickens, Elaine: Please don't tell the children. Young Children, Vol., 23, October, 1967.

PART FIVE

UNDERSTANDING BEHAVIOR

CHAPTER 15

Snail and His House (boy, 4 years)

FEELINGS OF SECURITY AND CONFIDENCE

Feelings of Security and Adequacy Are Important for All of Us

"Look here, teacher, I'm bigger than you think. I'm going to have a birthday soon. Let me do this by myself," said Katherine to a well-meaning adult who was trying to help her.

Her words remind us how often adults handicap children by acting as though children were unable to meet situations. A child has a difficult time developing confidence when he is surrounded by people who "help" him all the time. Children are often bigger than we think! Katherine was able to express her confidence in herself as a person able to do things. Few children can do this because they lack not only the verbal ability but the feeling itself.

As adults, most of us probably wish that we had more self-confidence. We realize that we are likely to do a thing better when we feel confident than when we are afraid of failing. We realize, too, that we get more pleasure out of doing something when we feel adequate and are free from anxiety. For all of us, feelings of insecurity and a lack of confidence are handicapping. They do not arise entirely from lack of skill, for the person who has confidence in himself may enjoy undertaking something new in which he lacks skill. But most people are not free enough of doubts about themselves to feel that the unfamiliar is a challenge to them.

As we observe people in nursery school, we will look for the meaning of their behavior in terms of the degree of security revealed by it. As we work with the children, we will seek for ways of strengthening their feelings of confidence and security. We will ask ourselves at least three questions. First, where do feelings of security and confidence come from and what helps or hinders their development? Second, how can we identify these feelings in people? Third, what can we do in the nursery school to increase these feelings?

Security refers to the feelings that come with having had many experiences of being accepted as we are rather than rejected, of feeling safe rather than threatened. Security results from a person's relationships with people and the way these relationships have been experienced by the individual. Confidence refers to the feelings which an individual has about himself, his concept of the kind of person he is. This concept, too, grows out of the responses other people make to him. Security and confidence are closely related. The secure child trusts himself and others. He dares to be himself and to discover more about himself.

FOUNDATIONS FOR FEELING SECURE AND CONFIDENT

First, where do feelings of security and confidence come from?

We have already suggested some of the important areas. They arise out of the way the child's basic needs are met, his experiences with feeding and later with toileting, the kinds of responses he gets from other people, the satisfaction he finds in exploring the world. Out of these early experiences the child builds a feeling of trust in the world, his first task developmentally. Having learned that he can trust others he is ready to trust and have confidence in himself. The attitudes and feelings of his parents are the most important factors in building confidence because he depends largely on his parents for the satisfaction of his basic needs.

If the child's first experiences have made him feel secure and confident because his wants were satisfied, if he has obtained response from people, and if he has had satisfying sensory experiences, he has laid a firm foundation for confidence and security. If, on the other hand, his wants have been unsatisfied and if he has failed to get response when he needed it, he has already experienced insecurity and felt inadequate. If he constantly heard the words "no" and "don't" when he reached out for experience, he has already grown to distrust his own impulses. The world does not seem to him a place where he can feel safe, and he builds a picture of himself as a person who is not very adequate to cope with the problems it presents. He may think of himself as a person who is likely to do the wrong thing.

INFLUENCE OF ADULTS

Children Are Influenced in Their Feelings by the Attitudes of Adults

Children tend to behave as they feel they are expected to behave, or according to the concept of self they have built up out of the responses of other people to them. Charles, for example, thinks of himself as a boy who gets into trouble. As he and his father came into nursery school one morning, his father remarked, "See how nice and quiet this place is until you get here!" What is a boy like who hears words like these? He is a boy who is noisy and defiant and "difficult." He lives up to the picture his father paints.

When Jim's mother brought him to nursery school, she explained to the teacher as Jim stood beside her, "Perhaps he'll learn to ride a tricycle here. He doesn't know how yet. He doesn't like to learn things. He just tries for a minute and then gives right up." It was not surprising that Jim lacked confidence, and did not persist, and was unfriendly with both children and teachers.

Ella was timid, too. She didn't join other children in play, but she did like to paint. She was at the easel painting carefully around the edges of the paper when her mother came for her one day. Her mother saw the picture, and she said half scornfully, "Nobody paints like that!" How can one have much confidence if one is considered a "nobody"? Ella didn't expect to have an important place in the group.

In contrast we see Michele. Michele is just four years old, new in the nursery school, eager for experience, but lacking in skills. Climbing fascinated her. One day she tried very hard to climb way up in the tree even though she was afraid. With some help from the teacher, she finally managed to reach a high limb. Delighted, she called out to everyone, "Look, I'm up here as brave as ever." We see in this incident the elements of healthy personality development. Michele sees herself as "brave." She has made an effort and mastered a difficult feat. She wants to share her delight. She is sure that there will be someone who cares.

Leighton and Kluckholn in *Children of the People* make an interesting comment on the attitudes which appear in another culture than our own. They describe the way the Navaho people treat young children in these words, ". . . the Navaho toddler is given self-confidence by being made to feel that he is constantly loved and valued.* Would Ella and Jim have behaved differently if they had lived under conditions in which they were "constantly loved and valued"? There are many children in our culture who are "constantly loved and valued," but there are many others who are treated as "nobodies," like Ella and Jim, even though there is no conscious intent on the part of parents to treat them this way.

We live in such a highly competitive society that it is often hard for us to recognize the values that may exist outside of achievement. Parents feel the pressure for accomplishment. They want children who will learn to ride tricycles or who paint good pictures. They push their children, even their toddlers. They do not value them as they are.

---

*Leighton, Dorothea, and Kluckholn, Clyde: Children of the People: The Navaho Individual and His Development. Cambridge, Massachusetts, Harvard University Press, 1947. p. 33.

We Tend to "Nudge" Children

Dr. James Plant described this tendency of parents to push their children as quickly as possible from one stage to the next as "nudging" the child in his growth. We are likely to "nudge" children on rather than allow them to take time to satisfy their needs in each stage. We do this even though it has been demonstrated that growth proceeds in certain sequences, one stage following another, and that the soundest growth occurs when the child is given time in each stage, "living it out completely" before going on to the next. Dependency, for example, precedes independence and the child who is most independent in the end will be the one whose dependency needs have been most completely met, not the one who was pushed the soonest into being independent. "Nudging" a child from one stage to the next serves to make him feel less secure and more defensive. Children who have been pushed through a stage frequently have to go back and experience it again before they are free enough to go on, before they are secure enough to develop further.

We Make Children Feel Guilty

Children sometimes find it hard to develop confidence in themselves because they feel they are to blame for things that happen. A child may enjoy an experience, such as playing in the mud or exploring a bureau drawer, only to find that what he has done is considered very naughty by the adult. With little basis for real understanding of adult values, with a great need to please adults because of his dependency on them, he comes to feel uncertain about himself and his behavior. Many times he thinks that his mistakes are much more serious than we really consider them. He suffers from a load of guilt that may be very great. When we blame him for what he does not understand or understands only in part, we damage his feeling of confidence and trust in himself.

By making events conditional on a child's good or bad behavior, we may increase his sense of uncertainty and lack of confidence. He may feel responsible for events which have no connection. Betty said, "Next week if I'm a real good girl, know where we're going? To the beach!" Let's hope that her parents were not too busy or tired that week or that nothing interfered with their plan. If a child can bring about a trip to the beach by being good, he can cause a calamity by being bad.

Pam arrived at nursery school one morning and didn't see the ducks. She was very interested in them and inquired anxiously, "I can't see the ducks." Then she added, "I made a noise. Do ducks get headaches?" She has evidently had to bear a feeling of guilt for causing headaches. Without enough experience to correct his concepts, the child is the victim of his misapprehensions. We may not suspect a child's real feelings or the heavy load of guilt he may feel for events.

We Are Afraid of Spoiling Children

Sometimes people are afraid to accept children as they are and to meet their needs because they are afraid of "spoiling" them if they do. They needlessly deny and interfere with children because of ignorance of the growth process. They

Courtesy of Myron Papiz.

The teacher tries to understand and comfort.

make it hard for the child to think of himself as an adequate person. "Spoiled" children are, in fact, those who get attention *when the adult wants to give it* rather than when the child himself needs it. They are those children who are subject to inconsistent interferences rather than given the support of consistent limits by parents who are willing to take responsibility for limits. A "permissive" type of handling which allows the child to live on his own level tends to build secure feeling in the young child rather than to "spoil" him. It reduces to the minimum the denials and interferences which are likely to shake a child's confidence in himself. It accepts him as he is. It helps him feel adequate.

What Does "Permissiveness" Mean?

The word "permissiveness" is misunderstood or at least interpreted very differently by different people. It may be worth explaining what we mean by it. By a permissive type of handling we do *not* mean handling that allows the child to do whatever he likes and that leaves the entire burden of responsibility for his behavior up to the child. Few of us as adults are mature enough to take this much responsibility. We find that laws are necessary, and police are needed to enforce them. The adult who lets the child do just what he wants is an adult who is avoiding his own responsibilities.

Children need limits set for them to protect them from acting in ways which will have damaging consequences or frighten them. But the limits sometimes are set at quite different points. One person will not interfere with a child or stop him in what he does unless he or she feels sure the child's action will result in undesirable consequences. The child is thus free to explore and experiment with materials, to act in all kinds of childish ways and learn for himself. Another person will interfere or stop a child unless he or she feels sure that what the child is doing is desirable. There is much less room for discovery and for trying out ways of acting under this method. The first person's attitude is a "permissive" one in contrast to the restrictive attitude of the second person.

By permissiveness we do not mean indulgence. Instead, we mean leaving children free to explore and discover and create and find their own way insofar as possible within acceptable limits. We also mean a generous quality in giving to the child, not a niggardly giving. "Of course you can," rather than, "I guess you can but I wish you wouldn't"; or, "Take all you need," rather than, "Don't take much"; or, "There's plenty for everyone," rather than, "No one can have more than one piece." When we give generously, children grow less anxious. They need less. They are more secure. By "permissiveness" we refer to a "giving" attitude, but one with no lack of firmness when this is needed.

Children are not helped to build confidence by parents who are indulgent, who give in to them rather than face the unpleasant behavior of a thwarted child. Both parents and child need to learn to face unpleasant realities in constructive ways, rather than avoid facing them.

Parents Need to Be Secure People

Accepting the child as he is and meeting his needs freely are easier for people who are themselves secure. A secure person is relaxed, comfortable, permissive, and giving. He or she does not feel so much need to make demands on others. Secure people are likely to create the kind of environment in which it is easy for the child to think of himself as an adequate person. Mike, for example, has lived with comfortable parents. He is free of defenses. He looks at the puzzle he worked on the day before and says, "That one was hard for me." He is a secure child.

Insecure people are defensive and often demanding. They are likely to set standards which the child can meet with difficulty, if at all. They are likely to be very concerned with what other people say about them as parents. If they are to accept children, parents need to be secure people; yet there are many reasons why parents have a hard time feeling secure today. They are handicapped not only by economic insecurities, tensions, and conflicts in the world, by inadequate housing and limited community resources in health and recreation, but also by an education which offers little guidance in understanding the parent-child relationships. Charles' father, who spoke in such a belittling way to his son, is typical of many parents. He wants to be a successful parent, but he is without experience or preparation for his role. Like most people, he values success highly and is striving for it in a professional field. His concept of a successful parent is one whose child behaves like an adult. He feels his failure to achieve this goal with Charles. His love for the child is hidden under his constant criticism. He is not a secure parent. He makes Charles an insecure child.

A Child May Be Offered Many Different Kinds of Experiences by Adults

By the time the child reaches the nursery school he will have had many experiences which will determine how secure and confident he feels. He may have come from a home where he has been accepted by secure parents, or he may have come from a home where his parents are too insecure themselves to be able to accept his immaturities. The experiences that he will have in nursery school will add to the foundation he has laid. The acceptance he finds in the teachers, the care with which experiences are adapted to his readiness to meet them, beginning with the experience of entering the school itself, either will bring growth in the direction of being more secure and adequate or will handicap this growth. We will consider further the significance of his nursery school experiences as we discuss ways of strengthening his positive feelings.

RECOGNIZING THE CHILD'S FEELINGS

We will raise the question here of how we may recognize a child's feelings. How do we identify feelings so that we may be of help to a child?

Children reveal their feelings through behavior. Sometimes they do it openly and directly. They act as they feel. Sometimes their feelings come out in ways that

Security comes from having a teacher who cares.

Courtesy of Suzanne Szasz.

are harder to identify. We must learn to understand; then we can recognize how plainly they speak to us through behavior.

Perhaps the first step in understanding the meaning of behavior is to be able to look at the way a child behaves without feeling a necessity to change his behavior. We must learn to look at behavior as it is rather than in terms of what we want it to be. We are likely to confuse the meaning of a child's behavior with our own feelings if we try to judge it, if we decide that the child should or should not be behaving as he is.

There Are Clues to a Child's Feeling in Behavior

We have already pointed out how children differ in the kinds of adjustments that they make in new situations. These differences have meaning. The person who wishes to understand a child will observe carefully how he responds in a new situation. He will not decide how the child should respond and try to force this pattern of response on him. If he does, he may damage the child and his development.

Children reveal characteristic attitudes in everyday, familiar situations, too. These may be seen in such things as in the way the child walks, runs, holds his hands, in his posture, and so forth. Posture is, of course, influenced by constitutional and environmental factors, but over and above these, reflections of the child's emotional patterns can be seen in his muscle tensions. One child's hands are relaxed, and another's are tense and constantly moving. One child clutches our finger tightly as we walk along with him, a sign of his need for support and the intensity of his feeling. Another lets his hand lie limply in ours, suggesting perhaps the nongiving quality of his relationships with others, in contrast to the warm, responsive grip of still another child who welcomes closeness without clinging to it. These are all clues to help us understand the child's feeling.

Sometimes a conflict the child is feeling is expressed in the movements of his hands, as in the case of the child who is watching finger-painting. He may stand at a distance, wiping his clean hands on his shirt or wringing them together, showing us the conflict he feels between the desire for sensory experience and the force of the restriction he has known against satisfying this desire.

There Are Clues in a Child's Speech

Voice quality and speech offer clues to feeings. The quality of a child's voice may be strained and tight, or relaxed and easy. It may be loud and harsh, or soft and faint, or it may be confident and well modulated. Even the amount of speech may give some indications of the extent of the child's assurance or of his hesitation. One child talks very little; another chatters almost constantly. These extremes may be a reaction to strains and pressures which are making them feel less confident and less secure than they should feel. Many insistent, needless questions are sometimes a symptom of insecurity, a seeking for reassurance more than for any specific answer. Too often these questions meet an impatient rebuff, not calculated to satisfy the need they express.

Spontaneous singing usually indicates confidence and contentment. The child who sings at play is probably comfortable, and it is worth noting the times and places when singing occurs spontaneously. We can learn from this in what areas or on what occasions a child feels secure. We can provide more of these kinds of experience. We have an important clue here.

The child who asks the teacher, "Do you want to go outdoors with me?" may really be saying, "I'm afraid to go out by myself. It would help if you wanted to go with me." The teacher needs to understand the meaning back of what he actually says.

The child who says happily, "Isn't this going to be a good gate? I'm building it all myself," is telling us something about what comfortable feelings he has about himself. This same boy's father once remarked about him, "I think he's one of those fortunate people who like themselves." The child liked himself—and everyone else, and was one of the most likeable children one could meet. He had been "loved and valued" in his family as the Navaho toddler is in his.

There is a real consciousness of an emerging self in these words of Katherine—the same Katherine who is "bigger than you think"—when she says, "I'm different from all the other people. When other people laugh, I don't, even if it's silly." Katherine feels secure enough to be different.

Patterns of Behavior Give Us Clues to the Child's Feelings

Children who feel insecure are likely to face a new experience or a difficult experience by defending themselves. They retreat or avoid the experience, or resist, or attack. Their defensiveness may make it difficult for them in the situation. Children who feel secure, on the other hand, do not feel the need to defend themeslves. They are freeer to look for ways of coping with the situation. They often seek out new experiences.

Bill, whom we mentioned earlier, was able to cope with Kim's interference at the blackboard in a variety of ways. A less secure child might have defended himself by crying or attacking. Ralph bursts into tears when someone knocks against the tower he is building, and then he hits out frantically at the offender. He has little confidence in his ability to cope with interference. It is worth noting that Ralph feels sufficiently secure with a few children in the group to be able to accept interference when he is with these friends, without being overwhelmed by feelings of helplessness.

When people lack confidence in themselves, they usually act defensively in many situations. Jane, who is new in the nursery school, begins to cry when the teacher asks her to be quiet at rest time. She is too insecure yet to accept any indication that she is behaving unacceptably. The teacher's suggestion that it was time to settle down and rest would have helped a child who felt at home in the school. The comfortable child can cope with demands. The insecure child tries to defend himself against them.

The secure child finds it easy to be friendly. He can share with others because he does not fear loss. He does not need to defend his rights. The insecure child cannot afford to share. His problem is not one of selfishness or unfriendliness but one of degree of security. We need to handle the real problem, not the symptom, in such cases.

Sometimes the Clues Are Indirect Ones

Peter was nearly four, but he had a hard time separating from his mother when she started to leave the nursery school. He cried and protested. His mother was distressed and felt she could not leave him. One day he had this conversation with his teacher as she was helping him get ready to go home:

Peter (half teasingly): Miss Williams, will my locker be here when I come back?
Miss W.: Yes, Peter, it will be right here waiting for you.
Peter: If my locker starts to run away, will you hold it?
Miss W.: Yes, I'll hold it tight and tell it to stay right here because Peter is coming to-morrow.
Peter: You just hold it. I want it right here.

As the teacher thought about the conversation, she felt that in an indirect way Peter was telling her that although he wanted to run away home, he wanted more to stay at nursery school. He needed more help from her in resolving the conflict he felt in separating from his mother. He wanted her to "hold" him, like the locker.

She telephoned his mother and suggested that the mother try leaving, even though Peter protested, for Peter really was enjoying school and might be ready to stay by himself. The mother left him the next day, a bit reluctantly, for he was crying and struggling. Almost immediately he relaxed and was ready for play under the watchful eye of his teacher. She had given him the help he wanted.

John shows us what a name tag can symbolize to a child. He was proud of the name tag he wore to help the assistant teachers identify him. He reminded the teacher to stick it on each morning. During the morning, one of the teachers reproved him for something he did. John said nothing, but a few minutes later this teacher observed that he had taken off the name tag. She felt that it was as though he did not want his name to be associated with misbehavior. He could remove his guilty self.

Thumbsucking May Be a Symptom of Insecurity

When we are in nursery school, we may see a child sucking his or her thumb at rest time or when the group is listening to a story or even during a play period. Like all behavior, thumbsucking is a symptom and may indicate a need in the child for more reassurance and greater security than he has found in his experience. It may be a difficult world for him because he is expected to be more grown-up than he is ready to be. He may be expected to be quiet, to inhibit his impulses for touching things, to take over adult ways of behaving at the table or in social situations, to comprehend and maintain the rules for property rights, and so forth. The strain of living up to all these demands, or of failing to live up to them, may be so great that the child seeks an infantile source of comfort. He turns to his thumb as a refuge.

The child is telling us something through his thumbsucking, and we need to understand. We should not increase his strain by taking away the avenue of comfort that he has found, but we should try to make his life simpler and more comfortable. We should try to reduce the tensions he is under and offer him a greater chance for feeling secure and adequate, so that he may seek other kinds of satisfactions.

Mary Lou Took Her Own Thumb Out of Her Mouth

Mary Lou was a round little girl of three who sucked her thumb most of the time at nursery school. She was timid and often held onto the teacher's skirt with her free hand. She didn't venture into activity with other children or even play alone actively.

Mary Lou was the oldest of three children and had always been a "good" girl according to her mother. She had been easy to care for and could even be depended on to watch out for her little sister while her mother was busy with the baby. She seemed content with little to do and never disturbed the babies. It was not hard to imagine that Mary Lou had had very little chance to have the satisfactions that usually come with being a baby. She had had to grow up very quickly, and had had to seek approval by behaving in unchildlike ways.

She remained dependent on the teacher at nursery school for many weeks, but her interest in the children was plain as she watched a group having fun together. Sitting close to the teacher she sometimes became part of a group at the piano or at the clay table. She had a real capacity for enjoying experiences and a sense of humor which was evident as she felt freer to act. She thoroughly enjoyed the sensory experiences at the clay table, in the sandbox, and in the mud hole in the nursery school yard. She often played alone in the doll corner after she felt more at home.

Later she ventured into more active play. She still stood around with her thumb in her mouth part of the time, but she was busy in the sandbox or riding the tricycles more of the time. The most marked change came in her behavior after she gained enough courage to use the slide. Sliding was a popular activity, and Mary Lou would often stand watching but resisted any suggestion that she join the group at the slide. At last on a day when no one else was at the slide, she tried it, with her favorite teacher near to hold her hand. It was an effort but she succeeded and went down again and again. She waved gaily to her mother when her mother came that day and showed off her newly acquired skill. From then on she participated more freely in every group. Mastering the slide seemed to give her a great deal of confidence. She even did a little pushing to hold her place in line there and began to stand up for herself in other ways. She was busy and happy. She hardly ever had time for her thumb. By the end of a year some of the adults had even forgotten that she used to suck her thumb. The fact that she no longer needed her thumb told a great deal about the change in Mary Lou and what nursery school had meant to her.

All Nervous Habits Are Symptoms

Other children may express the tensions they are feeling by biting their nails, twisting on their clothes, or sucking other objects. Masturbation is another means of finding satisfaction and a defense against strain. We may do a great deal of harm by attacking the symptom directly and denying the child an avenue of expression while he is still feeling tension and seeking relief and satisfaction. We need to look on all of these so-called nervous habits as symptoms whose cause must be sought and treated before the symptom itself can be expected to disappear. Treating only the symptom will tend to make some other form of expression necessary for the child and increase the strain he feels. The thumbsucking child may become a nailbiting child or a masturbating child, for example, if the symptom and not the cause is attacked. We must keep in mind the fact that all kinds of behavior have meanings which we cannot afford to ignore.

Speech Patterns Reveal Adjustments

Through his manner of speech, a child tells us something about himself, too. In the nursery school we are likely to hear children whose words tumble out in broken rhythms or with many repetitions. Preschool children are just learning to talk, and they often cannot form or recall the words as fast as they wish to get their ideas across. In some children this blocking is marked and begins to resemble stuttering.

Because children's speech is in its formative stage, it is especially important for us to handle its development with understanding. The repetition and broken rhythm which sounds like what we call stuttering or stammering is in itself a sign of strain and tension in the child. These strains may be temporary ones such as the piling up of unusual experiences which have fatigued the child or too much excitement just at the point in his growth when he is making rapid progress in learning to talk. Speech may be the most vulnerable spot at the moment, and it breaks down under the strains. Or the strains may be of long standing, such as conflicts over relationships in the family or the piling up of hostilities which are allowed no avenue for expression.

If the emphasis is put on the symptom—the imperfect speech—the result may be a serious and lasting speech disorder. It is important to avoid asking him to "stop and say it more slowly" as many people will do. It is important for us to accept his speech and attack the conditions which are causing it. We can make it a point to stop and give the child our full attention when he is speaking, so that he will not feel the need to hurry. We can speak slowly ourselves, so that we will set a pattern in speech that will be easier for him to adopt successfully. But most of all we need to accept the fact that speech like this is a sign that pressures and demands made on this child must be reduced if his speech patterns are to change.

Infantile mispronunciations are common and reflect patterns of feeling as well as of speech. They may indicate that the child is clinging to babyhood. The independent experience of going to a nursery school will itself be of help to the child. We need to read and talk a great deal to the child whose speech has defective sounds in it, enunciating clearly as we speak.

It is of interest that types of speech defects vary in different culture patterns. Among certain Eskimo and Indian tribes, for example, no case of stuttering has ever been recorded. In our culture, stuttering is much more common among boys than girls, while there are cultures where the reverse is true. Speech seems to be a sensitive index or response to the pressures which an individual feels. We need to try to understand more than just the words which are spoken.

ACCEPTING THE CHILD'S FEELINGS

In all these ways, a child shows us how he feels. After we have learned to recognize the child's feelings, we must find ways of adding to his feelings of security and confidence and reducing his feelings of insecurity.

What are some of the ways in which we can do this in the nursery school?

We Must Face and Accept Feelings If We Are to Help

The most important step is to make sure that we really accept the child's feelings — that we do not condemn or blame him for feeling as he does. Perhaps he feels afraid or angry or unfriendly. These may be feelings of which we do not approve, but approval and acceptance are different things. Acceptance means recognizing without blaming. It does not mean permitting the child to act out his feelings as he may wish, but it does mean acknowledging that he has the right to feel as he does without being ashamed of it. We may not approve, but we must accept the feelings that the child has if we are going to help him with them. Our very acceptance often reduces the feeling and makes the child less defensive about his fear or his anger or his hostility. Instead of hiding his feelings, he can bring them out where he — and we — can do more about them.

Accepting Our Own Feelings May Be Difficult

We usually find it difficult to be accepting about feelings which we have had to deny in ourselves. When we were children, we often felt jealous or resentful or hostile, but we may not have been permitted any expression of these feelings. They were not accepted by the adults around us. We had to act as though we loved a little sister, for example, and were willing to share our dolls with her, or we had to let the neighbor boy ride in our wagon because the adults insisted that children must be generous. Resentment piled up inside us, as well as guilt for the feelings that we knew existed in us. Now, as adults, we find it hard to be accepting of the child who refuses to share her doll or who pushes another out of the wagon. We feel like punishing the little girl who doesn't want to share her doll or her wagon. This helps us to deny that we were ever like this little girl. But if we handle our feelings by denying them, we cannot offer help to children who face problems with their feelings.

The story of what goes on unconsciously is oversimplified by the description we have given, of course, but we can be sure that whenever we feel strongly rejecting of a bit of behavior, there are deep emotional reasons lying in our experience for such a rejection. For some of us there will be more of these emotionally toned areas than for others, and our feelings will be stronger. Few of us will have escaped without some areas of behavior about which we find it hard to be accepting.

If, on the other hand, we were helped to accept our real feelings when we were children, we will now find it easier to be accepting of children as they show their feelings. If the adults with us when we were children said, "It's easy to get mad with someone who takes your things, I know," instead of saying, "She's your sister and you must love her and share with her," then we would have felt understood and could have faced our feelings with this kind of support. It would have seemed easier to feel and act more generously. This is the kind of help that we want to offer the children we are caring for today.

It is important if we are to help children in this way that we free ourselves of our old defenses. As adults we can now take the step of accepting the reality of any feeling that exists. We know that we all find sharing and loving hard at times. Some jealousy is almost inevitable as children adjust to changing patterns in the family or at school. It is not necessary to deny the existence of feeling. Hostile, aggressive feelings exist in all of us.

Acceptance Helps the Child

The child who refuses to share a toy is not helped by disapproval and shaming. Neither is the child who is afraid. All these children need to be accepted as they are if they are to feel secure. There is always a reason for their behavior. As we work with the little girl who refuses to share her doll or who pushes her companion out of the wagon, we will accept her feelings and use her behavior as a clue to understanding. We will ask ourselves some questions. What kind of little girl is it who is trying to keep the doll? Is she craving affection and substituting the doll for the love she seeks? Does she depend on possessing things to give herself a feeing of security? How can we help her?

We Can Voice Our Acceptance of Feeling

We can express our acceptance in words: "I know how you feel. It makes you cross because it's Timmy's turn on the swing and you want it to be yours," or, "It makes you feel cross to have your blocks tumble over, I know," or, "You're pretty mad with me right now because I can't let you play outdoors." Words like these help if they express a real acceptance of the feelings which exist. They are different from words like "You didn't mean to hit Bobby, did you?" which are untrue, as the child's reply, "I did, too," tells us. We must be honest and state what is true.

CONFIDENCE THROUGH EXPRESSION

Feelings Must Be Expressed

Next comes the question of what can be done about a feeling after it has been accepted. The answer is that feelings must be expressed in some way if we are to be secure and confident. If feelings are not expressed, they remain with us to be carried around until they come out unexpectedly in ways that may make us unhappy and less sure of ourselves.

Feelings must be expressed, and they are best expressed at the point when they occur. The child who says, "I'm afraid," is already less troubled by the feeling of fear. The child who says, "I don't like you," to someone who frightens him may be managing his feeling better than the child who says nothing but then bursts into tears when the person tries to make his acquaintance. The child who is angry needs to do something about the way he feels at the time, rather than keep his anger hidden where it may come out in more damaging ways later; by that time his anger may have grown and spread.

When we can do something about the way we feel, we are more confident. Psychiatrists tell us that the child who has been aggressive in his early years and whose behavior has been met with understanding has a better chance to make a good adjustment in adolescence than the submissive child. The aggressive child has done something about his feelings and has had a chance to identify them and to learn how to manage them.

We should encourage expression of feelings at the time they arise. Expressing a feeling at the time it occurs helps us identify it and keep it manageable. We can be much clearer as to what the feeling is really about. We can be more confident because we are likely to manage it in ways that are appropriate.

It Is Essential to Express Feelings in Words

There are many ways in which feelings can be expressed. The most important way for all of us is to express our feelings in words. It is essential to learn to put negative feelings into words if we are to manage them constructively. When children can use language to drain off negative feeling, they have taken a step in control of feeling. Their later responses will be more reasonable.

As adults, we often put our feelings into words to ourselves, silently, but we know how we feel then. We feel still better if we have chance to talk to a friend about our feelings. Getting a feeling into words makes it seem more manageable. It helps drain it off. Most important, it makes the feeling clear to us. Knowing how one feels is tremendously important. It is a dangerous thing to try to fool oneself about the feelings one has. We must understand and face our feelings if we are to be secure, comfortable people.

The child needs help in understanding what he feels, and he also needs help in putting the feelings he has into words. We should welcome his verbal expressions of feeling, for this way of expressing feelings means a step in his growth towards maturity and control of feelings. Children usually find it easy to talk things out directly, on the spot. They call people names or shout insults to one another. They may be using the best means of handling feeling that they have at their disposal. They are not grown-up people yet. They are controlling the impulse to hit or attack. They are expressing, not hiding, their feelings.

Clinical workers have reported that when they have been able to help young children express their feelings in words rather than acts, the children have seemed to gain in feeling secure. Expressing strong feeling in words rather than actions has led to more spontaneity and a higher level of behavior in general.

Putting Her Fears into Words Relieved Jill

Jill gives us an example of what putting feelings into words can do for a child. Jill had been in nursery school about six months and had been developing very well. She was a friendly, active child who enjoyed play with other children, and she was eager and curious.

Courtesy of Jean Berlfein.

Children who are friends can discuss plans freely together.

During one holiday period Jill had an experience in the doctor's office that had left her very frightened and upset. Her parents had comforted her as well as they could and tried to interest her in other things. Since they were very disturbed themselves about the affair, they preferred not to talk about it. They did not mention it to the teacher when Jill returned to school after the holiday. The teacher noticed a change in Jill's behavior. She was quiet and passive. She clung to the teacher and cried easily. Her teacher felt sure that something was wrong and asked the parents for a conference. They were glad to come and talk with her, and they told her about the incident. They, too, had felt that Jill was acting differently, and they were eager to help her. The teacher pointed out that it was very important for Jill to feel able to talk to someone about her fears. Jill's mother seemed very understanding, although she felt it might be hard for her to talk with the child about the matter. The teacher suggested that the next time Jill got upset and cried, her mother might tell her that she, too, had been upset in the doctor's office, that she understood how Jill had felt, and that it was good to talk about the matter.

A few days later the mother telephoned to report that she had had a talk with Jill the night before. The parents were preparing to go to bed and had found Jill still awake. She seemed unhappy. The mother had gone into the room and, sitting on Jill's bed, she had begun to talk with her about the frightening experience. She said that at first Jill did not seem able to put anything into words, but as they continued talking she became freer and finally went over all the details. Her mother told Jill that whenever she felt unhappy and afraid, she could come and talk with her, that she would understand, for she felt the same way sometimes.

At rest time that day in school, Jill said to the teacher, "You know what happened? Last night I was unhappy and I told Mummy." The teacher asked, "And Mummy understood?" "Yes," said Jill, "she asked me why I was unhappy and I couldn't say, but she knew it was about the doctor." The teacher answered, "Mummies do understand and know, and you can tell Mummy when you feel that way again." Jill went on, "And she said that at night when I am unhappy to come and tell Mummy and Daddy, but I wasn't unhappy anymore. I was just a little unhappy, and now I'm happy." The teacher repeated, "Mummies and daddies do understand, don't they! You can always tell them."

That evening the teacher telephoned Jill's mother to tell her about the conversation. Jill's mother could hardly believe that Jill had repeated this conversation, even using the same words that the mother had used to her. She realized that it had made a deep impression on the child. She felt that she herself could talk to the child more easily now. In nursery school and at home Jill's behavior began to change rapidly. She had played and laughed that day at school, jumping in and out of a box with two other children. She began to assert herself more and to take her place in the activities of the school. She became more like her old self. It seemed wonderful to the teachers, too, that a conversation with a mother who understood could do so much to relieve a child. Putting her fears into words with the help of someone she trusted had drained off much of the disturbing feeling and had left the little girl free to grow as before. Her mother had learned from the experience. It gave her confidence. She knew better how to help her child.

There Are Other Ways to Express Feelings

In Crying

Crying is another good way to express feeling, yet many times we hear people say to a crying child, "That didn't hurt. You're too big to cry." The crying may come because there have been too many failures or too much deprivation or frustration. Whatever the reason, the feeling of wanting to cry is there and needs to be accepted, not denied. No one can handle with wisdom feelings he isn't supposed to have. Words like "I know how you feel," when they are said by a person who really accepts the feeling help a good deal more than words like "You're too big to cry."

In Movements

Motor forms of expression of feeling are common forms for expression. Expressing feeling through movements or muscle activity is a way often used by young children to express feeling. A young child may kick or hit or throw. Our job is to help him use motor outlets in a way which will not be damaging to others. He may even need to be put by himself so that he can act in these ways without hurting anyone. If he is older, he may be able to take a suggestion about using a punching bag to advantage. Vigorous physical activity, such as pounding, or throwing a ball hard against something, will serve as an outlet for feeling.

If there is a warm, understanding relationship between child and adult, the child can accept many types of suggestion for draining off negative feeling. The teacher may be successful when she says, "You feel just like hitting someone, I know, but you must not do it. Try hitting the target over there with these bean-bags. See how many times you can hit it. I'll count the hits." The child may be able to handle his feelings with the help of an understanding, accepting teacher. Our job is to see that he does not use destructive outlets. It is also our job to direct him to outlets that are possible and acceptable.

Through Creative Media

Materials which offer possibilities for creative expression can be used to drain off feelings and make them more manageable. Finger-painting, painting at the easel, working with clay, playing in water, even the sandbox or a good old mud hole, will help a child to relax as he expresses feelings through these media. Music offers still another possibility and is often used this way by children.

Creative materials should be freely available to children because of the value they have as avenues for the expression of feeling. Adults use these same outlets. The child who has found he can turn his feelings into such creative channels has discovered an outlet which will serve him all his life. A child is more secure if he has many avenues of expression open to him. He grows as he can express himself and his feelings through art media. When he is denied self-expression in art media because patterns are set for him, he loses a valuable avenue for the relief of feeling which might help to safeguard him all his life.

The child is able to concentrate on making his picture in a secure environment.

The Timid Child Learns How to Express His Feelings

We will often see a timid, inhibited child swing over into unduly aggressive behavior as he begins to gain confidence in himself. This may be the first step in gaining confidence. He must first express his feelings and find acceptance for them. Then he can proceed to modify them. The child who has been inhibited may express his feelings in clumsy and inappropriate ways in the beginning. His first expression of feeling may seem exaggerated. It may belong at a much younger level than his present chronological age level. But if his timidity developed in an earlier period because he was afraid of his feelings and the way people would react to them so that he was not able to express feeling, he will need to go back and act as he wanted to act earlier. With understanding guidance he will come through this stage quickly, but he must "live out," for however brief a time, a period of expression at the less mature level. He must try out being "bad" and discover that he is accepted and that his badness does not frighten the adult. It can be managed.

"Transitional Objects" Give Security

Children sometimes use "transitional objects" to help themselves feel more secure and better able to cope with new or difficult experiences. With some children it may be a blanket they have had from babyhood. With others it may be a cuddly toy. But whatever the object they use, it should be treated with respect. Carrying it or knowing that it is easily available may help the child weather the strains he feels in moving from one stage of growth to another. The object is a device for coping with a difficult world. It has symbolic value for the child.

Transitional objects help in the "weaning" process that is part of growing. They are useful in periods of change when the child must let go or leave behind his old sources of security. They signal to us the child's need for support, as well as indicate the effort he is making to deal with change. One two-year-old in a group could not part with his sweater for several weeks after he entered the group. It may have represented his mother or his home. He wore the sweater, or carried it, and became very anxious if it was out of his sight. The way a child uses a transitional object gives us clues as to his feelings.

A Child Feels More Secure When He Is Having Satisfying Experiences

The child whose needs are being met is more likely to be confident than the one whose needs are not met. This applies to his experience in the nursery school as well as at home. If the school is providing satisfying, stimulating experiences, it makes it easier for the child to be happy and secure. The whole program of the school, as well as the equipment provided, will contribute to the child's growth in feeling more secure and more adequate. Experiences adapted to the child's level of development, equipment which fits him and makes it easy for him to solve problems, support from adults who understand what his needs are, all make it easier for a child to gain the feeling of security and adequacy that he needs.

Most important of all, in the nursery school the child is thrown with people who are on about the same level of development. He can have fun doing things with other children. Among this group of equals he does not need to feel inadequate, for he *can* keep up with them. He can do things as well as many of the others. He gains strength from the feeling that he is like others, from being able to identify himself with people who are at his stage of growth. Belonging to a group of equals constitutes one of the best forms of insurance against feeling little and helpless. We will discuss this point at greater length later, but we mention it here because of the important contribution it makes to feelings of adequacy in a child.

The child needs to find teachers in the school who will accept his positive feelings, too. As teachers, we must be ready to return his smile, to take his hand when he slips it into ours, to take him into our arms when he seems to feel the need of such closeness. We must respond to his warm, friendly feelings. If it is his need and not ours that we are meeting in doing this, we can be sure that he is helped to be more independent by what we do. He will gain confidence as he feels sure of having a warm response from us when he wants it.

GOOD TEACHING CONTRIBUTES TO
DEVELOPMENT OF CONFIDENCE

By the techniques we use as teachers we will also help the child grow more secure and confident. Let us take the situation of a child climbing on the jungle gym as one example, and see what it may mean.

Two-year-old Joan, just learning to climb, cautiously and awkwardly manages to get halfway up in the jungle gym and then calls for help, "Help me. I want

Courtesy of Jean Berlfein.

Conversation between friends at snack time in a comfortable atmosphere.

down." An adult comes to her rescue and answers the cry by lifting her down. Joan is on the ground safe, but with all feeling of achievement lost! On another occasion a different adult comes to the rescue. She stands beside the child and says reassuringly, "I'll help you, Joan. Hang on to this bar and put your foot here," thus guiding Joan's climbing back to the ground. Safe on the ground, Joan is elated. She starts right up again and this time is successful in reaching the top. When her mother comes, she can scarcely wait to show her this new achievement.

If, when Joan starts to climb the jungle gym, her mother says in a disgusted voice, "Come on, Joan, you've had all morning to play. I'm in a hurry. You can show me tomorrow," Joan may again lose the feeling that she is a person who can achieve. But if her mother is eager to share the experience and watches her, exclaiming, "That's fine, Joan, you've learned to climb way up high," Joan takes another step in growing confident.

SUMMARY

Let us summarize briefly some of the things that we can do in the nursery school to increase a child's feeling of security and confidence.

1. We can *accept him* as he is, his feelings and his behavior, knowing that there are reasons for the way he feels and acts. We will recognize that hitting and other forms of motor expression of feeling are normal for the young child. We will stop his unacceptable actions without blaming him or shaming him. We can expect him to change his behavior, but he has a right to his feelings. We want him to respect himself and have confidence in himself. If he is able to do this, he must feel that we have confidence in him.

2. We can help him find *acceptable outlets for his feelings*. We will help him put his feelings into words not only as a way of identifying what he feels but also as a step toward control. We can help him use many avenues for the expression of feeling, especially the creative avenues, but we must be sure that feelings are expressed. The really destructive feelings are those that have no recognized outlets.

3. We can try to *meet the child's needs* as he indicates what his needs are, and we can leave him free to develop in accordance with his own growth patterns at his own rate. Thus, we will give him confidence and the feeling that he is an adequate person. We will refrain from "nudging" him. Instead, we will try to understand him.

4. We can *acquire skills in handling him* which will increase his confidence, making our suggestions to him in a positive way, reducing the difficulties of the situations he faces, adjusting our demands to fit his capacities, forestalling trouble when we can.

SITUATION FOR DISCUSSION

*Gilbert: Feelings are Strong**

9:35 Ginger, a student, had brought her riding equipment into the playroom. The saddle, the bridle, her riding boots, and a brightly colored horse

---

*Recorded by Jane Martin.

blanket were on a low table. The children crowded around the table, pointing and talking about the articles there.

As Ginger showed the children the blanket, Gilbert, a three-and-a-half-year-old, reached out and patted the blanket, saying, "Pretty, pretty." He pushed another child aside so that he could touch the saddle also. He ran his hand along the leather side of the saddle caressingly. "Mine, mine," he shouted at Nels when Nels tried to climb on the saddle. Glaring at Nels, Gilbert pushed him away and climbed up on the saddle himself, hanging on as tight as he could. "Mine, mine," he repeated. Without a word Nels walked away. Pam and Ann tried to get him to give them a turn in sitting on the saddle. The answer each time was an emphatic "No" from Gilbert.

9:48   The teacher entered the situation. "Gilbert, let's put the saddle across this plank (a board with ends resting on two chairs). Then when you sit on the saddle your feet will fit in the stirrups," she said. Very reluctantly Gilbert climbed off the saddle and turned his attention to the blanket and the rest of the equipment on the table. Many of the children tried "riding the horse," climbing on and off the saddle. Gilbert stayed by the blanket, rubbing it with both hands.

10:00   Ginger's mother came into the playroom to help Ginger take the equipment to the car. She picked up the blanket along with the boots and walked into the hall. Gilbert rushed after her, grabbing the blanket and shouting, "Mine, mine." Softly Ginger said, "Gilbert, we must take the blanket home to the horse." Gilbert screamed, "No, no," as he tugged at the blanket and began to cry, to the surprise of Ginger's mother. Connie, another student, picked Gilbert up and said, "Come, Gilbert. I'll read you a story." He kicked at her, screaming, "Mine, mine." Connie had no success in trying to quiet him. He sobbed for about ten minutes after Ginger had left. At juice time Gilbert joined the other children there.

Comment

How Might This Situation Have Been Managed to Make It a More Constructive One?

We find a child who evidently is deeply involved in the sensory aspects of experience. He is attracted to the brightly colored blanket, "Pretty, pretty." He feels the leather saddle caressingly and rubs his hands on the blanket.

What he enjoys, he also seems to want to possess. "Mine, mine," he shouts. His feelings are strong as he reveals by the long period of sobbing. He shows little confidence in his ability to possess what he wants, so he must act aggressively, pushing other children, glaring at them and shouting.

Our goal in this situation will be to preserve the sense of pleasure Gilbert feels and at the same time help him gain confidence that there is enough for him and for the others to enjoy, in other words, to help him feel better able to share experiences with others while still enjoying them himself.

The first opportunity to help came when Gilbert pushed Nels away and climbed into the saddle himself. At this point Ginger might have stepped in, saying, "Nels is taking his turn on the saddle. It will be your turn next." To help Gilbert accept this, she might have put her arm around him and told him how she used the blanket and the saddle when she rode her horse, describing the hard, smooth leather so different from the soft blanket. She could have carried on a conversation with him, enriching the experience by her comments. Then she would make sure that Gilbert *did* have the next turn and that he did not have too long to wait. He might feel more confident if Ginger or another adult had maintained his right to sit there when the others wanted to use the saddle, "It's Gilbert's turn now." He might then have been better able to give it up when the end of his turn came.

It is not clear from the record whether Gilbert did have a turn after the teacher asked him to get off so that the saddle could be placed on the board. If not, this experience would have contributed to his despair at losing the blanket in the end. Gilbert had turned to the blanket after having to leave the saddle and seemed to be using the blanket as a comfort or security object, rubbing it with his hand. It became one more loss for him. We notice that, according to the record, there was no help given to prepare him for its loss and no explanation until *after* it had gone.

When he began to cry, Ginger told him that the blanket belonged to the horse, a fact, but not one that helped him with his own feelings. She might have said, "I wish I could leave the blanket here for you, but the horse needs it. It is his blanket." She might have given him a hug as she said, "Feel it once again before I have to take it." This might have been a way of showing him that she understood his feelings, that she wished she could give him what he wanted so much to have.

When Connie picked Gilbert up and offered to read a story to him, she was really denying his feelings and avoiding facing them. It was as though she did not understand what he was feeling. A child can face and manage his feelings with help. It would have been more help to Gilbert if Connie had knelt down, putting her arms around him rather than picking him up (which would have made him feel more helpless). She might have said, "I'm so sorry that they have to take away the saddle and blanket. We liked them, didn't we! It is hard to see them leave. Maybe Ginger can bring them again someday." If his sobbing lessened, she might continue, "What did you like best, the saddle or the blanket?" as she tried to get him thinking in different ways about the experience, recreating it and capturing the enjoyment in recall, recovering and dealing with the loss.

It is evident that Gilbert could make use of a greater variety of sensory experiences. The equipment in the play group might include a box with a variety of fabrics: a piece of velvet, silk, fine cotton, textured material; squares of brightly colored gauze; scraps of colored pieces; and scraps of leather. Some blankets for the cradle, in colors, could be added in the homemaking area. Plenty of opportunity to work with collage materials and to use paints should be satisfying to Gilbert. An excursion to the barn to visit Ginger's horse would add a great deal to the experience of all the children, including Gilbert, with some preparation beforehand about what to expect and about what the children would be allowed to do there.

PROJECTS

1. Observe and record three situations in which the guidance given by the adult was directed toward helping the child to feel more secure and confident. Estimate how successful it was in its effect on the child.

2. Listen to the quality and pitch of the children's voices. List the names of children whose voices are high-pitched or strained, soft and indistinct, loud and

somewhat harsh, and easy and pleasant. How would you relate what the child's voice seems to reveal with what you know of the child's adjustment and his feelings about himself?

3. Make a list of emotionally loaded words sometimes used in describing behavior of a child, such as spoiled, stubborn, selfish. Indicate briefly how the use of such words may influence objective observation of behavior. Give an example of some descriptive terms which might be used to describe the same behavior in the case of some of the words listed above.

REFERENCES

Arnstein, Helene S., in cooperation with the staff of the Child Study Association of America: What To Tell Your Child About Birth, Death, Illness, Divorce and Other Family Crises. New York, The Bobbs-Merrill Co., Inc., 1962.

Erikson, Erik: Identity and the Life Cycle. New York, International Universities Press, 1959. Vol. 1, No. 1, Chap. 2.

Fraiberg, Selma: The Magic Years. New York, Charles Scribner's Sons, 1959. Part 4.

Freud, Anna: The emotional and social development of young children. In Feelings and Learning. Washington, D.C., Association for Childhood Education, International, 1965.

Keister, Dorothy: Who Am I? The Development of Self-Concept. Durham, North Carolina, Learning Institute of North Carolina, 1973.

Murphy, Lois B.: The Widening World of Childhood. New York, Basic Books, Inc., Publishers, 1962. Parts 3 and 4.

Yamamoto, Kaorn (ed.): The Child and His Image: Self-Concept in the Early Years. Boston, Houghton Mifflin Company, 1972.

CHAPTER 16

Fire (boy, 4 years 4 months)

FEELINGS OF HOSTILITY
AND AGGRESSIVENESS

Hostility and Aggressiveness Are Problems for Individuals and Groups

The problem of what to do about feelings of hostility and aggressiveness is a difficult one for individuals and for groups. It is not likely to be solved by avoidance or by denying the existence of these feelings. As we have pointed out, the existence of a feeling must be accepted before there is much chance that it can be handled constructively. Only when we have accepted our hostile, aggressive feelings can we discover (1) the best ways to handle them and (2) the best ways to prevent them from multiplying.

The nursery school is a laboratory where we can study the problems of negative emotions and try to understand them. Resentment and hostility expressed aggressively are evident in the behavior of children whenever the situation is one which is not rigidly controlled by adults, whenever children are free to show us how

303

they feel, as in the nursery school. A child who is angry may address the teacher as "You dummy," and this teacher will be the one in whom he has some confidence. He is likely to be more polite to the teacher with whom he does not feel as safe. "We don't like you," sing out two children to a third. Occasionally, a chorus of "name calling" greets the visitor in the school. Some children do not reveal hostile feelings by such direct expressions, but they may have the same feelings. We can learn to recognize their less direct expressions, too. We can learn how to prevent more hostility and aggressiveness from developing.

Hostility and Aggressiveness Are Tied Up with Growth

In an earlier chapter we suggested that a certain amount of hostile feeling in all of us results from the growing-up process. As infants we were helpless and often our needs were not met. We felt threatened by the greater strength of the people around us. There were many frustrations and interferences for us all. Frustrations breed resentment when the frustrated person is little and helpless.

Some aggressiveness is necessary, for growth itself is a going-forward process which demands aggressiveness. Dr. Kubie states, "The acquisition of positive, self-assertive, commanding and demanding attitudes in the first two years of human life is an essential step in the development of every child."* But we now realize that much unnecessary aggressiveness, as well as hostility, is aroused by some of the traditional methods of handling children at home and at school. Healthy aggressiveness becomes unhealthy. Resentment develops which interferes with healthy growth. As we apply better methods of guiding children in the growing-up processes, we should be able to reduce the amount of hostility and unproduc-

---

*Kubie, Lawrence S.: The child's fifth freedom. Child Study, Summer, 1948. p. 67.

Courtesy of Myron Papiz.

Children meet many frustrations.

tive aggression in the world and to do this with increasing effectiveness as our knowledge and understanding grow.

Resentment Is Increased by Discontinuous, Nonindulgent Training

The amount of resentment and aggression, as well as the amount of confusion and guilt over these feelings, is perhaps greater in our culture than in some others because our training is discontinuous. In one situation the child is supposed to be submissive and obedient, as with parents at home. In another situation, as on the playground, he is expected to "stand up for himself" and come out ahead in highly competitive types of situations. The same bit of behavior is wrong in one place and right in another. These discontinuities make learning difficult for the child and may increase the number of his mistakes and the resultant guilt that he may feel.

Children in our culture also carry a handicapping load of resentment when parental management is nonindulgent and harsh and when standards are rigidly enforced. Such methods may arouse a great deal of hostile aggressiveness in individuals. We have usually refused to acknowledge the extent of these feelings while we have gone on multiplying them—in children and in ourselves. The result is that they are spilling over constantly in all kinds of unsuspected ways in our personal lives as well as in our group life. Few problems are more important than the problem of facing and reducing the hostility we feel.

Patterns of Violence in a Culture Make Control of Aggressiveness Difficult

Managing feelings of hostility and aggression in constructive ways is made more difficult for the child who is exposed to patterns of violence in behavior in the culture. Many children today are watching programs on television that are full of brutal attacks on people, of cruelty, and of unfeeling lack of respect for the dignity of human beings. The example set by these patterns of behavior in television programs or on the street makes it only too easy for children to follow these patterns themselves when their own controls break down.

There are uncontrolled, violent ways of expressing the negative feelings within us, and there are more "civilized" ways that require understanding and control. Feelings must be expressed, but they can be expressed in words or in art forms or in actions that do no harm to others. The energy aroused can be channeled into constructive achievements. There are many social battles to be fought, for example. We need to help, not hinder, children in the difficult task of learning how to release hostility and aggression in ways that are not damaging to others or to themselves. Much that children see today in the world around them and on television makes their task more difficult. These sights are especially damaging to those children who happen to be carrying a heavy load of resentment inside them.

Children Need to Express Hostile Feelings

It is safe to say that *all* children at times feel aggressive and hostile but that not all children act out these feelings. In the past we have tended to give approval to the children who did not act out their negative feelings. From what we now know about mental health, we realize that it is essential that feelings be expressed if a person is to remain mentally healthy. The problem is to discover avenues of expression which are not destructive, rather than to deny expression to these feelings. It is unlikely that we can have a peaceful world for long, while the individuals in it are carrying around a load of hostility with the added guilt that having such feelings and denying them is sure to create. We must help children to face and to express their hostile feelings.

It is worth quoting part of the same discussion by Dr. Kubie as follows:

... repeatedly in the early years of life anger must be liquidated at its birth or it will plague us to the grave.... If we are ever to lessen the neurotic distortions of human aggression, then it seems clear that the anger must be allowed and encouraged to express itself in early childhood, not in blindly destructive acts but in words, so as to keep it on the fullest possible level of conscious awareness. Furthermore such conscious ventilation of feelings must be encouraged in the very situations in which they have arisen, and toward those adults and children who have been either the active or the innocent sources of the feelings. Only in this way can we lessen the burden of unconscious aggression which every human being carries from infancy to the grave.*

Adults Must Accept Hostile Feelings in Themselves

The important job of parent and teacher, then, becomes one of encouraging expression of feeling in nondamaging ways and of diminishing the number of situations in which negative feelings are developed. Our ability to do this will depend in part on our ability to accept our own feelings or we will find ourselves meeting aggression by aggression and hostility by hostility. When a child calls us "You dummy," we must be able to accept the fact of his feeling of anger without getting it tangled up with our own angry feelings. This will be easier as we realize that his words offer no real threat to us as such words might have in the past or under other circumstances. We happen to be the recipient of his anger and hostility at the moment, but they have been generated by many factors in his past experiences just as our own have been.

To the extent that we were punished or shamed for the expression of our own hostile feelings, we may find it hard to accept the fact that the child needs to express such feelings. If our own defenses against such feelings are strong, if we have permitted ourselves little expression, it may be difficult for us to permit expression for others. But it remains important for us to achieve this acceptance if we are to be of help to the child.

Marvin Could Cope with Strong Feelings Because He Could Express Them

Let us look at an example of the steps one child took to master his anxiety and resentment as he prepared himself to cope with a situation. The year before, Marvin had attended a child care center for five days. He had objected to going and had cried each day. His parents had not stayed with him, but the director had

---

*Kubie, Lawrence S.: The child's fifth freedom. Child Study, Summer, 1948. pp. 70 and 89.

reported he was "a nice quiet little boy." However, the parents learned that on the fifth day he had climbed into a chair and stayed in it all day, clutching his teddy bear. He had not eaten lunch or taken a nap. As he was a lively active three-year-old at home, the youngest of three children, they realized that he had really been unhappy and arranged for his care with a baby sitter in the neighborhood while they were at work.

They talked over plans the next year and decided to try the center again. Marvin was now four, and there was to be another teacher in charge whom they knew. Here is the father's report of what happened when he broached the subject to Marvin.

FATHER'S REPORT

Marvin was eating his breakfast. He was in his usual exuberant mood while eating his cereal. He was dive-bombing his spoon into the bowl with appropriate sound effects.

"Marvin," I said, "one of Daddy's friends is going to be working in the nursery school you went to with Tommy. Would you like to visit her with me sometime?"

Marvin stopped eating, his spoon poised in midair. His eyes grew wide with alarm. His body tensed and he almost visibly drew into himself. He continued to stare at me and his lower lip began to tremble.

"If you take me to that school again I'll throw a bomb at it and break it all up!" he blurted.

"We could go just for a visit," I said somewhat uneasily, not at all prepared for the impact the idea of nursery school still held for him.

"They're bad there! Those children don't like me! That lady doesn't like me!"

"You liked Tommy. Didn't Tommy play with you?"

Marvin was breathing heavily. After a pause he said, "Tommy could come to my house and play with me. I won't go to that school again!"

"You didn't like that school?"

"No! I will take my axe and chop it all up!"

"You don't want to go there again."

He was a bit more relaxed. "No." A pause. "No. They don't have good toys. Or good boys and girls. Or good people."

"You didn't have fun there."

"No." He became quite agitated again. Then in a quiet voice he said, "I'm tired of eating." He put down his spoon, climbed down from his chair and walked into our bedroom. He climbed into our bed and covered himself up.

I sat down on the bed beside him. "Pat me," he said.

I patted him and told him we would not visit the nursery school until he wanted to and that I would stay with him while we visited when we did go.

"But not today?" he asked.

"No, not today," I agreed.

"Not for this many days?" He carefully arranged his fingers so that he could hold up three.

"Not for many days," I agreed.

He lay still for a moment. "I better finish my cereal," he said, throwing back the blankets. He climbed out of bed and went back to the table. "Not for *many* days," he said to himself as he climbed into his chair.

We see that Marvin's first response is a rush of strong feeling. Then he mobilizes his forces and asserts himself. He attacks aggressively, "I'll throw a bomb at it and break it all up." He will solve the problem by destroying it. Wisely, his father does not resist but retreats a bit. Marvin then tries to think of reasons why this going to school must not happen. He does this effectively. Not only is the school "bad" and the lady there "doesn't like me," but his friend could come to his house to play. His father tries to put Marvin's feelings into words more directly, "You didn't like that school." Marvin's aggressiveness returns, "I will take my axe and chop it all up." His father then states the heart of the problem, "You don't want to go there again." Marvin seems a bit more relaxed as it is put into words by his father. He can count on his father's understanding. This time he is less nega- tive. He says that they don't have good people there rather than saying they are bad.

His acceptance begins but his appetite has gone. He leaves the table and goes to his parents' bed, climbs in, and covers himself up. He goes to the most comfort- ing place available to him and hides himself. His father follows silently, taken aback by the intensity of the child's feeling, appreciative of the difficulty of the problem that the child must struggle with. "Pat me," says Marvin, needing and able to use the support he knows an understanding father can give. Now the fa- ther suggests a compromise. They will not visit until Marvin feels ready and he, the father, will stay with him. We see the "mutual regulation," the working out of a problem together which brings good solutions and good relations when there is understanding. Marvin tests it out, "But not today?" and his father agrees. Then Marvin asserts himself again, but this time it is in having a share in the decision. "Not for this many days," holding up three fingers. When his father says, "Not for many days," Marvin's response is, "I better finish my cereal." He climbs out of bed and returns to the table, saying, "Not for *many* days," as he climbs into his chair. He has coped with the situation actively and constructively. His self-respect and confidence remain. His father has stood by him in the steps he took to master his anxieties. One suspects there has been a mutual growth in understanding and both will be able to meet the situation when the "many days" are over and it becomes a reality. They are better prepared.

SOURCES OF HOSTILE FEELING

Let us discuss some of the common situations in which resentment is felt by children, how feelings develop in these situations, and how they may be "liqui- dated."

A New Baby at Home Creates a Situation in Which Hostility Needs to Be Liquidated

One of the commonest occasions outside the nursery school in which the child will feel hostility needing "liquidation" is when a new baby arrives in his home. Parents are often afraid that the older child will be jealous and may reas- sure themselves that he "doesn't seem the least bit jealous." Yet it is inevitable that an older child will resent in some respects the coming of a new baby however much he may also enjoy other aspects of the changed situation. Even Julia, the well-adjusted child in one nursery school, was not eager to receive a baby sister into her home. She was at school when her grandmother came with the news of the arrival of the long-awaited baby. After hearing about her and asking some questions, Julia reassured herself, "She won't come home today, will she?" and when her grandmother affirmed this, she added, "I don't want her to," and returned to her play. Julia could express her feelings.

If parents are afraid of a child's jealousy, he may have to conceal it from them. It can only come out indirectly, in his too rough hugging of the baby and some "accidental" hurting of it, and in an increased cruelty in his play with other children. These indirect ways are not as healthy as a direct expression, for they are less understandable and actually liquidate the feeling less. There is less need to be afraid of hostile feelings themselves than of what they do to us when we try to hide them and thus lose control over them.

Liquidating Hostile Feelings at the Nursery School

When there is a new baby at home, the child's feelings often spill out in his behavior at nursery school. He will act them out in the doll corner, perhaps, spanking the dolls frequently, smothering them with blankets, or throwing one on the floor and stamping on it. In this way he relieves himself by draining off some of the hostility he may be feeling, making it easier to face the real situation. A good nursery school should have some dolls that can stand this kind of treatment. A direct "draining off" of feeling in this way may be about the only means a child has of expressing the conflict he is feeling. Many parents do not understand and accept expressions of feeling at home as Julia's parents could.

If our interest is in sound personality development, it is not hard to see how little real value there would be in emphasizing the proper care of dolls at this point. If one did insist that dolls were not to be treated in this way, one would block for the child this avenue of expression, leaving him in an emotionally dangerous situation. There might be a good deal of trouble ahead for him in his relationship with the real baby. It is worth noting that anthropologists report that certain very gentle Indian tribes permit young children to show great cruelty to animals, which, they suggest, may serve the purpose of draining off some of the hostility which children feel, and account in part for the Indians' friendly behavior with each other.

Rubber dolls and other rubber toys serve as a good medium for the release of hostile aggressive feeling. They can be pinched and bitten with a good deal of satisfaction. One three-and-a-half-year-old, whose relationships at home had been tense and strained, had felt his position in the family threatened by the return of a father who was almost a stranger to him, and then even more threatened by the arrival of a new baby. His insecurity and hostility came out in the readiness with which he attacked and bit other children in the nursery school. The teacher had to watch him constantly to prevent his attacking others. She found that she could substitute a rubber doll and that he seemed to find relief in biting it. Biting, incidentally, is usually done by a child who feels helpless. He can see no other way to meet his problems. She carried the doll in her pocket for a time so that it would be instantly available, and she gave it to him when she saw his tension mounting, saying, "I know! You feel just like biting someone. Here's the doll. It's all right to bite the doll." The least interference or the smallest suggestion of a rejection filled his already full cup of negative feeling to overflowing. He had to do something, and biting on the doll served to reduce the feeling to more manageable proportions. The teacher's acceptance and her understanding of the way he felt gave him confidence. The day came when he ran to her himself because he knew that he needed the doll to bite. He could recognize his feeling and handle it in a way that was not damaging to the other children. He began to have more success and find more satisfaction in his play. Steadily he had less hostile feeling to handle.

During this time, he had been engaging in a great deal of verbal aggression against the adults in the school. When he was faced with the necessity of limiting his activity during the rest period, for example, he would lie on his bed and attack the teacher verbally, "cut her up, her legs, her head, her arms," and would sometimes, "put her in the garbage can," or sometimes, "put her in the toilet." His words revealed the extent to which he himself had been hurt and the anger and fear he had felt. Very slowly, with many avenues of expression open to him, he drained off some of his resentful feeling, and the acceptance and success he had in the school helped him to build other kinds of feelings. He discovered other kinds of relationships, and the warm, supporting relationship he had with his teacher left him free to find friends among the children. No child in the group was more responsive in the end to the love offered him.

Another Source of Resentment Is the Necessity for Keeping Clean

Another source of resentment in children, in addition to changing positions in the family, lies in the demands made on them to "keep clean" and the fear and guilt they often feel when they yield to the impulse to play in dirt.

Ruth was a child whose mother had emphasized cleanliness and proper behavior, including a strict toilet training regimen. Ruth showed as much hostility and resentment toward adults as did any child in the group at first. She refused requests or suggestions which came from an adult, even though they might be ones she really wanted to carry out. Her mother characterized her behavior as "just plain stubborness." Their life together had been a succession of issues over one habit or the other. The following incident occurred after she had been in school a year and had begun to participate in activities with confidence and was even affectionate with the teachers she knew, saying, "I like you," with real feeling. Even then she still grew disturbed and anxious when faced with a little dirt.

Ruth happened to be on the playground with a student teacher. She was swinging. It was muddy and as Ruth's boots swept through the puddle under the swing, they splashed mud on her and on the teacher. Ruth looked disturbed. "What will your Dad say?" she asked the student teacher anxiously. The teacher assured her that he wouldn't say anything and that it was just an accident and couldn't be helped. But Ruth answered darkly, "Oh yes, he'll say something."

She again tried swinging but once more they both got splashed. Ruth said warmly, "I'm sorry," and she repeated, "What will your Dad say?"

This time the teacher replied by asking Ruth what she thought he would say. Ruth answered, "He'll say you're all dirty and will have to clean up and take a bath," and then she added, "I'm going inside and stay in, if you don't mind." She went in and didn't come outside again during the morning.

Even though she expected no punishment for splashing the mud in this situation, it was a "bad" thing to her. It meant disapproval from the adults on whom this insecure little girl had to depend. Standards for behavior were high and punishment severe. Her anxiety was apparent in her words and her behavior. It was not hard to see why she had shown hostility and unfriendliness.

In this situation, a more experienced teacher not only would have recognized the extent of the anxiety the child was showing by her questions, but would have tried to help her put it into words so that it might have become more understandable and manageable — so that she would not have needed to run away from it. She might have verbalized in some such way as this, "Does your Dad get mad when you're dirty? Mothers and Dads often do, don't they, when children get dirty?" This might have given Ruth the help she did not find in the student's denial that *her* Dad would be mad. Ruth knew better about hers! It would have made it a common, shared experience, easier to face. The teacher might have continued, "Sometimes it is all right to get dirty because we can get cleaned up afterward just as we can now. Sometimes it's even fun to get dirty. I used to like to myself," and this might have relieved the child. She might have been able to stay outdoors and have fun. She might have been better able to trust herself.

The Clue May Be a Small One

Sometimes it is harder to identify the feeling that lies back of words or acts. The child may be afraid to express his hostility or his aggression openly. We have to find the meaning from a very small clue. Grace, for example, had always been very "good." This meant that she was not able to be very expressive or creative. In the nursery school she gradually began to find it possible to act with greater freedom. It was clear to anyone watching her that she often wanted to act differently but did not dare.

One day the teacher observed Grace carefully laying several chairs on their sides on the floor. The teacher made no comment, not understanding the meaning of this behavior. The next day Grace's mother asked anxiously about how Grace was behaving in school. She was worried because Grace had told her that the day before she had "knocked over all the chairs at nursery school." It was then clear to the teacher that this careful laying of a few chairs on their sides was in reality an aggressive act for Grace. It was as far as she dared to go in expressing her aggressive feelings, and she would have liked to have made it a much bigger act than it was.

Grace needed to be helped to see that she could express aggressive feelings, that she could really be accepted as a little girl who had "bad" feelings as well as "good" ones, that there were safe limits at school, too. Her parents needed to have more understanding of the importance of accepting all of Grace's feelings.

Dick, who was very timid, showed much the same kind of need when he declared, "I'm going to make a lot of noise," and then took one block and carefully threw it on the floor. His parents approved of quiet boys. He had few opportunities to be noisy, and he was trying to show that he really dared to be the kind of person he wanted to be.

Failure to Get Attention and Response

Failure to get attention and response will rouse resentment and hostility in children, too, especially in insecure children who are seeking reassurance through getting attention. Their feelings are involved in a way that makes them sensitive to failure. Situations are constantly arising in which children want attention from the teacher or from other children, want to feel important and needed—and fail. They are resentful and hostile as a result.

Whenever the situation is a competitive one, there is more chance for feeling these failures. A child may want the attention of the teacher and, not getting it, may attack the child whom he feels is his rival or the teacher whom he feels is deserting him. A child like this needs to have his confidence built up so that he will see others as less of a threat to him. He needs help in accepting and finding better outlets for his feeling. When it is all right to admit the feeling of wanting the teacher all to yourself, it becomes easier to work out a solution better than attacking others.

As teachers, we should be aware of the strong need most children have to feel sure of their place and to receive a share of our attention. When we give attention to one child, we need to remember that other children may be feeling left out. We saw an example in Betsy, who untied her shoe so that the teacher could tie it for her just as the teacher had done for another child. Not many children can deal with their feelings as directly as Betsy. They may need some help from us. A teacher may say, "I think you'd like me to do something with you sometimes. I've been doing a lot with Helen lately because she is new and isn't sure about what we do. Of course I like helping you, too. Remember when you first came and I had to show you what to do? Now it's different, and you sometimes help the new children." And she can add, "But you tell me when you really want me to do something for you and I'll do it if I can." This helps a child feel sure that there is a place for him and that he can have attention, too.

"Nudging" and Harsh Methods of Control

Children who have been "nudged" from one stage of development to the next, who have had high standards set for their behavior, who have been punished frequently may feel a great deal of hostility which they often cannot express directly. One way that these children may try to handle the hostility they feel is by reproving others. They try to identify with the teacher to escape from the feeling of being helpless. Tommy, for example, has received a great deal of punishment from parents who have never heard of any methods of discipline except the "good old-fashioned ones." Tommy was playing with Larry, and the two were building a block tower to dangerous heights. The teacher warned, "Not so high." Tommy immediately turned to Larry and said severely, "The teacher said no more blocks and when she says something you mind her." Thus he got rid of some of his resentment, but his "punishing" attitude makes it hard for any but the most comfortable children to play with him. Incidentally, in Tommy's behavior we get some insight into the quality of control which harshly disciplined people impose when they themselves are in power, and the need they often feel to identify with the controlling authority—the more arbitrary the better.

Sam Wanted Desperately to Feel Big

Sam is an outstanding example of a child who had been pushed around in many ways without much loving and giving on the part of the adults in return for their heavy demands. He was expected to behave like a little gentleman on every occasion when there were visitors at home, and he usually came to school in a suit instead of dressing in play clothes like the other children. His speech was more like that of an adult—even his vocabulary of swear words. He was advanced in his development, but he was also burdened with a tremendous load of hostility. It came out in the frequency and the cruelty with which he attacked younger children and animals, and in his many verbal attacks against the adults when he discovered that these would not be punished. Instead of trying to identify with authority, he fought it on every occasion.

As the group was coming in from the playground one day, he savagely attacked a friendly little boy who got in his way. The teacher separated them quickly and firmly. Sam exclaimed, "That was fun." The teacher merely said, "It wasn't fun for Jim. It hurts him," and told Sam to stay outside. As soon as the others were inside, she returned and sat down beside him. They knew each other well, and she felt sure that he could accept her presence without feeling threatened by it.

"I wonder why it makes you feel good to hurt Jim and the other children," she speculated quietly, not knowing whether he could give her any clue. He immediately launched into a description of how his uncle had brought him a gun, and he and his "little friend" (an imaginary friend) could use it.

Again the teacher answered, "I wonder if it makes you feel big to have a gun and it makes you feel big to hurt someone?"

With apparent relief the child answered, "Yes." They discussed how people wanted to feel big and how sometimes it wasn't fun to be little. The teacher mentioned that being friendly sometimes made people feel big. Sam stuttered as he talked and was near tears, something that almost never happened with him. He seldom dared to relax his defenses enough to cry.

At last the teacher told Sam that it was about time for them to go inside. He said, almost crying, "I could stay out here until afternoon." "Yes," she said, "you could." She busied herself picking things up and then asked, "Well, now you can either come in with me or stay outside. I wonder which you are going to do?"

He got up and said rather sadly, "I don't know." At that the teacher knelt down and put her arms around this hurt, bewildered little boy and for the first time he could accept her loving and nestled close against her, no longer "tough." She said, "I know how it is," and then suggested, "You might paint a big picture inside." He nodded and took her hand, and they went inside. He went straight to the finger-painting table where he knew there was a chance for him to express more of what he felt.

Sam did gain in the nursery school and became better able to play with others. He was imaginative and resourceful and found a place for himself as his hostility decreased. When he left nursery school, he was a less hostile child but still needed careful, understanding handling. Although his mother had gained some insight into the child's problems, his father would accept none of this "sissy stuff" and continued to rely on repression and a generous use of the rod to bully his little son into "good" behavior. Sam in his turn was a bully on the school playground, but he continued to use art as an avenue of expression. By the time he reached high school, he had received several awards for his artwork. He was also excelling in athletics and became a person of importance. He seemed more secure. He was coping with many of his problems.

To the Child, Even Friendly Adults May Seem to Be a Threat

All children, to some extent, are struggling with feelings of being little and helpless. Even friendly adults are so much stronger and more powerful than the child that they are potentially a threat. Children handle their feelings in different ways. When they are together in groups, they are quick to blame the adult for things that happen. We may overhear remarks like this. Ricky comes out on the playground and says to Dick, "Who covered up our holes?" "Oh, some teacher probably," replies Dick. Both these boys are friends with teachers, but they recognize in them the source of many interferences and frustrations as well as the source of needed support. They are glad to identify with each other against the teacher.

Larry gives us another amusing example. He happened to throw some sand, and it got into Celia's eye. Celia had to go inside and have the sand washed out of her eyes. When she came back on the playground, Larry was very sympathetic and wanted to look into her eye. He said to her comfortingly, "I should have thrown it in the teacher's eye and then it wouldn't have hurt you, Celia."

Two four-year-olds, Sandra and Jennifer, are playing in the doll corner. Jennifer has set the table. Sandra sits down, saying, "I'm the father." They go through the motions of eating soup and as they pretend to eat, they turn to the mirror hanging on the wall by the table and talk to their reflections. Sandra says, "Shut up and eat your soup."

We see thus some of the sources of the child's hostility and resistances, some of the situations out of which these feelings arise. As adults we are concerned with helping children to express these feelings in ways that will not be damaging and yet will serve to reduce them or turn them into constructive channels. We must understand what possible avenues of expression there are.

RELEASING HOSTILITY AND AGGRESSION

What Are Possible Avenues for Expression of Feeling?

Recognition of the feeling which needs to be changed is probably very important for the child if the feeling is really to be "liquidated at its source" as Kubie suggests. The teacher who stops a child about to hit another because this child has his favorite tricycle will say, "I know, John, you want the tricycle. It makes you cross at Bill because he has it, but you must not hit. When you feel cross at someone because he has what you want, you can go over and take a good whack at our punching bag. That may help you." By words like these the teacher is helping the child identify his feelings. The child needs to know what feeling he is taking out on the punching bag. He needs to be clear about the source of his feeling.

Motor expressions, of course, offer the simplest, most direct means of draining off feeling for children. That is why hitting, pushing, biting are common among young children. There are other more acceptable forms of expression along these lines that can be utilized instead as a direct expression of feeling. Pounding at the workbench, hitting a soft material like clay, using a punching bag, biting on a rubber toy, throwing against a backstop, even running and digging serve as an outlet for feelings in ways that do no damage to anyone. Sue, to

Courtesy of Henrietta Endore.

Making elaborate constructions with blocks is one way of reducing hostile feelings.

be described later, gave vent to her resentment at adult interferences by the hard pats she gave each piece of paper as she pasted.

The skillful teacher will suggest outlets which can be used instead of hitting and bullying. She will accept the feeling and put it into words: "I know. You feel like hitting him because he has the tricycle you want." But she will channel the expression in behavior. "When you feel like that, you can hit our punching bag or do some pounding at the table."

Language Is a Valuable Outlet for Feelings

Language is another type of outlet. The crying child relieves himself of a lot of feeling. So does the child who hurls angry words at an offender.

They may verbally destroy the teacher in all kinds of ways and tell her "to get dead." Such verbal expression relieves their feelings. They can see that it results in no harm to the teacher. She remains their friend. It is a satisfactory way at the child's level of "liquidating" feelings which might otherwise be a source of trouble. Later, as adults, these same children may fantasy this kind of thing but without the verbal expression and be helped in relieving serious irritations, as Chisholm indicates in his *Prescription for Survival.**

Art and Music Are Outlets, Too

Experiences with art and music offer avenues for the expression of feeling. These avenues of expression are important because they may extend into the

---

*Chisholm, Brock: Prescription for Survival. New York, Columbia University Press, 1957. p. 78.

Courtesy of Jean Berlfein.

Throwing newly mown grass is an outlet for energy and aggressive feelings.

adult years, as in the case of Sam, and serve as a protection against the emotional load which adults must carry. If art experiences are to have value as a means of release for feeling, they must be free experiences in which self-expression is encouraged, in which the child uses the medium in his own way. The child who paints a certain type of picture again and again is saying something about the way he feels through his pictures. He may do this through his work with clay or in music, too. We need to conserve the values of art experience as an avenue of expression of feeling. These values are lost if art experiences consist of copying patterns.

How the Teacher Meets Aggressive Behavior

When feelings have many avenues of expression, they do not pile up and become so unmanageable. The teacher encourages expression even though she may face problems within the group situation. How can the teacher meet the needs of individuals and of groups?

The Teacher Helps the Children by Her Example

For one thing, the teacher helps all children when she remains undisturbed herself in the face of aggressive behavior. Because of her example, the children will find it less disturbing to meet the inevitable aggressions which occur in their world. The child who is most disturbed over being called a name is probably a child who has been severely reproved for name calling himself. Adults have attached importance to this kind of behavior in his experience. But it is unfortunate to get upset over such experiences. Children are likely to meet some rejection and some angry responses wherever they happen to be. If their own aggressive behavior has been met casually, they will find it easier to accept unruffled the attacks they receive. They are less afraid and better able to take the world as it is. In responding to aggressive behavior, the teacher can say, "We all feel this way sometimes." She is not upset by it.

The Teacher Helps When She Accepts and Interprets Behavior

An important way to help is by interpreting to one child reasons why another child is behaving as he is. She may reassure him, by saying, "Never mind. He's calling you names because he's mad. It's your turn on the swing and he wants it to be his. It makes him feel better to call you 'dope.' You don't need to let it bother you." She may help a child by showing him how to meet the experience of being rejected by explaining, "They want to play by themselves. It's all right. I'll help you find another place to play and you can look for someone who does want to play with you."

She does not help when she blocks the children's expression and refuses to accept their feelings. She does not help the hostile child who has shouted at another child, "You go away," when she says, "But you must let him play." The newcomer will not be likely to have a successful experience with a person who feels unfriendly toward him. It is better not to force our way where we are not wanted. The teacher must work out a solution, accepting the feelings that are there.

There are solutions which protect the group while still respecting the needs of individuals. If the child who is excluding others is monopolizing the doll corner or the sandbox or some other area, the teacher can say, "It's all right if you want to play by yourself, but all the children use the doll corner or sandbox. You can make a house over in this corner and leave the rest for the children who do want to play together."

The Teacher May Need to Help Hostile and Insecure Children by Giving Them Techniques for Cooperating

Children who are hostile and insecure may need to be protected from facing repeated failures in their group experiences. They may need to have the difficulties of group living reduced until they can meet these with more chance of success. The teacher may need to help them play in small groups. She may need to help them by suggesting desirable ways of approaching others to forestall trouble for them. Suggestions such as, "He'll let you play if you'll wait for a turn," or, "You might get a block and help him build the walk," may succeed for such a child, and bring acceptance for him where rejection would increase his resentment. The teacher often helps when she interprets the meaning of an approach by another child as, "He wants you to help him." In this way she prevents the hostile child from being unfriendly and ensures for him a more favorable place in the group.

Children need protection when they are unsure and suspicious of others, not denial of the way they feel. The demands of group life are complex. Children who are hostile and lacking in social skills may not be able to play with more than one child at a time. They may need to exclude others. The teacher helps when she accepts this and makes it possible for them to be successful at their level.

The teacher helps the aggressive, resentful child when she is confident and firm in her management. The child needs firmness, not punishment. He may want to feel that someone else is to blame, but his teacher will accept only his need to wish that this were so; she does not accept this as fact. She is sympathetic but she is firm in dealing with his behavior and in facing the reality of the situation. She states it clearly for him. She has confidence that he will be able to face it, too. She tries to help him deal with his feelings directly, in a constructive way. Her firmness helps steady the angry child and reassure the insecure child.

MANAGEMENT WHICH DOES NOT CREATE HOSTILE FEELINGS

Suitable Environment

The teacher also helps the child handle the problem of his hostility and aggressiveness by avoiding increasing these feelings needlessly. She will do this by a thoughtful planning of environment and program in the nursery school. In a physical setup which is designed for him, the child will feel less hostility because he will meet fewer frustrations. He can wash his own hands, get his own coat, find the play materials he wants within reach, solve his own problems in many ways, and submit to fewer limitations. The program, as well as the physical setup, can be designed to reduce, rather than increase, interferences and frustrations. If it is flexible and imposes only essential limitations, it meets individual needs in a way that minimizes hostility. Under this kind of program, teachers become people who help rather than people who interfere with the child.

Unsuitable Environment

The child who is very destructive, or even just hyperactive, is often the child who has lived in an environment which is not well adapted to meeting his needs. His behavior is only the expression of the hostility and resentment he feels, as in the case of Rex. His mother came for help because at the age of two he was already very destructive. As she described matters, "He gets into everything, pounds on the furniture, breaks his toys, and has even broken a window once or twice." She reported that he climbed up on the stove or turned on the radio because he knew these things were forbidden. She had punished him severely, but he persisted in spite of the punishment until she was desperate. As in many similar cases, Rex's mother had limited him severely in his early attempts to touch things; she had never played with him or "spoiled" him by giving him much attention. It was hard for her to understand now why he was wet almost constantly and demanded constant attention if he was to be kept out of mischief and destruction. Nap time, for example, was a struggle, and she usually had to spank him several times before he would stay in his bed. But one could see what few satisfactions his environment offered him—how many limitations had been imposed with very little offered him in return. He was responding by expressing his resentment and hostility actively and vigorously through his destructiveness and his resistances. He was making her pay attention to him.

Punishment Adds to the Emotional Burden of the Child

Punishment does not help a hostile, resentful child. It only increases his burden of feeling. But firm action on our part may be essential for him so that he does not hurt others and thus add to his burden of guilt. The teacher acted firmly, for example, in the case of the resentful child who used biting as a way of attacking. She knew she must be responsible for preventing biting when she could. She had to do this while she was also helping him to use acceptable means of relieving himself of the tremendous load of resentment and the feeling of helplessness he carried. If she had punished or rejected this child because of his behavior, she could have offered him no help. The already overburdened little boy would have had to find his way out alone, or fail.

We should act promptly to stop some kinds of behavior, but we need not do this in a punishing way. We can remove a disturbing child from the group or hold him firmly, but we do not have to blame him for his actions. We do not try to make him feel more ashamed or even to apologize. Making a child say he is sorry usually means making him say something false. Truth is important. Later he may say he is sorry when he really feels this way. Our responsibility is to help him find nondamaging channels for the expression of the resentment he is feeling. When he is relieved of this feeling, he is ready for other feelings and other expressions of feeling.

Some Children Need Special Help

When a child is very seriously burdened with hostile feelings, he may need special help. He may be given this help within the group by assigning one teacher or an aide to be with him and to help him manage his feelings. With this kind of individual help, he may be successful. An aide reported this experience with a child who attacked others on little or no provocation. He had had a great deal of punishment and little real discipline. As he started to hit out savagely at another child who interfered with him, the teacher caught his arm and held it firmly, saying at the same time, "I think you must feel very mad." He looked at her in surprise, without resisting, and then nodded in agreement. Suddenly he turned and hugged her. The teacher knew how he felt and he was safe. She returned his hug and added, "Next time you feel mad, I will try to help you again."

Every group will contain some children who are likely to express hostility in aggressive ways. Most of them can be helped within the framework of the group to handle their hostile feelings in acceptable ways. An occasional child may need individual therapy outside the group in addition to help within the group.

The child who acts out his hostility may be serving a function for the whole group. He is acting it out for them, in a sense, and they learn what happens by watching him and the way his behavior is handled. If it is handled firmly, without anger, all children feel more comfortable. They have more confidence that their own angry feelings can be managed, if not by them at least by the teacher. We can see this in the way that some other child may take the place of the one who misbehaves if the latter child is absent. There is always a "difficult" child. The children are learning how to manage their feelings by observing each other and by responding to others.

Group Experience Has Special Value for the Timid Child

The value that group experience possesses for many timid children is worth attention. Timid, inhibited children are greatly helped in expressing their feelings by the safety they find within the group. It provides them with an environment in which it is easier for them to accept their hostile emotions. These children will benefit greatly from the "freeing" of expression that comes in a good nursery school experience. Children in groups may resort to verbal defiance of the teacher when there is some reason for resisting her. They feel strength in being together, and this feeling is one of the values that group experience holds for them. With people of their own age who are also feeling and expressing hostility, they are no longer so afraid of their feelings and behavior. Not as "good" in the conventional sense, they become healthier from the mental hygiene standpoint and capable of achieving a higher degree of emotional maturity in the end. We will look at this aspect again in the chapter *Relationships in Groups*.

Ben was an example of a child who grew able to express his real feelings in the nursery school. He was a quiet, timid child who remained dependent on the teacher for a long time after he entered the school. He usually found a place beside her when she sat down, and often held onto her skirt when she moved around the school. When he played, he would select the small toys and take them into a corner. He was not active and vigorous and was never aggressive toward others. Very slowly he began to join the other children in play and to identify himself with the group. He seemed pleased when they shouted names or chanted silly or "naughty" words. Finally he dared to express himself in this way, too. One day he was even a member of a group who defied the teacher from the safe height of the jungle gym.

It was about this time that some movies taken at the school happened to be shown one morning. A picture of Ben's teacher appeared on the screen. Laughing, Ben went up to the screen and slapped her image. It was probably no accident that he chose the teacher's image. That act may have symbolized the strength and the freedom to be aggressive which he was feeling. With that slap he proved that he had left his dependence behind. His relationship with the teacher was a friendly one, but he was no longer tied to her skirt as he had been in the beginning. Ben had known plenty of love at home but not much chance to express the resentments that he inevitably felt. As soon as he dared to be aggressive, to express what he felt, he became more active and social. He had no great amount of hostility to release. He was soon able to maintain and accept the limits which the teachers set for the group. He developed rapidly.

SUMMARY

We may summarize what we have been saying about hostility and aggression by pointing out that (1) we must accept the existence of these feelings; (2) we must see that they are expressed in some acceptable way, but as directly as possible, so that the individual will be freed from the emotional load they will otherwise represent; and (3) we must learn how to handle children without creating in them unnecessary feelings of hostility and resentment which make good social adjustment difficult.

Reducing the amount of frustration a young child has to meet, building up his feelings of security and confidence, accepting him as he is rather than "nudging" him into being something different will all help in the solution of the problems which these feelings present to any individual or any form of group life.

PROJECTS

1. Observe and record two situations in which a child faced frustration (was unable to carry out a purpose). How did he try to cope with the situation? What feelings did he express at the time? Later?

2. Report an observation of a child using an appropriate defense; an inappropriate defense. Give reasons for your evaluation in each case. Describe the different kinds of defenses which you have observed children using. Why were they used?

3. Observe and record a situation in which a teacher helped an angry child to put his feelings into words.

REFERENCES

Erikson, Erik: Identity and the Life Cycle. New York, International Universities Press, 1959. Vol. 1, No. 1, Chap. 2.
Escalona, Sibylle: Understanding Hostility in Children. Chicago, Science Research Associates, 1954.
Isaacs, Susan: Childhood and After. New York, International Universities Press, 1949. Chap. 3.
Redl, Fritz: When We Deal with Children—Selected Readings. New York, The Free Press, 1966.
Winnicott, D. W.: The Child and the Outside World. New York, Basic Books, Inc., Publishers, 1957. pp. 167–175.

CHAPTER 17

Car, Policeman, Stop Light (boy, 4 years 4 months)

AUTHORITY AND THE SETTING OF LIMITS

For Many People the Problem of Authority Is a Confusing One

"You're the boss of the whole school," remarked Susan to the teacher as they sat eating lunch together one day, and she added with deliberation, "Last year the school was all the bosses itself."

Susan had evidently been trying for some time to figure out who was "boss" at the school. She had been raised on "issues" at home, and her parents were still trying to show her who was "boss" in their house. She must have been puzzled about the school situation at first until she picked the teacher as the source of authority.

For many people, as for Susan, the problem of authority is a confusing one and remains so all through their lives. As children these people have been made to feel that the role of boss is the most important role. When they are grown, they struggle to do some bossing themselves or to resist being bossed by others. This struggle interferes with their solution of other problems. They hurt themselves and often the people they love in their efforts to boss or to resist bossing.

Discipline that leads to a struggle over who is going to be "boss" is damaging to anyone. It does not help people to respect themselves or others. It is better adapted to preparing them for life in an authoritarian world rather than in a democratic one. Like Susan, people who have met this kind of discipline have little concept of what it means to be a responsible member of a group. They are not ready for the self-discipline that democratic living demands.

Betsy, like Susan, had struggled against domination. The "boss" in her case was an older sister who interfered with almost every move the child made at home. In the freedom of the nursery school Betsy began to relax, but she was alert to resist anything that resembled domination. One day, irritated by something, she angrily threw a book on the floor. The teacher asked her to put the book on the table, but Betsy replied with feeling, "You can't always have what you want." The teacher was able to reply, "That's true. I can't always have what I want. I'll pick the book up myself this time, and we can go outdoors together." The teacher felt that this little girl needed to experience more mutual regulation in patterns of behavior, not just patterns of demands and refusals or submission, if she was to learn to live with others satisfactorily.

The matter of accepting authority, as well as taking responsibility for it, is more important in a democratic society than in any other. In a democracy, limits must be set and maintained by the consent of all. How can we prepare to solve the problems of authority in a democratic way?

POSITIVE VALUE OF LIMITS

We will start by reminding ourselves that the problem of authority or the setting of limits can be worked out in a way that has positive value for the individual. We sometimes think of the setting of limits as a form of interference because limitation has so frequently been experienced by us as "don'ts" and connected with punishment. In earlier chapters we have been concerned with the acceptance of behavior and permissiveness. We have tried to see the individual and his needs. We have tried to understand how to help him release and channel the creative forces within him, how to avoid blocking these forces. But to feel free, one must feel safe. Limits are essential if the young child, or if any of us, is to be safe.

Need for a Responsible Pattern of Authority

The child who feels confidence that his parent will stop him is likely to act with less hesitation, to explore more freely. If the stopping or the limiting is done with love and without humiliation, he is helped to trust himself, to develop as a spontaneous, creative person. He is free to act because he knows he will be stopped before he harms himself or acts in a way which would make him feel guilty or remorseful. He is free because he has parents who take responsibility.

When his parents set limits with confidence and with respect for the child and his problem, they are setting a pattern which he can follow as he takes over the task of setting and maintaining limits for himself. They give him a model to follow when they act as responsible people. They make it easier for him to act as a responsible person in his turn, a person able to see the value of limits.

There is evidence that the older preschool child may profit from a firmer discipline as he tests out limits and tries to discover for himself what is safe and what is acceptable. On the basis of a relationship of confidence, a clear-cut setting of limits helps him to find his place as a responsible person. Greater permissiveness with the very young child, on the other hand, gives him time to develop and extend his horizons, protected by the adult, before he takes over much responsibility. Too much disciplining too early or too little too late can interfere with growth and with a healthy solution to the problem of authority.

In discussing the subject of aggression, Winnicott points out the child's need for a "confident authority," saying, "It is the task of parents and teachers to see that children never meet so weak an authority that they run amok, or that they must, from fear, take over the authority themselves. Anxiety-driven assumption of authority is dictatorship....the calm adult is less cruel as a manager than a child quickly becomes when he is responsible for too much."*

Need for the Safety of Limits

The setting of limits, then, is an essential part of helping a child to act freely. The young child must depend on the adult to maintain safe limits because he is often too inexperienced to judge the consequences of his actions. The toddler may be fascinated by a long flight of steps, but he needs to be limited by a gate or a helping hand. Lack of such limits may result in a bad fall that frightens him and makes him less ready to explore freely.

When he has no limits, the child may feel very insecure. One of the most anxious children in one group of nursery school children was a child whose mother had tried to avoid any limitations of the child's freedom. The child had found little security in her world, in part because there were no limits on which she could depend. No one took responsibility for saying, "No," to her. She even put her feeling into words one day when she said to her mother, "I wish you would build a fence around my yard." Any child is more secure, freer to explore, when he is sure of consistent, confident handling that will set limits for his exploring and for his actions.

The child needs protection against the violence of his feelings, too, against his anger and its expression in destructive ways. He needs to feel sure that the adult will be ready to set limits to the way he expresses feeling, or he may be frightened and feel guilty about what he does. A young child's feelings are strong, and he reacts strongly with a temper tantrum, or in destructive ways. Only when he knows that the adult will help him to handle his strong feelings can he throw himself wholeheartedly into experiences and be spontaneous and creative. He needs to be sure of limits if he is to develop confidence in himself as a person.

The *way* he is stopped is important. If the limiting is done in a "punishing" way, it may arouse more angry feelings in him or fearful, anxious feelings. These feelings make it harder for him to develop his own controls. He may become defiant or dependent. His confusion makes him less able to be himself.

Responsibility for Maintaining Limits

Children who have met inconsistent authority which sometimes sets limits at one point and sometimes at another grow almost desperate in their efforts to find some sure limitation. Behavior which is interpreted as "contrariness" may only be

*Winnicott, D. W.: The Child and the Outside World. New York, Basic Books, Inc., Publishers, 1957. p. 174.

a seeking for the security of knowing where the limits for behavior really are. Children can accept known limits more easily — whatever these limits may be. The disturbed child will steady himself when a calm, confident adult defines the limits for his behavior clearly and enforces these limits.

Much of the defiant, "unreasonable" behavior of some children may be a result of their seeking for someone who has enough confidence to take responsibility for maintaining consistent limits. It is interesting to note, in this regard, that the child who frequently goes "out of bounds" himself is often the one who is most concerned when another child misbehaves. The child who does a lot of hitting is likely to be the child most disturbed by being hit. This reaction gives us a clue as to how he looks at his own hitting and the anxiety he may feel because of it. He needs someone to keep him from doing what he regards as a serious offense.

Pam, for example, at the age of four was an extremely anxious and insecure child. Without a confident teacher to steady her she went to pieces on slight provocation. One day she was at the clay table getting acquainted with a new teacher. This teacher was rolling and patting the clay on the table top. Pam looked at her seriously; "Clay is used on boards at this school," she said. The teacher said, "But I like to use the clay on the table. It's all right on this table top." In a minute Pam said in a pleading tone, "Use it on the board." The teacher complied, for she realized that Pam's self-control was so tenuous that the child felt the need for quite rigid limits. She did not feel safe with a teacher who was not maintaining limits strictly.

Even when people are older, they sometimes long, if unconsciously, to be free of the responsibility for limiting their own behavior. They try to return to the simpler situation where limits were set and maintained for them by others. Eric Fromm in his book *Escape from Freedom* discusses what may happen when people cannot accept the responsibility for being free. In many ways we all act out this escape in our daily living. We might mention the student who tries to put the responsibility for learning on the teacher, or the parent who tries to depend on the authority of a book. It is a real struggle for all of us to accept the responsibility for directing and limiting our behavior with wisdom and independence. It is not fair to the child to expect him to shoulder too much of this burden too soon.

DIFFICULTY IN SETTING LIMITS

Because of Our Own Experience with a "Boss" Type of Discipline

Because we know that authority can be damaging, breeding resentment, resistances, and hostilities, we may have a tendency to avoid exercising it even when we realize that it is necessary. When we react in this way, however, we are ignoring the positive value that limits have for individuals and for society. Rather than avoiding limitation we should try to understand what limits are suitable and how these limits may be imposed in constructive ways.

We may find it difficult to set limits with the confidence we should have because of our own experiences in growing up. We live in a culture that is not, on the whole, a permissive or "giving" one as far as children go. The emphasis in bringing up children is on restriction, on not touching, on staying dry and clean, on being quiet, on the kinds of things that may be damaging to individual growth. Relationships are often considered unimportant in comparison with objects. The needs of the child to assert himself and to find avenues of self-expression are not accepted.

From experience we know that a handicapping loss of self-confidence may result from these patterns. We want to avoid the old "boss" type of discipline. But in shifting to a more permissive type of handling we should not feel a sense of guilt when we sometimes have to act in a way that is *not* permissive. In shifting to a more permissive type of handling it becomes all the more important to remember that limits have a positive value if they are the right limits and wisely maintained. They can give support to children. We must be ready to use them with confidence. We must feel sure that sound discipline promotes healthy personality growth.

Because We Are Confused About Our Own Aggressive Feelings

For many of us there is another feeling which interferes with our ability to exercise authority with confidence. We face a problem because there is an element of aggressiveness in exerting authority. We ourselves may be afraid of aggressive acts. We may have tried to deny our own aggressive feelings. We may be unable to limit children wisely because we do not want to face the feelings which may come out in the act of limiting a child. In attempting to escape from being aggressive, we avoid accepting ourselves as people who can limit others.

Let us look at some of the feelings which may make it difficult for us to exercise authority.

Miss X was a teacher who was extremely "permissive" in an undesirable sense of the word. A group of children with her tended to be "wild," engaging in a great deal of destructive behavior. She was a sympathetic person with real insight, and she was skillful in turning the group's energies to constructive activities in time. After overturning the furniture, for example, the children usually did some fine building. They engaged in a lot of creative, original work and lot of group play, but some of the timid children suffered, frightened by the group behavior or by their own anxieties after they had participated in an episode of uncontrolled activity. Miss X was a person who had never been able to accept discipline herself. She had grown up as an only child in a strict household. She conformed outwardly but expressed her resistance in indirect ways. She was never on time; she never quite finished a task; she was absent-minded. As soon as she was grown, she left home. In her work with children she was determined that they should not suffer from the "boss" type of authority, as she had. Because she had not experienced authority as a help, she found it hard to use it in this way with her group. A sensitive, creative person herself, she gave her group freedom, but she could not meet their needs for the support of discipline.

Miss S was another teacher who resented bitterly the way in which she had been raised. She had experienced too often as a child a form of discipline which served only as an outlet for hostility and aggressive feeling. Her feelings against authority were very strong. She could not limit the children in her group because she would have disliked herself too much as she did it and perhaps disliked the children for making her act this way. She was unable to use discipline.

It is true that aggressive feelings often come out in the use of authority. People may punish because they wish to hurt, or in punishing they may pour out their aggressive, hostile feelings. A sensitive person feels guilt when this happens. But this is less likely to happen if we accept our own feelings. If we have faced the hostile, aggressive feelings we inevitably have, we can handle them and find safe or even constructive avenues for their expression. We can keep them where they belong. It is easier, then, for us to be clear about why we are imposing limits on the child. We can act with confidence when we impose limits if these limits are meeting the child's needs rather than serving as an outlet for our feelings.

ACCEPTABLE LIMITS

Setting Limits That Support the Child in Growth

Our problem is, therefore, to be clear about the value of limits as well as the value of permissiveness in handling children. As we untangle our own feelings in a situation, we are better able to exercise authority without feeling guilt in doing it. We can decide on the limits which will promote the most growth for each individual child at his particular stage of development. We can help the child to find these limits acceptable.

Discipline, for the child, is largely a problem of accepting limits. The child discovers that there are limits to the freedom with which he can follow his im-

Courtesy of Jean Berlfein.

The teacher, the parent and the child talk about acceptable and unacceptable behavior.

pulses; there are limits to the ways in which he can express his feelings. He must accept these limits if he is to be a member of a group, and there is value to him in belonging to a group.

The child finds it easier to accept limits if they are adapted to his stage of development. The two-year-old, for example, cannot accept comfortably many limitations on his urge to touch things, while the five-year-old can comfortably accept many more. The child will also find it easier to accept necessary limits if he has confidence in the person limiting him and if he finds satisfactions in relating himself to the group.

How do we set limits in ways that support the child in his growth?

We Must Set Only Necessary Limits

In the first place, we will set only those limits which are essential to protect and support the child and the group. We will avoid unnecessary limits. It is the many constantly recurring interferences which breed resentment in the child and make it hard for him to accept authority. Unfortunately, many interferences are common in a child's environment today. Our homes are built and furnished in such a way that the child's activities have to be restricted constantly. City streets are hazards and make further restriction necessary. The child often lives under circumstances which thwart his spontaneous, creative activity until he feels resentful. He resists or withdraws. Wise handling will include a change of standards or of furniture whenever possible to make these fit the child's need until he is older and better able to meet frustrations. When we observe children who have been restricted in many ways, we observe that they are often more intent on defying authority than in taking responsibility for limiting their own behavior—whenever outside pressure is withdrawn. Too many limits, imposed too early, breed resistance and lack of self-control rather than acceptance.

Unintentional Limiting and Interference

Children in nursery school may suffer from unintended and confusing interference when many adults are involved in supervision. They may be given directions more than once; the directions may be inconsistent; they may be unnecessary. The adults are well meaning but not well informed about what has already taken place. There may be a real need for some thoughtful analysis of the kinds and amounts of pressure that children are receiving in a situation. These pressures can only be known by systematic observations at intervals. It is a good exercise for the teacher to do such observing. She may be surprised at how many times some child may have received directions from several different people with the result that he is no longer listening.

We Must Be Sure That the Child Understands the Limits

In the second place, the limits which are necessary should be maintained in such a way that they are clear to the child. This means that they must be put in simple, concrete language rather than in general terms. Too often we assume that a child grasps a point when he really lacks the experience and the vocabulary necessary for real understanding. We must be ready to repeat and to define things in specific terms. We must help the child to understand what each limit means in terms of what he is expected to do.

We Must Be Consistent Without Being Inflexible

Obviously it is easier for the child to understand a limit which is maintained consistently. We should help the child by being consistent, but we must not confuse consistency and inflexibility. The person who says, "I wish I hadn't said that but I can't give in to him now," is probably being inflexible rather than consistent. When we make a mistake, we should be able to shift to a position more consistent with our goals. A parent may feel that her child is ready to stay at nursery school without her, for example, but when she leaves him there, she finds that he is not ready to stay by himself. She will help him most by continuing to stay with him. If she feels that staying with him is "giving in," she is taking a stand that is inconsistent with mental health principles. She is being inflexible. Phil's mother, mentioned earlier, helped him grow more independent when she really accepted his need and stayed with him at nursery school.

Resistance may be the beginning of a better attitude on the part of the child toward authority. The child may gain in some cases because a usual limit is not maintained but is disregarded. For example, Peter was a quiet, passive child who spent most of his time watching. He listened to records and joined the story group but engaged in few activities. He was concerned about "bad" behavior, calling the teacher's attention to things other children did which he thought they shouldn't be doing. For many weeks he remained outside the group, engaging in only a few safe activities like playing records or wheeling a doll buggy and watching others. One day he took a ball and carefully, deliberately, threw it over the fence. The teacher observed this and felt that it might represent a step in overcoming his fear of misbehaving. She smiled and said, "You threw it over the fence. Do you suppose I can get it?" She went outside and threw the ball back to him. After she returned, he threw it out again. She went out and returned it, throwing it very high, to his delight. This was repeated several times and another child joined and they began playing with the ball together and the teacher left. Peter seemed far less afraid of risking himself in play after this incident.

We Must Maintain the Limits We Set

Just as obviously, we do not help a child when we shift to a different position because we may be afraid or unwilling to handle the consequences of our stand. John, for example, may scream and kick when he is thwarted, but if the adult sees him about to take a tricycle from a child who cannot defend himself, she is responsible for stopping John even if he does scream and kick. She may stop him in different ways, some of them more skillful than others. She may step between the children before John has the chance to take the tricycle and direct him to another one, or she may have to restrain him; but she will be ready to accept his emotional outburst even though she is careful not to add to it by blaming him or reproving him. When she restrains him, she is accepting her responsibility and need feel no hesitation. She is helping him to face a necessary limit which is consistent with his goals for growth as a person. For the same reason the child who runs out in cold weather or in the rain without a coat must be brought back. Only when the adult is unafraid to take this responsibility will the child be safe and secure. The child is helped when these limits are clearly defined and consistently maintained.

Giving a clear definition of what is expected should never be confused with making a threat. The child who is being noisy at the table may be told that noisy behavior at the table makes it hard for others to attend to eating. If he wants to be noisy, he can move into another room where it will be all right to make all the noise he wants. This child would not be helped to control his own behavior if the choice were presented to him as a threat, "If you can't be quiet, you'll have to eat in another room." This kind of statement is a threat used to control behavior rather than a definition of limits to help the child manage himself.

We Must Feel Comfortable When a Child "Tests Out" Limits

We must feel comfortable about a child's need to test out the limits we set. The tremendous urge to be independent and to show initiative, which Erikson considers the important developmental task of the nursery school years, means that the healthy child will not conform passively to our demands. If he is to acquire the ego strength he needs, he must assert his difference from others. He must disagree: "I don't like that." He must reject: "Get out of here." He must defy: "I'm not going to." The fact of his resistance is healthy. We can accept his right to resist but we will not feel threatened by it. We will not be afraid to maintain our position.

In many situations we cannot allow the child to act out his resistance. When it's time to go home from school, for example, he has to leave. But we can maintain this necessary limit with full respect for his right not to *want* to leave. We can value his strength in asserting himself as a person even though we must help him to leave. In maintaining the limit, in this case the necessity for leaving, we can act in such a way that he does not feel blamed for his defiance or any less loved because of it. When we respect his urge to assert himself, we make it easier for him to accept himself along with the necessary patterns of authority. We make it easier for him to see authority as a constructive force, easier for him to be responsible for exercising it in his own behalf and for the sake of others some day. Resistance is healthy in a child, but accepting his need to resist does not mean permitting him to act on the resistance. Feeling is one thing and acting is another. The child has a right to feel in any way he wishes. It is good to *feel* able to assert oneself and to test out limits. But often he does not have the right to *act* in the way he wishes. We are responsible for limiting his action. We should feel comfortable both about his testing out and about the need for our maintaining the standards of acceptable behavior.

We Must Adapt Our Limits to the Needs of the Individual

The limits we set must be adapted to the need of the individual as he is at the moment if they are to contribute to his growth. We have mentioned the difference that a variation in age levels makes in what can be expected of children. But even the same child can be expected to accept demands differently at different times. If he is tired or ill, he will be less ready to face limits than at other times. His readiness to accept limits will depend on the circumstances he finds himself in as well as his physical condition. In a situation where he is unsure of himself, he may be unable to accept a limit which he could face easily under familiar circumstances. The child who feels confident and adequate can accept many more limits without suffering damage to his growth than the child who is insecure.

We will keep adjusting the limits we set to make them fit the needs of the child. A child who is just beginning to feel strong enough to assert himself may need to be quite free of restrictions for a time. Richard was given a great deal of freedom in asserting himself at the table until he was reassured about being accepted by the teacher. For Jean, who was already secure, such permissiveness would have been unnecessary and undesirable.

We Must Give the Child Time

When we set limits, we must give the child time to accept them. We should avoid forcing them or imposing them on him immediately. If we say to a child, "You need to put your boots on before you go outdoors," we do *not* need to see that he marches right over to get his boots on. He may have to protest a bit until he convinces himself that there is a limit which will be maintained. We can stop him if he starts to go out without his boots, but we can also give him time to decide to accept the limit. We help him in making the decision if our attitude is friendly and accepting. We may add, "I'll be glad to help you with your boots." We must respect his feelings as he struggles with the conflict between the urge to assert himself and the necessity of conforming to an adult demand. He doesn't realize that little boys sometimes catch cold with wet feet. The occasional child whose need to assert himself is very great may decide that he won't go outdoors if he has to wear boots. He should be helped to feel comfortable staying inside, so that he may feel really satisfied about asserting himself and gain strength from the experience. The key to helping a child is often just to give him *time* to accept what has to be accepted. Our own uncertainty or our own need to control only too often makes us want to push the child into unwilling acceptance.

Here is another example of effective guidance. Erik has gone outside and is playing in the sand, having removed his shoes. He is quite clearly enjoying it, moving his toes in the dry sand. The teacher thinks it is too cold outdoors for bare feet, so she goes out. She sits on the side of the sandbox quietly and says, "It feels good, doesn't it, Erik," and she smiles, enjoying it with him. She continues, "I wish you could play in your bare feet out here today, but I think it is too cold. You'll have to get your shoes back on this time. When the weather gets warmer, you can take them off." She adds, "I used to like to take my shoes off when I was a little girl. Now I'll help you put yours on." Together they get the shoes back on while she tells him more about what she liked to do as a child. Erik is a very independent child who has often resisted direction. Because his teacher takes time to feel with him and let him know that she understands, he can accept the necessary limit without loss of self-respect. In this case there was no need to act quickly, as there is in the case of the child who is hurting someone or being destructive. Just waiting a moment often helps a child to accept necessary restrictions.

We Must Respect the Child's Feelings

We must impose limits in a way which will respect the child's feelings. Shaming him, blaming him, frightening him, all show him that we do not respect the way he feels. When we use these methods, we make it harder for him to accept the limitations. Let us take a simple situation in which there is a necessary limit, such as the necessity of leaving school at the end of the morning, and observe the different ways in which this limit can be imposed. Here are some examples which are typical of those constantly occurring in any school.

Lee is a roly-poly, somewhat immature little boy. His father comes in and says to him, "Are you ready to go?" "No," says Lee sturdily. His father answers, "Well, even if you're not, you're going anyway. Put your things away and come along." His smile relieves his words, but the words suggest a reason why Lee remains immature. He is treated as such a little boy. One senses that he feels helpless.

Dick says to his mother when he sees her, "I don't want to go home." His mother answers with a smile, "I know. I'm glad you like it here and you want to stay, but we have to go now. We'll be back in the morning." Her words show that she accepts his feeling and it isn't hard for Dick to leave.

In any situation, limiting can be done in a way that shows respect and consideration for the child, or it can be imposed without consideration for the child's feelings. Even the baby who cries because he cannot touch something and wants to do so can be given something else to handle. It is the satisfied child, rather than the resentful, frustrated one, who learns to accept authority.

We Must Not Permit Undesirable Behavior

The child does not have the right to act in all the ways he may wish. He finds out what acceptable behavior is from what we permit. We are responsible for *not* permitting him to act in undesirable ways such as hurting others or disregarding the rights of others or being destructive. We help him when we provide a situation in which it is relatively easy to behave acceptably, in which things are manageable, without needless frustrations. We help him by giving him time when it is possible and by recognizing the way he feels. We help him by being consistent and confident in our action. We help him by stopping his undesirable behavior on the spot, where it occurs, without making more of it than is there, without adding to it our prejudices or our angry feelings.

It is usually easier for us to stop the child quickly and firmly when we realize that it can be done in a matter-of-fact way. Some misbehavior is inevitable as healthy children are growing and learning. When he behaves in unacceptable ways, we can say, "No," so that the child knows we mean it. We can hold him firmly, if necessary, to prevent an act. We may take away the stick he has used to hit with or the toy he has misused. In this way he discovers what is acceptable and what is not acceptable.

He may protest. He may resist. He may be very angry with us. He has a right to feel in any way he wishes, as we pointed out earlier, but he does not have a right to act in any way he wishes. We are helping him to learn the difference between the inner world of feeling and the outer world where behavior must be controlled and limited.

It is well for us to be aware sometimes of the fact that the child who is defiant and resistant may be playing an important role in the group. He is finding out for himself and for others what is acceptable and what is not. Other children are aware of how the teacher meets his behavior. He acts for them, in a way, for they are all concerned with the problem of authority. How far can one assert oneself? How does the teacher feel about it? The child at the top of the jungle gym refusing to come down will be replaced the next day, if he is absent, by some other child.

There may be individual children who are "difficult" for particular teachers, in which case the teacher needs to consider thoughtfully the reasons for her feelings about the child. But there is always some "difficult" child in the group if the group is learning about behavior. It usually helps a student or an experienced teacher too if she can keep her sense of humor as she deals with the situation. It helps to realize that both children and adults have problems with respect to authority and maintaining limits in behavior.

Acceptance of Limitations Depends on Mutual Regulation in Relationships

Last, and among the more important considerations in setting limits, is the relationship which exists between the child and the person doing the limiting. If the child has confidence in the adult, if he feels accepted by her, he can accept limitation by this adult more readily.

It is well worth taking time to build a relationship in which there is confidence before we act in a limiting way toward a child. If it is possible to wait until a child has had time to develop confidence in us before we limit him, we avoid creating unnecessary fear and resentment in the child. Our goal is to help the child accept and assume responsibility for limits. We make this difficult to achieve if we assert authority before there is a foundation of understanding. In the situation described the teacher would not have handled Sam in the way she did if she had not felt sure that he understood that she accepted him. She could not have helped this angry, hostile four-year-old with his feelings as she did, except on the basis of the relationship they already had established.

We set different limits at different times, and do this in different ways because the ability of children to accept limitation from us varies with the relationships we have with them. The familiar teacher in whom the child has confidence can step into a situation and help an emotionally disturbed child limit his behavior in a way that a person unfamiliar to him cannot expect to do. An unfamiliar person may use the same methods with the child, but she may only increase his resistance and his difficulties. Because relationships are so important, we will want to consider the effect of what we do as we work with children on the friendliness and confidence it builds between us and them. Good relationships make the acceptance of authority easy — and lack of good relationships makes it difficult.

Good relationships are never built on methods of control which depend on fear, especially fear of loss of love. "Mother won't love you if you act like that," or "I'll have to go off and leave you if you don't hurry," may be effective in getting immediate results, but such words are disastrous in their effect on the child as a person and on his relationships with adults. They deprive him of confidence in them. He is dependent and helpless and he resents being controlled through this feeling.

Exploiting a feeling does not build a sound relationship either. A parent once commented on how much her child liked milk, saying, "In fact she likes it so much that we can make her eat other things by threatening to take her milk away from her." Psychologically, as well as nutritionally, such a course has nothing to commend it. About the only defense a child has in such a case is to keep himself from liking anything very much so that he will have no vulnerable points. But he will resent this kind of control.

Parents must accept the necessity for not being able to give a child what he wants at times. They must be ready to face calmly his angry response when his demands are not met. The child who has been freely given to when giving is possible and appropriate can face and bear the inevitable disillusionment of not getting what he wants and may once have had. Jack's mother reported an incident that occurred on the way to nursery school one morning. They had almost reached the school when Jack discovered that he had forgotten to take the blanket that he usually carried with him and occasionally used as a "security" measure when he was tired. He immediately demanded that his mother turn around and go back for it, but she refused because she had other errands to do and felt that there was not enough time. She usually tried to consider his needs, but on this occasion she felt that he really was about ready to take the step of weaning himself from his blanket. He was using it less and less since he had been going to nursery school. Jack cried lustily in protest at her refusal. Then he said accusingly between sobs, "You *knew* I wanted it and you wouldn't go back." "Yes," she replied, "I knew you wanted it and I would like to have gone back for it, but I don't have the time today. I'm sorry." Minutes later Jack was greeting the teacher cheerfully. He gave his mother a warm kiss as he said good-by to her. He had faced a disillusioning experience, put it into words, and then left it behind. He had a big balance of trust and confidence to fall back on, and the help of a mother who was loving but firm.

Fortunately, there are many children who live in homes in which there is sufficient mutual regulation between parent and child so that both are able to adjust comfortably to the strains of daily small frustrations. There are enough "safety valves" for both.

The Role Guilt Plays in Learning

Some feelings of guilt are probably necessary in learning to change behavior. We must truly feel sorry about our behavior if we are to change. We are sorry because we *care*. We love and want to be loved. A measure of guilt may be a first step in changing behavior, but a heavy load of guilt does not lead to desirable changes. The child must defend himself against too heavy a load of guilt. His controls may break down. In the end he may no longer care. Then he is in a position where he may destroy himself or others. We as adults are careful to avoid adding to the load of guilt children carry, just as we do not interfere when they must face feelings of guilt which are reasonable and within their capacity to bear. Children have a right to their own feelings.

A Child's Behavior Changes When Patterns of Authority Change

A problem may arise when children find themselves faced with a pattern of authority in nursery school which is different from the one to which they are accustomed. The environment of the nursery school is set up so that there should be fewer adult interferences than in many other environments. The child is free to do what he likes most of the time. He does not meet many frustrations in his physical environment or many interferences, relatively speaking, from adults. Toys are available on low shelves; there are hooks and washbasins within his reach, adults are generally permissive.

After their initial adjustment to the new experience, children who come from homes that are less permissive and more limiting often go through a period of being resistant to limits or authority of any kind. In school they change from being "good" and "easy" to manage, to being negativistic and resistant. At home they are more defiant than they have ever been. The are impudent and uncooperative. They try out all the "bad" words and deeds they have heard and seen at the nursery school.

It is no wonder that parents, and sometimes teachers, may question whether the nursery school is desirable for these children. Only if the meaning of this behavior is clear can adults accept it and handle it in such a way that the child really gains from the experience. If we can see this behavior as a sign of the growth in self-confidence that follows a sudden increase in freedom, then we can meet it wisely.

Expression of feeling in speech or action safeguards mental health and gives self-confidence. These are things that we want to achieve. The child who has been unnecessarily and unwisely limited may need time to unload negative feelings and acquire confidence. When he suddenly discovers he can express himself, he must be given time to gain assurance by doing this. It is important that we take this time so that the child will feel accepted as he is. It is important that we neither blame nor frighten him, but help him in positive ways to understand what the limits for his behavior are. It is really by his "misbehavior" that the child shows us that he is working through a change in his concept of the part he can play in a group. It is through this behavior that we have the chance to help him become a more responsible, self-directing person.

The period during which the child asserts himself and expresses his resentment is not an easy one, particularly for parents. By "cracking down" on a child at this point, they may increase his problem and make it very difficult for him to work out any sound adjustment to the problem of authority in a democracy. Home and school need to understand what is happening to the child and to work together.

Our Goal is Self-Control

The problem of authority is not simple. It is tied up with a child's total development pattern. In one child, defiance may be a constructive step forward. In another it may indicate distressing confusion and conflict. In both children it calls for understanding on the part of the adults involved.

Our goal is self-control, the only sound control in a democratic society. But self-control can be sound only when there is a stable, mature self. A mature self emerges gradually as responsibility is adjusted to the child's capacity to assume it. It is the result of mutual regulation between us and the child. We expect him to take increasing responsibility for controlling his actions. We assume responsibility for which he is not yet ready, decreasing our share as he grows, giving more to him as his understanding of consequences increases with added experience.

PROJECTS

1. Observe and record three situations in which an adult defined and maintained a limit for a child. Note why the adult set a limit, how she defined and maintained it, and the response of the child. Estimate the value of the experience for the child.

2. Observe and report a situation in which a problem arose because the adult failed to define the limit clearly. What was the effect on the child?

3. Observe and report a situation in which a problem arose because the adult, after defining a limit, failed to take any action to maintain it. What was the effect on the child?

4. Timing of help is important. Report a situation in which the child was helped to accept a limit because the teacher's help came at the right time. Explain. Report a situation in which the child did not accept a limit because the help seemed to come at an inappropriate time. Explain.

5. Look at your list of the kinds of behavior which you dislike or which you approve of highly in children (see Chapter 1). How was this behavior treated in your own childhood in each instance? Can you identify some sources of your feeling about the "rightness" or "wrongness" of behavior? How might these feelings affect your handling of children in a realistic or objective way?

REFERENCES

Becker, Wesley C.: Consequences of different kinds of parental discipline. *In* Hoffman, M., and Hoffman, L. N. (eds.): Review of Child Development Research, Vol. 1. New York, Russell Sage Foundation, 1964. pp. 169–204.
Fraiberg, Selma: The Magic Years. New York, Charles Scribner's Sons, 1959. Chaps. 5 and 8.
Ginott, Haim: Between Parent and Child: New Solutions to Old Problems. New York, Avon Books, 1969.
Redl, Fritz: When We Deal with Children—Selected Readings. New York, The Free Press, 1966.
Spock, Benjamin: Bringing Up Children in a Difficult Time. New York, W. W. Norton & Company, Inc., 1974.
Winnicott, D. W.: Playing and Reality. New York, Basic Books, Inc., Publishers, 1972. Chap. 11.

CHAPTER 18

I Like to Play with My Friends (girl, 4 years)

RELATIONSHIPS IN GROUPS

Group Relationships Deserve Our Study

The child's first sustained group experience outside the family is likely to be that which occurs in the nursery school. His experience at nursery school differs from his experience in the family because the school group is made up of comtemporaries whose interest and capacities are on about the same level as his own. Living with a group of equals is a significantly different experience for a child from that of being a member of a family group. As students in the nursery school laboratory we can add to our understanding of what relationships mean to people as we observe the children in their group living.

The same situation has a different meaning for each child, and he responds to it as it looks to him. Patty and Lois, who had been playing house together, took their babies for a walk. Lois, looking back, saw two boys in their play house. "Someone's getting into our house," she said anxiously. Patty turned around. "Oh, we have company," she exclaimed joyfully and hurried back to welcome the boys.

In any nursery school or on any playground, some children withdraw, some are defensive or aggressive, some are friendly and seem to expect friendliness from others. But out of these relationships with equals may come some of the deepest satisfactions in life. In spite of the conflicts and problems which occur, it is important that all children find success in relationships with people of their own age. Group relationships in the nursery school are worth our study.

READINESS FOR GROUP EXPERIENCE

The child's readiness for group experience will depend on two factors. The most important factor is the preparation he has had within his own family. The second is the nature of the group he enters and the help available to him in making the adjustments there.

Readiness for the Group Depends on the Preparation of the Child in His Family

The kind of life which the child has lived within the family will determine the adjustments which are possible for him outside the family. The child is better able to enter into play relations with other children if his parents have enjoyed play with him, beginning with playful relations while bathing or dressing him, and including peek-a-boo games and make-believe. If in this play his parents have understood and respected the stages in his growth, treating him with consideration, he is readier to play with other children. He is better able to accept the give and take of play with them and to consider their needs while still standing up for his own.

By a seeming contradiction which often holds in the field of mental health, the child is apt to be prepared for life in outside groups to the extent that he has felt sure of his worth and his acceptance in the family, rather than to the extent to which the family situation resembles the situation with contemporaries. If he has felt secure in possessing a love which has never been withheld, he will have confidence in undertaking the different experiences of entering a group in which he must win acceptance. He seems to need to be valued in the home without proof in order that he may have the courage to prove his value outside.

The question of "spoiling" a child may be raised at this point. Does giving a child what he wants prepare him to meet situations in which he cannot have what he wants? The so-called spoiled child is obviously handicapped in social relationships. He is far removed from reality in the value that he tries to place on himself. But if we understand his situation, we will usually observe that this child has not been truly accepted by his parents. He has not been given what he needs and wants most. He is likely to have been a child who has been showered with the things that his parents wanted him to have, or indulged because it was the easiest way for them to escape effort and responsibility. His parents, perhaps because of difficult circumstances or inadequate parenting in their own childhood, have been unable to provide the unselfish love and discipline that every child needs for healthy personality growth. His own real needs have not been met, but only the needs that they wanted to meet.

When a child is without a real feeling that he is loved and valued, he becomes very demanding and may never be satisfied. He continues to seek attention no matter how much he may have, and he turns away from reality. Other insecurities also may make a child demanding but lack of an accepting love leads to the deepest insecurity and results in selfishness and unending demands for attention in the vain search for satisfaction of this deepest need. Children whose needs have been met are not "spoiled" children.

It may be well to remember that the term "spoiled" is often used loosely. Some people use it to refer to any child who does not behave in a way that pleases the adult. If the adult happens to be a self-centered person, ignorant of child behavior, he may apply the term "spoiled" to behavior which is far more healthy for the child than behavior of which he approves. We will do well to avoid use of a term so heavily loaded with popular misconceptions.

Readiness to Enter the Group Depends on What the Group Is Like

The child's readiness to enter a group will also depend on the group itself and the help that he receives there in making the step from home to school.

If the child is to be successful, the group must be one in which he has a good chance for a satisfying experience. He must be able to identify with it rather than feel overwhelmed by it. He is likely to be helped in feeling that he can belong if the group is not large. He is often helped if he knows that he can depend on one adult. It is usually desirable to limit the time that the child spends with the group at first and to plan his beginning experiences carefully, as discussed in Chapter 9. All these are factors in making group experiences more satisfying.

Some of the advantages of group experience in a nursery school over that in an unsupervised neighborhood group lie in the greater likelihood that the needs of each child are being met. In this situation, experiences can be modified for individuals while preserving the values of initiative and resourcefulness which a free group offers. The unsupervised group may be a good experience for some children, but it may be a poor experience for others. There is little protection to an equal extent for all the individuals in it. Absence of conflict may simply mean that the weaker children have accepted the domination of a bullying child. There may not be much growth for anyone in this type of situation.

VALUES OF GROUP RELATIONSHIPS

A More Realistic Concept of Self

What does the young child gain from being with a group of other children?

One of the most significant values for the child in being a member of a group of equals lies in the fact that he has a chance to find out more about what kind of person he really is through his experience. He has an opportunity to build a more realistic concept of himself as a person apart from his membership in a family.

In the family group each of us is valued, or should be valued, because we belong to that particular family, regardless of what we may be or do. We do not need to prove our worth in order to belong to the family group. When the family situation is a favorable one, each member can count on receiving attention and affection freely.

In a group of contemporaries, on the other hand, the place each one of us holds depends more on our skill and what we have to offer the group. We must demonstrate our worth. We must measure ourselves against others who are like us, finding our strengths and facing our weaknesses, winning some acceptance and meeting some rejection. When we experience success, it is based to a great extent on achievement. The limitations we face are likely to be real rather than arbitrarily imposed. A favorable family situation helps us to feel secure, but experiences with our own age group help to develop an awareness of ourselves and of social reality which family experience alone cannot give. Both family and outside group experience are necessary for complete social development.

We should mention the effect of discriminations of any kind on the development of the sense of self or the kind of person one can become. When our position in the group does not depend on our worth to the group or the contribution we bring, we are likely to build a distorted sense of self. We may fail to value ourselves or others as we should. The distortions about self which result from discrimination and prejudice are reflected in a loss of potential contributions to society and in diminished individual growth.

Twins Have a Problem with Identity

A realistic sense of one's individual identity, of who one is, is important to everyone. Twins have some special problems in establishing this sense of individual identity. One mother reported that when her twin girls first began to look at themselves in the mirror, each would say the name of the other twin. Sara would say, "Jane," when she saw herself in the mirror; and Jane would say, "Sara." This mother wisely began to dress them differently. She found that when they went to school it helped for each one to have her hair cut in a style different from that of her twin, so that others could tell them apart.

The teacher can help twins by avoiding thinking of them or referring to them as "the twins." She can call them by their individual names and, although she will respect the special relationship they have with each other, she will arrange separate experiences for them whenever she can. She may place them at different tables at lunch time or take them on trips at different times.

Self-Confidence

Besides building a more realistic picture of who he is, the child begins to feel less helpless and little in a group of other children. In the world of adults the child really is helpless. In a group of children he is among equals. He may feel able to act in ways that he would not dare to on his own. Children gain from realizing that they are liked and can like others as children.

These feelings are evident in the following incident. Six children had gathered at a table and were doing puzzles, talking, and helping each other. The teacher sat near by. Suddenly Nancy remarked, "I like you, Andy," and Andy

Courtesy of Jean Berlfein.

Family play: a boy and a girl cook together.

replied, "I like you." Nancy went on, "And I like Jane and Larry and Linda and Debby." The others began naming each other as people they liked. Then Nancy began again, "But we don't like her, do we?" pointing to the teacher. "We only like little children." Everyone laughed and seemed very pleased.

It is difficult for a teacher to accept group defiance unless she appreciates what it may mean to the child. A small group of four-year-olds, for example, may climb to the top of the jungle gym when they are told it is time to come inside. They are playing a new role, doing the thing they may have wanted to do many times in the past. They are no longer helpless children, dragged away from play by a powerful grownup. They are powerful people, high above the adult, asserting themselves.

The teacher in such a situation does not need to panic or feel threatened in her authority, although it is easy to have this feeling. She can allow them their brief moment of power. Inside themselves, they know they are children and she knows that she is an adult, responsible for bringing them inside. She may perhaps manage the matter in a playful way, pretending they are spotters for enemy planes, while she waits for a report, or she may say, "I'm ready to pull you home in the wagon," or she may seriously discuss with them, "I wonder why it is that you don't want to come in now." To this question she may get some replies that give her a lot of insight into how things look to them and what they dislike about aspects of their experience. Teacher and children will learn from this method of resolving the situation to their mutual satisfaction. Everyone is the better for reaching a solution together.

Children who have confidence and do not feel helpless have less need to fight against adults. They can accept adults without feeling threatened by them. Jean, as a secure, confident child, seldom felt the need to be defiant or resistant with adults. Lester was ready to accept their limitations when he developed more self-confidence. Some children, on the other hand, never develop sufficient confidence to defy adults but remain anxious and dependent on them. They are "good" children, but not happy or emotionally healthy children.

Resistance May Be Expressed Indirectly

Children who are timid may use indirect methods of asserting themselves. They may urge other children to do things that they themselves dare not do. Jimmy was a child who kept urging other children to do things which he wanted to do but did not dare. At four he was the oldest of three children and seemed afraid to displease adults openly. He would encourage another child, "Hit him, Steve," or "Pour your milk on the floor." Too often the teacher, concerned with handling the child who hit or spilled at Jimmy's suggestion, overlooked Jimmy.

Jimmy needs help in accepting himself and not being afraid of his own impulses. He needs a teacher who will act quickly to keep the other child from following the suggestion, but who will give him reassurance with words like "Do you feel like hitting him? We all feel like that sometimes. I can't let you hit him, but you can do some pounding at the workbench," or "It's fun to pour. You can pour all you want in the washbasin or the sandbox, but you mustn't pour milk on the floor." He needs reassurance too that he is important and valued, but most of all he needs help in facing and not being afraid of his own impulses. Other children may be unable to use even these indirect methods in asserting themselves.

We Need to Value Children's Resistance

For many parents and teachers, as we mentioned earlier, the phase in a child's social development in which he is resistant and defiant is a disturbing one. It takes experience and confidence to see the value in behavior which is usually considered unacceptable. When a quiet little girl, for example, begins to "talk back" and resist suggestions, her parents may question the value of experiences which seem to produce this kind of behavior. They are likely to raise a question because the child's need to resist may have arisen out of their own need to control and dominate her. It takes insight to perceive that resistant behavior may mean growth for the child as a person. It takes insight both into the child's behavior and into our own behavior. It takes skill too to guide a child through this stage so that its values are retained and, at the same time, safe limits and a respect for the child are maintained.

We will try to achieve some of this insight and some of the needed skill as we study children's behavior and participate in the nursery school laboratory. We will remind ourselves that children may need to assert themselves by resisting us.

As in other situations, understanding children who are in this phase of development means understanding our own feelings. Because most of us have many areas of insecurity, we may find it hard not to feel threatened by resistance. The adult who meets children's attacks with, "I won't have that," or "You can't get away with that," reveals himself as an adult who is defending himself against feeling helpless rather than as one who is helping the resistant child.

The strength of our need to punish is likely to be in direct proportion to the helplessness we have felt in our past. It is important for us to realize that we are no longer helpless, that we can be strong enough to accept the child's behavior without feeling threatened by it, and that we can do something about his behavior without acting for the purpose of relieving our own feelings.

Children Find That They Can Share Attention and Like Teachers

Children in groups have the opportunity to face and manage the feelings they have about wanting a big share of the adult's attention. Sharing the teacher's attention with others is less difficult than sharing the attention of one's mother. If the teacher gives her attention freely and generously when children ask for it, she helps them feel that there is enough for all. They are less likely to feel deprived at the times when they cannot have attention. They are more likely to be satisfied. It may be easier to learn this lesson in a nursery school group than at home.

Children may also take a step in learning that it is possible to like a large number of people, adults as well as children. As their relationships with the teachers develop, they find they can like and depend on different people. A child usually finds a teacher on whom he depends as he enters the group. He may want this teacher and no other to help him and share experiences with him. He may seek her out when he comes to school. But as he grows more sure of himself, he has less need to depend on her. He begins to reach out to others, and it is important for him to feel that this is a good step to take.

Children gain from living in groups in many ways, not only by resistance, but also by accepting their right to like and be liked.

The Teacher Helps by Promoting Sound Feelings

The teacher's first task is to help the child feel good about himself. Children who are secure and confident and like themselves find it easier to like other people. They will be more skillful in social situations. Jean, for example, was secure and confident. She possessed a high degree of skill in getting along with others; whereas Charles, who had not found much acceptance at home, wanted to play with other children but managed his relationships with them poorly.

The "forms" of getting along with others are of little use when they are imposed on a background of insecurity and distrust of others. A common mistake of teachers and parents is to attack the lack of skill, the inability to take turns, or the tendency to exclude others, and to try to correct these things without first changing the feelings which have brought about this behavior. When we try to help a child to get along with others, we must first help him to feel sufficiently secure, adequate, and free of hostility, so that he can really like others and not act defensively toward them. Then he will be ready for techniques and can enlarge the horizons of his satisfactions with people.

The teacher helps a child feel secure by giving freely to him what he may need in the way of attention and materials. The child who experiences a generous giving by the teacher will be more likely to give freely to others himself. When the

Courtesy of Jean Berlfein.

The firefighters face a problem in cooperating with a ladder.

adult is niggardly in her giving of attention or of materials, she does not help the child feel like giving freely in his turn. For example, Bill asked the teacher to give him the box of nails which was up on the high shelf. Bill was working on an airplane. The teacher refused and gave him a few nails. Bill took them and returned to his work, but he guarded the nails closely and was careful not to let anyone else use them. While it may not have been desirable to let Bill have the whole box of nails, it might have been possible to give him a different feeling about "givingness." Group relations are different in an atmosphere where giving is done freely and generously and where even withholding is based on generous feelings.

The Teacher Helps with Techniques for Getting Along with Others

When there is a foundation of positive feeling, the child's progress in group relationships will be facilitated by our suggestions of techniques, such as ways of approaching others. As the child meets success in using desirable techniques, he will tend to use them oftener and will be accepted better by others. A child learns these things from experiences that are within the level of his comprehension, from situations whose reality he can understand.

What are some of the techniques that we can suggest to a child who is ready for our help? What social skills will be useful to him?

We can help children by suggesting good ways of approaching others or by helping them to understand the feelings which lie behind the approaches of other people—however clumsy these approaches may be.

An approach is usually more successful if the approaching child has some suggestion about what he might be or do, or if he makes some contribution to the play in progress. A straight request "May I play with you?" is often doomed to fail even if it is accompanied by the adult word "please." In helping a child the adult offers more help if she can suggest something specific to the child that he might be or do. Another advantage in this technique is that if one is rejected in one role, one can always find another role or a different activity to suggest. This way there is more protection against failure.

Sometimes the teacher may need to enter the play, taking a role herself, to help the less skillful child, and withdrawing when she is no longer needed. She may demonstrate a technique by saying the words for the child, "Doctor, I think my baby needs a shot," to help carry on "doctor" play. She may forestall difficulty by suggesting, "There will be more room for the building over there," when two builders are encroaching on the territory of others.

Children are often very realistic—and successful. Terry calls to Tommy, "Say, Tommy, you'd better let Doug play with us because he won't let me have the rope unless he plays, and I want it."

Possessing something desired by others is as much of a social advantage at three as at thirty-three. A wise teacher may utilize this fact in helping the shy child. Letting the child introduce a new piece of equipment, or bring something from home for the group to use, may help him feel more accepted and give him added confidence. Obviously, such a technique should not be depended on too heavily or for too long, but it can sometimes be the basis for a social start.

Offering something in return for something else one wants is a successful device. Some children have amazing skill in making a second object appear desirable when they want the first. Even secondary roles can be made attractive by an imaginative child.

Regan, for example, wanted to join the group playing "police officer," mounted on tricycles, but there were no other tricycles. Terry encouraged her to join anyway, saying, "You can be a walking policeman, Regan. They have walking policemen. You can play if you are a walking policeman," and he made it sound worthwhile, for Regan became a "walking policeman."

Some children are too compliant. They may need the teacher's help in asserting themselves. Matt (three years, eight months) seemed to find it hard to express his own desires. One day he and Mary were painting at the easels, side by side. Matt was very absorbed in his picture. Suddenly Mary reached over and painted a green spot on his paper. The teacher, observing this, asked him if he wanted Mary to do this. Matt only looked at it and said, "That's a funny spot." The teacher replied, "I know that is a funny spot, but do you want Mary to paint on your picture?" Matt hesitated a minute and then said, "No." "Then you can tell Mary you want to paint this picture by yourself," the teacher said. Mary was listening intently to the conversaion. She began to paint again on her own side. The two children went on to paint more pictures side by side, each more aware of the other.

The Teacher Helps by Not Interfering

Whenever possible the teacher leaves the children free to work out their own solutions. She does not interfere unless her help is needed.

Courtesy of Jean Berlfein.

Social relations shift quickly with children. Friends are painting together. You are in my way.

(*Continued*) Now I see what you were doing.

Cindy and Larry are riding tricycles. Debby wants to ride with them, but there is only a small tricycle left, which she doesn't want to use. She is unhappy and tries to take the tricycle from Larry. Cindy settles the matter by saying, "If there's not any big ones, then you can't ride one now. But if you will wait then Larry will get tired and then you can ride with me." Debby appears convinced and lets go of Larry's tricycle.

Adjustments like these are likely to be reached only when the children involved *like* each other. When they have had pleasant experiences together in the past, they can make compromises more easily to ensure their getting along in present situations.

Terry is already a past master at working out compromises. On another occasion he was busily building with blocks when Regan wanted him to play house with her again. He satisfied her by saying, "I'll live over there with you but I'll work here, and I'm working now," and he went on with his building. Terry has had many successful experiences of getting along with others. He has confidence, and his confidence shows in the way he meets his problems.

As we listen to children in their play, we find that they approach others in friendly ways far more frequently than we may have been aware. We may not have noticed their considerations for each other because our attention is more likely to be directed to the times when they hit or grab. We will find too that there is more friendly behavior in a group where the children are receiving courtesy and consideration from the adults. They adopt the patterns of those around them.

CONCEPTS TO BE LEARNED

Children in Groups Learn About Sharing and Taking Turns

An area in which children often need help from the adults is in learning about property rights and "taking turns." Living in a group of equals provides many opportunities for learning in this area, and the child's concepts develop from his experiences in the group.

Since property rights are considered very important in our society, the child must begin early to learn about possession. In his home he discovers that some things are not his to touch. The wise parent helps him accept this fact by giving him something that is his when she takes away something that he cannot have. She teaches him that some things are his, and she does not insist that he share the things that are his until he is willing and ready to share. Pushing him into sharing before he is ready will only confuse him and may prevent sound learning. She will find that he can share first with people he knows and likes, and then slowly he can broaden his ability to share in most situations.

The nursery school provides an excellent place for the child to continue his learning about sharing, taking turns, and possessions. Equipment at the school does not belong to individuals but to the group as a whole. No child feels as threatened by a sense of loss when he shares things like this as he might in sharing things that belong to him personally. Two simple principles can be established to cover most of the situations. First, when a person is through using a piece of equipment like a tricycle or swing, it "belongs" to the next person who may wish to use it. One does not continue to claim a thing one is no longer using. Second, after one has used a piece of equipment for a time one may have to let someone else use it even though one is not through, but one can expect to get it back again.

If these principles can be translated into very specific terms, they will be easier for the child to understand, as, "After he rides around the circle once, you may have a turn. You can ride around the circle once and then give it to him." Words like these are easier for the child to understand than, "You must take turns with him." A group at the slide will be helped more when the teacher says, "First you go down and then Jim and then Lucy." They may not understand when she merely says, "You must all take turns at the slide."

The teacher often needs to interpret situations to inexperienced children to prevent misunderstanding. Bill was pulling a wagon when he observed Rickey on the tricycle he had been riding earlier. Rickey was new in the group and uncertain. Bill approached him aggressively; "I was riding that," he said. Rickey just smiled, and the teacher replied, "You are pulling the wagon now, Bill." "Yes, I am," said Bill, half surprised but satisfied. In a few minutes both boys were playing together on the jungle gym.

When we try to teach children about "turns," we must be sure to follow through in the situations. If a child gives up a swing so that another child may have a turn, we must see that the first child gets it back afterward if he stills wants it. Even if he isn't standing there waiting, it may be wise to say, "Johnny, Jane has had her turn now and you can have the swing back again if you wish." This clarifies the concept and prevents the child from feeling that taking turns really means losing something.

A group of four-year-olds were playing with boats in a large pan of water where there were also two turtles. Michelle had a boat but wanted a turtle. She picked up the turtle that Davy was playing with. "Hey, that's mine," said Davy, and he quickly grabbed it back.

The teacher accepted his assertion of his right to the turtle, but she commented to Michelle, "It's hard to want a turtle and find that someone else is playing with it."

Davy then turned to Michelle, "Here, this one will be for both of us. I'll share it with you," and he shoved it across to her. It often happens that the child who can assert himself freely can also share easily when he perceives the situation. He can feel good about sharing.

Special Cases Arise Under This Concept of Property Rights

An interesting situation is sometimes created by the children themselves. An aggressive child may prefer a certain piece of equipment. Almost before the teacher is fully aware of what is happening, he may establish that it is "his," and the other children, fearing his attack, may prefer to leave it for him and give up their turn with this piece of equipment. The teacher must be alert to such situations and protect the other children in their right to use all equipment equally. She must see that they suffer no retaliation later. Charles, whose aggressiveness was making him unpopular, preferred a red tricycle. With his usual lack of awareness of the needs and feelings of others, he proceeded to take it when he could. It became important for the teacher to accept responsibility for maintaining the right of others to use the coveted red tricycle. It was important because Charles needed to have other children feel friendly toward him. No one in the group was more eager to be liked. The fact that there were occasions when he possessed the red tricycle legitimately made it easier for him to bear the limitation of not having it every time. It was also important for the teacher to watch this situation because the other children needed to be successful in standing up for themselves in the face of the threat Charles offered them.

A slightly different situation exists when a timid child may depend on a particular piece of equipment for a feeling of security. He may cling to a tricycle or a doll because he feels safer with it. It may happen to be the first thing he played with, or the toy with which he had his most satisfying experience. It is important for him to have the teacher protect him in his possession of this piece of equipment until he has found other areas of security. The teacher must suspend the rules in his case, interpreting to the other children with "We'll let him keep the doll because he's new in our school and still feels strange. Remember when you were new? When he knows that we're friends, he can take turns with us." In doing this the teacher helps other children to understand and accept differences too.

Bill, for example, was a quiet, thin child who held aloof from the children and the teachers. One day he discovered the large red wagon. It may have been like one he had at home. Whatever the reason, he began to play with it almost exclusively and could not bear to share it with another child. The teacher felt that it was important to protect Bill in his use of the wagon for a time. She helped the more secure children find a substitute whenever possible and allowed Bill time to grow more sure of himself at school before she expected him to take turns with the wagon.

The time comes, of course, when a child like this should be ready to accept the standards of the group. The teacher must watch for this readiness and, for the sake of his relationships with others, not prolong needlessly the child's dependence on one piece of equipment.

ADJUSTING TO THE GROUP

Children Find Their Place in the Group Step by Step

In finding their places in a group, children usually go through certain steps in adjustment. After they have been able to relate themselves to an adult in the school and feel safe with her, they move on to relationships with individual children. There are many ways in which the adult can help the child move on into play with other children. If she sits at the table with the child, she can make sure that there is a place for another child to join them. She can encourage a second child to join the activity and then quietly withdraw herself, not absorbing the child's attention longer than necessary. Friendships with contemporaries in nursery school are more important than friendships with adults, and the adult must give children every encouragement to move on into having experience with other children.

In the nursery school most children have relationships with other children that are temporary or shifting. Two children may play together for a morning or for a few days, drawn by a mutual interest in digging a hole, or playing firefighter, or setting up housekeeping somewhere. Then each will have an equally close but short-lasting friendship with someone else. But even in these shifting relationships there are likely to be certain children who are rather consistently antagonistic to each other or attracted for reasons we may not fully understand. We can help children better if we are aware of their feelings of liking and not liking, so that we can be careful to use the one wisely and not to add to the other.

Close Friendships Are Often a Source of Strength

A timid child often gains from a close relationship with one child in the beginning; and the new child too may be helped by contacts with individuals before he is ready to enter groups. Both the timid child and the one who is new may need to gain confidence in simple social situations before they are ready to solve the more complex problems which arise when several children play together. The teacher may need to see that their contacts are largely with individuals at first. It is safer to like individuals before one tries to like groups. It may even be dangerous to try to love humanity without loving individuals!

Sometimes children discover one particular friend, and from this close friendship they develop confidence and assurance. There is nothing much better at any age level than having a special friend. The confidence and assurance that comes from feeling that one is liked by an equal, sought after, depended on, makes possible a great deal of development. Such friendships are worth encouraging, even though at one stage they may mean that the pair exclude others. The friendship is likely to lead later on to a growth in friendliness. As friends, they can show consideration for each other's feelings.

Stephen and Francis are friends. Stephen ran out to the playground one day carrying an Indian hat and yelled, "Francis, here's an Indian hat. Put it on fast." Francis replied, "I don't need it. I'm a cowboy." And then he added, "But I'm your friend," and the two ran across the playground together. In rejecting the hat, Francis was careful not to let his friend feel rejected.

Arvin, burdened with a heavy load of resentful feelings, tended to withdraw from friendly approaches. Mary, an outgoing friendly child, was able to reach him but only after he had first expressed his negative feelings. Mary ran up to him one day and threw her arms around him. "I love you, Arvin," she cried in a burst of pleasant feeling. "Why did you do that?" Arvin said, drawing back. "I love you," Mary replied confidently. Slowly he answered, "I can kill you. I can kill everyone else but you," and together they went off to play with the turtles in the bowl. Arvin had begun to like people.

Close friends often have conflicts with one another, especially if they are beginning to play more with other children. They may quarrel frequently and call each other all the current names, "dummy," "mashed potato head," and separate with, "I won't play with you any more." But they are still best friends, quick to defend each other against outsiders.

Mickey can assert himself but remain friendly. Lisa had bumped her truck into Mickey's dump truck. Very angrily he said, "Hey, you can't bump into my truck. I don't like that; you can't do that," and almost in the same breath he added, "But you're a nice girl," and he blew her two kisses!

While close friendships offer real support to children, the teacher needs to be alert to offer help at the point at which one of the pair may be ready for new contacts. Janice and Jerry had both developed confidence after they began playing together. It was several weeks before Jerry began to assert himself. One morning he announced, "I'm going out." Janice had previously decided she didn't want to go out. Janice complained, "Jerry shouldn't go out when I don't go out." The teacher pointed out to her, "But you could go out." Jerry persisted, "But I want to go out. I'm going out with Timmy." Janice protested again, and Jerry finally went out. Neither child was very happy. A wiser teacher might have recognized the real problem which the situation presented for the two children. Instead of pointing out to Janice that she too could go out, she might have said, "You like to have Jerry with you, don't you? He's going out now, but he'll be back. You and he will play together again." She would then have tried to help Janice have fun away from Jerry, so that the two children might find satisfaction in greater independence while still remaining friends.

Lester Developed After He Found a Friend

Let us take Lester as an example of a child who developed rapidly after he found a friend, because he is typical of many rather quiet children who find it easier to work through the conflicts they feel when they have the support of a good friend.

Lester was the only boy in a family with three girls. He had received a great deal of anxious attention from his parents and steady dictation from his three sisters. It had been hard for him to be a person in his own way. When he entered nursery school he was defensive and self-conscious, holding back from activities. He watched the other children, often trying to belittle what they were doing. Tears came into his eyes if anyone made a disparaging remark about him or his efforts. He risked very little action anywhere. Even at the table he seemed to feel that he might spill something or do the wrong thing, and be subject to teasing or criticism. He sat without eating much of anything but toast. On the playground he would lean against a post, half hidden, unhappiness showing on his tight little face.

Lester had been in nursery school several weeks before he became friends with Albert. Albert was timid and unsure of himself too, but he did not seem to be as sensitive to his problems as was Lester. No one entirely understood what brought them together, but it might have been their interest in imaginative things.

Whatever may have brought them together, the two boys began to play with each other almost exclusively. The first one to arrive at school would wait around the door until the other one appeared and they would literally fall into each other's arms. It was as though no other children existed for them. The change in Lester's behavior was remarkable. He seemed to come alive and was purposeful, active. It was clearly an important experience for him to find someone who depended on him and who offered no threat to him. Soon the two began to challenge other children and to exclude others actively from their play where previously they had merely ignored others. Their passive behavior was replaced by defiance of the teacher and her suggestions. Instead of sitting in front of his food, Lester was noisy and sociable at the table—if Albert were there. It was as though from his friendship he found the security he needed to enable him to defend himself in a world that had previously overwhelmed him.

When the two boys left nursery school at the end of the year, they had begun to accept others and were playing successfully in the group, although they were still bosom friends. Lester had become a person in his own right and a most engaging person, who found fun in many situations. Out of the friendship with Albert, which was close and for a time exclusive, he had gained confidence. He became able to face and accept the demands of group living.

Some Children Never Find Close Friends

Not all children seem able to find this release and stimulus to growth through finding a close friend. Charles, who was in nursery school as long, never found any close friend. The aggressiveness he displayed undoubtedly handicapped him, but it does not completely explain his lack of close relationships. Children who are not aggressive may still fail to find close friends. Beth was like Charles in being without friends, but she was not at all aggressive. In fact, she sought affection from children and adults. She would run after any teacher saying, "Lady, I love you." She wanted children to play with her, but even in the shifting relations characteristic of preschool groups she seldom had much of a place. In spite of Beth's words her relationships with people were superficial and lacked warmth. What makes such differences?

One explanation lies in the quality of the relationships each child had experienced earlier. Lester, with all his handicaps, had still known a loving, warm relationship with his busy mother; while neither Charles nor Beth had found much warmth and acceptance in any of the adults with whom they had lived. Beth had even experienced a surprising amount of neglect in a home where some of the standards seemed high. Again we see how the relationships which the child has experienced in his home influence and limit the kind of relationship he is able to establish outside his home. Sometimes a teacher can supply the child with a relationship sufficiently warm to make up the deficit when there is one, so that he can achieve an adequate measure of social satisfaction, as in the case of the boy who used the rubber doll for biting. But this is only likely to happen when some measure of warmth and affection has been experienced earlier by the child.

OUR GOAL IS TO HELP CHILDREN TO LIKE EACH OTHER AND MAINTAIN MUTUALLY SATISFYING RELATIONSHIPS

If we were to sum up our goals as we work with children in groups, we might say that they all lead in the direction of helping the children like each other more rather than less because of what we do. We might use this as a yardstick. Will the children like each other better if we do this? If children are friends, they will find it easier to get along together. If the techniques they use are constructive ones, they will find it easier to live with others.

As teachers we may have to redirect children as they try to unload hostility onto other children. Louise and Stevie were washing their hands side by side. Louise was a child who carried a heavy load of hostile feeling and was always attacking others in a critical way. She said, "Stevie's a bad boy." The teacher replied casually, "Oh, he's my friend and you're my friend. Isn't it nice that I have two friends?" Stevie beamed, and Louise picked up the idea with, "and Anne's your friend and Mike and Jim." "Yes," said the teacher, "there are lots of friends here."

Isolation Should Not Be Used As Punishment

Following the example of some adults, children may be overly concerned with "bad" behavior. Giving undue attention to a child's undesirable behavior may make it hard for that child to find his place again in the group. We sometimes see a parent or teacher isolating a child as punishment for not getting along with others. We have come far enough in our discussion to be aware of the fact that punishment may be undesirable because of the load of resentment and hostility that may accompany it. While the child may not repeat a particular act after being punished, he is not likely to feel more friendly toward others or to get along better with them because of it. Isolation or being made to sit on a chair deprives him of the chance to have other, and perhaps better, experiences. It also labels him as "bad" in the eyes of the group and thus adds to his difficulties in getting along with others.

Isolation may be desirable when it is used with a child whose difficulties are the result of overstimulation and fatigue because of too many experiences. In this case, the teacher may accept the child's need of a simpler environment. She will try to achieve it without giving him a feeling that isolation is a form of punishment. She may suggest a story alone or a walk, or she may put him in a room with his favorite toy for a rest, explaining that he will get along better with the others after a rest. She may remove a child who is disturbing other children and put him where he can be free to do as he wishes, but she will not do it as punishment for his failure.

Judy is a tense child, very jealous of her twin brother whom she feels her parents prefer. She has trouble getting along with other children because she seems to see them as rivals. She put it this way to the teacher one day.

Judy: "I want to be a wicked witch."
Teacher: "I wonder why you want to be a wicked witch?"
Judy: "Because they cause spells on people."
Teacher: "You mean there are really too many people around and you would like to get rid of them?"
Judy: "Yes, there are too many, and I'm going to be a witch and get rid of them."
Teacher: "Sometimes it is hard to have so many people around. When you feel like that, we could go off by ourselves where it is quiet until you feel better."

They went into the teacher's office where Judy played with clay. By the time she had finished, she was quite relaxed. Her voice was pitched lower, and she said she wanted to go back with the others.

A Child Gains from Being Given Help in the Group

Usually a child gains more from being helped in a situation than from being taken out of it, because most of the child's learning about how to live in a social group comes from the responses of other children to him. As he faces, in the reaction of others, the consequences of what he does, he learns what is acceptable and what is not. We may need to temper these consequences for him, but for the most part we can leave the child free to find his own way if the group is one of equals. We help him most when we help him discover that being with other people is fun. Then he will want to modify his behavior to fit the pattern of the group in order to belong.

When the situation is too difficult for the child, he will show us by his behavior that he needs help. Aggressive, attacking behavior is often a sign that the child feels helpless and is seeking a way out of the situation. The teacher needs to step in with the words, "I'll help you." A child will stop hitting if he sees some real hope of getting help. He can wait while the adult helps work out a solution. But he cannot be expected to trust the adult if she blames him for the difficulty. He must have confidence in her acceptance of him and her willingness to help. Confidence is based on past experience, and we must remember that the present experience will itself become a past experience, helping or hindering the child the next time. To condemn a child, to blame him for his social inadequacies, will only lessen his chances of success and our chances of offering help that he can accept. He will like being with people less if we act in these ways when he is having difficulties.

Rivalry Creates Problems

One of the least helpful things that the teacher can do is to encourage direct competition among children. Competitive situations breed ill will. Comparing children, holding one up as an example to others, is unfair to all because of the hostility it arouses. "See who will finish first," or "See how much faster Jane is dressing," or "See how quiet John is"—all these comments are likely to make children like each other less rather than more. They make others appear to be rivals or competitors rather than friends.

The teacher must be aware that young children, in part because of their dependency, will be competing for her attention. Comparisons increase the rivalry they feel. She should be very careful to do nothing to increase jealous feelings. These feelings can cause real unhappiness. Often a child will misbehave at rest or at the table because he wants the attention which the teacher is giving another child. His teacher must be ready to reassure him by a word or a smile that she cares about him too.

IN SPITE OF CONFLICTS CHILDREN BELONG TOGETHER

Conflicts will keep arising when children are in groups because it is difficult to solve all the problems that exist when people actively play and work together. Because children are in the process of learning, they meet many situations which are beyond their limited skills to handle constructively. Even Terry could say, "Let's talk it over," only when he was with children whom he knew very well. It is the teacher's responsibility to help the children understand others and themselves better, so that they can meet their own problems.

As we observe children in the nursery school, we are aware that the satisfaction they find in all activity is enhanced by the fact that other children are sharing it, just as we ourselves enjoy experiences that we can share with others. Whether children play cooperatively or merely side by side, they show us that each experience has more meaning for them because it is a group experience. Children belong together.

Kay expressed in her own way what should be our goal in group relationships. She and another child were on a walk with their teacher when they met a stranger who stopped to inquire whether the girls were sisters. "No," replied the teacher, "just friends." Kay smiled at him. "We make friends out of people at nursery school," she said.

SITUATION FOR DISCUSSION

Discussion

In the situations at the end of some chapters three children, Davie, Nels, and Shaylan, appear several times. How would you characterize the behavior patterns of each of these children from the records? What patterns are similar in each situation reported and what patterns appear to be different? What characteristics can be observed when the child is with a group that might not appear if he is by himself? What values do you see in repeated observations of the same child?

PROJECTS

1. Observe and record five situations in which a child used a successful, constructive technique in approaching another child or group of children, or in enlisting the cooperation of another child in carrying out a purpose. Analyze to find possible reasons why the approach was successful in each case.

2. Observe and record a situation in which the teacher helped two children to settle a dispute or to forestall a difficulty in such a way that they liked each other more after the experience.

3. Observe and report a situation in which a teacher was involved in relationships with several children in a group, as in a story period. Did the children compete with each other for the teacher's attention? Did she seem to be aware of the needs of each? Discuss the possible meaning of what the teacher did and its relation to the children's behavior.

REFERENCES

Erikson, Erik: Identity, Youth and Crisis. New York, W. W. Norton and Company, Inc., 1968. Chap. 3.

Greenleaf, Phyllis T.: Liberating Young Children from Sex Roles: Experiences in Day Care Centers, Play Groups and Free Schools. Sommerville, Massachusetts, New England Free Press.

Isaacs, Susan: The nursery as a community. *In* Rosenblith, J., and Allinsmith, W. (eds.): The Causes of Behavior: Readings in Child Development and Educational Psychology. Boston, Allyn and Bacon, Inc., 1962.

Isaacs, Susan: Social Development in Young Children: A Study of Beginnings. New York, Schocken Books Inc., 1972.

Kohlberg, Lawrence: Stage and sequence: the developmental approach to socialization. *In* Goslin, D. (ed.): Handbook of Socialization. New York, Rand McNally and Co., 1968.

Mead, Margaret: Can socialization of children lead to greater diversity? Young Children, August, 1973.

Redl, Fritz: When We Deal with Children — Selected Readings. New York, The Free Press, 1966.

Sprung, Barbara: Guide to Non-Sexist Early Childhood Education. New York, Women's Action Alliance, 370 Lexington Avenue, 1974.

CHAPTER 19

Once Upon A Time Story (girl, 4 years 8 months)

DRAMATIC PLAY — AVENUE
FOR INSIGHT

Dramatic play is of absorbing interest to children. In it they relive and try to clarify situations they have met. By observing dramatic play we increase our insights into how children see the world and how they feel about relationships among people. Dramatic play is an important source of satisfaction and learning for children.

ENCOURAGING DRAMATIC PLAY

With time, with properties, with freedom from interference, the children act out what is important to them. Because of all its values the good nursery school encourages dramatic play by careful planning.

357

In planning it is important that the program be flexible, so that there is a chance for dramatic play to continue once it has started. The group may be absorbed in housekeeping, in playing firefighters, or in moving, over most of a morning or over most of a week or more. They need the chance for sustained play when they develop such an interest, so that they may work through all that they are thinking and feeling about the subject. Uninterrupted time is needed by children for developing their dramas—not just bits of time between scheduled activities. Supervision that is casual and unobtrusive is important too, if the play is to have meaning to the children. They often need suggestions, but they do not need direction.

Heading the list of desirable properties which encourage dramatic play are materials for homemaking play. Dolls, doll carriages, beds, tables, chairs, dishes, an iron and ironing board, and telephone are among the things which will be used. The doll family should be large and should include several "babies." In one group, the most popular doll was a baby doll with eyes painted shut as though she were sleeping. Black and brown dolls should be included.

Group play is often promoted by having at least two things of a kind—two beds, two telephones, two or more doll buggies, and plenty of dishes and chairs for company. All the equipment should be simple in construction and substantial so that it can take hard usage without the need for limits to save the equipment and perhaps lessen the value of the play for the children. If a bed is strong enough to hold a child, he can use it to act out the part, and thus enter more directly into the play and gain more from it.

Courtesy of Jean Berlfein.

The group is re-creating a social gathering with the usual telephone conversation to interrupt it.

Variety results from the introduction of materials which can serve many purposes, such as boxes and boards. These things can be used by a resourceful group in many ways. Barrels, large and small, have many uses, and even cardboard cartons will serve for a morning of play in endless ways. One group delighted in using the barrel to roll in, like the little pig in the story. A ladder and a short piece of hose may suggest a whole fire department and all its activities. A bicycle-tire pump and a short piece of hose may be the beginning of a "gas station" where wagons and tricycles are serviced by eager attendants. Empty cereal boxes, butter cartons, cans with smooth edges, paper, and string may transform a house into a store, with the wagons turning into delivery trucks. "Raw materials," such as squares of brightly colored cloth for costumes, bring variety into the play. The resourceful nursery school teacher will provide materials which suggest uses limited only by the imagination of the children themselves. With the guidance of an observant teacher, dramatic play situations can contribute significantly to the children's learning as was done by the teacher in the "store" play described in Chapter 14.

VALUES OF SOCIODRAMATIC PLAY

Smilansky,* after a careful study of children's sociodramatic or voluntary social play, concluded that, "Sociodramatic play behavior develops three main areas in a child, all of which are essential parts, not only of play, but also of the school game and the game of life.

1. The first main aspect is *creativity*, based on utilization of past experience and controlled by the demands of some framework." The imaginative "Let's pretend" which is based on past experience and modified by the necessity of adjusting to the ideas of others is an important part of living itself. This imaginative element in spontaneous play is part of the creative approach to experience so valuable in the scientist and artist.

2. "The second aspect is *intellectual growth*, which includes power of abstraction, widening of concept and acquisition of new knowledge." In playing together children share their ideas and concepts about the world around them. Language is important here, and children use language more freely in sociodramatic play than at other times (as mentioned in the section on language).

3. "The third aspect is *social skills*, which includes positive give and take, tolerance and consideration." These social skills develop in carrying on episodes of family or community life when children must use techniques for getting along with others for achieving purposes or constructing settings. As teachers we enrich the play by supplying needed accessories and by suggesting techniques that seem to be lacking in getting along with others. Thoughtful observation before stepping in to make suggestions or offer materials is more rewarding here than in almost any other area. Later, children will go on to playing group games with rules, a very different kind of play and one which emphasizes only a few skills at a time.

---

*Smilansky, Sara: Can adults facilitate play in children? Theoretical and practical considerations, pp. 42–43. *In* Play: The Child Strives towards Self-Realization. Copyright © 1971, National Association for the Education of Young Children, 1834 Connecticut Avenue N.W., Washington, D.C. 20009.

Courtesy of Jean Berlfein.

These boys use the telephone in comfort in the house they have constructed

THE MEANING OF DRAMATIC PLAY

The dramatic play at nursery school centers around episodes and relationships that seem significant to the children. Through play they reveal themselves and their concepts of the world to us.

What meaning does such play have for children?

Dramatic Play Is One Way to Handle the Problem of Being "Little"

We can be sure that children want to understand what it is like to be grown up and do grown-up things. In their play they are preparing themselves for these roles someday. Play is also one way to handle their own special problem of being "little" in a world of big people. In play they have a chance to be the big mother or father, or the important worker. They can escape from being little through identifying themselves with the "big" roles. Doing this has real value in lessening some of the inevitable frustrations of growth. Notice which child wears the holster and gun or the biggest cowboy hat. It is likely to be a small child or a child who is unsure of his place or a child for whom being little seems especially handicapping. These appendages help him to pretend that things are different.

It is usually difficult to find anyone willing to take the role of the "baby" in homemaking play unless being this baby is the only way to be accepted by sought-after playmates or unless the child's dependency needs have not been adequately met in earlier relationships. Being little usually stands for deprivation. "You can't because you're too little." Lois, who loves the pet goat at school and wishes she had one at home, says sadly, "I've never had a goat. I'm only a very little girl." Ruth looks at the clock and says, "It's eight o'clock. That's grown-up time." When someone wants to join her play she pauses, then asks, "How old are you?" The child answers, "Three," and she replies, "Only kids that are four can play here." Ruth has had her fourth birthday.

Few children are as able to accept their size as Damon is. Damon is small for his age. When Donald taunts him with "You're little. You're as little as my brother. You're only four," Damon defends himself, "I know I'm little but I'm going to have a birthday and I'll be five. You can be little and five too." One imagines that Damon's parents had not used the phrase. "You're too little to do that." Instead they had helped him feel comfortable about being just his size.

Play Makes Children Feel Less Helpless

Taking adult roles in play also gives the child the chance to feel in control of situations. He can make things come out as he would like in his dramatic play. He can be the one to put the baby to bed, to do the scolding and spanking, to make the decisions. Doing all this probably serves to relieve the sense of helplessness which sometimes overwhelms him. Things become more manageable because he can escape at times into play. He finds it easier to face the reality of his age and size, to accept being put to bed, being disciplined. Toilet training had been successfully completed for David mentioned later in this chapter. But some of the feelings built up in the process remained and came out in his dramatic play. There he was the one to impose restrictions, reprove, and finally forgive.

In dramatic play the child also has a chance to drain off feeling and work through anxieties. It is significant to note how many times children play out going to the doctor, giving "shots" to a doll.

Play which is repeated by individuals and by groups is almost sure to have meaning for them. We need to try to understand what its meaning is if we are to offer sound help. It is probably neither accident nor perversity that makes a child knock over things or throw them down. We must remember that he himself has tumbled many times. He has been startled, and perhaps hurt, by falling in the course of learning to walk. He may recover some assurance by making other things fall and thus reduce the threat which falls have offered to him. We know that children are frightened by sudden, loud noises and yet as soon as they are able, they pound and bang, making all the noise they can. In this way they may be better able to handle the fear they have felt. Because they can make noises themselves, they are less disturbed by noise. The child who lives with adults who disapprove of noisemaking on his part, or who consider knocking over block towers as destructive and useless play, may carry a burden of unresolved fear and anxiety.

Guns are one of the props in play which children use in coping with the feelings which go with being little or helpless. The smallest boy may be the one who uses the biggest gun or perhaps two guns. Guns are a part of the world we live in, and we can hardly deny them to children as they try to re-create this world. They serve a role in helping a child to overcome the feeling of being little and help in the efforts he makes to find his place in the adult world. We can, however, verbalize to him our own feelings about guns and our hope that someday they will not have such a place in the world. We can disapprove of guns just as we show our disapproval of expressions of violence. We can also set limits on where guns may be used, limits such as outdoors only, in order to reduce the stimulation which guns often produce and which sometimes becomes more than a hostile child can manage.

Play May Help Children Reconcile the Two Worlds of Fantasy and Reality

Francis is at the table playing with the play-dough. He rolls it with a rolling-pin and pats it. He talks softly to himself. "Is that a birthday cake? Where are some candles?" He reaches and gets some cut straws and places them on the play-dough. He then turns to a teacher sitting near and says, "I don't want to sing." The teacher assures him that it is all right to have birthday cake and not sing. He blows two very hard puffs and says, "I blew it out," adding "Where is the knife?" The teacher hands the knife to him. He says, "A *really* birthday because I'm cutting the cake. It must be real because I'm cutting it. I blew out the candles and I'm cutting it."

Teacher: "You pretended to blow out the candles, didn't you?"

Francis: "Yes, but I'm really cutting it." He hands the teacher a piece and he keeps a piece.

Teacher: "You really cut it but we'll have to pretend to eat it."

Francis: "Ya." A slight frown comes across his face. He then runs across the room to Jamie, who is building with blocks. "Superman, I cut the cake for you. I pretended it was my birthday." Jamie smiles but makes no comment. Francis runs back to the table, picks up the clock and runs to Jamie with it. "See what I got for my birthday?"

Jamie: "Why?"

Francis: "Because it's my birthday and it's brand new."

Jamie: "Not your birthday."

Francis: "I pretended. I made a cake."

Francis is coping with the problem of the real and the pretend and is well on his way to finding pleasure in both. He makes the distinction in "I cut the cake. I pretended it was my birthday."

Play Offers an Opportunity to Drain Off Negative Feelings

In their play children often act out aggressive, destructive feelings. These are the kinds of feelings which create anxiety and need to be drained off. It is important to accept them in play, being sure only that the children are safe and that the impulses are under control and kept on the "pretend" level. An adult may need to remain near to "steady" a group which is acting out negative feeling, as in a war game or a fire play. It is important to the children to know that they can stop or that they will be stopped before they do real harm. Without this help the play may not serve the purpose of draining off hostility and keeping it within manageable proportion. It may only increase the anxiety of some children about their ability to handle their impulses. As adults we should have no hesitation about making a suggestion, redirecting or limiting play which we can see is going "out of bounds."

In doing this, of course, we do not want to deny expression to negative feeling. We must avoid what is a tendency to want only "good" behavior. Here is an example. Ruth, Marilyn, and Gordon are playing they are lions. Marilyn, who is an inhibited child, says, "I'm a good lion." Gordon says, "Don't eat me up." Lions fascinate him because of their dangerous possibilities. Marilyn changes her role. It's safer. "Don't eat me up," she says. Ruth boldly says, "I'm a mean lion," and chases Gordon. Then she stops and asks him, "Are you a mean lion?" When he answers "Yes," Marilyn feels braver and says, "I am too." "Pretend you can't get us," says Ruth. Gordon answers with, "I'm going to eat you up." Unfortunately, at this point a teacher steps in and tells them to be "good lions" and they drop the lion play. It no longer serves a purpose for them. Marilyn, who has conformed to high standards of good behavior and has paid a price in loss of creativity, had just reached the point of joining Ruth and Gordon in daring to be a "mean" lion. The teacher's words close this avenue of escape from adult demands for Marilyn. It is interesting to get further insight into what Marilyn is seeking by watching her subsequent play. A few minutes later she climbs up high in the jungle gym and says, "This is dangerous."

Many Kinds of Feelings Are Revealed in Play

Unable to bring out feelings directly, children sometimes hide them under what they feel is the safer guise of pretending to make a joke, just as adults often do, or they may pretend that they are acting a part. A three-year-old, who had been hurt and frightened repeatedly by what had happened in his world until he could not bear to face reality, used to deny that he was "Bill" and insisted that he was an "elephant." As an elephant he felt free to trample over the other children's materials, to resist the adults, and to escape from being the poor, frightened little boy that he really was. In time he grew to feel more secure with one of the teachers and sure of her support. This brought him confidence. He began to drop the role of an elephant and dare to be Bill, and take some responsibility for his own behavior.

It is always interesting to note what children consider funny, for understanding humor is one clue in understanding the kind of adjustment a person is making. Children's dramatic play often has a humorous quality, but underneath the humor may lie disguised meanings. We must be aware that feelings of many kinds are likely to be expressed under the acceptable guise of a joke.

One child tickles another with a leaf that he is carrying. They both laugh, for his gesture expressed friendliness. Another child tickles a companion with a leaf and the child objects. He senses the attacking quality which exists under the apparent playfulness of the gesture and resents it.

David, who is struggling hard to establish a feeling for his masculine role in the world, is making a mask at Halloween. He says, "I want a *man* witch. I don't like girls." His father is a withdrawn person, defensive and aloof. His mother clings to David, is over-directive and possessive. But David is valiantly making the effort to identify himself with male things, even man witches. At times he dresses up in skirts and then tries to defend himself by rejecting all girls. These conflicts are revealed in his play.

It has been clearly established that dramatic play has therapeutic values for children. We need to recognize and accept this fact. Such acceptance does not imply that nursery school teachers are in a position to undertake play therapy in the more technical sense of the term. But in the nursery school we need to see that children have plenty of opportunity to play out feelings, try out roles, clarify concepts through their own spontaneous dramatizations. We can make sure that children have a chance to benefit from the therapeutic values of dramatic play.

Television is having an effect on the dramatic play of young children. Patterns appear in the child's play which are a reflection of what he has seen on the screen. In some of the portrayals of aggressive behavior on television shows, children seem to find patterns for playing out their own aggressive feelings. While we are not sure what the effect of television may be on young children, we can be sure that it is desirable for the child to re-enact what he sees on television shows. In this way he is doing something about what he sees, trying to understand it better and make it less frightening. It is better for him to express the fears which may have been aroused by what he sees. The evidence from studies so far suggests that parents are wise to protect young children from large doses of the terrifying, indigestible material which too often makes up television viewing for them.

EXAMPLES OF DRAMATIC PLAY

Some dramatic play takes place when children are alone. They may talk to themselves as they play with a small family of dolls, as they build with blocks, play in the housekeeping corner, or play with water.

Courtesy of Anne Read Smith.

A group plays house on a steep slope in their playground.

David is playing with some small doll figures and furniture, while the teacher sits near. He talks to himself as he plays. A comfortable, happy child, his words nevertheless reveal something of the conflict all children feel during the process of socialization. He puts the smallest doll in a bed, saying, "She has to stay right in her bed. If she makes a noise, I'm going to spank her little bottom—spank her little bottom—spank her little bottom." He turns to the teacher. "She's a nasty little girl because she got up and made a noise, didn't she? She's a nasty little girl. She has to go sound to sleep." He turns back to the doll and continues as if two people were talking together. "Quit doing that. I'm just going to stay downstairs all day. Shut up. It's not daytime. It's still nighttime. I want to stay up all day. Do you want to peepee or not? You're not going to peepee. Stay right in your bed." In this play David is handling some of his feelings about the training issues he has faced. He is probably reassured by the teacher's presence although she makes no comments. He feels her acceptance but she is there to steady him if the play should become too disturbing.

Here is an example of the play of two four-year-old boys which seems influenced by television in the beginning but turns into a familiar picnic situation in the end.

Kevin and Michael were playing together in the housekeeping corner. After rearranging the furniture, they picked up the suitcases. Michael opened his. It was full of clothes and articles. Kevin opened his and seemed disappointed because it was empty. Michael poured some of the contents of his suitcase into Kevin's. He then proceeded to put on some dark glasses and picked up the suitcase and left. Kevin called good-by to him.

Michael came back into the housekeeping corner, saying to Kevin, who was playing with a string of beads, "We're robbers. Come on, robber."

"They'll be here in seven minutes. Call the police," Kevin answered him.

Michael picked up the phone and pretended he was calling the police.

"They're coming right away," said Michael.

"Call the cowboys," said Kevin. " "Come on, let's hurry; go on outside and I'll be there in a minute before the cowboys come. Go on outside, don't walk on the lawn. I'll be with you in a moment." Michael went outside the housekeeping corner.

"Come on back in; we'll eat a light supper first," Kevin said. "Hurry up, now, hurry up. If you don't want to set the table, I will," he added. (All this time Kevin was separating the plastic beads as he talked.)

Kevin told Michael to get some more silverware and put it in the suitcase. Michael made a sound like a siren.

Kevin said, "Put more silverware in the suitcase."

"Let's take the plates, too," Michael replied. He got the cups, more plates and silverware. They worked together to shut the suitcase.

"Now let's go," said Kevin and they ran out of the housekeeping corner into the adjoining room and unpacked the suitcase.

"We're having a picnic," said Kevin. Kevin filled the sugar and creamer with water. They set out the dishes. Michael had previously put a phone in the suitcase, so he took it out. They pretended to eat. Michael picked up the phone and made a call. "Let's drink some more tea," said Kevin and they did.

"Would you help me snap these beads together, Michael?" asked Kevin. "You'd better."

So Michael started putting the beads together. "You make you a string and I'll add onto mine," Kevin said.

Michael replied, "Leave a lot for me. Here I'll put some more in a cup for you and some for me." They put the beads together, working very hard.

Kim came in and Michael popped up and said, "We're playing house and you can't come in."

Kevin repeated this.

Kim stood on one side watching. Kevin and Michael then packed everything in the suitcase and returned to the other room.

These boys are friends. Each makes suggestions which the other accepts. They try to fit ideas together. Although Kevin is perhaps the leader, he does not dominate. He says, "If you don't want to set the table, I will." They start with concepts which may have come from a television show and go on to what they know about, picnics and playing house. Kevin continues his interest in the beads and draws Michael in finally. They enjoy being together but they do not accept another child, Kim. Instead, they move back to where they began. One feels that they are ready to end this experience. They have participated as friends who understood and accepted each other.

Kim, Nancy, and Barbara are playing house under a tent made of two little screens covered with a blanket.

Kim: "There is a lion outside the house. We are frightened so we stay in."

Barbara: "Yes, and we have to take care of baby sister too, or else the bad lion will get her."

Kim comes out of the house. She finds another child, Bonnie, standing near the tent. Kim goes up to her, takes her hand and says, "You are a bad lion. You frighten people, so they lock you up in a cage. Now you go to your cage"—Pauses, leads Bonnie to the other room, saying, "Come, I will make you a cage." She puts four long blocks together and tells Bonnie, "Now you get in there. That's your cage." Bonnie stands in the enclosure and Kim goes back to the house. She says, "The lion is locked in the cage, so we are safe."

In the meanwhile, Barbara, still in the house, says to Nancy, "Now you better listen to your big sister like a good girl or else the lion will catch you. Mommy will be back home soon." Kim, returning home, calls out to Bonnie from inside the tent. "You have escaped from the cage. You have unlocked the cage and you have escaped."

As Bonnie walks toward the tent, Kim shouts to the others, "The lion has escaped, the lion has escaped." They all three scream and shout.

Kim: "I must call the zoo and tell the manager." She picks up the telephone and calls. "There is a big lion escaped from the zoo and he is frightening us. Please get him, will you?" She puts down the receiver.

Barbara: "Now they will come and get him and put him back in the cage, Ha! Ha!"

Everything quiets down and the play shifts.

Nancy: "I am the mother."

Kim (pointing): "No. You (Barbara) are the big sister and you (Nancy) are the little sister. You are eight and she is five. You better mind her while I go out." She goes out for a few seconds and comes back.

Kim to Barbara: "Did she (Nancy) mind?"

Barbara: "No, she was a very bad girl."

Kim to Nancy: "Mommy is not mad at you, but next time you must mind."

Nancy: "I will."

Kim goes out for a few seconds and returns. Kim to Nancy: "Did you do what mother said?"

Nancy: "Yes."

Barbara says, "I know. When you go somewhere like downtown, we could play ring around roses."

Kim answers, "But be careful, big sister, because she is only three and she might fall down and get hurt."

Kim to Nancy: "You didn't behave and we spanked you—not real hard—I'll show you how———It doesn't hurt does it?"

Nancy: "No—But don't spank too hard, OK?"

Kim: "And then you played with the telephone."

Barbara to Nancy: "You better not. You are too little to play with the telephone."

Kim to Nancy: "You were playing in the street and we caught you."

Nancy: "I have to go out to pick berries."

Kim: "No, because you fooled us—(pauses)—Why do you have to pick berries?"

Barbara: "I want to call Grandma." Picking up the telephone receiver, dials 1, 2, 5, 8.

Puts down the receiver. "I called but the line is busy."

Barbara: "I am going to pick berries."

Kim to Nancy: "You also go to pick berries. When we are not looking."

Kim: "We must sleep now. Curl up, honey."

Nancy walks out on tiptoe. Suddenly Kim and Barbara rush out shouting, "Where is she? Where is she?" Both of them run out looking for Nancy. Barbara finds Nancy behind the door and shouts excitedly, "Here she is Mom—Hurry, Mommy." Barbara and Kim hold Nancy's hands on either side and drag her into the house. Kim pretends to lock the door of the house and tells Nancy, "You have been a bad girl. Now you have to stay in all day."

Here again we see the children's concern about misbehavior, playing with the telephone, playing in the street, running away, taking care of siblings. They cope with the problem of being little and the temptations they face by creating a "bad lion" and dealing with him and by being the punishing parent themselves. The re-create their world, only this time they are in control. Dramatic play serves to build confidence in them as they deal with and master the situations they re-enact.

THE BEGINNINGS OF GROUP GAMES DEVELOP OUT OF DRAMATIC PLAY

In addition to revealing feelings, dramatic play sometimes shows us how children can share experiences with each other. We see the beginnings of group games developing in their spontaneous play—forerunners of the more organized games which they will enjoy later.

When Kay and Jill played with the rings and discovered that they were "taking turns," they were developing a game with a clearly repetitive element. Group chants and play with word sounds are a form of dramatic play which comes with group consciousness. As we observe, we will see many examples of "games" appearing at the four-year level which have an "acting out" quality, characteristic of the growing ability of four-year-olds to be objective about experiences.

The more mature four-year-olds enjoy very simple activities in groups. Four or five children and a teacher may join hands in a circle on the grass in "ring around the rosy and we all fall down" with appropriate action. Marching becomes a group activity with a variety of instruments in the band. We need to guard against too much patterning or we may lose the spontaneous development of group feeling which holds much value for children. We should be ready to accept the nonconformists with their individual variations or the play may lose some of its meaning for the children.

As students in the nursery school laboratory, our task is to observe and interpret the meaning of the dramatic play which brings children so much satisfaction and through which they express so many of their feelings.

PROJECTS

During an observation period in nursery school, observe and record a dramatic play situation which occurs. What roles do the children take? Is there a leader? What seems to hold the group together? What ideas or feeling do they seem to be expressing? What kinds of satisfactions does the play seem to be giving them?

REFERENCES

Axline, Virginia: Play Therapy. New York, Ballantine Books, Inc., 1969.

Cuffaro, Harriet: Dramatic Play—The Experience of Block Building. *In* Hirsch, Elizabeth (ed.): The Block Book. Washington, D.C., National Association for the Education of Young Children, 1974.

Curry, Nancy: Dramatic Play as a Curricular Tool. *In* Sponseller, Doris (ed.): Play as a Learning Medium. Washington, D.C., National Association for the Education of Young Children, 1974.

Hartley, Ruth, Frank, Lawrence, and Goldenson, Robert: Understanding Children's Play. New York, Columbia University Press, 1952. Chaps. 2 through 5.

Smilansky, Sara: The Effect of Sociodramatic Play on Disadvantaged Pre-School Children. New York, John Wiley & Sons, Inc., 1968.

Smilansky, Sara: Can adults facilitate play in children? Theoretical and practical considerations. *In* Play: The Child Strives Toward Self-Realization. Washington, D.C., National Association for the Education of Young Children, 1971.

PART SIX

HOME – SCHOOL –
COMMUNITY RELATIONS

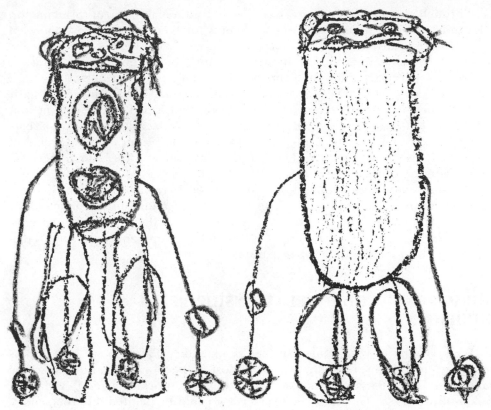

CHAPTER 20

Mummy and Daddy on Skis (boy, 4 years 7 months)

TEACHERS AND PARENTS
WORK TOGETHER

To bring up children in personal and tolerant ways, based on information and education rather than tradition, is a very new way; it exposes parents to many additional insecurities. . . .*

ERIK ERIKSON

Parents, or any of us, face difficulties in trying to follow new ways or patterns of behaving. The twentieth century has brought us so much that is new that we do not always appreciate how the role of a parent has changed.

*From Identity and the Life Cycle. New York, International Universities Press, 1959. Vol. 1, No. 1, p. 99.

Through the centuries there have been traditional ways of bringing up children in different parts of the world. Parents for the most part have followed these. Only recently has a body of knowledge been developing that might be useful for parents in the way that knowledge is useful to an engineer or a doctor. But being a parent is different from being an engineer or a doctor. Being a parent is a deeply personal experience as well as one that calls for information. It demands "personal and tolerant ways," as well as "informed ways," of functioning. We are just beginning to give attention to the possible ways in which parents can be helped, not only to gain the "information and education" available at present, but also to use the knowledge in their individual ways, with respect for the individuality of their child.

Parents have a tremendous job to do and do it remarkably well. Some of them face many obstacles because of health, housing conditions, the demands of their jobs, and many other factors. We are interested in the problems of parents. We are interested in how nursery schools or child development centers may be of help to parents in doing their job as parents.

THE PARENT—CHILD RELATIONSHIP IS SIGNIFICANT

We know that parents and what they think and feel and do are very important to the child. Ricky, for example, spent most of the morning in nursery school making a table. After he had made it, he painted it, working intently with long strokes of the brush. He asked the teacher if it could be painted different colors. When she agreed that would be a good idea, he used blue, yellow, orange, and then he painted a part with one color over another to make still a different color. He announced that he had made the table for his Daddy. He asked the teacher almost pleadingly, "Do you think my Daddy will love it?" "Yes, I think he will love it," she answered.

As he intently brushed the table with paint he said, "I am doing a good job. A painter should do a good job. I can paint better than other children." He seemed satisfied as he looked at the table, and he said hopefully, "We'll wrap it up with a string around so it won't come open. It is a surprise. Will he know what it is?"

The teacher answered, "If he doesn't, you can tell him." Ricky excitedly answered, "I *can* tell him it is a table for him." Here we see a child eager to please a parent, putting his best effort into a product, planning and anticipating, hoping it will be a good thing.

We Get Acquainted with Parents As They Come with Their Children

What do we see as we observe parents bringing children to nursery school? Here are some examples.

Jean and Her Mother

On their first day in nursery school Jean and her mother are obviously enjoying themselves. Jean has discovered the easel and uses the paints freely and sys-

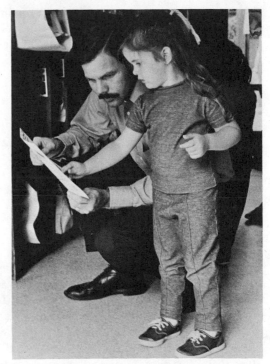

A parent admires his child's product.

Courtesy of Marianne Hurlbut.

tematically, one color after another in solid masses. She shows delight in the experience and calls her mother over to see. Her mother comes readily, interrupting her own exploration of the book corner where she has been looking over the books. She shows pleasure in Jean's painting, and they smile at each other. One gets the impression of two independent people, respecting each other and confident of the bond of love between them.

Jean's mother watches the other children, appears interested in the activities that are being carried on, and comments or questions the teachers as things occur to her. She is dressed comfortably in a simple dress which will not be hurt by fingers covered with paint or wet sand. She does not direct Jean's attention to objects or children. She does not attempt to tell her what to do. On one occasion when Jean is hit by another child, her mother appears to take it in a matter-of-fact way, neither approving nor disapproving of the behavior. Later when Jean pushes a child down, her mother shows no special concern. She leaves matters up to the teacher. She is friendly and outgoing. In her handling of Jean's vigorous protest at leaving, she is casual, "It has been fun, hasn't it! Of course you don't want to leave but we're going now and we'll be coming back tomorrow." Jean relaxes and smiles at the teacher as they go out.

After a couple of days of visiting, she and the teachers agree that Jean is ready to stay without her. Before the end of the week, Jean has stayed through the whole morning and has had her lunch there. In the following weeks Jean's mother often stays for a few minutes to watch. She greets the staff and the other children warmly and often shares incidents from home with the teachers. She reported with appreciation one morning that Jean had remarked, "Mother, you do have such nice kids," adding, "You know, she's right." Often she comes in slacks and sometimes she has to hurry off and does. She has a good deal to manage in a home with four children, but one feels that she respects herself and doesn't expect the impossible of herself or others.

Tommy and His Mother

Tommy and his mother arrive on the first morning with anxiety showing plainly on their faces. They had met the teacher, visited the school on an afternoon previously, but still they do not feel at all sure of what it will be like. Tommy's mother sits down on the chair the teacher indicates is for her. When Tommy finally leaves her to explore some trucks and calls for help, she only goes to him after she asks the teacher, "Is it all right for me to help him?"

She watches him closely and only occasionally appears to notice what other children do. She quickly turns away when she observes a dispute or children coming to blows. Once another child grabbed the small truck Tommy was using. He burst into tears and rushed to his mother who held him tightly and did not conceal her concern. One feels her disapproval of much that goes on and her uncertainty. She does not seem comfortable with the teachers and volunteers few comments. When she told about an incident, she added, "I know what I did was wrong." She seems to be passing judgment on herself and others and expects the same from them. Perhaps a school situation makes her feel this way even more than usual because childhood experiences of feeling failure and distance between herself and teachers are being revived.

For Tommy and his mother, the process of adjusting to nursery school is a slow, difficult one. It is a long time before Tommy feels sufficiently at home to stay alone comfortably. He continues to get upset when something unpleasant happens and to need his mother again. She shows anxiety over what is happening and continues to need the teacher's reassurance.

These are some of the parents one sees. These are some of the parents one must learn to understand. There are many others, responding in somewhat different ways, just as each of us would have a characteristic way of meeting the situation if we were accompanying a child to nursery school.

Parents Often Have Mixed Feelings About Nursery School

As we can see, the experience of having a child enter nursery school means different things to each parent. The school will offer each parent something different. The wise teacher needs to understand that the parent's feelings toward the school and the experience of having a child there may be somewhat mixed.

In bringing a child to nursery school, as we pointed out earlier, a mother is taking a step that will mean important changes in her relationship with a child who has only recently been a baby and completely dependent on her. Now the child will quickly become more independent than he has been. He will have experiences in which she does not share. If he is developing well, he will find satisfying relationships with other children and with his teachers. Parents may find it hard to share responsibility for the child with the teacher.

The mother who has enjoyed the period of her child's babyhood may find it difficult to accept his liking for nursery school and his readiness to leave her. The mother who may have found the care of a young child more than ordinarily difficult may also be reluctant to let him go. She may be afraid that she is shirking her responsibility. She finds it hard to accept her real need to have some time free from the demands that every young child makes. It is a reasonable need for parents and one for which they should make some provision. Nursery schools are a way of meeting this need while they are also meeting the child's need for independence and for companionship with other children.

The parent who is entering a child in school because she expects to be working outside the home will be influenced in her feelings by the way she feels about the job. She may be looking forward to working and may be satisfied about arrangements at home. She is likely to be glad to have the child enter even though she has some regrets about the necessary separation. If she wishes she did not have to work, she may find it very difficult to help the child enter into the group and she may need reassurance from the staff of the school. Most parents, of course, are able to help the child with the separation if they themselves feel confidence in the school or center.

Children who have had brothers or sisters in school previously usually enter more easily than those who have not, less because they themselves are familiar with the school than because their parents feel at home there. If the parent has accepted school experience for the child, the child is likely to find it easy to do the same.

Most parents enjoy watching the spurt in growth which usually occurs. All kinds of changes appear in the child's language, his social skills, his ideas about himself, and what he can do. He is no longer a baby, and he now appears more sure of this. As one mother remarked, she found herself enjoying her child much more after he started attending nursery school. He seemed more like a person to her.

Teachers Need to Be Aware of the Feelings of Parents

The parent-child relationship is one which is loaded with strong feelings. The teacher needs to be aware of these feelings. There are reasons for the way a parent feels, and it is important for the teacher to recognize and accept the parent's feelings. A mother will be helped if the teacher can listen and can understand her attitude toward the situation. The teacher's acceptance may free the parent so that she can look at the present and judge its meaning without being as entangled by emotions from the past.

Most parents also will feel strongly about matters pertaining to health. Frequently teachers are less alert than parents to adjusting a child's wraps to changes in temperature or activities or to avoiding drafts. They may be less concerned about wet feet or wet sleeves. Teachers are not the ones who are up at night with the sick child. They do not have the same heavy emotional investment in the child as the parent. Good parent-teacher relations are based on understanding on the part of each as to how a thing looks to the other. The inexperienced teacher must train herself to be very careful in matters involving health. With experience, she will come to appreciate the parent's viewpoint. If she is careful, she relieves the parent of a source of anxiety and makes better relationships possible.

Parents are sometimes defensive when they come into a school situation. Their childhood experiences with schools may make them expect to be judged or graded, and perhaps even fail to pass the test. Because they feel this way, they may expect the teacher to criticize what they do. They may react as if she had criticized them even when she says nothing. They are in need of reassurance before they can really learn to look at children as they are and learn more about children's behavior.

Parents who are older than the average parent of a preschool child, or parents who have a background of professional experience, especially people who have been teachers of older children, are likely to feel anxiety about the behavior of their children. They may have had little in their background to help them understand and have confidence in the growth impulses of young children. They are likely to see failure for themselves in the childlike behavior of their offspring. They need reassurance from a teacher who accepts children as they are.

In all her contacts with parents the wise teacher will remember that the relationship between a parent and a child is heavily loaded with feeling, and she will respect this feeling. She will do all she can to reassure the parents and to help them feel accepted in the situation of being a parent in the nursery school, just as she helps the child in the new situation.

Parents Want to Learn, but They May Be Critical

For parents, as for children, the nursery school can offer rich opportunities for learning. Parents, like children, are ready to learn at this point. They are interested in what happens to their child in his first school experience. As they come with their children, they watch the teachers and the other children and parents. They see rapid changes taking place in children. They have many questions.

Not all the changes taking place will seem like desirable ones to a parent. Growth seldom proceeds smoothly or in one direction. They may find a quiet, docile child becoming more aggressive and defiant after he has been in nursery school for a while. He may not share his toys as willingly as he did earlier. His vocabulary may be increasing rapidly, but it may contain words which the parents find quite unacceptable. Parents may be critical of aspects of the program.

Sometimes parents bring up criticisms directly. These criticisms should be considered carefully to see whether situations should be handled differently as well as to understand what may lie behind the criticism or complaint. It usually represents a step in growth when a criticism is expressed by the parent and accepted by the teacher and a mutual understanding reached. Negative feelings will appear but can be changed and cleared away by frank discussion so that they do not block the growth of more positive attitudes. Resistance is an important part of learning.

It helps if the teacher is aware of the part her own feelings play. She has her resistances to learning and changing. She may find herself acting defensively with parents, being most critical of them when she is most unsure of herself. Teachers need to feel comfortable about the things they are doing so that they do not act defensively. The teacher may need to say, "I have the impression that there are some things we do at school that bother you. Tell me what these are, please. We can talk about them." Teachers too can change. A competent teacher learns a great deal from parents. She is helped in her work with individual children as she comes to understand the child better through contacts with his parents. She may ask for the parent's help. Working together with parents can be satisfying and rewarding as we watch them learn and change and as we find ourselves learning and changing.

GOALS IN WORKING WITH PARENTS

In working with parents there are two main goals. The first goal is to help parents grow in confidence. The parent who feels confidence in himself or herself is better able to enjoy his or her child and to make creative and intuitively wise use of the experiences they have together. The confident parent is better able to learn about the needs of children. He or she is likely to use this knowledge more effectively.

The second goal is that of helping parents gain the insights and the knowledge that may improve their contribution to a child's development. The teacher who helps a parent feel more confident and who is skillful in providing sound information has achieved important goals in her work.

HOW DO WE HELP PARENTS GAIN MORE CONFIDENCE IN THEMSELVES?

There are many small but significant ways in which the school and the teacher may help parents feel that they are important.

Does the school provide a comfortable place for the parent to sit when he or she is waiting, a bulletin board with attractive, interesting material on it, and some magazines and books for browsing or lending?

In her informal contacts with the parents, does the teacher try to make the parent feel welcome at school? Does she take time to point out something of interest that is happening? Is she clear in the directions she gives about the arrangements for visiting, or the acceptable times to bring and call for the child, or the decisions that are hers to make and those that the parent should make?

The parent will feel more confident if she understands just what is expected of her as the parent of a nursery school child. She will gain confidence if the teacher takes time to listen to what she wants to tell the teacher. In listening the teacher will try to "listen with the third ear," to catch the meaning that may lie back of the words. She may ask herself why the parent is telling her this. It is important for the parent to feel that she is being understood.

The same principles for building confidence apply with adults as with children. The teacher will use these in her contacts with parents. She will show interest, give encouragement, avoid blaming or criticizing. She will comment with approval on sound methods. She will accept all the feelings the parent may have.

At times parents may ignore or resist the demands the school makes by continually ignoring the time for calling for the child, for example. The teacher must be able to meet negative attitudes and negative types of behavior with understanding and firmness. She does not feel personally responsible, for she knows that negative feelings are often displaced. She does not respond by blaming and rejecting the parent who is resistant or irresponsible. She faces the irritation she may feel, and deals with it, so that she can be of help to the parent in working out a more constructive solution for both of them.

In all our relationships with parents we must respect the deep feelings involved in the parent-child realtionship. We know that life with young children can offer much satisfaction, as well as much frustration at times. We must respect parents as people if we are to help them feel confidence in themselves as parents.

We must be people who are kind in the way we judge ourselves, too. We are less likely to judge others harshly if we are not harsh in judging ourselves. We need to feel a basic respect for all human beings, including ourselves, if we are to be of help to others. Good relationships are built on awareness and sympathy.

The Teacher Offers a Professional Relationship to the Parents

The teacher helps the parent largely because of the kind of person she is. Her friendliness, her genuine interest in the child and his family, in all that is important to them, her acceptance of them as they are, the way in which she refrains from passing judgment on what the parent says or does mean that she is offering a relationship in which the parent can feel secure and safe to be himself or herself.

But the relationship between teacher and parent differs from the personal relationship between friends; it is a professional relationship. Just as a child learns the possibilities of a new relationship when he starts to school and finds that the relationship with his teacher differs from that which he has with his mother, so the parent and teacher should discover and explore the possibilities of the professional relationship. Some teachers are unaware of these possibilities and seek only to make friends with the parents. In these cases, the teacher's own need for friendship and for closeness to people may stand in her way of developing a different type of relationship.

The teacher who can offer a professional relationship to parents must have a real understanding of herself. She must be able to recognize her own needs and feelings and the part they play in her relationships with others. She must have ways of handling these needs and feelings which leave her free to offer her interest and skill as a professionally trained person. She must be able to offer what she has in response to the parents' needs, not to satisfy her own personal needs. She accepts the parents, but she herself does not depend on feeling accepted by the parents.

The inexperienced teacher will need to guard against becoming entangled in personal relationships with parents of the children in her group. She will want to know them as people and be a person herself with them, but she will not seek to satisfy her own need for close, personal relationships through these contacts. She will be careful never to discuss the problems of parents with others outside the professional staff. She will try to understand and learn to use wisely the professional relationship.

WHAT KNOWLEDGE WILL BE USEFUL TO PARENTS?

Our second goal in working with parents is to help them gain more understanding about children and their needs. Along with the intuitive understanding most parents have about their own child, they can benefit from more information or added knowledge. Much of what we learn as teachers of young children will also be useful to parents. We have a responsibility for sharing our knowledge of child development with them and doing this in a way that does not interfere with the parent's own unique "knowing" about his or her child.

What knowledge may be especially useful to parents? What might be included in a parent education program? We will suggest here some information that might be included in a discussion program:

1. The values of play and of activity for the young child, with emphasis on letting the child touch things and explore as much as possible.

2. The kinds of play materials and play experiences that are appropriate at different ages and stages, with emphasis on simple, "raw" materials, dramatic and creative materials, and homemade equipment.

3. Ways in which a child is helped to develop competence with speech, including the importance of talking with a child and listening to his speech, the importance of experiences with books and stories, the importance of using "elaborated" speech with the child.

4. Information about the way in which a child learns, and the value of answering a child's questions, of helping him ask questions, of helping him to discover for himself.

5. Understanding about the kind of help that promotes good development, with points like giving directions or making suggestions in a positive rather than a negative way; giving a child enough, but not too much or too confusing, kinds of experience; letting him take his time; preparing the child for new or difficult experiences; playing a supporting role rather than a critical one.

6. The value of helping a child learn to distinguish between fantasy and reality while still enjoying and using his imagination.

7. The importance of putting feelings into words as a way of understanding and controlling action, and how this may be done.

8. The value of play with other children, and ways in which a child is helped in getting along with others.

9. Information about development and about growth needs, especially about the extent of individual differences in children.

With more knowledge, parents' expectations for the child become more reasonable. Parents can take more interest in the child's development, watching growth patterns unfold that are reassuringly similar to those of all children, yet unique and different in wonderful ways. They are better able to treasure the individuality of their child as a result of their increased understanding of growth.

How Do We Help Parents Learn?

Parents, or any of us, learn in a variety of ways. We learn by *observing* a skillful person as he performs a job. We learn by *discussion*, raising questions and expressing feelings and attitudes. We learn by *doing*, putting into practice what we have seen and discussed. When observation, discussion, and active participation take place under favorable conditions, they result in sound learning. A good parent education program will include opportunities for all three kinds of activities.

Observation

An important avenue for learning for parents is the opportunity they have to observe in the nursery school. Here they have a chance to see their child with other children. They may find he is like other children, not different as they feared. They see children under favorable conditions. They get suggestions for kinds of play materials and activities, for ways of managing situations. Sometimes the situations need to be interpreted by the teacher. She can explain why a situation was handled one way and not another, and what a bit of behavior may mean. Observation at the nursery school may make many things that children do seem more acceptable and less annoying. Observation may make clear the significance and value of behavior which has hitherto been unnoticed.

The teacher should encourage parents to observe and give them a chance to talk about what they see. If the school provides adequate observation space, perhaps a one-way vision screen, parents will find it easier to observe without distracting their child.

The teacher may wish to observe a child at home in order to gain more understanding of a particular child. She will arrange with the parent for a visit. The teacher gains a great deal from observing the child in his relationships at home with his parents and his siblings. Observing deepens her understanding of him.

For the child, the visit of his teacher may have a good deal of significance. She is giving him a special experience and showing that she values him and his home. The visit has meaning for the parents, too. It shows them that the teacher cares enough to come to their home. Even though a mother may feel somewhat anxious and strained, she may still appreciate the visit. Her relationship with the teacher should be a more comfortable one afterwards. It should be easier for the mother to bring up important questions and for the teacher to understand what these questions mean.

Discussions

Individual conferences represent one of the most profitable ways in which teachers and parents can share their experience. The nursery school teacher and the parent will hold many informal conferences at the beginning or end of the school day. Planned conferences will also be held in which there is time to raise questions at leisure and think through problems that have arisen, when both parent and teacher can become more aware of how each may be of help to the other.

Often the first contact will be one made by telephone. Initial contacts are important even if they take place over a telephone. The parent always hangs up the receiver with some kind of feeling which will influence her attitude toward the school and will somehow be conveyed to the child.

The next contact will probably be a conference between the teacher and parents. In most cases the first conference takes place without the child. It is very desirable but not always possible to have the conference with both mother and father. The parents have a chance to become acquainted with the teacher, and she has a chance to begin to know them. She will explain the general policies of the school, its regulations such as those in regard to health or to fees, the steps to be taken in entering school. She gives them a chance to raise questions and encourages them to talk about their child. She listens. Together they try to understand what the experience may mean to him and the roles each will play in it. She will try in this first conference to create an atmosphere in which communication is easy, so that future conferences will come as a matter of course.

In the conferences she has with parents, the teacher helps them approach problems, not by giving an answer, but by pointing out possible factors involved and perhaps suggesting several possible solutions. The parent may select a solution from those suggested by the teacher, but it will work in the end only if he makes it his own. He knows the child, the situation, and what he himself can do.

The responsibility for solving a problem belongs to the parent, and the teacher should not attempt to take it over, any more than she should solve the child's problems for him. She only tries to help the parent to solve his own problem through listening to him, asking questions to clarify a point, or suggesting factors which may be related. She may point out the possible meaning of a course of action and share similar experiences of others or of her own. The experienced teacher does not offer advice or pass judgment. Her interest and sympathetic understanding help the parent. The parent is also helped if the teacher is not anxious but seems to feel sure that there is a solution even if it takes time to find it.

Every teacher needs some training in conference methods. She also needs the opportunity, especially as a beginning teacher, to discuss the conferences she has with a professional person, such as a supervisor or a consultant. She learns from analyzing her actual experience and identifying the meanings in both her responses and those of the parents. In-service training is needed here. Only a beginning can be made in learning as a student.

At intervals while the child is in school and certainly before he leaves, the parents and teacher will want to confer and evaluate his progress. As they look at what is happening, and pool their thinking about him, they may see new significance in what he does and find new suggestions for helping him, as well as gain new appreciation for what he is like. Such evaluation is well worth-while.

Group Discussions

Another important contribution the nursery school makes to parents is the opportunity it gives them to have contacts with other parents. These contacts are not the same as those in the ordinary social event. They meet as parents, here. They can share their concerns. It is often a relief to them to know that they are not alone in facing some problems. They may get help from each other in solving a specific problem. A mother with young children is likely to be rather isolated and lonely, without many contacts outside her home. She needs contact with adults who are also interested in children.

In the group meetings held at school, the parents get together to talk about common problems. As a group they all have children at the same stage of development. They are all concerned with early childhood education. Each has taken a step in the process of giving a child more independence. With the support of other parents, a parent may find it easier to let the child be free. Since many adults live far from their own childhood families, they cannot turn to their parents and may be relatively alone in facing uncertainties which they hesitate to share with friends. They are in need of the "extended family experience" which the nursery school offers. It lightens some of the drudgery which is part of caring for children if experiences can be shared in conversations with people who have the same interests.

Group experiences may be of many kinds. Most schools have general group meetings. Held in the evening, they are for mothers and fathers. The more chance for parent participation, the more the individual parent will gain. Techniques can be used to bring about participation even when groups are large.

If there is a speaker, his talk can be followed by a question period or the group may break up into "buzz" sessions so that everyone has a chance to raise questions. There are many films which present good material on child development and family life. Discussion can follow the film showing. Reading one of the plays* written to bring out points relating to family problems is an excellent basis for discussion. The parents who read the play or act in it will usually gain a good deal. Spontaneous acting-out of incidents as a way of presenting a situation for discussion is another device which may stimulate thinking and sharing, especially if after the problem is presented, groups try out different solutions in this practice situation to see how they seem to work.

The whole matter of planning a series of programs for the year should be done in such a way as to bring out the real interests of the group and to provide for participation. If the parents share responsibility with the staff for making plans, or take on the responsibility themselves, the experiences are likely to come closer to what parents really want and thus be more valuable to them.

Sometimes parents bring up particular situations for discussion. It is only natural that parents will wish to discuss the particular problem of their own child, but the discussion leader will need to keep relating the specific example to general principles or group interests. "Is this a problem which occurs frequently?" "Have some of you met this problem in other types of situations?" "Shall we look at reasons why this behavior appears in children just at this point in their growth?" Parents may be encouraged to bring in *typical* situations for discussion at a meeting.

It may be helpful to have some agreement before discussion starts on the length of time any one person should talk and what the group wishes to do about handling questions on personal problems. It is seldom wise to have a discussion of more than an hour and a half. Frequently small groups will stay to talk more informally about points which have been raised, and this is a valuable part of the experience for them.

Other types of meetings include discussion groups held when the children are in school. These may be informal "coffee hours," with a discussion led by

---

*American Theatre Wing Community Plays. Distributed by the National Association for Mental Health.

someone on the staff when parents bring up questions, or they may be planned to cover some definite subject. There are also "work meetings" in which parents and teachers repair equipment and talk as they work.

A lending library with books and pamphlets is useful to parents, as is a bulletin board where teachers and parents can share things which have stimulated their thinking.

Participation

Parents have opportunities to "learn by doing" as they live with their own children. They can also learn from participating in the nursery school or center.

Most schools welcome parents who come in as volunteers, helping with aspects of the program, such as an excursion or field trip, or bringing in a musical instrument to play, or providing objects of interest, or enriching experience through a cooking project, story telling, or dancing. Discussion and evaluation by parents and staff afterwards make this a valuable experience for all.

In parent-cooperative schools the parents themselves serve as assistants to the trained teacher they employ to conduct the program, while they also have the administrative responsibilities.

Other schools such as some Head Start programs employ parents as assistant teachers. The experienced parent has a great deal to contribute, but to ensure its being a good situation parents need to have a general knowledge of principles of child development and of nursery school philosophy. They also need an adequate

Courtesy of Marianne Hurlbut.

A parent makes cookies with a group in the center.

Courtesy of Robert Overstreet.

A parent assists the teacher.

orientation in the procedures of the program as it is carried on in the particular school in which they will be sharing responsibilities with a trained teacher. They need to attend regular meetings in which there is discussion of current problems, review and planning of experiences for the children, and a chance to bring up questions, especially those about their own uncertainties or resistances. In other words, they need the same opportunities the professionally trained staff members need if the experience is to be a learning experience.

In addition to the problems faced by teachers ordinarily, parents who participate in a group with their own child face the added problem of filling two roles, that of teacher and of parent. Doing this may be a formidable task and, in many cases, the parent faces it without realizing what is involved and without professional help readily available. Since both the need to learn about children and provide them with sound group experience, and the interest in learning on the part of parents is great, we may hope that better programs for parent participation will develop steadily.

Some Head Start programs have also demonstrated what older boys and girls working within a well-supervised program can offer young children as models for growing-up while they themselves gain from taking responsibility.

THE SCHOOL AS A CENTER WORKING WITH PARENTS

The nursery school has responsibility for acting as a center for the education of parents. More is being done today, and much more needs to be done in the future, as we learn more about ways of helping parents. A good way to think about the matter is to ask ourselves, "What would we like to find in a center to help us with the task of being a parent?"

Many schools have a waiting list with names of parents who hope to put their children in the school. These parents are interested, and the school can offer them opportunities for learning through discussion groups, through conferences and consultation services, and, in some cases, through home visits and home teaching. Classes for expectant parents have proved to be of value. Their content can be extended. Most schools need to be doing much more to help both fathers and mothers find success and satisfaction in carrying on their roles in "informed" ways.

Someday nursery schools may provide far more effective ways of helping parents to carry on a role that has so much significance, culturally and personally.

Parents who have lacked educational opportunities themselves can learn ways of helping their children's learning. In some experimental programs teachers are going into homes and helping mothers of infants and very young children find ways of enriching the experiences there. In other programs, teachers are going into homes to work with the child at home to augment what the school is doing and to demonstrate to the individual parent how she may help the child.

With more general awareness of the role of education, more parents are becoming aware of the role they themselves can play in the process of helping children learn. Children will benefit from this greater awareness by parents if *all* aspects of learning are emphasized, learning about onself and about other people, as well as cognitive learning. They will benefit if parents do not work too hard at trying to be teachers.

The nursery school teacher remains in a key position to help parents. She can help the parent value what the child is and does. She can help the parent see a relation between a single bit of behavior and the total growth pattern. In this way she may help the parent gain a perspective and yet keep a sense of closeness to the child. She will not stress techniques. Techniques are not enough, however good they may be. They may even interfere with spontaneous relationships. It is not so much what people do as how they feel about what they do that is important. "What parents need all along is enlightenment about underlying causes, not advice and not instruction as to procedure."*

As the teacher works with different parents, she will strive to understand the differences in their feelings. She will gain much in working with them that will help her in her own understanding of children. She, in turn, may help the parents in their understanding of children. Working together, teachers and parents will find the satisfactions that come with confidence, skill and understanding.

PROJECTS

1. Observe a group of children at the end of the school day. Note what individual parents do and say as they call for their children. What differences did you

---

*Winnicott, D. W.: The Child and the Outside World. New York, Basic Books Inc., Publishers, 1957, p. 10

observe? What meaning do you think the parent's behavior has for the child in each case?

Note the response of the children to their parents' coming. What differences did you observe? What meaning do you think these differences have?

2. Attend a group meeting of parents and teachers and report briefly. How would you characterize the general atmosphere of the meeting? Which parents participated in the meeting? How did they participate? What problems were brought up? What role did the teachers seem to play? What values did the meeting hold for parents? For teachers?

REFERENCES

Almy, Millie: The Early Childhood Educator at Work. New York, McGraw-Hill Book Company, 1975. Chaps. 8 and 9.

Auerback, Aline.: Parents Learn Through Discussion: Principles and Practices of Parent Group Education. New York, John Wiley & Sons, Inc., 1968.

Bromberg, Susan: A beginning teacher works with parents. Young children. Vol. 24, No. 2, December, 1968.

Ginott, Haim G.: Between Parent and Child: New Solutions to Old Problems. New York, Avon Books, 1969.

Goldman, Richard, and Champagne, David W.: Some speculations on parent-school-child interactions. Children Today, March-April, 1975.

Gotkin, Lasser: The telephone call: The direct line from teacher to family. Young Children, Vol. 24, No. 2, December, 1968.

Honig, Alice: Parent Involvement in Early Childhood Education. Washington, D.C., National Association for the Education of Young Children, 1975.

Hymes, James L.: Effective Home-School Relations. (Revised and updated.) Southern California Association for the Education of Young Children.

Isaacs, Susan: Troubles of Children and Parents. (1948). New York, Schocken Books Inc., 1973.

Kunreuther, Sylvia: Black mothers speak and a white teacher listens. Children Today, Vol. 17, No. 3, May-June, 1970.

Lane, Mary B.: Education for Parenting. Washington, D. C., National Association for the Education of Young Children, 1975.

Leventhal, Brigid and Hersh, Stephen: Modern treatment of childhood leukemia: The patient and his family. Children Today, May-June, 1974.

Murphy, Lois B.: The consultant in a day care center for disadvantaged children. Children Today, May-June, 1968.

Newman, Sylvia: Guidelines to Parent-Teacher Cooperation in Early Childhood Education. New York, Book-Lab Inc., 1971.

O'Keefe, Ruth Ann: Home start: Partnership with parents. Children Today, January-February, 1973.

Parenting. Washington, D. C., Association Childhood Education, International, 1974.

Pickarts, Evelyn, and Fargo, Jean: Parent Education: Toward Parental Competence. New York, Appleton-Century-Crofts, 1971.

Schultz, Florence: Helping parents of two-year-olds. Young Children, Vol. 23, No. 3, January, 1968.

Spock, Benjamin: Bringing Up Children in a Difficult Time. New York, W. W. Norton & Company, Inc., 1974.

Strauss, Bert, and Strauss, Frances: New Ways to Better Meetings. New York, The Viking Press Inc., 1955.

Winnicott, D. W.: Playing and Reality. New York, Basic Books, Inc., Publishers, 1972. Chap. 11.

Wolf, Anna: Parent education: Reminiscence and comment. In Solnit, A. J. (ed.): Modern Perspectives in Child Development. New York, International Universities Press, 1963.

CHAPTER 21

The Dancing Turkey (boy, 4 years)

ACCEPTING OUR COMMON RESPONSIBILITIES

All through this book we have been looking for ways to increase our understanding of children. We have discovered that observing them will teach us a great deal about human behavior. We have discovered that if we are to handle children widely we must understand something about ourselves. The kind of people we are influences what we do for children.

The longer we study, the more we appreciate the complexities of human behavior—the more we hesitate to propose ready-made formulas for solving problems or set standards as to what a child ought or ought not to do in a situation. We realize that as yet we know only a little of all that we need to know about people.

We have taken a big step forward when we have learned to *observe* children, to recognize the *uniqueness* of each individual, to search for the *meaning* back of an act, *to accept the child as he is,* and *to have confidence in his growth impulses.* We have taken a big step when we have learned to make our contribution to the child through reducing the difficulty of the problems he must face, through enriching the experiences he has, and through helping him to find avenues for creative satisfactions, rather than by depending on admonition and interference. We have also taken a big step when we can assume responsibility for defining and maintaining limits for the child's behavior with confidence because we understand his developmental needs and his level of readiness.

We need to keep in mind all that we have learned as we face the challenges today. Profound restructuring is occurring in many aspects of our living. New possibilities are open in many fields. There is freedom from many old restrictions. Education is playing an increasingly important role.

But many things have not changed. The Secretary-General of the United Nations has pointed out the tragic fact that more young children lacked adequate nourishment during the last decade than during the previous one. In spite of our advances, children today are in need of more help if they are to develop in healthy ways. Parents have been concerned about their children through the centuries, but today individual parents may be less likely than formerly to be able to provide their children with a healthy environment. Families are in need of more support if they are to fulfill their functions well. Not all changes have brought improvements.

Schools are an important part of a community. They reflect conditions there. The community that does good planning in the direction of ensuring adequate housing, adequate employment under conditions favorable for everyone, and adequate community services and facilities values its schools.

To the extent that a community fails to plan well, it handicaps the school in carrying out its functions. The school suffers, too, as a result of divisions and conflicts among the citizens, for the school does not exist as an agency apart from the community. Schools are nurtured by their communities. They in their turn should nurture community life. Along with the home, the school can facilitate change in a community.

The home and the school have a role to play in the betterment of the community. They share responsibility for being aware of community needs and for taking an active part in bringing about needed changes. The growing interest in such matters as reducing the amount of pollution in the world and the shift toward a more responsible stand on the part of some business firms are examples of such changes. The school as well as the home can support these efforts. Teachers and parents working together can support the positive advances that are occurring. They can also give leadership in identifying and working for other improvements in both local communities and the extended world community.

For more than fifty years teachers have been at work in the field of early childhood education. Books first published in 1930 have recently been reissued.* The material is as sound today as when first published. The title of a book published in the 1930's, *Parents and Children Go to School,*† indicates the early em-

---

*Isaacs, Susan: Intellectual Growth in Young Children. London. Routledge, 1930. Reissued by Schocken Books Inc., 1966; and Social Development in Young Children. New York, Harcourt, Brace and World, Inc., 1939. Reissued by Schocken Books Inc., 1972.

†Baruch, Dorothy: Parents and Children Go to School. Glenview, Illinois, Scott, Foresman and Company, 1939.

phasis on working with parents. Today early childhood education has been "redis-covered," and the discovery has brought many newcomers into the field. There is need for a restatement of goals. We need to reaffirm our faith in the "whole child" and in the value of thinking of his physical, mental, and social well-being together as a whole. We need to act more effectively on the statement from the Universal Declaration of Human Rights "Education shall be directed to the full development of the human personality and to the strengthening of respect for human rights and fundamental freedoms."[*]

One of the strengths emerging from the flux of change is the fact that parents and teachers are finding it more possible to work together in planning a favorable environment for children. Together, parents and teachers may be bet-ter able to help children find the satisfaction and fulfillment that is possible in life. We live in one world, and our concern must include all children and all parents and teachers.

With many choices open, we must evaluate approaches critically if we are to meet our responsibility for bringing up children well. Only as we continue to study children and learn from them, only as we try to understand ourselves bet-ter, can we expect to judge wisely what will benefit each individual child. This is our responsibility today.

As students and teachers and parents we must accept the challenge put by Chisholm, "Dare any of us say that he or she can do nothing about the desperate need of the world for better human relationships?[†]

REFERENCES

Biber, Barbara: Challenges Ahead for Early Childhood Education. Washington, D.C., National Associ-ation for the Education of Young Children, 1969.
Coles, Robert: Still Hungry in America. Cleveland, Ohio, The New American Library, Inc., in associa-tion with The World Publishing Company, 1969.
Erikson, Erik: Childhood and Society. (Revised edition). New York, W. W. Norton & Company, Inc., 1963. Chap. 11.
Erikson, Erik: Insight and Responsibility.New York, W. W. Norton & Company, Inc., 1964.
Senn, Milton: Early childhood education for what goals? Children, January-February, 1969.

---

*Universal Declaration of Human Rights.
†Chisholm, Brock: Social responsibility. Science, January, 1949, p. 43.

INDEX

Page numbers in *italics* indicate illustrations.

Acceptance, 20–21, 75–76, 163–164, 185, 291–292, 317, 387–389
Accommodation (Piaget), 55, 58
Accountability, 48
Activities, 24–31, 82–87, *82, 109, 125, 191, 198,* 211, *219,* 225–232, 248–259
  teacher initiated, 192–194
Adequacy, 279–280, 339–340. See also *Confidence, Security.*
Adjustment
  differences in, 136–137
  in a group, 337–353, *344, 346, 347*
  in new experiences, 135–156
  influence of past experience on, 17–21, 291–292, 376
Ages, of nursery school children, 66–68
Aggressiveness
  feelings of, 303–321, 326–327
  reducing, 190, 314–318, *316,* 320
  sources of, *304,* 308–314, 318–319
Aide, nursery school, 73
Animals, 87, *148,* 154–156, *217* 252–253
Anxiety, child's, 161–163, *202,* 324, 361–362
  parental, 161, 221, 375–376
Art, as avenue of expression, 260–261, 269–270
  in the program, 269–272
  models or patterns in, 105–106, 269, 272
Association for Childhood Education, International, 220
Attention, demands for, 153, 176, 180
  giving, 221–222, 236
Attitudes
  toward eating, 168–170, 172–174
  toward sex, 163–164, 253–256
  toward toileting, 160–164
Authority. See also *Discipline.*
  attitude toward, 322–327
  consistency of, 324, 329, 335
  goals of, 117, 121, 335–336
  maintaining, 324–325, 327–334
  patterns of, 323–324
Autonomy, 51–52. See also *Independence.*
Axline, Virginia, 37

Baby, new, coming of, 308–309
Baruch, Dorothy, 263, 388
"Battered" children, 34
Behavior, bad or good, 117, 160, 297, 311, 320, 335, 353
  interpreting, 319
  "testing out," 114–116, 330

Bernstein, Joanne, 246
Biber, Barbara, 193–194, 197
Birthdays, 258
Biting, 309–310
Blank, Marion, 239
Blocks, *11, 57, 65,* 82–83
Books, *29, 32,* 220–221, 244–248, *245, 247*
Brearley, Molly, 56–57, 216
Bruner, Jerome, 218–219
Building, nursery school, 79–81

Carpentry, *54, 69, 218*
Carroll, Vinette, 219
Case histories
  Alice, who was anxious to please, 167–168
  Charles, who is fighting to find his place, 5–7
  Ellen, who found it hard to trust, 11–13
  Helen, who was passive, 152–153
  Jean, who lived under favorable circumstances, 7–9
  Jill, who put her fears into words, 293–295
  Juan, who watches others, 9
  Lester, who found a friend, 351–353
  Marvin, who can accept his feelings, 306–308
  Mary, who was out to defeat "bossing", 166–167
  Mary Lou, who sucked her thumb, 289
  Mickey, who was ready for school. 149
  Nettie, who doesn't feel valued, 10–11
  Ralph, whose mother gave him time to feel secure, 149–150
  Ruth, who feels she must keep clean, 310–311
  Sam, who conformed, 167
  Sam, who wanted to feel big, 312–313
Cauman, Judith, 235
Child care center, 29–34
Child Development, Office of, 35
Child Development Associate, 33, 71–73
Chisholm, Brock, 315, 389
Choice, offering to child, 100–101
Clarke-Stewart, Alison, 32, 34
Clay, *53, 238,* 271–272
Cleanliness, 164, 271, 310–311
Clothing, *159, 164*
Cohen, Dorothy, 200–201, 204
Community responsibility, 3–4, 387–389
Competition, 102–103, 190, 270, 355
Concept formation, 54–57, 209–214, 225–236
Concept of self, 187, 281–285, 339–340
Conference, parent-teacher, 140–141, 380–381
  staff, 74–76

Confidence, 279–299, 377–378
Conflicts, *118*, 355
Conservation, understanding of (Piaget), 56
Consultant, 38, 89
Cooperative nursery school, 37–38
Crayons, 271
Creative expression
  in art, 260–261, 269–272
  in language, 261–264
  in music, 264
  values of, 260–261
Critical period, 50–53
Crying, *283*, 295
Culture patterns, 256–258, 290, 305
Curriculum. See names of specific subjects, e.g.,
  Art, Social studies.

Dancing, 267–268, *268*
Day care center, 29–34
Death, 253
Defenses, 152–154
Defensiveness, 97–98, 135–136
Dependency, 17–18, 176, 180, 282
Destructiveness, 318–319
Developmental stages, 50–57, 60–61, 138
Dewey, John, 46–47
Dialects, 239–241
Differences, individual, 5–14, 58–59, 136, 139.
  See also *Case histories.*
Directions, positive, 99–100, 187–188
Discipline, 52, 114–121, *120*, 322–336. See also
  Behavior, "testing out."
Discussion
  group, 381–383
  staff, 74–76
  with parents, 380–381
Dramatic play, *7, 8, 30, 66*, 85–86, 162, *191*,
  196–197, *202*, 205, *341, 344*, 357–367, *358,
  360*
Drawing(s), children's, *3, 24, 45, 64, 79, 97, 114,
  124, 135, 158, 183, 196, 208, 224, 279, 303,
  322, 337, 357, 371, 387*

Eating, *41, 52*, 168–175, *172, 174, 175*, 298
Education, for parenthood, 36–41, 377–385
  role of, 3–4, 58
Educational Policies Commission of NEA, 25
Elimination, 159–168, *162*
Entering nursery school, 137–151
Environment, adapted to child's needs, 218, 241
Equipment, *12, 65*, 81–87, *84, 86, 89, 90*
Erikson, Erik, 49–54, 180, 330, 371
Ets, Marie, 214, 256
Evaluation, 35–36, 48–49, 74–76, 381
Excursions, 258–259, *260*
Experiences
  completed, *72*, 192
  group, 337–355
  learning, See *Learning experiences.*
  new, 135–154
Expression. See *Creative expression* and *Feelings,
  expression of.*

Failure, 102–103, 188, 222–223, 311–312
Fairy tales, 247
Family, 17–19, 67–68, 338–339, 358
Fantasy, 214–215
Father, 50, 284. See also *Parent(s).*
Fear, 151–156, 201–203, 222–223
Federally supported programs, 34–37
Feelings
  ambivalence of, 21, 374–375
  clues to, 285–290, 311
  expression of, 194–195, 292–297, 305–306
  of parents, 142–145, 147
  sources of, 304–305, 308–314, 318–319
Fein, Greta, 32, 34
Festivals, 257–258
Finger paints, *27, 179, 230*, 271
Forestalling problems, 108
Fraiberg, Selma, 214, 254
Freud, Anna, 49–50
Freud, Sigmund, 49–50
Friendships, *175, 252, 294, 298*, 350–353, 355,
  360
Fromm, Eric, 325
Frustration, in growing, 18–19, 304, 321

Games, group, *198*, 205, 367
Giving, 115, 284
Goals
  at mealtime, 170
  in day care, 32
  in group experience, 353
  of discipline, 52, 117, 335–336
  of early education, 3, 58
  with parents, 377–379
Group experience
  adjusting to, 350
  goals for, 353
  readiness for, 338–339
  values of, 339–343, 348–352
Guidance. See *Teaching skills.*
Guides
  in action, 99, 105–112
  in discipline, 121, 321–322, 335–336
  in speech, 98–105
Guilt, feelings of, 52–54, 282, 326–327, 382
  role of, in learning, 334
Guns, 202, 361–362

Habits, nervous, 289–290
Handicapped child, programs for, 37, 70
Head Start program, 35–36
Health, 62, 71, 80, 111
Hearing, 229
Hill, Patty S., 47
Hitting, problem of, 312–314, 319–320
Home, visits to, 35, 380
Hostility, feelings of, 303–321
Housekeeping, 87–88
Humor, 261–262, 363

Identity, sense of, 340
Imagination, 215

Inadequacy, in new situation, 15–16, 97–98, 135–136
Individual differences, 5–14, 58–59, 136, 139. See also *Case histories.*
Insecurity. See *Security.*
Intellectual development, stages in, 54–57
Intelligence, 208–210
Isaacs, Susan, 47, 63
Isolation, as punishment, 353–354

Janitor, 22
Jealousy, 176, 308–309
Johnson, Harriet, 47

Keister, Mary Elizabeth, 56
Kindergarten, 66
Kluckhohn, Clyde, 281
Knowledge, implicit, 56, 210–213
Kubie, Lawrence, 304, 306

LaBarre, Weston, 3
Laboratory nursery school, 36–37
Language, 236–244, 261–264
Learning, process of, 54–57, *193,* 200–201, 208–259, *217*
Learning experiences, *25, 56, 139, 184, 193, 202, 217, 224–259, 231, 232, 233, 234, 235, 249, 250, 254–255*
Legislation, 36
Limits, acceptable, 327–333. See also *Discipline.*
Literature. See *Books.*

McAfee, Oralie, 241
McMillan sisters, 47
Manners, in eating, 171
Masturbation, 289–290
Mathematics, *193,* 249–251, *250*
Mealtime. See *Eating.*
Merrill Palmer Institute, 47
Mitchell, Lucy Sprague, 47
Montessori, Maria, 46–47
Mother, working, 33–34, 46. See also *Parent(s).*
Motivation, 61–62, 102–103, 216–219
Music, 264–267, *268*
Mutual regulation, 51, 333–334

Naps, 30, 92, 175–177
National Association for the Education of Young Children (NAEYC), 74, 79–80
Navaho, 281
Needs, basic, 17–21, 50–54, 279–280, 303–306
Negativism, 160–161, 166–167. See also *Resistance.*
Nervous habits, 289–290
Newberry, John, 247
Nudging, 282, 312
Nursery school(s)
  aides in, 73
  ages for,
  as a laboratory, 22, 36

Nursery school(s) (*Continued*)
  buildings, 79–81
  characteristics of, 24–28
  church, 38
  cooperative, 37–38
  definition of, 24
  entering, 140–149
  equipment, 81–87
  federally supported, 34–37
  Head Start programs in, 35
  history of, 46–48
  number of children in, 65–66
  observational records in, 126–129
  philosophy of, 58–62
  private, 38
  readiness of child for, 138–140
  scheduling in, 26–31
  selection of, 38–39
  staff in, 69–73, 183–186. See also *Teacher.*
  types of, 31–39
  visiting in, 141–142
  volunteers in, 73–74

Objectiveness, 15, 124–125
Observing, *25, 109, 111,* 111–112, 124–129, 205, 380
Office of Child Development, 35
Operations (Piaget), 57
Painting, *10, 28, 106,* 269–271, *296, 346–347*
Parent(s), 14, 21–22, 39, *137,* 143–144, *327,* 371–385, *373*
  as teachers, 383–384, *384*
  learning by, 35, 38, 379–384
Parent meetings, 40, 381–383
Parent-teacher relationships, 39–41, 140–148, 371–384
Parenthood, education for, 36–41, 379–385
Patterns, in art forms, 267, 269–270, 272
Perception, sensory, 267
Permissiveness, 115, 283–284, 326
Personality, basic tasks in growth of, 50–54
Philosophy, nursery school, 45–48, 58–62
Piaget, Jean, 49, 54–57
Plant, James, 282
Play. See also *Dramatic play.*
  equipment for, 82–87
  messy, 271–272
  role of, *12, 25, 30,* 196–206
  values of, 197, 200–203
Playground, 80
Poetry, 246
Position, of child in the family, 18
  of teacher for supervising, 109–111
Positive suggestions, 99–100, 187–188
Posture, 226
Prejudice, 185
Private nursery school, 38
Professional growth, 74–76
Professional relationship, 378
Program, nursery school. See names of specific subjects, e.g., *Art, Social studies.*
Projects, for students, 22, 43, 62, 78, 93, 113, 123, 131, 157, 180, 195, 206, 223, 273–274, 301–302, 321, 336, 356, 367, 385–386

Property rights, 348–350
Punishment, 116, 318–319, 353–354

Questions, use of, 101, 239, 253–254

Readiness
   for experience, 158–161, 171, 338–339
   for learning, 219
   for nursery school, 138–140
   for reading, 220–221
Reading, readiness for, 220–221
   to child, 29, 32, 244–248, 247
Records, types of, 126–129
Redirection of activities, 103–104
Reinforcement, 48, 58, 61–62, 189
Relations, human, 65, 71
Relationships
   group, 337–355
   home-school, 39–41, 372–385
   professional, 378
   social (children), 174, 175, 252, 294, 298
Resentment, 18–19, 305. See also Hostility.
Resistance, 20, 171–172, 329–330, 342–343, 376
Rest, 32, 175–177
Rhythm, 267–268
Rights, property, 348–350
Rivalry, 308–309, 355
Rooming-in, maternity, 169
Routines
   importance of, 159, 177–180
   mealtime, 168–175
   resting, 175–177
   toileting, 159–168
Ruggles Street Nursery School, 47

Safety, 110–111, 118
Schedule,
   for eating, 169, 174–175
   for program, 91–92
   for rest, 176–177
   for toileting, 166
Science, 193, 249, 250, 251–256
Security, 50–51, 68, 146, 279–299, 285
Seeing, 230–232
Self, concept of, 279–280, 339–340
Self-understanding, 15–22, 71
Sensorimotor experience, 5, 26, 53, 54, 128, 172,
   219, 225–232, 225, 230, 238
Sensorimotor stage, in development (Piaget),
   54–55
Sex, 163–164, 253–256
Shaming, of child, 102
Sharing, 144, 252, 348–350
Singing, 19, 67, 264–266
Situation for discussion, 41–43, 76–77, 112,
   121–123, 129–131, 154–156, 205–206,
   299–301, 355

Smilansky, Sara, 359
Social relationships, 12, 198, 252, 292, 294,
   337–355
Social studies, 256–259
Space
   amount of, 79–81, 81
   need for, 88
   use of, 88–91
Speech, 101–102, 237–239, 243–244, 290. See
   also Language.
Spoiling, of child, 282–284, 338–339
Staff
   discussions, 74–76
   evaluation, 48–49, 74–76, 381
   in a nursery school, 69–73, 183–186
Students, as teachers, 15–16, 17, 19
   feelings of, 15–21
Stuttering, 150, 243
Suggestions, positive, 99–100, 187–188
Supervision, 109–111. See also Teaching skills.

Task, developmental, 50–54
Teacher
   as model, 189–190, 241
   attitudes of, 185–186
   characteristics of, 183–185, 194, 283
   role of, 68, 69, 72, 120, 186, 188, 193, 194,
      217, 283, 285
Teaching skills, 97–112, 187–195, 213
Television, 203–204, 364
Theories, personality, and nursery school
      programs, 49–58
   teaching, 57–58
Thumbsucking, 288–290
Timing, of guidance, 104–105
Toileting, 159–168, 162
Transitional object, 199, 297
Transitions, 177–178
Trips, 258–259, 260
Trust, sense of, 50–51. See also Security.
Turns, taking, 348–350
Twins, 340

Understanding, 379–384
Universal Declaration of Human Rights, 381–382

Vision, 230–232
Visiting, at school, 141–142
   in the home, 380
Voice, effective use of, 101–102
Volunteer, 73–74

Washing, 59, 165
Water play, 82, 200, 210–213, 210, 212, 213
Winnicott, D. W., 51, 219, 231, 324, 385